SOCIAL DEFENCES
AGAINST ANXIETY

Tavistock Clinic Series

Margot Waddell (Series Editor)

Recent titles in the Tavistock Clinic Series
(for a full listing, please visit www.karnacbooks.com)

SOCIAL DEFENCES
AGAINST ANXIETY

Explorations in a Paradigm

Edited by

David Armstrong & Michael Rustin

KARNAC

First published in 2015 by
Karnac Books
118 Finchley Road
London NW3 5HT

British Library Cataloguing in Publication Data

A C.I.P. for this book is available from the British Library

ISBN: 978–1–78220–168–7

Edited, designed, and produced by Communication Crafts

Printed in Great Britain

www.karnacbooks.com

CONTENTS

SERIES EDITOR'S PREFACE

Margot Waddell

Since it was founded in 1920, the Tavistock Clinic has developed a wide range of developmental approaches to mental health which have been strongly influenced by the ideas of psychoanalysis. It has also adopted systemic family therapy as a theoretical model and a clinical approach to family problems. The Clinic is now the largest training institution in Britain for mental health, providing postgraduate and qualifying courses in social work, psychology, psychiatry, and child, adolescent, and adult psychotherapy, as well as in nursing and primary care. It trains about 1,700 students each year in over 60 courses.

The Clinic's philosophy aims at promoting therapeutic methods in mental health. Its work is based on the clinical expertise that is also the basis of its consultancy and research activities. The aim of this Series is to make available to the reading public the clinical, theoretical, and research work that is most influential at the Tavistock Clinic. The Series sets out new approaches in the understanding and treatment of psychological disturbance in children, adolescents, and adults, both as individuals and in families.

Social Defences against Anxiety is an extraordinarily significant volume and, as Series Editor, I am very proud to be adding it to the Karnac/Tavistock list of publications. The chapters included here are, in themselves, both impressive and instructive in the huge range of different areas of work and expertise represented in them. They also, individually and collectively, mark another milestone in the history and evolution of the ground-breaking work done in the late 1950s by Elliott Jaques and Isabel Menzies Lyth. As the Editors, who are both steeped in organizational and psychoanalytic thought, say in their Introduction, they feel that there is now a question in the air as to whether, nearly six decades later, the original paradigm "risked becoming a dead metaphor". These thoughts were provoked in the context of a rapidly changing landscape in the worlds of organizational consultancy, education, health, welfare, and elsewhere.

As can clearly be seen here, this rapidly changing landscape was, predictably, not only in the areas of technology and socio-technical systems approaches, but also in the inevitable social changes brought about by globalization, the information economy, and different forms of management, governance, and consultancy. Furthermore, psychoanalytic theory in relation to both individual and group processes has itself been developing at pace since the original paradigm was formulated. Yet at the centre remain, as we see here, the original insights into the role and impact of unconscious mental processes, especially those of anxiety and the nature of defences against it, on organizational and institutional, as well as personal, life.

The breadth, depth, and subtlety of thinking and scholarship to be found here are remarkable. The collective wisdom expressed throughout these pages, especially in the ease of passage between theoretical writing and everyday idioms, is reliably and thoroughly informed by expert research in a huge variety of different settings.

My own feeling is that the book represents a line in the sand that will not easily be erased or washed away. A more accurate metaphor might be "conceptual benchmark" in the ongoing development of work at the Tavistock and elsewhere. This Institution has, itself, always espoused the importance of a way of thinking that goes both laterally—across social, cultural, and familial dynamics—and also vertically—from conscious head and heart to unconscious mental functioning. *Social Defences against Anxiety* will very significantly ensure the continuation of that particular hard, necessary, and fruitful joint endeavour.

ACKNOWLEDGEMENTS

T he origin of this book lies in a two-day research colloquium "Rethinking Unconscious Defences against Anxiety", which took place in September 2013 at St John's College Oxford, to re-examine the ideas first set out in Isabel Menzies famous paper "A Case Study in the Functioning of Social Systems as a Defence against Anxiety: A Report on a Study of the Nursing Service of a General Hospital". Most of the chapters in this book are developments of presentations that their authors first gave at that event. We would like to acknowledge the valuable contributions of all those who took part in the colloquium.

We are grateful to the Independent Social Research Foundation, and its Research Director, Louise Braddock, to the St John's College Research Centre and its then Director, Professor Paul Tod, and to Tavistock Consulting, and its Director, Judith Bell, for their generous support for the colloquium. We would like to thank Margot Waddell, Series Editor of the Tavistock Clinic Book Series, and Oliver Rathbone and his colleagues at Karnac, for their enthusiastic support for this book. We are particularly grateful to Eric King for his outstanding work as text editor of the final manuscript.

The original intention of this project was that it should initiate further research in this field, both theoretical and empirical. All editors' and authors' royalties from this book are being set aside for this purpose, and we hope that further work will follow this publication.

ABOUT THE EDITORS AND CONTRIBUTORS

David Armstrong is an Associate Consultant at Tavistock Consulting. He trained as a social psychologist at the Tavistock Institute of Human Relations and worked in action research and organizational consultancy at the University of London and The Grubb Institute before returning to the Tavistock in 1994 to join a newly established consultancy service at the Tavistock Clinic. A Distinguished Member of the International Society for the Psychoanalytic Study of Organizations (ISPSO), he is the author of *Organization in the Mind: Psychoanalysis, Group Relations and Organizational Consultancy* (2005).

Philip Boxer brings over 30 years of consulting experience to his work with clients in public, private, and not-for-profit sectors. His practice develops clients' capabilities for competing in turbulent environments and uses approaches that enable clients to increase their agility and their ability to scale learning across network organizations. He has published in the fields of organizational and social dynamics, management studies, and systems engineering. He is a member of the Centre for Freudian Analysis and Research and received a BSc from London University, an MSc from the London Graduate School of Business Studies, and a PhD from Middlesex University.

Andrew Cooper is Professor of Social Work at the Tavistock Centre and the University of East London. The work of Isabel Menzies Lyth has informed many of his writings, which include cross-national studies of child protection systems and practices and (with Julian Lousada), *Borderline Welfare: Feeling and Fear of Feeling in Modern Welfare* (2005).

Maxim de Sauma is a Fellow of the British Psychoanalytical Society, Full Member of the British Psychoanalytic Association, Member of the American Psychoanalytic Society, and CEO and Clinical Director of the Brent Centre for Young People, London.

Peter Elfer is Principal Lecturer in Early Childhood Studies and Convenor of the Master's Programme in Early Childhood Studies at the University of Roehampton, London. He has a long-standing interest in the well-being of babies and children under 3 years in early years settings. Much of his research concerns the experience of staff who work with young children and how they manage this complex work, with its daily demands and challenges as well as pleasures. He has published a number of academic papers on this theme and was co-author (with Elinor Goldschmied and Dorothy Selleck) of *Key Persons in the Early Years: Building Relationships for Quality Provision in Early Years Settings and Primary Schools* (2011).

Marcus Evans is the Associate Clinical Director of Complex Needs in the Tavistock and Portman NHS Trust. He is a Consultant Adult Psychotherapist and a Registered Mental Nurse. He was appointed as head of the nursing discipline at the Tavistock and Portman NHS Trust in 1996 and was given responsibility for its development. This was a role he held until taking on his present role in 2011.

Sarah Fielding is a Member of the British Psychological Society, a Specialist Mental Health Worker, and a Service Manager (Clinical Administration) and Executive Assistant to the CEO and Clinical Director at the Brent Centre for Young People, London.

Jo Finch is a Senior Lecturer in Social Work at the University of East London (UEL), where she leads the MA in Social Work and the Post-Graduate Diploma in Social Work (Step-Up). She is also a course tutor on the Professional Doctorate in Social Work at the Tavistock Clinic and also teaches research methodology to students on the BA (Hons) and MA Social Work programmes at UEL as well as on the doctorate. She has a long-standing research interest in the issues raised by students struggling or failing in practice learning settings in social work and other professions where there are assessed practice learning requirements.

William Halton is a freelance organizational consultant, executive coach, and supervisor, and he has consultancy experience in the public, private, and voluntary sectors. He is a former member of the Tavistock Consultancy Service and "Consulting to Institutions" Workshop. His special interests are in mediation work, personal development programmes, and group relations conferences. He has a professional background in child and adult psychotherapy. He is a contributor to *The Unconscious at Work* (1994) and to *Working below the Surface* (2004) and has published in the *Organisational and Social Dynamics* journal.

Larry Hirschhorn is a founder of CFAR, a management-consulting firm in Philadelphia and a past principal. He currently works part-time with the firm. He is a founder and past president of ISPSO. He is the author of several books and many articles on the psychodynamics of organizations, including *The Workplace Within* (1988) and *Reworking Authority* (1998). He is currently researching the experience of risk in a postindustrial society.

Paul Hoggett is Emeritus Professor of Social Policy at the University of the West of England, Bristol. He has contributed to the emergence in British universities of Psychosocial Studies, in which psychoanalytic theory and methods are applied to social science research. He is a psychoanalytic psychotherapist and member of the Severnside Institute for Psychotherapy. He was the founding editor of its journal, *Organisational and Social Dynamics*. His most recent book is *Politics, Identity & Emotion* (Paradigm Publishers, 2009). He now chairs the Climate Psychology Alliance.

Sharon Horowitz is an organizational psychologist who specializes in the financial services and technology industries. She has over 20 years' experience advising senior leaders and their teams including strategic business development, performance management, the psychology of financial risk taking, leadership/team creativity, and performance, succession planning, and portfolio partnership structures. She is an executive coach with expertise in on-boarding role transitions/promotions for women on Wall Street. She is a confidential advisor for founder/

owner firms, focusing on either end of the career spectrum—from growth to leadership advancement to succession strategy, to post-succession enjoyment of life.

Emil Jackson is Head of Child & Adolescent Psychotherapy in the Adolescent and Adult Departments at the Tavistock Clinic where he works clinically and has a central role in training child psychotherapists. His expertise combines 18 years' experience as a psychotherapist with children, adolescents, and adults, with 14 years' experience as an executive coach and consultant. His coaching and consultancy work spans public and private sector organizations, with a special interest in education. Since 1999, he has developed the application of work discussion groups extensively within schools, working with teaching and support staff, middle leaders, and head teachers.

Sebastian Kraemer is a Consultant Emergency and Liaison Child and Adolescent Psychiatrist at the Whittington Hospital, London, and an honorary consultant at the Tavistock Clinic, where he worked as a clinician and trainer for 25 years. He writes and lectures on paediatric mental health liaison; the role of fathers from anthropological and modern social perspectives; family therapy, psychoanalysis, and therapeutic change; the fragility of the developing male; dynamics of professional groups; and attachment and inequality in social policy.

James Krantz is an organizational consultant and researcher from New York, where he is a Principal of Worklab, a management consulting firm. He has a PhD in Systems Sciences from the Wharton School and a BA in Philosophy and Economics. He is past president of the ISPSO; Fellow, A. K. Rice Institute; member, OPUS; and currently Director of the Center for Socio-Analytic Studies at The Institute for Psychoanalytic Training and Research. His writing focuses on the unconscious background of work life and on the socio-psychological challenges posed by new forms of organization.

Deborah Langstaff is the Matron for the Trauma Service at Oxford University Hospitals NHS Trust. She has over 30 years' experience in the speciality and has a particular interest in systems of ward-based nursing organization which are patient centred yet supportive of those responsible for care delivery. Her publications include work on patient and staff experience and leadership within the context of acute care.

Amanda Lees is a Research Fellow working at the universities of South-ampton and Winchester. The work of Isabel Menzies Lyth inspired her recently completed doctoral research, which investigated social work-ers' perspectives on information sharing in the context of multi-agency working to safeguard children.

Susan Long teaches and supervises research at INSEAD Singapore, the University of Divinity Melbourne, the Melbourne Institute of Creative Arts Therapy, the National Institute of Organisation Dynamics Austra-lia (NIODA), and the Grubb Guild in Australia. She also works as an organizational consultant and is a member of the Board of the Judicial College of Victoria and of Comcare's advisory board for the Center of Excellence for Research into Mental Health at Work. She was founding President of Group Relations Australia and a past president of ISPSO. Her research has attracted grants through the Australian Research Council and industry. She has published six books and many journal articles.

Aideen Lucey is an independent organizational consultant and execu-tive coach. She is also a Visiting Consultant and Coaching Practice Director at INSEAD European Business School. Previously she was a principal consultant at Tavistock Consulting. She consults to indi-viduals and groups from a wide range of professional backgrounds including public services, the not-for-profit sector, and large corporate organizations. Her particular areas of interest are in leadership, group dynamics, and the social context of work. She has written several papers on organizational and social dynamics.

Nick Papadopoulos is an organizational change consultant and execu-tive coach specializing in leadership development and the relationship between an organization's culture, strategy, and leadership practices. He is in the final phase of completing his doctorate, focusing on the relationship and relative contribution of social and psychological fac-tors in diagnosing organizations for the purpose of change. He is an MA graduate of the Tavistock Institute's AOC program and also holds an MA in Executive Coaching. Prior to becoming a consultant in 2000, he trained and worked as a psychoanalytic psychotherapist.

Michael Rustin is Professor of Sociology at the University of East Lon-don and Visiting Professor at the Tavistock and Portman NHS Trust. He is an Associate of the British Psychoanalytical Society. He has published widely on the interrelations between psychoanalysis and society. His books include *The Good Society and the Inner World* (1991); *Reason and Unreason* (2002); *Narratives of Love and Loss: Studies in Modern Children's Fiction* (1987, 2001) and *Mirror to Nature: Drama Psychoanalysis and Society* (2002) (both with Margaret Rustin); and *The Inner World of Doctor Who* (2014) (with Iain MacRury). He is a founding editor of *Soundings* journal and a co-author of *After Neoliberalism? The Kilburn Manifesto* (2013).

Jason Schaub is a social work academic who teaches and researches in social work education, gender/sexualities, and safeguarding. He has a growing writing profile about gender/sexualities and about practice learning and other aspects of social work education. He is a senior lecturer at Buckinghamshire New University.

Mannie Sher is a Principal Social Scientist and Director of the Group Relations Programme at the Tavistock Institute of Human Relations. He leads organizational development and change projects and consults to boards and executive teams of organizations on leadership and strategic change. His research and consultancy focuses on the impact of thought on the dialectic relationship between social constructivism, the unconscious, and liberal democracy. He has published on consultancy, leadership, organizational development, group relations, ethics, and corruption. His latest book is *The Dynamics of Change: Tavistock Approaches to Improving Social Systems* (2013).

Jon Stokes is a leadership psychologist and coach who consults and advises at board and senior levels. He is co-director of the leadership development firm Stokes & Jolly, providing leadership development, assessment, consultancy, and coaching services to senior leaders. He trained and worked as a psychologist at the Tavistock Institute and Clinic, where he was Chair of the Adult Psychotherapy Department and the Founding Director of Tavistock Consulting. He is an Associate Fellow of Oxford University's Said Business School, where he teaches on leadership, and an Associate at the Institute for Government.

Simon Tucker is the Executive Director of OPUS. He is an experienced manager, coach, trainer and organizational consultant. He is also a teacher, consultant and associate organizing tutor on masters' and doctorate programmes at the Tavistock Clinic. He originally trained as a social worker, and his background includes over 25 years' experience of management in a variety of services within social care and the NHS, including Child Mental Health Services. It was in this role that he developed a network of consultancy to frontline professionals including head teachers, whose experience was the focus of his doctoral research.

Liz Tutton is a Senior Research Fellow at the RCN Research Institute, Warwick Medical School, University of Warwick, and the Trauma Unit, Kadoorie Centre, John Radcliffe Hospital, Oxford. She has spent many years in nursing, education, and research. Her research interests include patient and staff experiences of care; recovery and treatments; and core concepts of care such as comfort, participation, and hope. She currently has a particular focus on recovery from traumatic injury and older people.

Anne Zachary qualified in medicine and then psychiatry at the Royal Free Hospital. She is a member of the British Psychoanalytical Society and for more than 20 years, until 2010, also worked as a consultant psychiatrist in psychotherapy at the Portman Clinic (Tavistock & Portman NHS Foundation Trust). From there she consulted to various medium secure units and prisons and then to the high secure Broadmoor Hospital (2003–8). She has also built up a private psychoanalytic practice in Kew. She has published journal papers on puerperal breakdown and the menopause and on firesetting and homosexuality, as well as a chapter on murderousness. A reminiscence appeared in the *British Journal of Psychotherapy* in the autumn of 2013.

Introduction:
revisiting the paradigm

David Armstrong & Michael Rustin

Origin of this book

This book has its origin in an invited symposium[1] whose aim was to revisit one of the founding paradigms of a psychoanalytically informed approach to the practical understanding of institutions. The paradigm to be reconsidered had been first set out in writings on the subject of unconscious defences against anxiety by Elliott Jaques and Isabel Menzies Lyth, in papers published in 1955 and 1960, respectively.[2] Underlying this aim was a perception by the editors that this paradigm now risked becoming a dead metaphor, since although its key ideas had been considerably developed[3] and were often alluded to, it was not clear that it was any longer able to generate new insights in a landscape that had changed considerably during the time since they were first advanced.

Thus, the intention was to bring together a group to share reflections arising from their own work, on ways in which this paradigm continued to inform them, had potential for extension, refinement, or revision, and might be able to take account of both conceptual and contextual changes since it was first put forward. This group included organizational consultants, researchers, educators, and professional practitioners in the fields of education, health, and welfare, all of whom were known to be interested in these ideas.

In a Framing Statement, "Revisiting the 'Unconscious Defences against Anxiety' Thesis", at the symposium, the editors had identified some questions and considerations that they suggested might usefully be engaged with. These included developments in psychoanalytic theory which had taken place since the paradigm was first set out; advances in the socio-technical systems approach to organizations, including the analysis of primary tasks and the anxieties that might be evoked by these; and consideration of more pervasive social changes that had taken place since 1960, in the direction of, for example, globalization, the information economy, neoliberalism, and new forms of management and governance. All of these we believed might be relevant to the renewal of the "unconscious defences against anxiety" paradigm. We also proposed that it would be valuable to examine different institutional and professional settings, to explore empirically whether and in what ways anxieties were being evoked in different fields of work, and how they were giving rise to defences.

Finally, we suggested that a research programme to investigate this field needed to be one that was committed to bringing about change in social practices and institutions, and not merely in describing them. As in psychoanalysis, understandings are achieved through the process of change itself, rather than as its "objective" precursor. In this tradition, a main resource for learning about prevailing anxieties and defences has been researchers who have engaged in reflection on experiences within their own work, as practitioners and/or consultants. It follows, we argued, that a research programme to investigate this field should be one that actively involves its subjects and aspires to a democratic communication of ideas.

This Introduction sets out the issues raised in the Framing Statement, linking them with the contributions made in the following chapters. We first revisit the original thesis that has shaped this entire tradition of thought.

Probably its most well-known expression was Isabel Menzies Lyth's 1960 paper "A Case Study in the Functioning of a Social System as a Defence against Anxiety: A Report on the Nursing Service of a General Hospital". There she described the dysfunctions of a particular social system and explained them as the effects of unconscious defences against the anxieties evoked in staff in the work of nursing. She argued that nurses were exposed to intense mental pain through the impact of patients' suffering, and also from the necessity to confront situations of physical intimacy with patients for which they were emotionally ill-prepared. The states of pervasive anxiety aroused by this situation were largely unrecognized by the senior staff members responsible for managing this system. Unconscious defences against such anxiety were socially constructed and maintained, and they were institutionalized as inflexible routines and practices into which trainee nurses were social-ized and to which they were expected to conform. This regime took the form of a minimization of personal contact with patients (even though it was an expectation of being able to give personal care to patients that had motivated many to become nurses), a displacement of sensitive forms of nursing by the ritualistic following of rules, and the mainte-nance of rigid hierarchies which required unquestioning obedience to superiors, significantly restricting the exercise of judgement and discre-tion. Correspondingly, nurses were given little opportunity to reflect with more experienced staff on their feelings about their work. Men-zies Lyth argued that in the absence of opportunities to become aware of and to work through the anxieties inherent in their tasks, nurses responded by retreating from their painful situation, the latter taking the form of high levels of absence and sickness and of withdrawal from training of about a third of trainees. It was dysfunctions of this kind that had led to the original invitation to Menzies Lyth to conduct an investigation within a particular hospital.

Three chapters in this book explicitly discuss Menzies Lyth's seminal paper on the system of nursing. In the opening chapter, William Halton critically views this study, identifying a key neglected element—that of obsessional defences—in his analysis. In chapter 7, Liz Tutton and Debbie Langstaff review academic research on nursing practice since its publication. They point out that attention was paid to Menzies Lyth's study in the years after it was published (perhaps more than she herself realized) and that it contributed to a significant shift towards the more personal care of patients by nurses which came about in the 1970s. But they show also that some of the lessons concerning the need for the relationship-sensitive nursing which were learned then are now being unlearned, under the pressures of scarcity and of depersonalizing forms of management. Marcus Evans (chapter 8), responding to the Francis Report (2013) on serious deficits in the care provided in British hospitals, draws on his observations and experience to describe regres-sive changes in the contemporary practice of nursing. It seems that although hospital systems have changed considerably since Menzies Lyth wrote her paper, they often retain a defensive function of keeping at a distance the emotional experiences of the nursing task.

Psychoanalytic theory and its social applications

Explanations of social and institutional behaviour as a consequence of unconscious mental processes have generally been regarded with some suspicion in the mainstream of social science. Difficulties in observing and accounting for unconscious processes, which are of their nature hidden from everyday view, have made the disciplines of sociology and psychology reluctant to incorporate these dimensions of mental life and social behaviour into their models of theory and method. The idea that unconscious or irrational motivations might have relevance can usually gain a hearing only when more conventional forms of explanation seem to fail, or to need some supplement. Menzies Lyth's original paper retains its impact on contemporary readers because the discrepancy between what the hospital she studied set out to do (train nurses, provide care for patients) and what she observed actually happened within its walls was so great. It was this that provided scope for the explanation she gave in terms of extreme states of mind and the institutional defences constructed to hold these at bay. One of this book's purposes is to consider other settings where awareness of unconscious dimensions of thought and action can deepen understanding of institutional processes.

Unconscious defences against anxiety:
explanations from "inside" and from "outside"

The concepts of unconscious anxiety and unconscious defences in the description of psycho-social processes, central to the work of both Menzies Lyth and Elliott Jaques, had their origin in contributions by Melanie Klein and her colleagues to the field of psychoanalysis and its applications (Klein, 1935, 1946). Klein differentiated between paranoid-schizoid and depressive forms of anxiety, holding that the former characteristically belongs to an earlier and more primitive phase of development in which the infant self feels persecuted by its environment, with the loved and hated aspects of its objects being radically split from one another. Depressive anxiety was a consequence of a greater integration of the personality such that the severity of splitting between good and bad—the loved and the hated—was lessened and the self became capable of care for the well-being of its objects and capable also of remorse and a desire to repair the damage that in phantasy it inflicted on them. Jaques gave more attention than Menzies Lyth to the differences between paranoid-schizoid and depressive anxiety and their significance, although both these concepts are relevant to the understanding of anxieties in the context of nursing.

There were, however, significant differences between Jaques's and Menzies Lyth's formulation of these issues, as they emerge in and shape organizational dynamics. Jaques's (1955) view was that "*one* of the primary cohesive elements binding individuals into institutionalized human association is that of defence against psychotic anxiety" (p. 479, emphasis in original). He argued correspondingly that the defensive apparatus is imported into the organization, as it were, from outside, arising from the psychopathologies of its members. As he put it later (in the process of repudiating it), "individuals unconsciously or collusively concoct organisation as a means of defence against psychotic anxieties, thereby generating a fundamental cause of problems within these organisations" (Jaques, 1995, p. 343). This view tends to split off the emotional world of the organization from its actual setting in the engagement of individuals within particular structures and in given social, economic, and political contexts.[4]

Menzies Lyth, in contrast, saw defensive processes as elicited by anxieties that were, instead, intrinsic to the particular work that an organization undertook—nursing in her original study. On this view, the defensive structure of the organization is not, as it were, imported into the organization by individuals *de novo* but is, rather, generated within it and is experienced by new entrants as a something to which they have to adapt. "This means in practice that she (the new entrant nurse) must incorporate and operate the social system more or less as she finds it, restructuring her psychic defences as necessary to match it" (1960/1988, p. 74.)

Bion's theory of container and contained (Bion, 1963) throws light on this difference, since he argued that the relations between the two are reciprocal, the container influencing the contained, and the contained influencing the container. The mother–baby relationship is a prototypical case, the mother's containing functions and capacities being shaped in response to the baby and its particular qualities. Another is the psychoanalytic setting itself, in which the containing frame of the analysis has to accommodate whatever the analysand brings to it. We can think of the psychoanalytic process as itself constituting a social institution, in which both internal realities (those of analyst and analysand) and "external" ones (those arising from the setting and the traditions of psychoanalysis) have influence.[5] The setting and its effects may become most visible when it is at risk, which may be for internal reasons ("acting out") or because of external disruption. Jaques and

Menzies Lyth gave different emphases to the influence of the external and the internal (analogous, perhaps, to the duality of culture and personality[6]) in the understanding of the origins and consequences of unconscious anxieties for institutions. These differences are addressed by Philip Boxer (chapter 5) and Nick Papadopoulos (chapter 6) in this book, each arguing that institutional processes, and not individual states of mind, should be seen as the principal sources or generators of anxiety and defence.

Paul Hoggett (chapter 3) outlines an approach to the psycho-social which seeks to take account of both internal and external forces contributing to irrational states of mind, insisting on their necessary synthesis. He extends the consideration of states of anxiety from the workplace and the particular social institution to the larger society. Hoggett gives an unconscious dimension to Raymond Williams' concept of a structure of feeling, and he draws on psychoanalytic theory, in particular the idea of an internal establishment, as resources for the analysis of collective states of mind. He argues that "late modernity" has given rise to a pervasive state of anxiety, manifest in the panics that get into organizations and governments as they respond to perceived risks of many kinds.

The psychoanalytic concept of anxiety

Anxiety was a significant concept for Freud, the central topic of his *Inhibitions, Symptoms and Anxiety* (1926d [1925]), and it became even more important in psychoanalytic theory as a consequence of the influence of Klein. It is the Kleinian formulation of anxiety which was taken up by Jaques and Menzies Lyth in their development of these ideas in institutional settings. One can question the grounds for continuing to give centrality to this idea. Susan Long (chapter 2) and Paul Hoggett (chapter 3) each argue that this concept is too narrow and that there is a need to broaden the paradigm, to include (in Hoggett's words) "a variety of feelings that threaten to be overwhelming". Many examples of the effects of overwhelming feelings, and defences against them, are indeed described in this book. Emil Jackson (chapter 17) discusses the sexual anxieties evoked in teachers by adolescent pupils; Mannie Sher (chapter 10) explores the dynamics of containing sexual violence in the work of a Sexual Assault Referral Centre; Simon Tucker (chapter 16) describes the fear of failure engendered in primary school head teachers who feel both isolated and persecuted; and Maxim de Sauma, Sarah Fielding, and Michael Rustin (chapter 20) describe the feelings of shame, humiliation, and anger that threaten to overcome the young offenders with whom they work.

Larry Hirschhorn and Sharon Horowitz (chapter 12), in a departure from the predominantly care-focused concerns of many chapters in this book, view anxiety from a more positive perspective. They argue that, in contemporary society, risk-taking activities—from extreme sports to trading in financial markets—are positively valued by many and that the anxieties engaged by these pursuits can be exciting and energizing. Like Papadopoulos and Boxer, they argue that in "turbulent environments" (Emery & Trist, 1965), such as those of the present day, anxieties may have a different form and function than in more stable and hierarchical systems. These arguments, like those of many other contributors, locate the sources of anxiety in social processes that extend well beyond any single institution. Hirschhorn and Horowitz describe the need to differentiate between what they call protective frames—cultural constructions that enable risks to be managed rationally—and the unconscious defences that are resorted to when these break down. The protective frames they identify in the context of extreme sports are the specific discipline of a sport, its skills, and its good equipment. In financial trading, they are the understanding of the market as a game, an enjoyment of the process of trading, and a belief in the capacity of the partners as a pair. What ensues when these protective frames break down (as they did for their clients) seems to be something akin to the "manic defences" of psychopathology. One might think of the consultancy practice they described as enabling clients to discriminate between protective frames and unconscious defences against anxiety.

More generally, given these broadening frames of affective reference, a question arises as to whether there are still good reasons for encompassing this "wide variety of feelings" within an overarching concept of anxiety, or whether they should be thought of as each requiring a separate formulation and analysis.

For Freud, anxiety was experienced whenever the ego, or the rational part of the mind, felt at risk of being overwhelmed. Anxiety is, we might say, the signal that unconscious desires and fears are threatening to take control of the personality. This basic idea is consistent with the later developments of this concept in psychoanalysis, including the theory of unconscious defences. Anxiety is what threatens to swamp the capacity for understanding and thinking, and the sense of self. Neurotic anxiety gives rise, in Freud's view, to certain symptoms, to which the unconscious social defences described in Menzies Lyth's nursing paper are analogous. Psychotic anxiety disrupts the mind altogether, and it detaches the spheres of unconscious fantasy and reality from one another, leaving the self at the mercy of the former.[7]

Nevertheless, it seems fair to say that Freud struggled in his writings to give consistency to this concept, returning to the topic many times (De Bianchedi, Scalozub De Boschan, De Cortiñas, & De Piccolo, 1988). Freud states in *Inhibitions, Symptoms and Anxiety* that "anxiety has an unmistakable relation to *expectation*: it is anxiety *about* something" (1926d [1925], p. 163). But whereas "fear" is of a known object, the object of "anxiety" is a response to a situation of danger that is not understood by the subject. Freud's original concept of anxiety is a quantitative idea, of psychic equilibrium being disturbed by excesses of desire from within, then being managed through the diversion of energy into phobias or other neurotic symptoms. In 1926 Freud locates the site of anxiety in the ego, and this allows him to recognize the different kinds of relation to objects in which it occurs. In the *New Introductory Lectures* (1933a), he suggests that a particular determinant of anxiety (defined as the response to a situation of danger) is allotted to every age of development: "The danger of physical helplessness fits the stage of the ego's early immaturity; the danger of loss of an object (or loss of love) fits the lack of self-sufficiency in the first years of childhood; the fantasied danger of being castrated fits the phallic phase; and finally fear of the super-ego, which assumes a special position, fits the period of latency" (1933a, p. 88). But although his theory of anxiety does acquire a relational dimension, its primary focus remains on danger to the self.

It is with the object-relations school of psychoanalysis that the fully relational concept of anxiety, and its wider social applications, emerges. Klein did not disagree with Freud about repression—indeed, she extended his understanding of the harmful effects of an excessive superego. But because she held that from the beginnings of life the human being was in an emotionally charged relationship to others (initially, its maternal object), the focal concern became the nature of these relationships and, in particular, the balance that prevailed within them of feelings of love and hate, both of which dispositions, according to Klein (and indeed Freud), were innate. The development of the concept of anxiety in Klein's work, and in particular the ideas of paranoid-schizoid and depressive anxiety, shifted its emphasis away from the force and fear of instinctual impulses. Unconscious anxieties are about risks to the survival not only of the self, but also of its objects. The bodily dimension of anxiety does not disappear—Menzies Lyth describes her nurses as deeply disturbed by feelings—for example, of desire and disgust—aroused by their proximity to the exposed and damaged bodies of their patients. But it is an essentially relational idea of anxiety, deeply influenced by Klein's formulations, that is taken up in the social defences paradigm.

Later developments in the concept of anxiety

In the Framing Paper it was noted that, in recent decades, an evolution of the concept of unconscious defences against anxiety has taken place, primarily in a clinical context, through the idea of narcissistic defences or "borderline" states of mind. Psychoanalysts including Henri Rey (1994), John Steiner (1993), Ronald Britton (1998b), and Edna O'Shaughnessy (1981, 1992) evolved this idea to explain a particular form of unconscious psychological defence in patients. This borderline state of mind, sometimes referred to as a psychic retreat (Armstrong, 2005b; Steiner, 1993), is adopted as a refuge from unbearable anxieties of paranoid-schizoid or depressive kinds, or both. These anxieties are liable to be disavowed, repressed, or split off since they threaten to be overwhelming to the psyche. In this formulation, the place in the mind of knowing and understanding, and of not-knowing and not-understanding, has become more central, following the influence of Wilfred Bion. Whereas in classical Kleinian theory, it was the balance of love and hate which was crucial in determining the state of the psyche, Bion, developing Klein's idea of an epistemophilic instinct, added a third fundamental disposition—namely, the desire to understand—whose inhibition or destruction was liable to be damaging or even catastrophic for the personality, as he showed in his descriptions of his analytic work with psychotic patients (Bion, 1967). Bion links his account with Freud's early understanding of psychotic states as characterized by a loss of connection between mind and reality.

This idea of a borderline or narcissistic defence against anxiety has been recently made use of by colleagues in the UK to understand various crises in the welfare system—for example, in the failure of agencies responsible for child protection to intervene when children's lives were at risk. One such instance was the death of Victoria Climbié in 2000, a case that attracted great public attention. Following the official Report by Lord Laming which described its circumstances in detail,[8] it was argued (Cooper, 2005; M. E. Rustin, 2005; M. J. Rustin, 2004) that it was a refusal to know, a form of "turning a blind eye" (a phrase used by Steiner in his characterization of a borderline state of mind), that had allowed this catastrophe to take place. They suggested that it was the forms of relationship and cultures which dominated these occupational settings which were the key factor. Procedures could themselves sometimes become a form of unconscious organizational defence, just as they had been in the hospital studied by Menzies Lyth. Andrew Cooper and Julian Lousada (2005) have explored the use of this "borderline" concept in relation to the contemporary health and welfare systems more widely, in their book *Borderline Welfare*. Andrew Cooper and Amanda Lees's chapter in this book (chapter 15) revisits this field of practice. It is likely that the focus of public attention on a single scandalous case when abuses of this kind are revealed, and an institutional reluctance to investigate the systemic contexts in which failures occur, is itself evidence of the resilience of such defences of not-knowing.[9]

A related development in psychoanalytic theory relevant to this paradigm is the theory of destructive narcissism. Herbert Rosenfeld (1971) developed this idea to explain the form of narcissistic defence in which contempt for others was mobilized to sustain a sense of omnipotence, a damaging instance of what John Steiner (1993) calls a pathological organization, dominated by hatred and destructiveness. Both Rosenfeld (1971) and Donald Meltzer (1973) wrote of the phenomenon of the internal gang, or gang in the mind, as such a form of unconscious psychological defence. Such a formation may be keeping at bay overwhelming feelings of guilt caused by the real or phantasied damage caused by the self to its primary objects of attachment. Where the self can feel justified and supported by its internal gang in its contempt for victims, guilt can be repressed or projected on to others.

To the concepts of persecutory and depressive anxiety and "borderline" or narcissistic states of mind may be added even more primitive anxieties concerning survival itself. Bion's (1963) theory of the container–contained relationship and his idea of nameless dread, Esther Bick's (1968) observations of infants and her concept of "the second skin" as a defence against the fear of "falling to pieces", Frances Tustin's (1981) and Donald Meltzer's (1975) work on autism, and Thomas Ogden's (1989) concept of the contiguous-autistic position are all resources for the exploration of extreme anxieties whose origin may lie prior to the formation of paranoid-schizoid personality structures. In this book, Aideen Lucey's discussion in chapter 13 of the second-skin defence adopted by corporate managers in response to a performance culture draws on Bick's ideas; Boxer, drawing on Lacan's writing, develops a concept of "existential anxiety", distinct from "performance" or "annihilation anxiety". Hoggett's reference to an almost universal fear of risks in late modern capitalism points to pervasive anxieties about survival itself.

Developments in the understanding of the mechanisms of defence have accompanied exploration of these extreme and disordered states of mind. Particularly important has been "projective identification"— the idea that individuals may project into and then perceive in others attributes that they find intolerable to recognize as parts of themselves. Bion saw such projective communications as sometimes merely evacuative, getting rid of unwanted parts of the self into its objects, and as sometimes expressing a desire to communicate. Such communications take place in the relationship between "container and contained" (Bion, 1963), both in the maternal and the psychoanalytic situations, as well as in group and institutional contexts.

Several contributors in this book make use of the concepts of projective identification and the countertransference to understand particular forms of anxiety and defence. Jo Finch and Jason Schaub (chapter 19) explain the inability of assessors of social work training placements to make appropriate judgements about performance (sometimes almost no student is allowed to fail) as an effect of their being overwhelmed by the projective identifications of their students. Anne Zachary (chapter 11) describes the cut-off states of mind of staff she encountered in a visit to a Special Hospital, and their disorienting effects on her, which she interprets as their unconscious defence against the anxiety provoked by their patients. Maxim de Sauma and his co-authors (chapter 20) describe one of the main issues in their group work with young offenders as the risk of becoming overwhelmed by the projected mindlessness and depression of their patients.

These ideas of projective identification and the countertransference give us resources to understand the larger transmission of anxieties in organizational systems, since distress and pain felt in any one part of a system are liable to be projected into other parts. Thus, in Finch's and Schaub's studies, it is ultimately the distresses of disadvantaged and marginalized social work clients which are being unconsciously transmitted to social work trainees and, from them, onwards to their teachers. In the original Menzies Lyth nursing study, the projections were firmly organized so as to operate in the opposite direction. Upwards communications about emotions from patients and junior nurses were blocked, and the obsessional defences and latent hostility towards patients that are noted in Halton's chapter as having become embedded in the nursing hierarchy were pushed downwards into the front-line nurses. This concept of the mirroring effects of anxieties transmitted across different levels of an organization is one of the most powerful psycho-social ideas to have emerged from the understanding of the processes of projective and introjective identification.

It will be evident that there is a large variety of states of mind that can become overwhelming in social settings and that are liable to give rise to unconscious structures of defence. Developments in psychoanalytic thinking, most often based on clinical experience, have provided new resources for reflecting on anxieties and defences arising in social settings. It is because it makes possible such subtle explorations of different kinds of relations between persons and their objects that psychoanalytic thinking remains a valuable resource for the study of institutional processes.

Varieties of institutions

We next consider the different social and institutional contexts to which the original paradigm has relevance. The anxieties and unconscious defences described in the original paradigm were located in two particular settings: the industrial conflicts of a factory and hospital nursing. But there are many other social institutions to which it has relevance, as is shown in contributions to this book. What conceptual and methodological resources can be brought to bear on understanding the institutional contexts of defences against anxiety?

From the beginning, socio-technical systems theory has been central to this work. Two of its key concepts are: the transformative process by which inputs from various elements of an institution's environment are transformed through work into its outputs; and the idea of the "primary task", which identifies the principal goals of an institution or sub-group within it and directs attention to the organizational prerequisites of these being either fulfilled or not (Miller, 1993; Miller & Rice, 1967). It should be recognized that the primary task of an organization is constructed, not given, and is often disputed. The term is most valuable as an analytic resource, for clarifying the connections and interdependences between different elements of a social system, and should not be taken as a moral or political endorsement of any particular institution's goals. Gordon Lawrence (1985) valuably differentiates between the *normative* primary task, the *existential* primary task, and the *phenomenal* primary task of an organization. The normative is what members of organizations feel they *ought* to be doing, under the direction of authority; the existential task is what they *believe* they are doing; and the phenomenal is what it is hypothesized that they *are* doing, perhaps outside their conscious awareness. These distinctions are analytically useful in getting to grips with belief, fantasy, and reality in the behaviour of organizations and their members.

Organizations are often internally diverse. There may be no single primary task that captures their complexity. Hospitals, for example, include different environments of care. An operating theatre, an accident and emergency room, a long-stay ward for children suffering from serious illnesses, and a ward populated by patients suffering from dementia all make different emotional demands on their staff and their patients, although there are responsibilities common to all caring environments. In many institutions, there will be more than one principal goal or value, and its definition may be contested, leading to conflict. For example, in schools, the goal of maximizing the achievement of the most capable children may compete with commitments to children with average or low academic ability. Or in an institution such as a prison, the goals of administering punishment (by means of confinement and other measures of deprivation) may be in conflict with the aim of achieving rehabilitation and reform. Such conflicts can lead to serious problems of organizational identity.

Clarifying the inputs, outputs, and transformative processes within organizations, and what accompanies these in terms of their structures, cultures, and relations to their environments, provides a useful method of analysis. But from the perspective of unconscious defences against anxiety, there is a further question—namely, where organizations have distinct primary tasks as their condition of operation, are there also distinct forms of anxiety that are evoked by them? We suggest that this well be the case and propose the hypothesis that many primary tasks are liable to have associated with them a corresponding primary anxiety.

Contributions to this book give grounds for thinking that the dominant anxieties of, for example, primary school teachers, investment bankers, hospital nurses, lawyers, policeman, and prison officers are different from one another. For example, a significant anxiety for teachers must be that their students fail to learn; this may lead teachers to fear that they are failing too. This is linked to the larger anxiety inseparable from learning itself, which inherently involves the risk of "not-knowing" and the vulnerability that comes from this. This may indeed be the central anxiety, intrinsic to learning, present in all educational environments. It is then one of the essential tasks of educators to contain the vulnerability of learners, so that they can tolerate not-knowing for long enough to be able to learn and change. When this anxiety becomes overwhelming, unconscious organizational defences are liable to emerge. These may include the scapegoating of failure, expressed through an excess of blame or exclusion; mechanistic prescription and regulation of how learning is to take place; and the displacement of complex learning by concerns about external recognition or disgrace.[10]

"Defences" are constructed as a means of coping with such anxieties, and they become embedded and enforced within the structure, rules, and cultures of institutions as routine assumptions and practices that become taken for granted "as the way things are done here" (Trist, Higgins, Murray, & Pollock, 1990). They are learned and adopted during the process of socialization of new entrants to an institution (who may have joined initially with rather different expectations than are realized in practice) and are then passed on to their successors. Institutions will select for those who find their defensive structures and cultures tolerable or welcome and will tend to marginalize or expel those who find themselves resisting them. Jon Stokes (chapter 14) discusses this phenomenon in the context of the recruitment and socialization of lawyers.

Such defences, like the symptoms of neurotic or psychotic anxieties which Freud described in individual patients, can be expected to have a positive function of some kind, displacing or reducing the anxieties to which they are a response. Thus an apparently superficial and purposeless symptom (e.g., an obsession, a hysterical anxiety, or a phobia) gives a more-or-less manageable form to desires or fears that unconsciously threaten the integrity of the personality. While social defences are unlikely to be helpful to an institution or to its members in achieving their primary goals or outputs, they may nevertheless perversely contribute to their psychic survival.

One aim of this book is to explore differences between organizational contexts and to clarify the particular states of anxiety and defences which emerge in them. Institutions described in the chapters that follow are engaged in different kinds of work, often designed to meet the needs or risks to well–being of distinct populations of clients. These include hospital patients, school pupils, infants and young children in day nurseries, young offenders, offenders detained or in treatment because of diagnoses of severe personality disorder, and vulnerable families deemed in need of attention by social services. While the focus may be on the professional staff providing the services, rather than on the users of their services, the clients are nevertheless an implicit presence in these accounts as the ultimate "objects" of professional work. Where the organizations in question are businesses, the principal goal may be the achievement of a financial surplus or profit, although there may also be "intrinsic" commitments to the value of whatever is produced in pursuit of this end.

Contributors to this symposium were from different locations, and some differences of perspective emerged. Some were committed to (or perhaps nostalgic for) the containing structures of the welfare settlement of post-war Britain, with its commitment to social integration and care. From this position the marketization and governmental regulation of autonomous professional practices were seen as sources of anxiety. But for others, perhaps more accustomed to work in the private sector and to the culture of the US, exposure to new forms of competition and risk-taking, and socio-technical changes arising from the knowledge economy, were viewed in a more hopeful spirit. What was shared, however, was a commitment to the psychoanalytically informed analysis of social institutions.

A changed social environment

A third element of our approach was concerned with understanding broader social changes that had taken place during the last half-century. The question here was, what implications did these have for the understanding of anxieties? The original studies had taken place in strongly boundaried, hierarchical settings in the 1950s. Much has changed in Western (and other) societies since then. Social structures have in significant respects become weaker, and individuals are required to depend more on their own initiative for survival. Substantial de-industrialization has taken place, and a large proportion of employees no longer work in large-scale physical manufacturing but, instead, in service, knowledge, or digital industries or are self-employed. Financialization of the economy has occurred, demanding more pressing attention to profit in many organizations, both public and private. Control by extended hierarchies has been to a degree replaced by networks, systems of market exchange, or devolved autonomy, in which discipline is imposed through rewards and sanctions for competitive success or failure. This change in the modalities of power has been described as a move from government to governance, and its practices theorized as the new public management (Clarke, Gewirtz, & McLaughlin, 2000; Du Gay, 2005).[11] That is to say, regulation and control are achieved less through direct instruction and command, and more by inspecting, measuring, and auditing the activities of units expected take responsibility for their performance.[12] Many organizations are required to be concerned not merely with the adequacy of their performance according to defined criteria, but also with its standard relative to that of competitors, with published league tables to make visible a hierarchy of merit and achievement. Consumers and service users are supposed to be empowered, through being able to exercise choices that reward success and punish failure among providers. Such systems exercise formidable pressures on organizations and are the source of anxieties no doubt of both productive and destructive kinds. Occupations have emerged that exercise the responsibilities of audit and inspection. Whereas the main function of earlier inspectorates, such as Her Majesty's Inspectors (HMIs) in the British school system, was to provide expert advice and support, the new inspectors are *de facto* the enforcers of government policies, including those that give priority to financial solvency. (This emphasis is particularly fierce in the British NHS.) It is widely held that permanence and security of employment has been diminished by these changes and that "precarity", as with the emergence of zero-hours contracts, is becoming a common experience. There is much to be investigated in regard to the different pressures that now bear down on individuals and organizations in the era of neoliberalism. Several chapters make direct or indirect reference to this context. In the socio-technical systems tradition, the seminal concept referring to these changes was the "turbulent environment" (Emery & Trist, 1965).

Theories of globalization and individualization developed by social scientists such as Ulrich Beck (1992), Anthony Giddens (1994, 1998), and David Harvey (1991, 2005) go some way to explain the changes noted above. They describe the erosion of social structures that formerly provided some protection to large numbers of people from the pressures of competition. Improved means of communication, both physical and virtual, enabled corporations to escape from national and local constraints on their operations. Deregulation of labour and financial markets has altered the balance of economic and social power to the advantage of capital. Ulrich Beck's idea of the risk society emphasized the exposure of citizens to new threats to well-being, from which collectivist structures were now less able to insulate them. Giddens took an optimistic view of these changes, seeing them as potentially empowering citizens to exercise greater choice and agency in their consumption of what we might call the welfare goods of education and healthcare.[13] A concept of modernization essentially favourable to the enhanced role of markets and consumer choice was influenced by these conceptions, and it has dominated the approaches of governments in Britain and the US since 1980.

Anxieties and defences against them may be generated in this context at opposite poles of the social spectrum. At one end, there has been the "irrational exuberance"[14] seen in the financial system, which contributed to the near-collapse of the banking system in 2007–8. Of interest to researchers into unconscious defences against anxiety must be the states of mind and behaviours observed within the financial sector in this period (Stein, 2011; Tuckett, 2012). At the other, we have the re-emergence of food banks for the poor; there were also the Summer Riots in London of 2012, in which large numbers of young people engaged in disorder and looting on a scale and with a rapidity that owed much to the role of new media of communication.

Related to these perspectives is a literature on the displacement of vertical by horizontal forms of connectedness in recent decades—sometimes described as the emergence of the network society. Information technology is assigned an important role in these changes. A positive view of their potential has been put forward by Manuel Castells (2012) and Paul Mason (2013. They explain the recent emergence of rapidly forming protest movements, such as those of the Arab Spring, in part through the wide availability of instant lateral communication, through social media and the phenomena of texting, blogging, and email, which enable collectivities to form and dissolve in rapid and apparently spontaneous ways. Mason has used the evocative metaphor of swarms and swarming to describe this phenomenon.

There are also the broader consequences of information technology to be examined. On the one hand, this makes information openly available at an unprecedented scale and immediacy. On the other, these "virtual" resources can be deployed in perverse and exploitative ways, engendering new forms of addictive, delusional, and sometimes violent behaviour. The impact of these technologies and the behaviours to which they give rise on family dynamics, as well as on the relations between generations, are another field to be investigated. James Krantz's chapter examines these issues (chapter 4).

What are the consequences of the emergence of these new environments for anxiety and systems of defence? Several chapters explore such contexts—for example, examining the anxieties of senior entrepreneurs and managers working in financial services (Hirschhorn & Horowitz), in the legal profession (Stokes), and in corporate management (Lucey) and of primary school head teachers (Tucker) now exposed to wider entrepreneurial responsibilities than they were prepared for by their earlier career as teachers.

It may be argued that anxieties are more often the product of these external contextual conditions than of psychological responses to distressing work. On this view, the main source of anxiety among the nurses in Menzies Lyth's study did not arise from their unmetabolized response to their patients' suffering, but, rather, from the impact of a hierarchical form of authority typical of its time.[15] The hospital's unresponsiveness to mental pain thus merely reflected the usual way in which emotions went unnoticed and disregarded.[16]

Some contributors argue that explanation of defences against anxiety needs to focus more on societal factors and less on the interpersonal dynamics that they believe had too large a place in Menzies Lyth's and especially Jaques's approaches. Boxer argues that the nature of anxiety has been transformed by the erosion of hierarchies and by the increasing "turbulence" of organizational settings, which are now exposed to many "lateral" pressures. He compares the organizational environment to the complex ecology of a coral reef and argues that a kind of "existential anxiety" (i.e., unstructured and always present) is the consequence of such wider exposure. Lucey adapts the psychoanalytic concept of the "second skin" to describe the defences she observes in corporate managers to a pervasive performance culture, which she sees as an effect of neoliberalism and the culture of consumer capitalism. Nick Papadopoulos (chapter 6) proposes that the "cultural theory" based on the work of Mary Douglas can add a valuable sociological dimension to the original paradigm (Douglas, 1970; Thompson, Ellis, & Wildavsky, 1990). Stresses in organizations on this view are as likely to be the outcome of contradictions and confusions of "thought styles" (between four competing patterns of competition, hierarchy, collective enclave, and fatalistic individualism and their hybrids) as of the unconscious anxieties evoked by the tasks performed by their members.

Giving inadequate recognition to external forces can explain why interventions to address unconscious defences, like that of Menzies Lyth, may fail. Alastair Bain's (1998) concept of domain anxiety was relevant to this. He addressed the problem of why organizational defences seemed sometime to be so embedded that local improvements apparently achieved through consultancy interventions could be short-lived, as defensive structures dominant in the wider environment returned to re-take possession of a now-deviant and therefore threatening setting.

These contrasting emphases on internal and external explanations echo differences between psychoanalytic and socio-technical kinds of explanation which emerged at the Tavistock Institute of Human Relations in the 1970s, and which led to serious divisions within it. We, however, hold that both of these levels of explanation—one locating the sources of anxiety in the organization of different kinds of work, and the other in the effects of an external social environment—are equally relevant and that they should not be seen as alternatives to one another.

Occupations and their practices and cultures are shaped by the larger social system in which they are located. But they also contribute to the shaping of that system and are not merely its passive effects. The occupations and institutions that were most powerful in the era of the European welfare state differ from those that dominate in the era of neoliberalism, and each of them was active in shaping its respective period of hegemony. For example, the mining industry, employing 734,000 workers in Britain in 1950 and virtually none today, and the financial and insurance sector, employing 1.1 million in 2012, exercised influence larger than their numbers in shaping its social system in these two periods.

Practical understandings of anxieties and defences

As well as investigating the nature of unconscious anxieties and defences in organizations, our symposium was interested in how they could be practically addressed. This was the normative or ethical commitment of the originators of this paradigm. Jaques sought through shared understanding to find solutions to some of the pressing problems of industrial conflict at his time of writing. Menzies Lyth hoped that a shared understanding of the hospital social system as an unconscious defence might lead to improvement in the well-being of both patients and nurses.

The contributors to this volume seem all to share this commitment. Jackson describes the role of a work discussion group with teachers in a school in thinking about the anxieties evoked by the sexualized behaviour of adolescent pupils, noting its calming and containing effects. Peter Elfer (chapter 18) reports the considerable take-up of this method in the day nurseries, as providing space for staff to reflect on the emotional dimension of their work with children and parents, improving the quality of care. Sebastian Kraemer (chapter 9) describes the difficulties of maintaining space for reflective practices in institutions such as hospitals. While strongly committed to this perspective and its benefits, he draws attention to the fragility of such spaces, drawing attention, as Freud had done, to the human proclivity to conform to the group in contexts of conflict or danger. (The anxieties aroused by situations where thought is unfettered by authority or convention explains the fate of Bion's Northfield Experiment in the British Army: see Bion, 1961; Harrison, 2000.) Long provides an unexpected extension of Bion's idea that there is a primary instinct to understand, or for knowledge, to be added to the previous duality of Love and Hatred (L, H, and K in Bion's notation) (Bion, 1962a). She describes what she has learned from her training of horses about how learning can take place. Horses are, like human beings, social animals and are trained most effectively when both their need for security and safety and their curiosity and initiative are engaged. Consultancy, she proposes, should function more in the mode of "whispering", in a conversation—and less in the mode of shouting. Finch's and Schaub's attention to the functions of projective identification in the practice assessments of social work trainees is plainly given in the hope of modifying the toxic processes they describe. Lucey found that her leadership development work with managers was able to provide some containment of their anxieties and restore contact with their more reparative and authentic selves, though she describes this as addressing the symptoms rather than the causes of the anxieties that manifest themselves in their second-skin defences.

There is a methodological as well as a normative dimension to the commitment of this tradition to practical understanding. A conception shared by clinical psychoanalysis and psychoanalytically informed consultancy is that understanding is best achieved in the activity of seeking change. There are ontological reasons for this, where the primary objects of understanding are unconscious states of mind, understood as real structures perceived mainly through their effects. The power and effect of unconscious formations becomes evident principally in the context of interactions, which create space (e.g., through the transference and countertransference) for observing the discrepancies between manifest and latent structures, as well as between external reality and its representations or misrepresentations. For the most part, the work in this book continues a tradition of action research which was initially inspired by a dictum attributed to Kurt Lewin, "The best way to understand a system is to change it."

There is also an epistemological and communicative dimension to this paradigm, in both its original and its contemporary forms. The epistemological aspect lies in the necessity to describe and capture the experience of human objects of research in their own terms. The anthropologist Clifford Geertz (1983), advocating a conception of research that can capture the culture- and meaning-making capacity of its subjects, referred to such descriptions as "experience-near".

The communicative aspect arises from the fact that in both clinical psychoanalysis and organizational consultancy, it is only when those whom psychoanalysts and organizational consultants are trying to understand begin to understand themselves that change takes place. Researchers in these linked traditions therefore have to be adept at formulating ideas that may well draw on theoretical or technical conceptions, but also have to be intelligible and accessible in the language of everyday life.

This book contains both writings that are primarily theoretical and others that in their descriptions (whether of head teachers, young offenders, or indeed partners in a hedge fund) remain close to the experiences of their subjects. A capacity to translate freely between theoretical and everyday idioms (recognizing, of course, that each influences the other) is intrinsic to this field of work.

Another way of putting this is to say that the model of research that underlies this paradigm is a democratic one. This bears on the distinction between horizontal and vertical forms of communication which is made in this book. One form of knowledge, which is appropriate to many medical, scientific, and technological fields, is top-down in its usual application. Expert research is undertaken and is implemented in policies for the benefit of unavoidably inexpert and passive citizens. The contemporary "nudge" approach to public policy is a crafty attempt to achieve policy goals with a minimum of coercion. (Thaler & Sunstein, 2008). Another form of knowledge, more strongly represented in this book, is generated interactively in dialogue and through practical action, and its dissemination is more horizontal than vertical. Those working within this paradigm are generally committed to interactive, inclusive, and egalitarian forms of communication, on grounds that it these that facilitate learning and support consensual and democratic forms of authority.

* * *

The book is arranged in four sections. The first is mainly theoretical, and its chapters analyse, revise, and develop the original paradigm in the light of developments in both theory and society . The three subsequent sections focus on particular fields of application: healthcare and nursing, the private sector, and education and welfare. However, theory and its contextual applications overlap throughout. For example,

William Halton's opening chapter both argues for a theoretical revision to Menzies Lyth's original thesis, and makes a contribution to the understanding of health systems. Hirschhorn and Horowitz's chapter reports an experience of consultancy in the financial sector of business and challenges a negative view of risk and anxiety, which it sees as implicit in the "social defences" tradition. An underlying assumption of this work is that theoretical understanding can only be advanced by engagement with particular contexts. It is through such a dialogue between the investigation of what Cooper and Lees call complex particulars that we hope that the unconscious defences against anxiety paradigm will be advanced.

Notes

1. This took place at St John's College Oxford in September 2012, with the support of the Independent Social Research Foundation, Tavistock Consulting, and the Research Centre of St John's College. Its precursor was an earlier symposium, celebrating the life and work of Menzies Lyth, which took place at the Tavistock Centre in 2009 and whose proceedings were published in the *British Journal of Psychotherapy*, 26 (No. 2, 2010), pp. 138-226, edited by D. Armstrong, T. Dartington, M. Rustin, and A. Zachary.

2. Isabel Menzies Lyth's 1960 paper, which appeared in *Human Relations, 13* (2): 95-121, was published under her maiden name, Isabel Menzies, as were her other publications prior to her marriage in the mid-1970s. In this book she is referred to throughout as Menzies Lyth.

3. For example, by Menzies Lyth and her associates' own work on nursery care (Bain & Barnett, 1986; Menzies Lyth, 1989), Hinshelwood and Skogstad's *Observing Organisations* (2000, pp. 1–11, 155–166), Miller and Gwynne's *A Life Apart* (1972), Tim Dartington's *Managing Vulnerability* (2010), and papers by Obholzer (1994b), Bain (1998), Hoyle (2004), Stein (2000), Long (2006), Cooper (2010), Khaleelee (2010), Krantz (2010), and Hoggett (2010).

4. One wonders, however, how well this formulation by Jaques of his earlier position corresponded to his own explanatory practice. His account of the depressive and paranoid-schizoid states of mind of managers and trade unionists in conflict with one another in the factory he studied (Jaques, 1955) suggests that these have origins in a structured social relationship and can by no means be seen solely as the projections of the unconscious anxieties of individuals. At issue in this debate is the adequacy or otherwise of methodological individualism in the explanation of social processes.

5. We are indebted to Margaret Rustin for this suggestion.

6. Eric Trist (1950) refers to this debate.

7. Those who have worked in psychotic environments, whether of a clinical or even political kind, know how terrorizing these can be.

8. http://webarchive.nationalarchives.gov.uk/20130107105354/http://www.dh.gov.uk/en/Publicationsandstatistics/Publications/PublicationsPolicyAnd Guidance/DH_4008654

9. Many other examples of this phenomenon could be given—for example, the practice of paedophilia occurring unnoticed or unhindered in public institutions (O'Hagan, 2012).

10. Pruitt and Barber (2004) give an account of these dilemmas from a US perspective.

11. Foundational to the earlier system is Weber's theory of bureaucracy (1948), to the later is Foucault on governmentality (Burchell, Gordon, & Miller, 1991).

12. Although these new systems are justified as conferring freedom on both service users and providers, they are sometimes experienced as more centralized and authoritarian than those they replace.

13. Giddens (1991, 1992) also argued for the utopian possibilities of individualization in the personal sphere, through a concept of the "pure relationship" unfettered by constraints. For a critique of these ideas, see Craib (1994).

14. This is the famous phrase of Alan Greenspan, Chair of the US Federal Reserve from 1987–2006, during the key decades of financial deregulation.

15. Critiques of authoritarian institutions were common at that time—for example, E. R. Goffman's description of "total institutions" in *Asylums* (1961) and the movement for de-carcerization that he influenced.

16. The impact of the Robertsons' films on the experience of young children in hospital, where their distress at their separation from parents had been completely unnoticed, is an instance of this kind (Robertson & Robertson, 1953, 1958).

PART I

Theoretical

CHAPTER ONE

Obsessional–punitive defences in care systems: Menzies Lyth revisited

William Halton

Isabel Menzies Lyth's landmark account of a nursing service, "A Case Study in the Functioning of Social Systems as a Defence against Anxiety" (1960), is well known, and it contains a fundamental truth that seems to elicit instant recognition from every kind of reader. In revisiting this paper for a colloquium on social defences, I became aware of several aspects of the paper that I had not previously noticed. Although she describes the social defence as a protection for nurses against the impact of the nursing task, the stress and anxiety that it created in them was far from protective. Furthermore, although the paper refers to primitive anxiety in general, it never actually names the specific anxiety nor the specific defence that is embodied in the care system. The data are provided but not the conclusion. Would it be possible, I wondered, to take this missing step now? With this question in mind I re-read the ten sections that describe the nursing techniques, and I was struck by the use of language associated with obsessional mechanisms. Was the social defence that Menzies Lyth had in mind—but did not name—one of obsessionality? If it was, then perhaps naming the defence would also disclose the unnamed anxiety. The first question is: how far does her description of the social defence correlate with obsessional mechanisms? Answering this question will involve recapitulating some familiar territory.

What is a social defence?

In 1953, four years before Menzies Lyth started her consultation, Elliott Jaques had addressed the question: What makes organizations gel? His answer was: "social defences" (Jaques, 1953). Bion (1961, p. 166) had described social defences in singleton small groups in terms of basic assumptions that provided small-group cohesion, but he had not considered coordinated relationships between several groups. Building on Bion, Jaques described an organizational social defence as an emotional configuration that promoted cohesion and collaboration between multiple groups. It comes into existence when members of an organization align their personal defences with each other and with the structure and culture of the organization. For example, he says, a paranoid social defence existed at the company Glacier, where conflict and suspicion between "bad" managers and workers was allocated to management–union negotiations, and cooperation with those same "good" managers operated on the shop floor. Examples of depressive social defences occur when those attending a funeral forget the bad aspects of the dead person and retain the memory of the person's good qualities, or when an organizational culture of emphasizing exclusively positive feelings is used to keep depression about destructiveness at bay. A social defence then is a shared pattern of loving and hating the same things or the same people. It is a shared configuration of emotions that promotes cohesion between multiple groups in an organization. Jaques called it "the phantasy form" of the organization. Although Menzies Lyth uses Jaques's concept of social defence as one of her theoretical references, it emerged that there was insufficient alignment between the nurses' personal defences and the social defence of the hospital—the best nurses left the hospital.

What was the Kleinian theory of obsessionality at that time?

In 1952 Klein published a paper, "Some Theoretical Conclusions Regarding the Emotional Life of the Infant", giving her final overview of the stages of child development, as follows. In the early stage, which is characterized by splitting between good and bad objects, aggression and death-wishes are given free rein to attack bad objects that become retaliatory as an internalized punitive superego. The cognitive integration of split objects into whole objects occurs by the end of the first year, and in this stage the need arises to preserve them from previously unbridled aggression. However, from the point of view of emotional development, the capacity for love is still too weak and immature to rein in and integrate aggression. Menzies Lyth refers to the child who fears that his inability to control his aggressive impulses would lead to "utter chaos and destruction" (1960/1988, p. 47). The alternative to integrating aggression is to repress it. But repression is only a partial solution, and it brings its own problems—namely, that unconscious aggression is still active but is now out of conscious control and may return. In order to reinforce repression, obsessional mechanisms are mobilized to assist in the control of unconscious uncontrollable aggression. At a later stage of the depressive position when love has developed more strongly, aggression will be contained, integrated, and modified by love. Reparation as an expression of love will become the appropriate defence. At that later stage, obsessional mechanisms will be outgrown.

The main obsessional mechanisms familiar from Freud's writings are: the disconnection of all emotion from ideas and actions in such a way that feelings do not arise, known technically as isolating; ritual behaviours designed to undo previous aggression and prevent a future occurrence, known as undoing; chronic indecision combined with checking and rechecking trivial matters in case they unwittingly involve aggression and death-wishes; and, finally, an "exceptionally severe and unkind" superego (Freud, 1926d [1925], pp. 111–123).

So, in Kleinian theory, when the stage of integrating whole objects is reached there are two methods for managing aggression. The first is by repression reinforced with obsessional mechanisms and a punitive superego. The second, more mature method, when love is more developed, is by integration of aggression and reparation. Menzies Lyth found that the social defence at the hospital was based on the first method—namely, repression—but we can see that the personal defences of the best nurses were based on the second method—namely, integration and reparation.

Background to the consultation

In 1957 King's College Hospital was under stress because there were too many patients. In the eleven years since the founding of the NHS there had been an increasingly rapid turnover of patients, an increasing proportion of acutely ill patients, an increasing range of illnesses, and an unpredictable variation in patient numbers (Menzies Lyth, 1960/1988,

p. 63). Feeling overwhelmed by demand, the nursing managers were moving student nurses rapidly from one unit to another in response to a constantly changing workload. The external regulator, the General Nursing Council, had complained that students were not spending the regulation twelve weeks in each unit. Menzies Lyth, a Kleinian psychoanalyst and founder member of the Tavistock Institute of Human Relations, was invited to help with the nurse allocation problem.

Start of the consultation

Menzies Lyth treated the failure to provide adequate training for nurses as a presenting symptom of some wider systemic issue, shifting the focus away from the client's primary concern and creating for herself what turned out to be a self-assigned impossible task (Roberts, 1994). Extensive interviewing revealed a high level of anxiety among the junior nurses and a high drop-out rate. Menzies Lyth refers to the emotions stirred up by the primary task of caring for sick, injured, or dying patients and the impact of anxieties projected onto nurses by relatives. As well as being the real people that they are in the external world, the patients are also the symbolic representatives of the internal parents of childhood, whom the nurses had loved as well as injured by aggression and death-wishes. Through this symbolic connection, the nurses' desire to make reparation to the parents of childhood is transferred to nursing current patients. But, she says, none of these current emotions arising from the nursing task nor the reawakened feelings from childhood accounted for the nurses' high level of anxiety. This was caused by the way their feelings were dealt with by the defensive nursing techniques (1960/1988, p. 50). She writes: "By the nature of her profession the nurse is at considerable risk of being flooded by intense and unmanageable anxiety. That factor alone, however, cannot account for the high level of anxiety so apparent in the nurses. It becomes necessary to direct attention to the other facet of the problem—that is, to the techniques used in the nursing service to contain and modify anxiety" (p. 50). She then describes these techniques in ten sections, using the language of obsessionality.

Isolating emotions from actions and their repression

The first three sections go straight to the heart of the matter: the isolating of the emotions of care from the actions of care. She describes how the removal of emotion from patient care was achieved. The nurse is given a list of tasks, the actions of care, and performs them for up to thirty patients in an emotionally disconnected way—that is, without the emotions of care. Menzies Lyth writes: "This prevents her, the nurse, from coming into contact with the totality of any one patient" and "It is hardly too much to say the nurse does not nurse patients" (1960/1988, p. 51). As the nurse moves from bed to bed, re-making beds, washing faces, or performing other intimate tasks, there is no time to talk or develop a relationship or even know the name of any particular patient. Detachment and denial of feelings prevent any form of attachment taking place, leaving the nurse free to be moved rapidly from patient to patient, or from unit to unit or building to building. Emotional outbursts are met with disapproval and punishment. She writes: "Interpersonal repressive techniques are culturally required and typically used to deal with emotional stress". "Sympathetic handling . . ." is replaced by "repression, discipline and reprimand from senior to junior" (p. 54).

In these first three sections, the central mechanism of obsessional-ity—isolating feelings from actions and their repression—correlates with the nursing techniques. As a socio-technical system, the technical tasks of nursing are achieved but the social system obstructs the nurse–patient relationship. Blocking out an empathic nursing relationship leads to an emotionally empty interaction between a depersonalized undifferentiated nurse and a depersonalized undifferentiated patient. It produces a psychological absence in role (Kahn, 1992). As well as being an obsessional defence, this was also fractionated Taylorism,[1] existential alienation, role depletion, dehumanization, and multiple indiscriminate caretaking—everything Menzies Lyth was determined to change.

Rigid ritualization and excessive anxiety about trivial matters

In sections four and five, Menzies Lyth describes how the tasks them-selves are ritualized. She writes that each individual task has to be performed "in a way reminiscent of performing a ritual". "Precise instructions are given about the way each task must be performed, the order of the tasks, and the time for their performance, although such precise instructions are not objectively necessary or even wholly desir-able" (1960/1988, p. 55). There is only one right way to wash a face or make a bed or lift a patient. Trainers reinforce the importance of the rituals by implying that their correct performance is almost a matter of life and death. Each separate task on the list has to be performed in the same predetermined way by every nurse for every patient on every ward or the consequences will be catastrophic. Outside of these pre-scribed rituals, an equally excessive anxiety is attached to unregulated decisions, such as booking a room or making a rota. These discretion-ary decisions led to extensive checking and re-checking and referral upwards, even, she says, when "the implications of a decision are of only the slightest consequence" (p. 56).

Here again there is a close correlation between Freud's description of obsessional mechanisms and the description of the nursing tech-niques, such as ritual behaviours that must be scrupulously enacted and the displacement of anxiety onto trivial matters. Outside the prescribed rituals, the nurses display chronic indecisiveness and an inability to make even minor decisions.

What about Freud's "exceptionally severe and unkind" superego?

Freud's punitive superego can be found in the manner of enforcing hospital discipline described in sections six, seven and eight. And here Menzies Lyth is writing fifteen years ahead of Foucault's *Discipline and Punish* (1975).The surveillance function of the punitive superego was carried out by a regime of peer surveillance in which nurses watched and reported on their peers and on all nurses junior to themselves. Menzies Lyth writes: "Every nurse is expected to initiate disciplinary action in relation to any failure by any junior nurse" (1960/1988, p. 59). All nurses feel like breaking the rules—for example, by skimping repetitive tasks or by forming an emotional attachment to a patient. She writes: "Irresponsible behaviour was quite common, mainly in tasks remote from direct patient care" (p. 58).

Surveillance leads to punishment. "Discipline is often harsh and sometimes unfair, since multiple projection also leads the senior to identify all juniors with her irresponsible self. . . . Nurses complain about being reprimanded for other people's mistakes while no serious effort is made to find the real culprit. A staff nurse said: 'If a mistake has been made, you must reprimand someone, even if you don't know who really did it'" (1960/1988, p. 58). One nurse was reprimanded four times by senior nurses for a mistake that had hastened a patient's death. She had to visit her old headmistress for comfort.

The fear of reprimand led nurses to betray what they felt were the common-sense principles of good nursing, like the nurse who had been told to give a patient a sleeping pill and, finding him asleep, woke him up to do so (1960/1988, p. 69). Rigid compliance with instructions takes precedence over the nurse's own discretionary judgement and personal initiative in response to the needs of individual patients. Compliance reduces the quality of care. The nurses complained that they had been given more responsibility at school than they had in the hospital.

In these three sections we can see that the administration of discipline correlates with the punitive superego of obsessionality. The fact that innocent nurses deserved punishment shows that nurses as a class were treated as guilty. Some nurses colluded with the system by identifying with this punitive regime. The harshness of the discipline drives out kindness, compassion, humanity, and common sense, and fear of reprimand adds to the chronic indecisiveness. The punitive system tends to promote passivity and inaction. Enforcing prescribed actions of care under the threat of punishment is self-defeating because it reduces the responsiveness to individual needs. The safe option is to make no decisions, to take no initiatives, and to blame your juniors whenever possible.

The last two sections, nine and ten, deal with the lack of professional development through individual tutorial support and group seminars and, finally, the resistance to change, because change means changing social defences.

Naming the defence and its underlying anxiety

As we review these ten sections, the correlation between the defensive nursing techniques and obsessional mechanisms with their punitive superego falls readily into place, as if what we might name as an obsessional–punitive social defence was exactly what Menzies Lyth had in mind. As stated previously, psychoanalytic theory in the Freud–Klein model tells us that at the threshold of the depressive position the cognitive integration of a whole object is in advance of emotional integration and that obsessional–punitive defences are used to control unintegrated aggression. Using this theoretical model, we can say that the existence of an obsessional–punitive defence indicates that the underlying organizational anxiety was about inappropriate emotional contact between junior nurses and patients—whether loving or hating or their derivative emotions. Some feelings of aggression towards patients, whether latent or experienced, are an intrinsic part of the clinical situation, as Winnicott had earlier described in "Hate in the

Countertransference" (1947). In addition, overwhelming numbers of patients had led to managers receiving a complaint from the General Nursing Council, which may also have stirred some anger towards patients (and student nurses). The purpose that Menzies Lyth ascribed to the social defence was to protect the nurses from the impact of the nursing task (1960/1988, p. 51). It is true that enforcing an emotional disconnection between nurses and patients did protect the nurses in that way. But the data that she provides are more consistent with protecting the patients (and the hospital) from the aggression in the system, attributed to the nurses by a process of projection.

The downwards projection of a phantasy of uncontrolled aggression resulted in a lack of trust in all junior nurses as a class. The obsessional–punitive social defence was management's response to its own anxiety about junior nurses making an uncontrolled and damaging emotional response to patients. Junior nurses were subjected to having no relationship with patients, to repression of feelings, to obsessional rituals, and to harsh discipline in order to protect patients from the danger that junior nurses supposedly represent. She comments: "Senior nurses do not feel they can fully trust their subordinates in whom they have psychically vested the irresponsible and incompetent parts of themselves" (1960/1988, p. 60). As a result junior nurses felt disempowered. She writes: "We were struck repeatedly by the low level of tasks carried out by the nursing staff and students in relation to their personal ability, skill and position in the hierarchy" (p. 59). Menzies Lyth found no inappropriate attachments or out-of-control aggression in the junior nurses that posed any threat to patient care.

The conclusion of Menzies Lyth's inquiries and observations was that the high level of stress, anxiety, and fear felt by the nurses was not caused by the nursing task but was a result of a systemic downwards projection onto the nurses of imagined aggression towards patients, giving rise to mistrust and followed by obsessional controls and punitive sanctions. This obsessional–punitive social defence was not a Jaques-type social defence that aligned the personal defences of the nurses with structure and culture in such a way as to create collaboration and cohesion across multiple groups. Some junior nurses colluded with it; however, a large number of good nurses left. At best the obsessional–punitive social defence was partially successful in that at least the actions of care were carried out, but predominantly it was an aggressive management defence against its own anxieties, phantasies, and projections.

Outcome of the consultation

The nurse allocation problem was solved by creating a reserve pool of nurses to deal with variations in the workload. Other changes tended to reinforce the existing social defence (Menzies Lyth, 1960/1988, p. 79). Menzies Lyth proposed that specific patients should be assigned to specific nurses so that each nurse could, in her words, "realise to the full her capacity for concern, compassion and sympathy, and for action based on these feelings which would strengthen her belief in the good aspects of herself" (p. 75). In other words, she wanted to put "human relations" back into nursing. Compassion and sympathy are based on identification with the patient as a person like oneself: vulnerable, frightened, and separated from home and facing unknown consequences (Black, 2004). A compassionate nursing relationship requires time for talking to patients and involves the psychological presence of the nurse in role (Kahn, 1992). Menzies Lyth's vision was to move the defence system to a more advanced stage of the depressive position in which nurses would be empowered to engage in reparative work commensurate with their skills and abilities and be helped through tutorial support to manage any difficult feelings that might be stirred up. Professional development and patient safety would be secured through the painful acknowledgement of aggressive feelings that would lead to their integration and modification. Senior nurses would have to move their superego function from control and punishment to support and guidance. Her suggestion would have established nursing practice based on an integration of relationships, feelings, and actions, instead of being based on repression and punishment. It would have brought personal defences, culture, and structure into alignment to form an appropriate social defence for the nursing task. But her proposal was rejected.

As for the self-imposed impossible task of changing the "phantasy form" (Jaques, 1953) of the whole organization, Menzies Lyth failed to persuade senior managers to withdraw their scapegoating projections onto the junior nurses. This would have required them to take ownership of their own feelings of aggression towards patients and of the guilt for any failures of care due to understaffing and the pressure of increased patient numbers. At a more conscious level, in personal conversation with Menzies Lyth senior nurses showed understanding and sympathy. "But", she writes, "they lacked confidence in their ability to handle emotional stress in any other way than by repressive techniques" (1960/1988, p. 54). This was a social defence system that was self-perpetuating despite the personal discomfort of all the participants, both senior and junior.

Impact of the consultation on Menzies Lyth

In its detailed charting of inhumanity, cruelty, and lack of kindness and common sense, Menzies Lyth's paper is a record of a painful formative experience as a consultant, and in later papers she makes many unfavourable references to it. It gave her a lasting sense of the damage that institutions can do (1988, p. 21). From then on she referred to consultancy as the art of the possible. She was more successful in a later assignment at the Royal National Orthopaedic Hospital in an action-research project with a much smaller part of the system. Here she used attachment theory to develop a practice of nursing care for children in which, in the absence of the mother, they were cared for by named members of staff with whom they had a close personal relationship. Her report on the project (Menzies Lyth, 1976) demonstrates the value of her consulting methods in promoting the painful discussion and acknowledgement of "less acceptable ideas and feelings such as unconscious wishes for damage" (1976, p. 42). She says that the changes that were made were due to the willingness of the people concerned to "bear the doubts and uncertainties of change" (1988, p. 203) and, in particular, were due to the capacity of the ward sister to trust her subordinates sufficiently "to give them freedom to operate, even on occasion to do something of which she disapproved or make a mistake for which she, the sister, still had ultimate responsibility" (1988, p. 195).

Some links to today

Finally, what links can we make from Menzies Lyth's paper to present times? That so many people recognize their own work situation in this paper suggests that the features of an obsessional–punitive social defence are currently a widespread phenomenon. The rigidly prescribed obsessional rituals that control how work is done, known as the "auditable surface" (Cummins, 2002), and the methods of surveillance, such as multiple targets, statistics, inspections, and so on, may be different, but the aim is the same—namely, to control the relationship between practitioner and patient. Following Menzies Lyth, behind this control is the projection of society's ambivalent feelings onto practitioners, who then become, like the nurses, objects of suspicion and mistrust.

External regulators threaten managers with financial sanctions for non-compliance, and managers in turn threaten practitioners with punitive levels of disciplinary sanction. This creates tension between managers and practitioners. As a result, care systems have become increasingly rigid and fearful. For example, Dame Fiona Caldicott is recently reported as saying "The culture in the health service has unfortunately become one of anxiety, some say fear . . . " (Chris Smyth, *The Times*, 13 September 2013); Professor Sir Mike Richards, Care Quality Commission's chief inspector of hospitals, said of Barts Health NHS Trust that "Too many members of staff of all levels and across all sites came to us to express their concerns about being bullied, and many only agreed to speak in confidence" (Ross Lydall, *Evening Standard*, 14 January 2014).

As Menzies Lyth showed with the sleeping-pill incident, care systems in which prescribed rituals have diminished the practitioner's authority to respond to individual needs do not provide the best quality of care. Recently senior doctors were complaining that "inflexible procedures get in the way of common-sense" and reduce the quality of care that they could offer patients (Chris Smyth, *The Times*, 13 September 2013).

Far from making patients safe, obsessional–punitive systems, devoid of empathic relationships, increase the danger to patients of poor care, neglect, or abuse, when these systems are under strain or management is absent. For example, when the actions of care were overwhelmed by patient numbers and lack of staff at Mid Stafford Hospital, the absence of compassionate feelings and relationships was exposed, and over a period of years hundreds of patients died, as was said at the Francis Inquiry, "with a lack of dignity or respect" (Francis, 2013, Vol. 1, p. 237). The widespread lack of empathy is evident in other care systems. It has been reported that in social care homes during the last ten years, over one thousand patients suffered from dehydration-related deaths and three hundred and eighteen from starvation or undernourishment, while nearly three thousand deaths were linked to bed sores (Ben Riley-Smith, *Daily Telegraph*, 2 December 2013).

A more specific example occurred at a nursing home in Lancashire that had "a lax regime with weak and inadequate management" and where elderly residents with dementia were "pelted with bean bags, mocked and bullied on the assumption they would not remember the abuse" (Peter Walker, *The Guardian*, 11 January, 2014). When an obsessional–punitive system breaks down, the repressed unbridled aggression resurfaces and the absence of integrated empathic relationships puts vulnerable clients at risk.

Or to take a different example related to indecisive decision-making and child protection: David Pelka, aged 4 years, was starved, tortured, and killed by his mother and her partner. At their trial it was reported that "local police, teachers, social workers and doctors missed at least 26 chances to save him" (David Leppard, *Sunday Times*, 18 August 2013). Could it be that the obsessional–punitive culture had disabled these professionals' capacity for making discretionary decisions by inducing a state of mind of fearful indecisiveness and inaction? In terms of disciplinary action, court hearings, and public inquiries, there is a current of thinking that making a wrong decision is more risky for practitioners than failing to act at all. In this example and in other similar cases, the feelings of care may have been present but the decision-making that forms a link to the actions of care was missing. Mistrust and disempowerment of practitioners contributes to a lower quality of care and greater risk for clients.

What Menzies Lyth has shown in her study of the hospital is that an obsessional–punitive culture can be more anxiety-provoking for staff than anxieties arising from the nature of the task. It blocks the development of an integrated empathic relationship, reduces the quality of care, and increases the risk to clients. As long as it persists, it will continue to contribute to high levels of stress, staff turnover, and practitioner/patient/client/child casualties.

Note

1. Taylorism is an organizational philosophy also known as scientific management, the machine theory of organization, or machine bureaucracy. In his book *The Principles of Scientific Management* (1911), Frederick Taylor aimed at making organizations run like "a complicated and delicately adjusted machine" (quoted by Mintzberg, 1988, p. 177). According to Taylor's principles, thinking about and organizing work are done by management. Integrated tasks are broken into segments that are allocated to different employees to be performed in accordance with precise instructions. Workers are interchangeable. Taylor was criticized for reducing workers to automatons, depriving them of all initiative (Morgan, 1986, pp. 30–32) and for disregarding their "essential humanity" (Rice, 1963, p. 180). The human relations school, to which Menzies Lyth belonged, was strongly opposed to the Taylorist approach.

CHAPTER TWO

Beyond identifying social defences: "working through" and lessons from people whispering

Susan Long

Anxiety and defences

According to Freud, anxiety is a signal that something to be feared is about to happen. The thing to be feared may be external, or it may be a thought or feeling within inner life. Nonetheless, whether external or internal, anxiety signals the likelihood of something that we have previously learned to fear or that is instinctively threatening. The fear may be as primitive as the loss of mother. Some say anxiety is the fear of the unknown or of death or of falling to pieces. Perhaps it is all of these.

Psychoanalysis demonstrates the power of anxiety by showing how we create ways to dispel, fight, or avoid it. Jaques and Menzies Lyth showed how we create social defences against anxiety—ways of organizing our social structures and cultural activities to dispel, fight, or avoid anxiety. Menzies Lyth especially showed how such defences are against the anxieties created by the work done in our workplaces. The tasks we organize themselves create anxieties and so paradoxically deflect, through social defences, their very purposes. Scholars following Menzies Lyth have demonstrated how groups, organizations, and even countries unconsciously create structures and cultures to defend against anxieties (both depressive and paranoid). And most often the defensive structures and cultures so created have themselves caused problems either of deflecting the initial purpose and tasks of the groups or creating new problems with attendant anxieties that have in turn to be defended against. Different institutions by the very nature of their work create different defences.

But anxiety is not the only fundamental shaper of organizational structure and culture. Stein (2000) argues that envy has been much neglected in the organizational literature and is central to Bion's (1970a) ideas about the parasitic relation in groups. Envy, he argues following the work of Klein and Bion, goes beyond the defensive and is decidedly aggressive. The idea of defences against anxiety, Stein argues, has been taken as central to the group relations literature and linked in an almost fixed way to Bion's basic assumptions, while Bion himself did not restrict the basic assumptions or group culture to this paradigm. And defences against envy have been explored by sociologists such as Schoeck (1966) who argues that democratic processes are based on defences against envy.

But the same might be said of other strong emotional states. Fay (2008), for example, explores the notion of derision from a Lacanian perspective and its role in several organizational control mechanisms.

> The structure of derision . . . is twofold: first the false promise that one will be treated as a subject, i.e. a person whose otherness, subjective voice and desire are acknowledged (openness), and, second, the disappointment of this expectation with the suffering realization of being treated as an object, a resource or a number (closure). Derision provides a new critical understanding of a whole range of managerial and organizational control mechanisms such as appraisal, job interviews, quality certifications, benchmarking. [p. 831]

Flynn (2001) explores social defences against shame in a rehabilitation organization, where case managers unconsciously felt responsible for their clients' shortcomings and feared shameful exposure of their poor performance, and subsequently the organization defended against this through an avoidance of looking at the "hard" data around client success. Shame about performance was a parallel process between clients and staff, intrinsically linked to the task of the organization.

I have explored emotions (pride, greed, envy, sloth, and anger) within the context of perverse organizational structures (Long, 2008) and argued that perverse structures develop through the expression of such emotions and consequent defences against exposure.

Moreover, a whole theoretical edifice has been built by René Girard (1972) and his followers around the idea of social organization (one might say defences) developed against violent reprisals such as found in feuds and intergroup and international enmities. His is a theory of scapegoating as a primitive way of handling reprisal and, in turn (in more developed societies), social law as a way of preventing scapegoating. In this vein, Boccara (2013) has demonstrated how policy and law may act as a defence in support of what he calls the "country romance"—a narrative built in a defensive way to protect a nation's self-identity. It is as if the task of policymakers becomes a defence of country identity in the face of projections from others.

Emotional life generally, then, especially viewed negatively as a sign of weakness or aggressiveness, may, it seems, give rise to organizational defences. The Freudian paradigm may well argue that the emergence of all such emotion gives rise to anxiety as a signal, and hence the defences are fundamentally against the experience of the signal anxiety. Technically this could be correctly argued, but in practice I tend to agree with Stein (2000) that the fundamental paradigm of defences against anxiety *per se* has led to neglect of the effects of other strong emotions in organizations. This is a pity because the paradigm of organizational defences, both primary and secondary, is powerful and well applied to an analysis of many emotional states that function in different ways. I hope this debate leads to a greater exploration of the effects of many and different dynamics stemming from both the expression of and defences against many *strong* emotions in the workplace.

I want, however, to take us beyond an analysis of social defences against anxiety or other uncomfortable or dangerous emotions. I am interested in what we can do once we discover these dynamics. Unfortunately, just as in individual psychoanalysis, insight into anxieties, envy, pride, or aggression and their defences alone is rarely mutative. I have often, through my consultancy or research, given groups or organizations insight into the defensive structures and cultures that they have created. Very often, the people involved have nodded and agreed that my analysis is cogent. Too often, little is done and change is minimal. Surface changes occur, but most often the organizational culture is too deeply embedded into external cultures in the context of the industry, domain, or general culture.

However, just as structures and cultures are unconsciously created through social dynamics—that is, they are unconsciously co-created—

so might change best be seen through the lens of co-creation. Freud was clear on this when he said that insight alone was not enough for change. Real change is brought about by "working through". In psychoanalysis this meant a process of re-learning at a deeply emotional level in the analysis. In socio-analysis this means a process of re-learning in the organization. The Grubb Institute links this to authentic action through role, role being the place where person, system, and context meet and are connected through source (a spiritual purpose, if you like) and where action can occur.[1]

I often find that a metaphor from a completely different discipline helps me to understand the organizations that I work with. I offer one here.

A metaphor

I have recently been training a new horse. Work with the horse and our joint performance has provided me with a powerful metaphor.

First let us look at primitive nature and roles. To a horse we humans are predators. She is the prey. Occasionally she may fight to protect herself or her young, but flight is her first line of defence: she wants to join her herd and flee. Yet, when we are afraid of the horse, she sees us not as prey but as (1) the horse at the bottom of the herd hierarchy hence able to be dominated or (2) another horse who is signalling danger. In a herd, as in a large group, anxiety is infectious, and we may simply instil our fear into the horse and hence raise defensiveness.

The herd provides protection, and the herd leader provides direction. In building a working relationship with my horse, *I have to move out of the role of predator, or prey, or lower hierarchy horse into the role of leader of the herd*. To do this I have to be adept in her language. The term "horse whispering" comes from the notion that the human learns the language of the horse and clearly communicates in that language rather than forcing his or her own incomprehensible demands on the animal.

Temple Grandin, a professor of animal behaviour, herself growing up as an autistic child, understands animals not from the human perspective of dominance but from the psychology of the animal itself. She argues (Grandin & Johnson, 2009) that there are two main emotions in herd animals—fear and curiosity. Mostly humans try to control animals through manipulating their fear. Natural horsemanship or horse whispering builds on curiosity, lowers fear, and takes up leadership. This is a firm, decisive leader with clear and consistent communication.

The notions of fear and curiosity will be taken up later in this chapter. But the reader may note that for psychoanalytic and socioanalytic theories these emotions are central—in the forms of anxiety and the desire for knowledge (Bion's K: 1962a, 1963, 1965). First, how does one move from predator to leader?

Simple steps

First comes the *building of trust* in the relationship between horse and rider: lots of ground work together, as well as riding, together with consistency of communication and aids. The groundwork also uncovers the anxieties and defensiveness in the horse, and its bad habits. I wonder about the nature of "groundwork" in organizational research or consultancy. I think it is the close cultural analysis that we do as an initial step (Long, 2013).

This work also involves *containment*, because horses are herd/ flight animals. The rider has to learn to be the lead and to contain the flight reactions of the horse with hands (with good, not rigid) contact with the horse's mouth or head, and with leg movements lessening the horse's fear that she might fall on a sharp turn or other manoeuvre. Non-riders think you use your legs simply to kick and move the horse. No! They are communication tools or instructions for moves that have been learned, *and* they tell the horse you are there and allow some confidence that you know what you are doing. The containment tells the horse that I, the rider, have some confidence in myself and that I can act as leader.

But when learning or *developing new movements and routines* the rider gives the new aids and instructions, but it is up to the horse to start making the moves in order that he can be rewarded by his own sense of mastery and yes, enjoyment. The rider/coach/instructor can only indicate what is to be done. The horse must willingly do it himself.

The process of containing the horse while she takes risks is ongoing. These (containment and risk-taking) are not mutually opposed for horses or humans. Containment does not mean holding back (although it may be exhibited that way sometimes). It means, I'm here with you! I'm right with you. I can provide correction if needed but also I can let you take a new move and reward you. You can stretch your own command of the movement so long as we are in communication. I can give the aids, but the first move is up to you.

In sports coaching and horse training, the coach/trainer has to take the lead and have ultimate authority, although with the eventual interplay of the partnership this is very finely tuned. In the organizational consultant/client partnership or the manager/subordinate partnership, the authority shifts and flows between the two—but it should always be tracked. I am increasingly looking to think in terms of co-creation in any partnership. But let us take it a little further. I am sure you, the reader, are making many of your own links. The group leader who exercises good authority has an important role in containment and clear communication while aiding risk-taking.

Predator–prey

As noted earlier, at a primitive level humans are both predators and prey. They share the fear and curiosity of prey animals but also the predatory focus and aggression of the predators.

Although predator–prey relations in nature exist between populations of different species, Hegel (1806) describes something similar in human culture in his famous master–slave dynamic. The master needs the slave to do his bidding, and the slave needs the master for his own survival. The dynamic of recognition is involved. In the eyes of the master, the slave is reduced to almost nothing, yet the slave is never totally a non-being. The master needs the recognition of the slave in order to be a master, just as the slave needs the recognition of the master. These ideas are taken up by Jessica Benjamin (1988) and others as a basic dynamic in interpersonal psychoanalysis. Through my metaphor, we can see that the role of master (and the population of all masters) needs the role of slave (and the population of all slave roles) just as in the predator–prey populations the predator population needs the prey population, and vice versa. Domination is mediated by the need for recognition and the existence of the other. It is interesting that some authors see narcissism and narcissistic leadership as motivated by the need for recognition, while for non-narcissistic leadership and followership, the motive is for love (e.g., Maccoby, 2000). Freud (1921c) saw this when he analysed group cohesion as libidinal while the leader's motive was seen as more narcissistic.

Within the herd there is hierarchy. Human cultures also demonstrate hierarchy. When this occurs creatively the hierarchy demonstrates good authority—that is, authority in the service of the purpose and task of the group; authority that guides and leads the work group and recognizes members as equals in all other ways. In other words, the hierarchy serves purpose, safety, and creativity.

All this occurs, unless the authority is perverted. When perverted, authority serves domination. Predators turn on their own, enlist accomplices, and others within the population become prey. We see this in bullying and other perverse behaviours (Long, 2008).

Working through

Working through in psychoanalysis is the deep emotional re-learning that occurs in the relations between analyst and analysand. It is not a simple cognitive process based on insight, however important that insight might be as a first step. Working through brings about emotional change through the collaborative efforts of the analytic pair. It involves the parties in active listening, in authentically surfacing thoughts and emotions and discovering the truth existing in the analytic experience (what Bion referred to as "O").

In my metaphor, the working through involves moving away from the predator–prey relation towards becoming the herd leader: talking the body language of the horse; providing trust and containment; encouraging and rewarding risks; and finally developing a mutual partnership. The whole process of role change for the trainer is predator → herd leader → partner. What, then, is the process of "working through" in an organization? Can this clinical description of the emotional work in analysis be useful in organizational work?

First, I think much more research needs to be done on the nature of emotional work in organizations. Simplistically just attempting to get people to "love and trust" each other is naive. Working through requires a realistic appraisal of the risks and dangers faced in the work of the organization: a socio-technical appraisal as well as a cultural analysis of anxieties and defences. It might involve multiple parties in active listening, authentically surfacing thoughts and emotions, and discovering the truths existing in the systems of which they are a part. It also requires clear, containing leadership that promotes risk assessment as well as risk- taking alongside rewards. Hirschhorn and Horowitz (2013) have recently argued that a major shaper of organizational culture and leadership in the current global and fast-changing environment is the capacity to take risks. They liken successful organizational players to extreme-sports athletes. But such athletes and their managers have to realistically appraise the risks they take, even if they do push the limits, before going for the adrenaline buzz they get as a reward.

Some of this research might focus on the role of curiosity at work. Bion (1961) argued that humans are herd animals, and, as such, following Temple Grandin (Grandin & Johnson, 2009), we have the primary motivations of fear and curiosity. (These later become more refined: anxiety, ambition, love, hate, etc.) Fear and curiosity are certainly the ingredients present in the primal-scene phantasy and in the child's sadistic impulses directed at the contents of the mother's body—seen as containing all that is both good and bad (Klein, 1930). These phantasies pertain to the family but also, I would contend, in the family writ broadly—in the tribe or group. The child's curiosity about the adult world—about sexuality and violence, and, through the projective mechanisms described by Klein and Bion, about the child's fears of retribution for desiring to be part of that—might be seen through a wider lens. There is *in* the group curiosity *about* the group: the pairings, the political and libidinal alignments, motivations. Such curiosity lies behind the "epistemophilic instinct" (Klein, 1930): the desire to know and to do. Also, curiosity lies at the heart of Bion's K (knowledge) that motivates much behaviour. Such curiosity informs creative risk-taking to find answers to what needs to be known and done in the workplace. The theory of social systems as defensive is more about fear and anxiety; about fear of reprisal for one's envy, aggression, and pride; and fear of the attacks from within giving rise to shame and guilt. Moving beyond identification of such fears towards mastery requires that we get in touch with our curiosity and risk-taking. "Leadership . . . concerns the authorization of curiosity and the deployment of resources—time and space—toward that end" (Krantz, 2013, p. 42).

People whispering

You can see now through my metaphor that I think we need to move beyond an identification of the basic anxieties and defences in an organizational culture towards a process of "people whispering", which leads to the move from leaders as predators to leaders as good authorities. It also leads to "working through". What are the processes involved?

1. An analysis of anxieties (or other destructive emotions) and their defences is helpful because it is the first step. It begins to name that which was previously un-nameable. Most critically, it begins building trust in possible co-creation. The most rewarding end to a cultural analysis is when the client says, "You've understood who

we are and have given us back the data in our language. You've said what we know but haven't put into words."

Too often however, this trust is eroded because the naming of the un-nameable (the "unthought known", in Christopher Bollas's terms; 1987) *also promotes hope*—something has been uncovered together by the consultant and/or leader and the group. If this hope is not sustained through change and consistency, then hopes are dashed and trust is lost.

2. Alongside building trust is the work of understanding the context. What is the primary task of the organization? What are the risks and opportunities in the broader economic, social, and political environments? Critically, we as psychoanalytic thinkers and prac-titioners have to work and research alongside systems thinkers and management thinkers from other perspectives. Organizational problems are usually "wicked problems" insofar as they cannot be approached simply through the lens of one discipline alone. Multiple lenses are required. Clinical understanding of human psychology is useful, but not in isolation.

3. Working through must follow. As in my metaphor, the working through is done through a hopeful pairing with the consultant and/ or leader. Containment, clear communication (in the language of the group) and clear roles, boundaries, and authority are required. All this is needed to enable new behaviours to be discovered by the group/organization and then for these to be rewarded—by appro-priate rewards, themselves agreed by the groups involved. The whispering is done through a close process of mutual communica-tion: learning what the other means in each situation through lis-tening, sharing, and mutual reflection; finding the right cues while learning on the job; discovering the appropriate rewards, which include having discretionary authority in all work roles; activating clear leadership that is supportive and containing—which includes holding others (subordinates, peers, and leaders) accountable for their work, while also encouraging risk-taking with appropriate guidance. Working through is never done by leaving people to their own devices; it is a process of mutual support. Most importantly, it involves a change of mind, a change in the way of being with oth-ers at an emotional level. Curiosity (about the other and about the world) is more basic than primary trust. Erikson (1950) did say that it was just as important to mistrust as to trust. Curiosity allows for such a discernment.

4. Too often, organizational leaders find the collaborative process too slow for the changes they believe need to be made. Indeed, in rapidly changing environments, clear direction is needed. This can be done when strong trust has been developed. Nonetheless, to build a culture able to work through the anxieties and fears inherent in their work (as per Menzies Lyth's description), organization members must take risks and learn for themselves within a supportive culture.

The defensive culture can be transformed into a creative culture if "people whispering" is valued, just as the defensive, prey horse can be transformed into a partner.

I use my horse-training metaphor in my consultancy work primarily through work with organizational leaders. Senior leaders in large organizations must not just be good team leaders but fundamentally able to manage the (often unconscious) large group that is in every organization, the large group being the unorganized form of the hierarchy that can appear. My emphasis is to aid leaders to move from predatory leader—experienced as overly critical, non-consultative, out of touch with the coalface work of the group, perhaps overly narcissistic and self-serving—to leader of the herd, with clear communication, consultative and empathic, understanding the nature of the work, providing good boundaries and containment, and exercising good authority.

I also work to allow the large group to become creatively organized. In a recent change-management process, I emphasized that the change process was a temporary organization in itself, requiring its own management and leadership, and this proved a model for the new structure that the department was moving into. This aided the managers to learn new ways of leading within the temporary project team that could then be taken out to the new structure.

People are more complex than horses—their languages, rewards, group relations, and fears are different. But the importance of deeply knowing the other—"tuning in" to their emotional life (as Harold Bridger used to say; personal communication, 1990) and attempting to speak their "languages"—is the same. It is the "curious" side of our natures that brings the deeper emotional change. The context that allows curiosity to thrive is a patient one. It gives time and attention as gifts. Moreover, the working through of change needs to be guided by a leader who becomes a partner and yet can move back to decisive leadership when needed *and* who can discern when these role changes

Curious and responsive leader who knows the group and its work enough to discern when the following role changes are needed:

Containing yet decisive and clear leader → collaborative partner → containing yet decisive and clear leader → collaborative partner → etc.

Box 2.1

should come about (Box 2.1). Such discernment can only come through knowing the herd—oops, I mean the group/organization—and through knowing the anxieties likely to occur in the institution where they work.

We must learn to whisper, rather than shout to one another.

Note

1. www.facebook.com/pages/The-Guild-powered-by-The-Grubb-Institute

CHAPTER THREE

A psycho-social perspective on social defences

Paul Hoggett

Psycho-social studies

Over the last fifteen years there has been an unprecedented revival in the application of psychoanalysis to the social sciences in the UK. This development has gone under the heading "psycho-social studies" and has led to the emergence of research centres and groupings working under this rubric in over a dozen British universities and the launch of a new national learned society, the Association for Psychosocial Studies. Several important publications have emerged, including Wendy Hollway and Tony Jefferson's (2013) seminal *Doing Qualitative Research Differently: A Psychosocial Approach*, and a special issue of the journal *Psychoanalysis, Culture and Society* (Layton, 2008) was devoted to exploring some of the differences within this UK development (including the question of whether psycho-social should be hyphenated or not). Arguably this is the first time we have seen the application of psychoanalytic theory and method to mainstream social science since the flowering of the Tavistock Institute of Human Relations in the 1950s, a flowering in which the work of Isabel Menzies Lyth on "social defences" figured prominently (1960).

One of the common themes in psycho-social studies has been the attempt to use psychoanalysis to illuminate the interpenetration of

psyche and society—that is, to combine psychoanalytic with social scientific ways of thinking without giving either one undue prominence. The following contribution has two aims. The first is to apply a psycho-social lens to the concept of social defences. The second is to consider how developments in psychoanalytic and sociological thinking since 1960 enable us to extend and deepen the original concept that Menzies Lyth bequeathed us.

Early theorizations were psychologistic and undersocialized

The original theorization of social defence by Elliott Jaques was not psycho-social. Jaques saw the organization as a container for the anxieties of its members. As he put it, "individuals may be thought of as externalizing those impulses and internal objects that would otherwise give rise to psychotic anxiety, and pooling them into the life of the social institutions in which they associate" (Jaques, 1955, p. 479). This is essentially a psychologistic account in which organizational life is seen to embody the persecutory and depressive anxieties that Jaques, following Klein, saw as inherent to the human condition. The direction of movement is from the psyche (in)to society.

An alternative theorization, one that originates with Menzies Lyth (1960) and has been in much currency in systems psychodynamic thinking, sees anxiety arising from the so-called primary task. While I do see this as no longer psychologistic, it nevertheless remains an undersocialized account. In Menzies Lyth's case study of the organization of nursing in a London teaching hospital, the role of society in constructing the psychic meaning of the nursing task was underplayed (a society whose influence was mediated through a set of gendered institutions—that is, the nursing profession of that time). I do not believe there is any such thing as a primary task; the task of a team or organization is always problematic, contested, and socially constructed (Hoggett, 2005). There is no such thing as "the primary task" of teaching, nursing, policing, governing, nor even parenting; to say that there is essentializes these phenomena, rendering them timeless and context-free.

We need a theorization that is neither psychologistic nor undersocialized. A psycho-social perspective is neither purely psycho nor purely social but draws upon both, the overlapping space, the space in between, the space of the hyphen (Hoggett, 2008).

So what candidates do we have to qualify as psycho-social concepts? The following come to my mind:

» Social unconscious (Hopper, 2002)
» Social dreaming (Lawrence, 2005)
» Structures of feeling (Williams, 1977)
» Social defences

In this chapter I wish to focus on the last in this list, but in doing so I also give some consideration to "structures of feeling". I have deliberately avoided using the fuller title "social defences against anxiety" as I believe that it is an open question whether these are just defences against various forms of anxiety or whether the defences may be erected in the face of a variety of feelings that threaten to be overwhelming. Taking a psycho-social perspective, it is clear that the character of a social defence is partly informed by our psycho-logic (defences against overwhelming feelings include rationalization, reaction formation, denial, projection, etc.) but is also partly informed by wider social processes.

In this chapter, I first consider developments in the way in which psychoanalysis thinks about psychic defences, which could deepen our understanding of social defences. I then argue that if we are to avoid psychological reductionism, then we must also strengthen the societal dimension of this concept, specifically by drawing on the idea of "structures of feeling".

Pathological organizations: systems of defence

Menzies Lyth's paper was based on research undertaken in the late 1950s just before she became a training analyst at the London Institute of Psychoanalysis in 1960. It is likely that she was in analysis with Bion at the time the work was undertaken (Pecotic, 2002). It is revealing that even at this time she speaks of "the social defence system", and in this sense I think perhaps she anticipates later developments in post-Kleinian thinking. Until the 1970s, British psychoanalysts within all three traditions had tended to think of defences in their singularity, but in recent decades the idea has emerged that the psyche itself contains organized systems of defence, something captured most vividly by Steiner (1993) in his concept of the "pathological organisation".

One can trace two sources for this idea. The first is from Rosenfeld's concept of "destructive narcissism", the valuing of that which is anti-life and which therefore stands against dependency and therefore interdependency. As Rosenfeld notes, "the destructive narcissism of these patients appears often highly organized, as if one were dealing with a powerful gang dominated by a leader, who controls all the members of the gang to see that they support one another in making the criminal destructive work more effective and powerful" (Rosenfeld, 1971, p. 174). It is important to stress just how innovative this way of thinking was at the time, as it began to draw a picture of the psyche as an internal society, analogous to the picture Bion draws of the struggle between the scientist and the liar in his book *Attention and Interpretation* (1970a). The other source for Steiner's concept of the pathological organization appears to be Meltzer's (1968) notion of an internal establishment, an imaginative development of Bion's concept of "basic assumption" mentality revisited in his last works, particularly *A Memoir of the Future* (Bion, 1991). It was this idea of an internal establishment that I took up in my paper to the Bion Centenary Conference in Turin in 1997 (Hoggett, 1998).

Right at the start of his *Psychic Retreats* (1993), Steiner argues that pathological organizations can be conceptualized in two ways: (1) as systems of defences; (2) "as highly structured, close-knit systems of object relationships" (p. x). Such pathological organizations are universal, existing in severely disturbed and normal patents. Interestingly enough, Steiner suggests that the function of pathological organizations is "to bind, to neutralize, and to control primitive destructiveness whatever its source" (p. 4). Like Freud, Steiner sees defence being triggered by impulse, but his line of reasoning then follows Klein rather than Freud, who, for much of his life, saw anxiety primarily as a reaction to the work of the sexual rather than destructive impulse. Steiner notes that all defences achieve, at best, a kind of compromise, and pathological organizations are as much an expression of destructiveness as a defence against it (1993, p.5).

What, then, of the highly structured system of object relations inherent in pathological organizations? Rosenfeld thought of this in terms of the gang in the mind. I think the idea of an establishment in the mind is a little more nuanced, an establishment that offers protection to the patient so long as the patient colludes with it. In other words, the pathological organization offers a perverse form of containment (Steiner, 1993, p. 8).

So the key things to take away from this are:

1. the pathological organization is an organized system of defences;

2. the system can be thought of as an internal establishment which operates for the most part on the basis of consent but which, if threatened, can unleash considerable violence;

3. there is something perverse about the way in which the system operates, not only in terms of the collusion that it invites but in terms of the tendency to be contemptuous of the patient's more loving, needy, and thoughtful aspects.

Steiner's theory can deepen our understanding of social defences, but we must be wary of sloppily talking about hospitals, firms, and so forth as "pathological organizations". In contrast, I believe Susan Long's concept of the "perverse organisation" is a recent successful attempt to build upon Steiner's way of thinking (Long, 2008, p. 21), particularly in terms of (1) the way in which it draws attention to collusive processes in organizations in which different actors and agencies become complicit in deviant and sometimes criminal behaviours, (2) the organization of denial, in which disturbing truths are simultaneously recognized and disavowed, and (3) the way in which the organization creates a twisted moral order built upon self-deceiving propaganda similar to the one described by Margot Waddell and Gianna Williams as the "Fair is foul and foul is fair" mode of inversion and distortion (Waddell & Williams, 1991).

Enactments and embodiments

Another development of Bion's psychoanalytic theory may also deepen our understanding of the variety and nature of social defences. In a stimulating essay on Bion's concept of containment, Ronald Britton (1992) argues that if experiences cannot be held in the mind, then they are either somatized and embodied, hallucinated/projected, or enacted (p. 106). If a powerful feeling such as resentment is projected, then the feeling is displaced onto substitute targets, or scapegoats; it is the other who is seen as resentful, ungrateful, or envious, not ourselves. When a feeling such as anxiety is embodied, it literally becomes inscribed upon the body—faces line, muscles tighten, stomachs knot, and so on. And when we talk about a feeling being enacted, we refer to the way in which attempts are made to get rid of a feeling such as irritation through action—someone who acts without thinking is often enacting in this way.

I have found Britton's development of Bion's thinking helpful in understanding the process of government. My argument is that if governments cannot contain public anxieties (which crucially involves retaining a capacity for thoughtfulness and a commitment to dialogue about a risk that has suddenly become perceived as threatening), then they will project, enact, or embody these anxieties. So how does a government enact anxiety? Enactment occurs when a government faced with a panic of some form succumbs to the intense pressure to be seen to be doing something. This is very much the territory of Edelman's (1964) "symbolic policy making", where government interventions, including legislative action, are rushed through, partly in the search for a quick fix, only to be quietly abandoned once the public panic has receded. A whole range of recent examples come to mind including Zero Tolerance in the US and the Respect Agenda in the UK.

How might a government come to embody anxiety? To think of the state embodying anxiety may at first seem puzzling, but when we start to think in terms of the "body of the organisation" then things become clearer. Indeed, I believe that Menzies Lyth's (1960) classic study in King's College Hospital in the late 1950s examines how nursing was trapped within a rigid, tight, and anxious organizational body. The health service in the UK has long been the focus for powerful social anxieties (Obholzer once called it the "keep death at bay" service; 1994b, p. 171), and the nursing task is itself typically one that arouses powerful anxieties in nurse practitioners (tending wounds, cleaning bodies, providing comfort in the face of the fear of dying, etc.). Menzies Lyth found a nursing profession in a state of singular denial about the emotional challenges it faced and therefore unequipped to support the nurses in their emotional labour. As a consequence, nursing at St Thomas' had become organized along the lines of what Menzies Lyth referred to as a "social defence system". This comprised a series of unreflexive practices designed to minimize emotional contact between nurse and patient—including the "task/list" system of fragmenting nursing tasks so that each was responsible for one minor function across the entire ward, reducing the possibility of contact with a patient to a matter of minutes. So, drawing from Menzies Lyth, we can say that the analytic question concerns the way in which the state and its institutions may come to embody social anxieties through its rules, systems, structures, and procedures, creating a kind of "thick skin".

I have been interested in the way in which child protection social work in the UK has taken on a similar kind of organizational form (Hoggett, 2013). For a variety of specific reasons, for more than two decades the protection of children at risk of abuse has become the source of considerable public anxiety in the UK (Cooper & Lousada, 2005). During the last period of Labour government, particularly after 2000, the much publicized deaths of a small number of young children from abuse became the focus for a series of public panics. Each successive scandal led to a knee-jerk response from government—that is, the search for someone to blame (projection) and the further tightening of systems and procedures. It was as if these latter reactions were guided by the illusion that highly complex family/community systems could be subject to such control that the possibility of failure could be entirely removed. As a consequence, by 2010 child protection social work had become so massively proceduralized that social workers appeared to spend more time in front of computers than engaging in face-to-face work with children at risk and their families. A complex structure of rules, systems, and procedures had come to embody public anxieties rather than contain them. Each perceived "failure" led to the further formalization and proceduralization of the field, so that a virtual and electronic child came to replace an actual child engaged in real relations with professional staff (Hall, Parton, Peckover, & White, 2010; Wastell, White, Broadhurst, Peckover, & Pitthouse, 2010; White, Hall, & Peckover, 2009).

Structures of feeling

Some of our feelings are uniquely our own, unique to our biography, to our character. But some of our feelings we feel in common with others. Bion's basic assumptions describe configurations of feeling that all members of a particular group may experience at a given moment. We also know that crowds may be gripped by specific feelings and by religious, social, and political movements—messianic hope, for example, or terror, or resentment. After the demise of early crowd psychology, social theory has only recently begun to develop ways of theorizing the social organization of feeling.

We began with Jaques and his belief that anxieties inherent to the human condition were constantly externalized into groups and organizations. Against this psychologistic account we considered the possibility that certain work tasks were inherently anxiety-making. This perspective, illustrated by Menzies Lyth's classic study, avoided the psychologism of Jaques but underplayed the role of social context. However, the reader may have noticed how, in the previous section, I have already started to speak of "social anxieties" and "public panics". What, then, of the possibility that powerful anxieties may be located "out there" in society and become taken into the organization (a direction of movement opposite to that envisaged by Jaques)? This perspective has become legitimized by advances in sociological thinking which have demonstrated the way in which powerful patterns of affect can characterize the lives of communities, both local and national and organized along spatial and non-spatial lines. Raymond Williams (1977) developed the concept of "structures of feeling" as a means of understanding "the particular quality of social experience and relationship . . . [that] gives the sense of a generation or a period" (p. 131). Following Williams, we can use the concept of structures of feeling as a device for understanding the existence of enduring configurations of affect that characterize the subterranean sentiments of an era or epoch. The differentiation of affect from emotion is now common in sociological accounts of human feeling. Whereas an emotion such as jealousy typically has a fixed object and is therefore more anchored in language and symbolic thought, an affect, such as anxiety, is more unformed, visceral, and fluid and shifts from one object to another; hence, it is one of the basic constituents of social contagion (Crociani-Windland & Hoggett, 2012). I believe that there is a particular structure of feeling that has become characteristic of Western society since the Second World War, an epoch that is sometimes referred to as late modernity, and anxiety constitutes its affective kernel (Hoggett, 2008). This anxiety is connected to perceived moral, physical, and existential risks, risks that periodically assume the form of collective panics, particularly moral panics (e.g., children at risk of abuse) and risk panics (e.g., genetically modified foods, bird flu, extreme weather events linked to climate change). I believe that these anxieties, particularly when manifest as panics, get into the life of organizations, and not just public ones, where they may be contained, embodied, enacted, or projected.

Social defences are not just against anxiety

Going back to Britton's reading of Bion (Britton, 1992), the point is that, for Bion, from birth all human experience (good and bad) threatens to overwhelm the apparatus that the person has for containing it. Anxiety is one important aspect of human experience, but there are many others—hope, resentment, love, envy, and so forth—that can easily overwhelm us. It follows that we defend ourselves not just against anxiety, but against any experience that threatens to overwhelm us. Perhaps the same is true for institutions. Alongside social defences against anxiety, might we need to consider the possibility of social defences against resentment, or social defences against envy (Stein, 2000)?

Conclusion

I am not offering a more sociological account of anxiety as an alternative to earlier perspectives. I believe that anxieties inherent to the human condition are externalized into the group, that the group itself may generate "group anxieties" (this seems to be what Bion has in mind in his 1961 book *Experiences in Groups*), and that the nature of the work that the group has to undertake may also generate anxiety. In other words, anxiety in group life is over-determined, but it nevertheless behoves us to try to distinguish between each of these possible influences when we study actual organizations.

In this chapter I have tried to outline an approach that is psychosocial—that is, one that can enable us to understand how the group/organization is situated in the space in between the psyche and the social world. You could say it occupies the place of the hyphen, the place of overlap and interpenetration. There are other sociological theories I could also have introduced, particularly the study of "emotional labour" which was kick-started by Arlie Hochschild's (1983) seminal research. There are also many other important social processes that bear upon organizational life, not the least the division of labour, Taylorism, and occupational and professional forms of organization. I find myself wondering occasionally whether there is not a kind of relationship between social and psychic structure which is analogous to the anaclitic relationship that Freud believed characterized the relationship between the sexual and self-preservative drives. In other words, emotional dynamics lean upon or are propped up on pre-existing organizational structures, but because these dynamics involve both conscious and unconscious agency they also influence that structure in an iterative way.

CHAPTER FOUR

Social defences
in the information age

James Krantz

My questions in this chapter have to do with the meaning and nature of social defences in the twenty-first century. In the background is a concern whether systems—psychodynamics in general, and social defence theory in particular—will be relevant in the "information age" that is upon us. I think the jury is still out. It remains to be seen whether we will be able to adapt our concepts to new conditions and dynamics. I come to this with many questions and little insight, hoping that others will join me in the kind of research that helps us understand what social defences mean in the digital world.

Social defences: a legacy

Social defences are about containment, as conceptualized by Bion (1970b). Containment is about how we process lived experience and the fragmenting psychic effects of being unable to work with emotional experience. It refers to psychic processes through which painful experiences can be converted into reflective understanding rather than function as propellants for primitive defensive processes as described by Klein (1946). It happens through unconscious interaction with an "other". Some entity—a mother, family, group, organization, or established order—holds the painful aspects of experience that are projected into it and hopefully modifies them so that the disturbing experience can be re-internalized in a fashion that enables thought.

Menzies Lyth (1960) developed the idea of social defences by fusing Bion's concept of containment with Fenichel's (1946) observations about the external influences on neuroses. He recognized that while institutions are created to satisfy the needs of people, they take on characteristics that are independent of them. They have an independent reality that shapes people as well as being shaped by them: real, enduring, and impersonal qualities. Social defences, for Menzies Lyth, are not simply forms of group regression, such as widespread splitting or scapegoating, but are anchored by the building blocks of organizational life.

The genius of Menzies Lyth's concept is in showing how the non-human aspects of organizational life—structures, practices, policies, technologies, work methods, patterns of decision-making, the distribution of authority, and so forth—can be incorporated into the cycle of projection and introjection in a way that reinforces people's defences against task-related anxiety by functioning as containers of psychotic anxiety.

What makes social defences so effective is that the organizational arrangements either eliminate situations that expose people to anxiety-provoking activity altogether or insulate people from the consequences of their actions. The nursing service was an ideal setting for crystallizing the concept. Its approach to scheduling, decision-making, and work assignment created a depersonalized and fragmented pattern of care. Coupled with infantilizing management practices, the system promoted dependency, ritualistic work, impersonal relationships with patients, and other characteristics that had the effect of shielding nurses from the painful anxieties stimulated by close and intimate contact with patients and their families.

Social defences enable people to metabolize their emotional experiences through creating meaningful connection, or they encode psychotic anxieties into organizational culture by fostering detachment and repression. When social defence systems promote mindsets that repudiate the struggle inherent in sophisticated work, they help people conceal what is ambiguous or unknown through projection, denial, and projective identification.

How the idea of social defences, which provided such a rich window into the issues underlying organizational life, map onto the emerging conditions of twenty-first-century organizations depends on our understanding of the aspects of the new organizations that are more than just the people who animate them. The organizational building blocks that anchor the projective processes are undergoing major change. How emerging organizations—the new virtualized, digitally rich, computer-mediated, and knowledge-based systems—can contain and modify anxiety must be asked anew. The limits of our understanding are shaped by our attachment to our images of the past, but more so because the new configurations, new tasks, and social systems are only beginning to take shape.

The information age upon us

Many of the constructs we inherited from Eric Trist, Fred Emery, Ken Rice, and their Tavistock colleagues came from efforts to make sense of deep shifts that were occurring in the social, economic, technological, and political spheres. They detected elements of a then ineffable future by noticing new patterns—workers needing more than subsistence; destabilizing environments; shifting values, service, and knowledge orientations; and the impact of new technologies on social systems. With the late stage of industrialization, known as post-industrialism, the world moved towards a constant-change gradient, resulting in conditions of continuous transitional states.

Today we are in the midst of another change, one in which the gradient of change is shifting again, now from linear to nearly exponential. The full emergence of the information age is unfathomable. Its effects are likely to accelerate change to such an extent that we will see as much change in the next 10 to 20 years as we saw in the entire twentieth century, requiring profound realignment and restructuring of our technical and social systems.

Many of the most emergent qualities of organizations are frequently discussed: Fixed boundaries are evaporating along with the stable small groups, requiring new strategies of containment. Organizations, per se, are being superseded by networks and eco-systems. Global interconnectedness amplifies local vulnerability and confronts us with otherness in new and extreme ways—horizontal rather than vertical sources of authorization, strategy that is emergent rather than centrally directed.

Symbol systems involving family, social, and political authority, sexuality, birth, death, and the ordering of the life cycle are in disarray.

Repeated betrayal by organizations, failed dependency, and massive social disturbance seem to have become the norm. Cumulatively, these traumatic events have created a climate of existential anxiety, which is engendering despair and, alongside it, new forms of hope in a transformed future. While the information utopians and the information doomsayers are locked in ongoing debate, the changes we face are of a magnitude that requires working through the disruptive psychological effects on the deep levels of personality.

Digital immigrants

We are "Digital Immigrants" (Palfrey & Gasser, 2008; Prensky, 2011). Discerning the nature of social defences and the containment of anxiety in new settings requires understanding the world of the "Digital Natives". Digital natives spend their lives surrounded by computers, videogames, digital music players, video cams, cell phones, and the tools of the digital age. Digital natives *think and process information differently* from their predecessors. Their defensive manoeuvres will be shaped by immersion in the digital sphere. The groups, structures, and rituals that contained anxiety in the receding world will no longer hold the meaning that enables them to function in the same manner in the emergent world.

We digital immigrants have much to offer digital natives. It is an essential bridging function needed to bring systems psychodynamic thinking into the new calculus. I see this as the litmus test of whether systems psychodynamic thinking is relevant only to the twentieth century or whether it has something to offer in the information age. I have to admit to some dismay about whether my immigrant tribe will be able to make these linkages. Viewpoints about the new information-based world that seem to be defensively avoiding the exposure and vulnerability required of embracing new and unfamiliar realities seem all too common.

Typically these viewpoints take one of two forms. The first is the view that the increasing dominance of digital life, virtualization, information technologies, and social media in social life entails a downward turn of civilization and reversal of progress. Implicit in this posture is the idea that we were the peak of human civilization—that it rose to us and is in decline after us. It is strikingly common to see sentimental analyses of the "new" that are actually descriptions of what is felt to have been lost.

The second viewpoint is an assumption that we can apply the same filters and frameworks to new organizational forms that have served us so well in the past. Philosophers remind us that when we observe something we are often tracing the frame through which we observe it. So many articles about the digital world adopt the images of organization, ideas of containment, assumptions about boundaries, ideas about basic assumption life, or notions of authority and leadership that pertain to our familiar systems. It is akin to what Trist (1989) called the assumption of ordinariness as a mechanism of denial, leading to a familiar impasse in which no learning takes place from what is being experienced.

It is a challenge, perhaps an affront, to recognize that the new conditions are beyond the reach of many of our established ways of thinking. To take a fresh look at the meaning of social defences in the new work systems, I believe we need to return to the most basic questions.

» What actually are the new building blocks of the emerging task systems, these impersonal dimensions that anchor the cycle of projection and introjection in such a way that individual's defences are reinforced?

» What does containment mean in the context of networks, eco-systems, and virtual groups whose members and resources are dispersed but which function as coherent units through the use of the cyber-infrastructure. We certainly know something about how relationships can facilitate sentient cultures of cohesiveness and reality-testing. And we also know about how the absence of requisite sentience provides fertile ground for persecutory fantasies. But how does this actually function in virtual environments and network structures?

» And, crucially, what anxieties are stimulated by the tasks and systems that comprise these new work structures? I see this question as the ground zero of the viability of social defence thinking into the twenty-first century.

Speculations on the future

Exploring the question of social defence systems in the twenty-first century requires looking at how tasks are shaped and work gets done. As a starting point I would like to focus on three related features of emerging work systems: knowledge work, globalization, and virtualization.

Knowledge work

The information age brings an increasing pervasiveness of knowledge work. Automation is expanding rapidly to handle many tasks formerly requiring people. Knowledge work is something about which we know a lot. What we know goes to the heart of questions about unconscious defences against workplace anxiety.

Unlike the industrial factors of production—land, labour, and capital—knowledge is a resource that must be coaxed, not forced. Climates in which employees volunteer their creativity and expertise do not depend on the traditional tools of control and accountability. Creating and sharing knowledge are essential to fostering innovation. They require climates that build trust and contain the anxieties involved in the personal risks of working through one's knowledge.

Knowledge work takes place through conversation. It often emerges through relationships. Knowledge workers learn, innovate, contribute, and change by talking and listening. Knowledge work is intensely personal; it begins with the self and involves intuition and experience. In every conversation, knowledge workers test an aspect of their own personal take on the world—the system-in-the-mind. Sophisticated work occurs where people can learn publicly, risking personal exposure in the service of developing shared understanding and collaborating in such a way that vulnerability is neither hidden nor pathologized, as Larry Hirschhorn (1988) has so eloquently addressed.

To join with the development of humane, creative systems, we must find a way to bring our deep understanding of the primitive anxieties stimulated by knowledge work into communication with an understanding of the networks and forums that now contain these conversations. The phantasies and anxieties stimulated both by the vulnerability of knowledge work and by the collaboration that depends on linking minds clearly contribute to the rigid sterility of many corporate environments. How primitive anxieties are expressed and defended against in the networks and forums that contain these conversations is worthy of serious research. Supporting the creative and sophisticated abilities of their members will require new strategies for containment and an approach to social defences that fosters integration.

Globalization

The conditions under which knowledge work happens are changing as well, in some ways profoundly. Where and how knowledge work occurs is going through its own transformation. Increasingly knowledge workers are able to perform tasks anywhere, disrupting aspects of social defence systems that are anchored in sentient ties.

New models of connectedness to organizations have emerged. Because a great deal of knowledge work can now be systematized and modularized, vast task systems are often broken into very small and discreet tasks. Virtual freelancers are hired to do discrete tasks that do not rely on real-time collaboration. While it is creating great flexibility for both organizations and workers, it also poses psychological challenges. The mechanisms of coordination and the computer infrastructures themselves most likely replace the earlier aspects of organization and take on social defence functions as well. The choices involved in designing these systems and mechanisms will take on this extra significance.

More embedded in organizations are itinerant corporate workers who are untethered to any place, moving around from "hotspot" to "hotspot" without any fixed "home base". There is an exponential increase in this model. IBM estimates that it has more than 45% of its 400,000 contractors and employees working remotely. While this provides for many of the dependency needs that are absent for freelancers (i.e., healthcare, retirement benefits, career trajectory, etc.), it also poses significant questions about the management of anxiety in the absence of sentient ties.

Many highly dispersed, rapid-paced global organizations develop sterile, rigid, or persecutory climates. Where people are so transient, relationships do not form. The sense of connection then requires over-reliance on relatedness and under-reliance on relationship to maintain connection (Krantz & Gould, 2005). Relatedness is the internal image of the organization. Relationships are the actual interpersonal connections between people. Relationships, with the reality of connection they provide, facilitate cohesiveness, gratification, and reality-testing. When relatedness (relationships-in-the-mind, not modulated by direct face-to-face contact) dominates the interpersonal landscape, it produces a fertile ground for persecutory fantasies.

One hypothesis is that the increasing dominance of such fantasies gives the culture of many contemporary organizations a distinctly paranoid–schizoid coloration, particularly since countervailing forces—those that bring people together—are in decline. Reflective, more balanced, integrated, and nuanced processes associated with meaningful relationships are diminished. In the absence of sufficiently rich relationships, and the containing function they serve, the human resource (HR) function is mobilized to mediate the social sphere.

What often emanates from HR is a prescriptive, normative idea about correct behaviour, the management of feelings, and the creation of "proper" attitudes. This can be seen as a form of social defence against the anxieties associated with the anonymous experience of these environments, together with the diffusion of more authentic relationships.

In the absence of genuine human connectedness, HR can become an instrument for creating a humanizing veneer. Take as illustration the massive proliferation of psychological and behavioural training in emotional intelligence. It is a trend to "normalize" and regulate relationships in contrast to fostering authentic, and often messy, relationships. Another trend that supports similar outcomes is the extensive use of 360° feedback mechanisms, which privileges consensus, adjusting oneself to the views of others, and "getting along" as dominant behavioural values.

At the same time, organizations that span institutional and national boundaries have become central to the accomplishment of highly sophisticated, non-linear, non-routine knowledge-based work, especially in science and engineering. Coordinating work and knowledge across time and space requires mechanisms that enable effective knowledge sharing and learning. Crucially, it requires developing the means by which sophisticated deliberation can occur.

Many organizations have begun to realize that virtualization was compromising some important benefits of more traditional workplace benefits. Too much division and distribution of labour diminished natural collaboration, including innovation arising from serendipitous encounters and hallway conversations. Work lives often lack a sense of community and the richness of collaboration. (Apparently someone joked that IBM stands for—"I'm by myself".) Experimentation is occurring with new approaches to co-working spaces, often organized around communities of practice rather than geographic or functional similarity, in order to restore some sense of community containment. Being distributed across space and time requires dynamic structures and processes and collaboration support systems that attend to all levels of analysis: individuals, groups, networks, organizations, and social ecologies.

Virtualization

A virtual organization is a group of individuals whose members and resources may be dispersed geographically, yet who function as a coherent unit through the use of cyber infrastructure. How this affects the individual is a topic of immense importance. Virtual organizations and groups are themselves socio-technical systems, where the social system is comprised of transient virtual connections and the technical system largely of computer code.

The internet and virtualization raise many psychodynamic concerns. Does it provide an easy avenue for avoiding meaningful relationship and help people avoid the distressing reparative dimensions of authentic experience? How does the illusion of proximity in time and space distort our connection to the world? Does "knowing" things instantaneously, instead of having to tolerate the discomfort of not knowing, impair thinking? Does computer mediation tend to convert subjects into objects, the "self" into the "itself" (Turkle, 2011) or promote borderline personality development (Guignard, 2014)? Does it amount, as some argue, to a breakdown of the authority of reality, resulting in less repression, diminished ability to cope with reality, and reduced sublimation?

Marshal McLuhan (1964) explored ideas that resonate with those of Fenichel and Menzies Lyth by pointing out that we create tools and then the tools create us:

> The printing press, the computer, and television are not . . . simply machines which convey information. They are metaphors through which we conceptualize reality in one way or another. They classify the world for us, sequence it, frame it, enlarge it, reduce it, and argue a case for what it is like. Through these media metaphors, we do not see the world as it is. We see it as our coding systems are established. [McLuhan, 1964, p. 173]

However, his work also suggests that virtualization, which entails a shift from emphasis on the written word to emphasis on the image, suggests a deeper transformation in the self and the psyche than is readily recognized. As David Patman (2013) suggests, the exploration of unconscious processes in groups and organizations may need to be refocused on the applications and social media that are increasingly binding people in common tasks. Given their pervasiveness, they may well begin to serve containing functions that have been previously located in familiar organizational structures.

Take the example of algorithms, which function as the backbone of the cybersphere. These equations, which instruct the computers how to behave, are actually pictures of the world, in the mind, converted into computer code. Each contains its own assumptions about human behaviour and needs. We shape them, they shape us. How does the adolescent relatedness underlying Facebook affect the world? There are significant anxieties that come with computer-mediated collaboration which are attached to the potential loss of the self and engulfment in the large group. I am curious about whether and how particular algorithms function as social defences.

Conclusion

A number of years ago, Tom Gilmore and I wrote an article about "The Splitting of Leadership and Management as a Social Defence" (Krantz & Gilmore, 1990), arguing that there seemed to be a pattern whereby the lionization of managerialism or leadership, and the corresponding denigration of the other, functioned as a social defence. Alastair Bain (1998) later built on this paper to conjecture that social defences were increasingly appearing at the level of the domain rather than at the level of the enterprise. More recently, I conjectured (Krantz, 2011) that people will increasingly manage their relatedness through a sense of citizenship in professional communities of practice rather than in organizations or groups. Today, it seems to me that now that they are moving into the digisphere as coordinating mechanisms, computer applications and social media will become the location of social defences.

The wellsprings of psychotic anxiety in task systems are intensified by the breakdown of familiar containing structures. At the intersection of systems psychodynamics and twenty-first-century information-based organizations, many mainstay concepts are becoming outmoded, such as small groups as the primary mediating structure between individuals and the larger context. What we understand far less is that there is also enormous creativity, sophistication, and generative relatedness in these unbounded systems. How do we account for the containment that this depressive-position functioning implies? To my mind, it is urgent that we get hold of this question. How new structures and work methods will interact with individual's anxieties and whether they can be used to promote creativity and integration rather than institutional-ize more primitive relations is a question of great import.

To be a meaningful part of these conversations, our theories, concepts, and practices must be adapted accordingly. We need to learn how the new work systems, which are without stable boundaries, well-defined task systems, and thick interpersonal contact, can foster depressive functioning. We need to discover and join with what is developmental in these systems. We need to engage and live among the digital natives. And we need to find ways to identify with—perhaps even love—native digital cultures, as is necessary to work well with our clients and patients.

We are faced with a paradox. Only by recognizing how little we know about the new conditions of work will we be able to mobilize the enormous expertise represented here to address twenty-first-century organizations.

CHAPTER FIVE

Defences against innovation: the conservation of vagueness

Philip Boxer

An individual newly joining an enterprise may experience it as a social defence system to which he or she must react and adapt. For the nurses in Isabel Menzies Lyth's study, "in the process of matching between psychic and social defence systems, the emphasis was heavily on the modification of the individual's psychic defences" (1960, p. 115). A social defence system is, however, also "a historical development through collusive interaction between individuals to project and reify relevant elements of their psychic defence systems" (p. 115). Menzies Lyth underlines that the use of the organization of an enterprise as a defence against anxiety is operated only by individuals.

This approach has brought its clinical concepts, practices, and focus on to what enables interventions to be effective, approaching organizational entities either through addressing the individual's experience within a single enterprise, or through the metaphoric use of psychoanalytic concepts to the enterprise itself *as if* it were an individual (Arnaud, 2012). Either way, the enterprise has been presumed to exist as a sovereign entity, paralleling the presumptions of a sovereign ego. How, then, are we to think psychoanalytically about the way in which the development of an enterprise interacts with an individual?

Consider this metaphor: an enterprise is like a coral reef, and the people whose employment depends on that enterprise are as the organisms that colonize the habitat created by the coral reef. In these terms, the organization of the enterprise used by its employees in support of their psychic defence systems is like the reef habitat used by its colonial organisms in support of their individual niches. The dynamic relationship of the coral reef with adjacent environments affects what forms of colonial organism it can support, but so too do the forms of colonial organism affect the topography of the coral reef. How does this translate into the individual–enterprise–environment dynamic?

All reef systems are open systems, but the extent of their openness to exchange with adjacent ecosystems varies, reflected by their organization as habitats that may themselves be more or less dynamic. To study such reef systems as isolated ecosystems, their internal processes must dominate over their cross-boundary conditions. Extend the spatiotemporal scale, however, and the topography of the reef itself becomes, for example, a function of the ocean-swell regime. Here, the cross-boundary conditions dominate over the reef system's internal processes. Thus, "ecosystem processes can be defined and measured at many scales not just that of the whole reef, depending on the question being addressed and the observer's perception" (Hatcher, 1997, p. 82).

This chapter considers the psychoanalytic implications of considering how cross-boundary conditions come to dominate intra-enterprise dynamics. We need to clarify what constitutes the enterprise–environment interaction, however, before considering the interaction of these cross-boundary dynamics with the individual.

The enterprise–environment interaction

The enterprise–environment interaction was less essential to the socio-technical challenges facing the machine cultures of the post–World War II era; a "machine culture" describes an enterprise culture focused on maximizing machine performance (Rice, 1958, p. 241). At that time, the primary task of an enterprise was defined as the task that the enterprise had to perform if it was to survive (Miller & Rice, 1967, p. 25). Thus, when A. K. Rice originally wrote about the Ahmedabad experiment (Rice, 1958), the primary task of the workers at Calico Mills involved managing a group of looms. The nature of the technology of production constrained the ways in which primary task could be defined (Miller, 1959).

By the latter part of the twentieth century, primary task was that organization of an enterprise that could form the basis of sustainable competitive advantage. Technology does not constrain the enterprise in the same way in the twenty-first century. The constraints come more from the nature of each situation and circumstance—for example, in healthcare, organizing an appropriate care pathway for an elderly person. The design of the organization is constrained by the situation and circumstance of the person rather than by a prior assumption of a primary output, such as of woven cloth.

Effective individual care must be organized on a one-by-one basis, the primary task of the care in each case depending on the nature of the individual situation and circumstance for which it is designed. The enterprise providing care must be capable of simultaneously organizing many different responses through the use of some repertoire of possible services and treatments, not necessarily all provided by itself. The cross-boundary conditions dominate the intra-enterprise dynamics.

In the place of one supply-side definition of primary task, the enterprise must support many simultaneous demand-side definitions, each one potentially defining its response differently—for example, in healthcare, through the provision of a variety of care pathways (Boxer, 2014). Given this proliferation of demand-side definitions of its primary task, an enterprise providing such a service must define its survival differently to the supply-side definitions of Miller and Rice (Miller & Rice, 1967).

The twenty-first-century pull towards having to respond to customers one-by-one

The need to do many different things at the same time is not unique to healthcare enterprises; it is apparent in any industry impacted by digitalization. This requires a shift in an enterprise's locus of innovation from its supply-side to its demand-side, enabled by the increasing ability to connect everything digitally. In the place of markets, digitalization enables a focus on the demands of customers, each within his or her context-of-use.

This demand-side focus means that an enterprise subject to these competitive pressures must place greater emphasis on its ability to create new and multiple forms of collaboration in order to generate value. As a result, it must itself operate within networks of other operationally and managerially independent enterprises, forming ecosystems with which it must collaborate in varying ways. Within these ecosystems, an enterprise must adopt strategies enabling organized networks to become the new economic entities shaping competition, their economics being organized around the contexts-of-use in which demands arise. In the case of the care enterprise, the pathway supporting an individual's care becomes just one pathway through an organized network.

Organized networks rely on task systems that have become increasingly modular. The agility of these networks is the variety of pathways through the network that they can support (Boxer, 2012). An enterprise aligns these pathways dynamically to customers' demands through contractual networks and creates dynamic complementarities with other enterprises. In this way, its identity becomes increasingly independent of institutionalized boundaries. The horizontal task linkages that can be established across these organized networks become dominant with respect to institutionalized vertical accountability linkages, and cross-boundary conditions dominate intra-enterprise dynamics. The dominance of these cross-boundary dynamics produces the conditions in which the dynamic behaviour of the ecosystem exhibits complex adaptive behaviour (Kurtz & Snowden, 2003).

Decoupling the individual from enterprise–environment interactions

One symptom of the impact on the individual of the dynamic nature of these enterprise–environment interactions has been a call for deep changes to educational and entrepreneurial systems. A study of the US economy since the end of World War II showed that output and productivity had become decoupled from jobs and wages in the last twenty years (McAfee, 2012). People doing routine forms of work had become increasingly decoupled from enterprise–environment interactions.

During this time, enterprises were responding to massive changes in their environment with changed strategies and boundaries redrawn by divesting peripheral businesses. These enterprises focused on core areas while outsourcing selected activities, and they merged at a historically unprecedented rate (Wulf, 2012). The resultant elimination of layers in an enterprise's organizational hierarchy ("flattening") was associated with increased control and decision-making at the top enabled by massive investments in information technology.

With these changes in how enterprises were being organized came new perspectives on the nature of competition as dynamic specialization and a more dynamic understanding of the way markets themselves were organized to serve particular interests. Michael Porter, a dominant influence on competitive strategy during the 1980s and 1990s, concluded that a fundamentally different approach was needed to create value, an approach that gave priority to creating value for the customer as well as for the supplier (Porter & Kramer, 2011). Put together, these changes reflected an unprecedented period of technological change, setting loose unprecedented demands for innovation across every industry, whether privately or publicly owned. In the reef metaphor, cross-boundary conditions were having a huge impact on the organization of the reef ecosystem/enterprise.

The effects of the decoupling can be seen in the persistent levels of high unemployment in Western economies, so that jobs that can be mechanized or computerized are gradually lost. One view is that this leads to new kinds of job created for "new artisans". These "new artisans" are workers who "combine technical skills with interpersonal interaction, flexibility and adaptability to offer services that are uniquely human" (Autor & Dorn, 2013). Another view is that this argument is itself a manifestation of neoliberal thinking and that neoliberalism is the ideological corollary of this decoupling. With neoliberalism, the well-being of each citizen can best be advanced by "liberating individual entrepreneurial freedoms and skills within an institutional framework characterized by strong private property rights, free markets, and free trade" (Harvey, 2005, p. 2). In effect, each citizen becomes a consumer personally responsible for the state of his or her life in an environment presented as if it were "natural".

Neoliberalism as a symptom of the decoupling

Neoliberalism for the very rich makes perfect sense, given that the rich have the power to shape markets to serve their interests. For those less fortunate, however, neoliberalism's offer of personal fulfilment lies in the shadow of varying degrees of anomie. Anomie is experienced as anxiety about what to do in the face of a withering away of norms, norms understood as "mental" givens. This anomie is existential anxiety or angst involving a "loss of meaning", a loss of a sense of direction and of knowing where even to begin to make meaning. Such existential angst is anxiety *without* an object. It is to be contrasted with annihilation anxiety—anxiety *with* an object that is an extreme form of performance or signal anxiety (Freud, 1926d [1925]). Neoliberalism from the perspective of this existential angst can be understood as an attempt to neutralize a critique of the aesthetic shape taken by an individual's life (Boltanski & Chiapello, 2005). Such a critique is based upon the importance attached to personal liberation, authenticity, and being-true-to-oneself, in clear echoes of the 1960s. This critique is taken up by a neoliberal rhetoric that is *vague* in theory, with no direct link to practice. In practice, markets are not "free" and the citizen is never wholly able to exercise sovereign rights over the shape of his or her life. The neoliberal rhetoric is enacted by enterprises and the state *as if* it is true (Bloom, 2013).

Looked at from the perspective of social defences, neoliberal management practices may have created some kinds of job while destroying many others. Their effect in the public sector, however, has been the standardizing and mechanizing of patient care, to the point at which the care can only be described as being provided in bad faith (Rizq, 2012). It is as if the perverse enterprise (Long, 2008) is offering a social defence in the form of jobs that can serve as psychic retreats (Steiner, 1993), displacing social anxiety onto the enterprise itself with its rules, systems, structures, and procedures (Hoggett, 2013). With some of its more recent political manifestations as "austerity", we may even see neoliberalism as banally evil in that its adoption as an ideology enables individuals knowingly to inflict the suffering of anomie on others (Alford, 1997). Neoliberal rhetoric responds to changing cross-boundary conditions as if the focus on protecting the existing organization of niches within the reef ecosystem/enterprise should be intensified.

The neoliberal focus thus remains on the individual, while the interactions of the enterprise with its adjacent environments remain the concern of others, kept safely "other" through narcissistic ide-alization of the enterprise itself (Schwartz, 1992) or through envious attack as a narcissistic defence against unbearable otherness (Stein, 2000). It is in this sense that neoliberalism may be seen as a symptom of the decoupling. It is a way of giving meaning to what-is-going-on that conceals what-is-"really"-going-on. At the level of the enter-prise itself, neoliberalism can result in an organizational miasma, in which there is "an incapacitating ethos of self-criticism, an inability to maintain boundaries between public and private lives, a silencing of organizational stories, a compulsive scapegoating and, above all, a paralysis of resistance" (Gabriel, 2012, p. 1139). It was this paraly-sis of resistance that was the focus of Menzies Lyth's work on social defences.

Menzies Lyth's work on social defences
as co-opted to this symptom

The original study of a nursing service by Isabel Menzies Lyth considered how the standardization of working practices could be used "to give substance in objective reality to characteristic psychic defence mechanisms" (Menzies Lyth, 1960/1988, p. 101). The study was criticized by a Registered Mental Nurse who argued that while standardization of a nurse's work might be used as a defence and might be useful in training, the social organization of a nursing service could not be "above all" for support in the task of dealing with anxiety (Registered Mental Nurse, 1960).

Menzies Lyth acknowledged this by drawing on Jaques's work (Jaques, 1956). She pointed out the effects of removing discretion from the way a job was defined: "nurses felt insulted, indeed almost assaulted, by being deprived of the opportunity to be more responsible" (Menzies Lyth, 1960, p. 112). She argued that to be effective, changes emerging from work with individuals and small groups needed to be counterbalanced by changes in surrounding areas (1990, p. 468). Menzies Lyth's focus was, therefore, as much on the organization of the institution as on the uses made of it by the individual. She nevertheless concluded that "resistance to social change is likely to be greatest in institutions whose social defence systems are dominated by primitive psychic defence mechanisms" (1960, p. 118).

A focus on the role of primitive psychic defence mechanisms involved focusing on the individual–enterprise interaction within the context of the overall aims of the enterprise (Armstrong, 2012b). The criticism made by the Registered Mental Nurse was more a prophecy of this focus on the individual–enterprise interaction, therefore, enabling the "defences against anxiety paradigm" (Stein, 2000) to be a perfect candidate for co-option in support of neoliberalism.

Co-opted in this way, the problem that needed solving was the interaction between the individual's attachment to forms of psychic defence and the organization of an enterprise. It became a way of thinking about the relationship between the individual and the enterprise, paralleling the organism's relationship to the reef ecosystem defined as the organism's niche within the ecosystem habitat. The psychoanalytic nature of the cross-boundary dynamics needs to be examined more closely to escape from this co-option.

The impact of cross-boundary dynamics

Jaques's original work on social systems as a defence against anxiety described the social system in terms of roles occupying different levels in a hierarchy corresponding to different timespans of discretion (Jaques, 1956). His work was concerned with getting precision in the structure of a managerial hierarchy. He later took this further by defining an enterprise as an interconnected system of roles with mutual accountabilities and authorities based on the requisite organization of the enterprise in relation to its environment (Jaques, 1989). His conclusion was that it was badly organized social systems that aroused psychotic anxieties rather than *vice versa* (Jaques, 1995).

This focus on the enterprise–environment relation did not sit well with the Tavistock paradigm (Palmer, 2002), in which the dominant approach was on the individual–enterprise interaction, working through self-managed teams and semi-autonomous work groups (Kirsner, 2004). A polarization emerged between Jaques's hierarchical approach to the enterprise–environment interaction and an argument for the value of the psychoanalytic approach to the individual–enterprise interaction by examining the transferential processes implicit in working relationships (Amado, 1995).

The dangers in pursuing an approach focused on the individual–enterprise interaction became apparent in the work that Emery and Trist did with the top management of a merged aerospace engine maker, which faced significant technological developments in its environment. They found that the team faced anxieties that were

> . . . existential rather than interpersonal. The issue that the team faced was one of survival. In a turbulent environment, the issue is survival. The need is to stop the flight into personal paralysis and interpersonal discord and to replace these by participation in a process of group innovation. In systems of organisational ecology, the locus of innovation is in the set of the partners involved. [Trist, 1977, p. 164]

In these turbulent environments, the laws connecting parts of the environment to each other were themselves "often incommensurate with those laws connecting parts of the enterprise to each other, or even with those which govern the exchanges" (Emery & Trist, 1965). The impact of turbulent cross-boundary dynamics on the individual–enterprise interaction was experienced by top management as existential anxiety or angst, distinct from anxiety attached to their performance as individuals in their roles. Faced with such dynamics, consideration of interpersonal anxieties constituted a flight into consideration of personal defences against anxiety. The challenge here was to address the sources of the existential angst.

The double challenge facing the enterprise

With psychoanalytic understanding comes a presumption that there is more going on than is accessible to what may be said. From the early years of the Tavistock paradigm, the work group was distinguished from its other existence as the "basic group" (Rice, 1958). In this other existence, the "basic group" exhibited basic-assumption behaviours as manifestations of its individual members' relation to the unconscious (Bion, 1961). The starting point for working with enterprises within the Tavistock paradigm was thus an entity with boundaries around an inside (Palmer, 2002) and a "workplace within" through which the individual governed his or her actions (Hirschhorn, 1988). The dependence of this approach on an *a priori* definition of the work group limited it, however, to addressing only the individual's relation to the work group as constituted "vertically" by the enterprise—that is, to addressing the individual–enterprise interaction.

Consider the position of Bert, a care worker within an enterprise set up to provide in-home support to the elderly mentally ill, supporting a person called Agatha. A role consultation with Bert would focus on how he was able to take up a role as it had been defined by the enterprise. The consultation would not go beyond that, however, to re-defining the enterprise within which the role was itself defined (Huffington, 2008). Bert's experience of his relation to his employer would be one of being constrained. In considering what was constraining, such things would be included as the employer's articles of association, organizational roles, contracts, assets, systems, archives, accounts, buildings, affiliated or contracted enterprises, customers and advisors. The objects in this open-ended list would have many possible linkages between them, the structures they formed being social structures of meaning as well as physical structures. The constraining effects produced by these social and physical structures would "subject" individuals like Bert at the same time as the behaviours of Bert also "structured" others' experience, such as the care that Agatha might receive (Miller, 1968).

The services with which Bert can respond to Agatha are structured "vertically" by the way their enterprise has been set up, in turn structuring the experience of Agatha "horizontally" through the way they are delivered. In a turbulent environment, however, competition demands that services delivered have increasingly to be structured by the choices Agatha can make "horizontally", presenting the care enterprise with a double challenge. The enterprise subjects those working within it to "vertical" constraints, assimilating them to its ways of organizing its work. The enterprise is also itself subject to "horizontal" constraints, imposed by the choices of those to whom it provides services. In turbulent environments, these "horizontal" constraints become at least as important as the "vertical" constraints if the enterprise is to accommodate itself to its different customers' demands in order to remain viable.

The significance of the twenty-first-century pull towards having to respond "horizontally" to customers one by one is that it increasingly presents enterprises with this double challenge. This places particular demands on a Bert in an "edge" role, who experiences this double challenge in terms of how he responds to cross-boundary dilemmas about how to provide care to an Agatha. The limitation of both the hierarchical approach and the approach focused on the individual–enterprise interaction is that the focus of analysis is too limited. It has to include the interactions between all three parts of the ecosystem defined by individual–enterprise–environment. Under these conditions, Bert becomes critical in determining how to manage the cross-boundary dilemma that the enterprise must contain as part of a larger ecosystem. It is also in the context of this dilemma that Bert's subjection to his unconscious emerges, because it is in relation to this subjection that existential angst arises as a symptom of the challenges facing the individual–enterprise–environment interaction.

The double challenge meets double subjection

In his paper on the two principles of mental functioning, Freud tells of a man who, following his father's death, dreams that his father is still alive (Freud, 1911b, p. 225). Freud uses this to show how an individual is *doubly subjected*, subject to reality as represented by inter-subjectively agreed social structures of meaning, and subject to the unconscious manifesting itself here in the form of a wish as a dreamer. This double subjection leads to the experience of being divided: "The point is not to know whether I speak of myself in a way that conforms to what I am, but rather to know whether, when I speak of myself, I am the same as the self of whom I speak" (Lacan, 1966b), p. 430). Double subjection describes the Freudian topology of the relation between the ego and the id: "where id was, there ego shall be" (Freud, 1933a, p. 80).

In the English translation of this quote, the emphasis is on enlarging the organization of the ego "so that it can appropriate fresh portions of the id" (p. 80). The emphasis via the original German ("*Wo Es war, soll Ich werden*") and its French translation, however, is on the "there" where the id was in order to capture something of the nature of the id as being always elsewhere, never fully "drained" by the ego (Lacan, 1975, p. 194). This quality of the radical Otherness of the unconscious as "being elsewhere" provides us with a way of distinguishing the performance or annihilation anxiety associated with performance that is subject to familiar social structures, and the existential angst aroused by the disruption of these structures by cross-boundary dynamics. To the extent that Bert's role supports his self-identity, the organization of the enterprise serves as a defence against performance or annihilation anxiety. With the double challenge comes a potential disruption of the current organization of the enterprise, and any resultant disruption to Bert's role gives rise to existential angst (Armstrong, 2007).

The effect of the double challenge facing the enterprise, therefore, will be to affect the way the individual is subjected to its social structure (Figure 5.1). The necessity to accommodate itself to "horizontal" constraints causes potential disruption to the vertical constraints constituting the current organization of the enterprise. Such divergence (Figure 5.1, bottom right) will lead strategy consultation in order to consider new ways of competing as an enterprise. Divergence in the double sub-

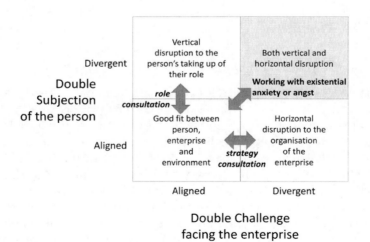

Figure 5.1. Double subjection and double challenge

jection experienced by the individual within an existing social structure (top left) will lead to role consultation relating his or her performance to the expectations of the enterprise. It is divergence in both (Figure 5.1, top right), a characteristic of turbulent environments, that gives rise to existential angst.

In the turbulent environments identified by Emery and Trist, the failure by an enterprise to include horizontal forms of disruptive inno-vation as part of its normal behaviour will prevent it from engaging in the kinds of dynamic adaptation demanded of it. To be effective, the enterprise has to take into consideration the forms of existential angst precipitated by the failure of existing vertical forms of subjection. It has to enable individuals at its "edges" to "mind the gap". Within these environments, the new perspectives on the nature of competition as dynamic specialization demand that innovation becomes part of the way of doing business, no longer left to a separate world of "entrepre-neurs" (Foss & Klein, 2012).

If Bert can bear his existential angst and the group in which they work is able to innovate, they will together develop new horizontal ways of organizing the group's relation to individuals in the envi-ronment of the enterprise, including Agatha. With such work-group innovation, an enterprise ceases to be a pre-existent entity defined top-down, instead becoming an effect of its emergent relationships with its customers arising from a continuous process of innovation by its work groups. Such innovation requires a different relationship to the detail of what-is-going-on at the "edge" of the enterprise and a differ-ent approach to the governance of the enterprise itself, in which "edge" roles such as Bert's become critical (Boxer, 2014). Innovation comes to depend on those in "edge" roles being able to bear disruption to the way their work group and ultimately their enterprise supports their identities. To understand what is involved for Bert to bear the effects of this disruption, it is necessary to examine its impact on their subjection to the social structures of the enterprise.

On the disruption of subjection
to social structures

An individual in an "edge" role is at an intersection between the way vertically organized and horizontally organized systems interact with each other. Such an individual is likely to be in roles within multiple overlapping horizontally organized systems while at the same time being in vertically defined enterprise roles. An individual experiences his or her subjectivity within these systems in relation to others, subject to both horizontally defined and vertically defined systems, "through subjection to roles in these systems" (Long, 2006, p. 287). The difference is that in roles defined horizontally, two-way horizontal relationships co-determine how the individual is subjected. In contrast, enterprise-defined roles are ones in which one-way vertical relations determine the way in which the individual is subjected.

Double subjection means that, alongside their subjection to these systems, defences associated with their subjection to the Otherness of the unconscious may also operate which the individual experiences as his or her subjectivity under threat (Long, 2006, p. 288). Such threats come from an experienced loss of support to their self-identity pro-vided by both vertically defined and horizontally defined social struc-tures supporting their relation to the unconscious. In these terms, how is the experience of existential angst to be understood?

Subjection to social structures as a relation to thirdness

Subjection by social structures is evidenced by shared mental models. From the perspective of subjection, the relation to these shared men-tal models may be expressed as a relation to "thirdness" (Benjamin, 2009). Thirdness was originally Charles Peirce's way of referring to the mediating context within which attributions of meaning were made (Murphey, 1993). Thirdness is a way of describing the shared set of assumptions and constraints implicit in the structured relations to which an individual is subject, referred to as a shared mental model or a shared matrix of thought (Bion, 1961).

The relation to both vertically defined and horizontally defined systems has this property of "thirdness" in the way they subject the individual, even though the origin of the mental models in each case may be different and disjoint. With hierarchically defined roles, the origin will be in the founding assumptions and constraints of the enterprise to which the individual is "vertically" subject ultimately through his or her employment. In contrast, with horizontally defined systems, the origin will be in the nature of the situation in which the two-way co-creating is taking place, shaped by assumptions and con-straints that are felt to be appropriate to the situation itself. Under-stood in terms of double subjection, however, their relative authority for the individual will also depend on the nature of the libidinal investment that each supports, arising from the individual's relation to the unconscious (Stavrakakis, 2007).

In these terms, the conservation of forms of thirdness that constitute resistance also involve the conservation of particular forms of libidinal investment. The potential for resistance will arise in the cross-boundary dilemma faced by Bert in his relationship with Agatha. What will be at stake is the relative dominance of one or the other's libidinal investment in particular forms of thirdness. The horizontal resistance of Agatha would be to the vertical forms of thirdness being conserved by the enterprise to the exclusion of other possible forms of thirdness. By looking more closely at the organization of thirdness, something of the differing nature of vertically or horizontally derived forms of libidinal investment may be deduced.

Distinguishing vertically and horizontally derived forms of thirdness

For an enterprise to be available for use as a social defence against anxiety, there have to be current forms of thirdness that will support those defences. Throughout the twentieth century, the theory of the enterprise developed based on largely static and "closed" forms of thirdness. These static and "closed" forms of thirdness to which the employees of an enterprise were subject reflected the founding assumptions and constraints that established an enterprise as competitively viable. They authorized ways of composing asset structures consistent with its top-down definition of primary task.

Innovation involves enabling this thirdness to give way to different forms of thirdness rooted in different processes and values (Lane & Maxfield, 2005). For this to be possible, the physical and social structures to which individuals are subjected have to be decomposable and capable of re-composition within different forms of thirdness (Foss & Klein, 2012). Disruptive innovation involves disrupting existing forms of thirdness to change the "ontological scaffolding", with its taken-for-granted kinds of entities and interactions, within which individuals' actions are aligned with each other (Lane & Maxfield, 2005). Within the socioanalytic field, such innovations may be described as abductions (Long & Harney, 2013) or hypotheses that attempt to make new kinds of sense from experiences (Murphey, 1993).

Peirce's pragmaticist reframing of pragmatism situated abduction as taking place within the context of beliefs that were held acritically—

that is, without question—but which nevertheless constrained the ways in which the individual made sense of his or her experience (1905, p. 484). These indubitable beliefs were *vague* in the sense that, while constraining the ways in which the individual made sense, they could not themselves be made determinate in their meaning, their effect being indirect through the way they constrained the way a person reasoned (p. 486). A belief that was vague could therefore apply to contradictory statements. For example, to understand what was meant by "I want you to be happy", "happiness" could be related by the speaker to outcomes in the situation that appeared contradictory. Reducing vagueness involved understanding this dependency on "what the person meant in the situation".

Peirce introduced the concept of invariant forms of vagueness in order to give an account of the ways in which indubitable beliefs shaped an individual's reasoning (1905, p. 481). Indubitable beliefs were thus like fixed points in the ontological scaffolding within which individuals worked. Unconscious libidinal investment in the organization of a mental model can thus be described as evidenced in acritically held relations to these indubitable beliefs, paralleling the way symbolic equation unconsciously restricts the relation between an object-signifier and the object-signified (Segal, 1957). Thus, even if an object-signifier is not itself subject to symbolic equation, indubitable beliefs evidence the unconscious constraining of an object-signifier's relation to other object-signifiers. For example, Bert and Agatha may come from different backgrounds. When Bert asks himself to tea at Agatha's home, what is implied for Agatha may be a whole set of expectations concerning time of day, dress, and behaviour. These expectations are vague in the sense of reflecting Agatha's particular beliefs in how to organize her life. When the meeting in question is about planning Agatha's future care, a failure by Bert to understand these forms of vagueness constraining Agatha's understanding of "tea" will have serious consequences for the meeting. In order to avoid the potentially damaging effects of misreading what Agatha expects of him, Bert must be prepared to question the vagueness in his own understanding of the situation he faces. Moreover, in so doing he may be questioning assumptions that were formerly held by him as indubitable.

The distinction between horizontally and vertically defined forms of thirdness may therefore be stated in terms of whether or not vagueness may be called into question. This in turn enables the nature of the libidinal investment that is being disrupted to be restated.

Defences against innovation
as the conservation of vagueness

The forms of resistance to change that defend existing mental models go much further than resistance arising as a consequence of narcissistic attachment (Lakatos, 1970) or of perverse organization (Long, 2008). At stake is an unconscious libidinal investment in a particular organization of a mental model, expressed in terms of particular organizations of vagueness and mobilized in support of organizations of identity (Stavrakakis, 2007).

An infant's early experience of the maternal matrix is a prototypical experience of thirdness. Within this matrix there will be that about the infant's experience that she or he will repeat, but also that which she or he will not be able to repeat. Freud distinguished these by referring to two kinds of unconscious thing-presentation: *Sachvorstellung* and *Dingvorstellung*. *Sachvorstellung* was the thing-presentation that acted as support to word-presentation, potentially repressed by the ego through negation, but *Dingvorstellung* was that about the thing that was lost (Freud, 1925h, pp. 235–236).

This relation to the lost object is the relation to *objet petit a* (Lacan, 1966a, p. 690), which in its imaginary form *i(a)* covers over what is lost while at the same time standing in the place of what is desired (Lacan, 1959–1960, p. 54). An existing organization of vagueness will conserve an unconscious libidinal investment in a relation to what is lost. It will also constitute a relation to what is desired, a relation to what is yet-to-be-known and yet-to-be-experienced. While a vertical relation to acritically held beliefs conserves vagueness, a horizontal relation seeks to reduce it.

Peirce's purpose in producing his pragmaticist reframing was to understand the forms of practice through which vagueness might be reduced within the context of what remained irremediably vague (Peirce, 1908). His argument was that it was through the practice of critical reading of the conduct determined by "man's occult nature" that the limits of irremediable vagueness might be explored (Ochs, 1998). Thus, Bert can go to great lengths to ensure that he limits the benefit of the doubt he gives to Agatha by critically examining what he had previously left vague, even though in doing this there will remain an irremediable vagueness about the organization of Agatha's beliefs.

Disruptive innovation can be understood as the disruption of existing ways of managing vagueness, a disruption that uncovers the limits of what is irremediable vagueness, or the limits to understanding how

Agatha understands her needs. In contrast, defences against innovation will involve the conservation of vagueness, of the beliefs that are held indubitably. Social defences against anxiety will involve the conservation of acritically held beliefs giving rise to unquestioned forms of vagueness, leaving room for the person to do things "their way", shielded from performance anxiety by their unquestioned vagueness. Existential angst arises when this vagueness has to be *reduced* in order to uncover a focus for innovation that is also at the heart of the angst, a vagueness that demands innovation if it is to become bearable. Minding this gap between the vertical and the horizontal demands of Bert and his leaders a different kind of ethic founded in the desire arising in the situation at the "edge" (Lacan, 1959–1960). In the words of an extreme alpinist, innovation challenges us "to climb through fear, to point fear up instead of down" (Twight & Martin, 1999). In this way, existential angst acts as a guide "against its will" (Kierkegaard, 1980).

Conclusion

In turbulent environments, the cross-boundary interactions between an enterprise and adjacent environments become dynamic and two-way. This presents the enterprise with potential incommensurabilities between the current "logic" of its organization and that of individuals and enterprises within adjacent environments. The current conception of social defence becomes inadequate under these conditions.

Turbulence creates a double challenge for an enterprise in which vertically defined relations to prior founding assumptions must be balanced with horizontally defined assumptions needed to respond to new kinds of demand. This double challenge changes the focus of the enterprise from being defined solely by its boundary conditions to being defined by its multiple relationships one-by-one with adjacent environments. Given the individual's double subjection both to social structures of meaning and to the unconscious, the emphasis on support to psychic defences addresses only one side of the double challenge, in which the existing organization of the enterprise is conserved. On the other side of the challenge is the need for innovation, in which the existing organization of the enterprise is disrupted.

Vagueness refers to the ways in which the organization of a mental model is experienced as constrained, based on acritically held beliefs. Social defences against anxiety involve the conservation of this vagueness. Disruptive innovation demands that vagueness be questioned, through questioning an individual's unconscious libidinal investments in acritically held beliefs. Valency for innovation demands a questioning of how existing vagueness is maintained in support of psychic defences, through which opportunities for innovation may be identified in what was previously left unexamined by that vagueness. Achieving this involves creating the conditions in which the horizontal relations of an enterprise may dominate vertical ones. It also involves engaging in critical examination of existing vagueness in order to identify the dilemmas that vagueness keeps concealed, which may lead to new learning (Boxer, 2013). Such practices demand courage from leadership.

CHAPTER SIX

Reconceptualizing social defences for the purpose of organizational change: causes, consequences, and the contribution of cultural theory

Nick Papadopoulos

The theory of social defences has changed little since Menzies Lyth's development of Jaques's initial hypothesis. Yet despite its utility, the problem of bringing about organization-level change in the contexts in which its use was originally intended has remained. Arguably this is because it prioritizes the psychological dimension over the social causation and operation of social defences. Recent theoretical developments have contributed to this difficulty by emphasizing the ubiquity of social defences in all organizations as an inescapable consequence of the nature of most work and emotions arising in primary-task performance. This development should be treated as a background given and not the foreground explanation. To assume their inevitability and target their psychology draws the intervention focus on to the people involved and helps them to understand and work through what they are caught up in. While this is an important aspect of intervention, especially for personal and leadership development and training purposes, it can avert attention away from the social nature and operation of social defences, what they are a reaction to, or the potential consequences they may in turn generate.

Part of the theory's difficulty with change is its under-developed and under-utilized social side. Instead of focusing and intervening on the psychological nature and effects of social defences on individuals, what is proposed here is treating social defences in the first instance as symptoms of social or external causes that need to be explained, not what is doing the explaining. This allows us to see them as social entities in their own right and to treat them for analytic purposes as independent of the people involved. With this we can begin to trace their social triggers or what in their environments they are a reaction to and to hypothesize about their organizing logic, their "reason-for-being", and what in the wider organization they may in turn affect.

The Durkheim-influenced cultural theory of Mary Douglas is introduced as a sociological and political resource to supplement and bolster the social operation and consequence-generating effects of social defences. It can assist in hypothesizing about their political nature and the underlying values and assumptions informing the grievances driving them. We can then do the same for elements in the organization, including changing external conditions, new policies, practices, or leadership, and the unanticipated consequences that these can generate. Such elements are what give reason for social defences to develop. We can then hypothesize about where their potential consequences may be directed. To capture this, social defences are reconceptualized as social or structural entities in their own right as "informal institutions" that generate their own feedback processes and operate according to their own internal organizing logic that in turn affects and generates consequences back onto the people and organization.[1]

In its current state, social defence theory lacks a sociological and political perspective from which to draw out the purposive, political, and normative dimensions of behaviour within groups and organizations (see Emery, 1997). Such a political dimension is at best only implicit in Bion's use of Freud's secondary processes to differentiate between task and basic assumption behaviours. What can be missed are the political grievances and jostling that can occur in groups. These draw on social values about what is right and wrong, how the group should be organized, and what it should pursue and how. Such behaviour should not always be reduced to its psychology, which can miss its distinctive influence and signature on groups and outcomes. A social–moral–political perspective can act as an alternative lens through which to view and supplement psychoanalytic exploration and insight. This is an area into which the mature works of Trist, Emery, and Jaques ventured. Cultural theory offers one such alternative and theoretically consistent social, moral, and political lens.

I start with Menzies Lyth's innovation, differentiate between organizational and individual or team change, and look at the theory's problem of change before introducing the re-conceptualization. I then highlight some relevant contributions of Emery, Trist, and Jaques to open up the theoretical space, before introducing the central concepts of cultural theory and how they can be utilized as a practical resource to social defence theory and intervention. I finish by applying these ideas to Menzies Lyth's seminal case study (1960).

Menzies Lyth's innovation

Such a development is not inconsistent with Menzies Lyth's innovation of Jaques's hypothesis. She gives social defences their own *social quality*, which is independent of the individuals and their collective defences. She also gives them a *systemic component* that, through processes of feedback, loop back to influence the people involved and the organization. This is where she clearly diverges from Jaques, who emphasized how "all institutions are used by their members as mechanisms of defence against primitive anxiety" (1955, p. 496) which cohesively bind "individuals into institutionalised association" (1953, pp. 420–421). Instead, she stressed that social defences are more than a duplicate of people's unconscious psychological dynamics. Once these dynamics are triggered, they operate independently through being built into organizational structures, systems, operating cultures, and work practices. They become "an aspect of external reality that old and new members must come to terms with" (Menzies Lyth quoted in Krantz, 2010; see also Menzies Lyth, 1989, pp. 26–44).

However, she does not seize on the *social and systemic* implications of her innovation and subtly undermines them. She does this by placing the causality of what occurs within organizations on the needs of its members for social and psychological belonging and satisfaction. While I do not suggest that this view is wrong, what it does is turn attention away from the *social* causation and operation of social defences and how they may impact the organization. It turns the causal attention on to the people and their psychology, which then become the basis of change intervention. This translates into practice as a focus on what she initially called "socio-therapy", or helping individuals and teams come to grips with their situation.

Theorizing and initiating organizational change, however, is qualitatively different from and additional to individual and team change. It ultimately concerns where the causality in the relationship between psychological and social factors is placed. This in turn informs where the emphasis and design of change interventions is placed. To assume that changing individuals will change organizations ignores the influence of an organization's strategy and culture and its structures, systems, and leadership practices on people's thought and behaviour (Burke, 2011; Burke & Litwin, 1992). These are the social or structural conditions that broadly define the opportunities and constraints acting on people.

Social defence theory and the problem of change

A recurring problem of social defence theory and practice is the difficulty of bringing about organizational-level change in the contexts where its use was originally intended (Krantz, 2010; Long, 2006). Several reasons for this have been suggested. These include the ubiquitous nature of social defences found in all organizations (Bain, 1998) and how individuals need and use social systems as a means of "maintaining their identity and protecting themselves against intolerable internal conflict" (Miller, 1976, p. 20). This theorizing makes social defences difficult to change (Menzies Lyth, 1960) and explains only why change may be psychologically resisted (Long, 2006), not how change or stability come about. It bypasses the challenges of grappling with organizational-level change and, instead, attends to the psychology involved and to developing interventions directed at individuals or teams. The challenges of facilitating organizational-level change led Emery, Trist, and Jaques to re-focus their attention on the wider environment representing the causal influences acting upon organizations (Emery & Trist, 1965) and the organizational design or structural influences on behaviour (Jaques, 1995). These contributions do not bypass psychology but prioritize the role of social influences and causation. What this does is invert causality from psychological to social factors and treats unconscious psychological dynamics as the symptoms and starting points for further investigation and not the discovery itself. As symptoms, they represent the important early warnings of potential problems or change.

The reconceptualization

Developing the social side of the theory requires, first, an understanding of how the nature of social context can itself exert influence on thought, feelings, and behaviour. This can be done by utilizing institutional, systemic, and sociological models to supplement and build upon psychoanalytic methods. Second, it requires prioritizing that once social defences are triggered, they will exhibit their own distinctive characteristics and social dynamics. These are independent of the people involved and exert a causal influence back on behaviour and organizational outcomes. This was Menzies Lyth's innovation. Third, what is missing is the theory's ability to trace the social processes set in train and to predict some possible social consequences that the social defences may generate.[2]

What is needed, I argue, is a reconceptualizing of social defence systems as informal institutions that generate their own feedback processes back onto, and in turn influence, both the people involved and the larger organization within which they operate. They are reconceptualized as "institutions" to identify them as distinct social entities in their own right and as "informal" to stress their tacit and often unconsciously operating or loosely held nature. As institutions, they inherently carry within them the organizing logic and social values associated with one or a mix of cultural theory's elementary forms of social organization. As institutions, they can be seen as sets of behavioural practices that cultivate their own distinctive thought-styles, or ways of thinking, doing, and feeling on the people operating within them. The "thought-style" that is cultivated in turn reinforces the institutional practices from which they are generated and becomes the causal engine generating the effects that social defences have within the social contexts they operate.

What can appear as psychologically motivated behaviour may also be seen as the "thought-style" cultivated within social defences. Similarly, what groups do is to generate behavioural practices and a thought-style that feedbacks onto the individuals. This in turn reinforces the institution they have co-created even if it is at odds with their own values, beliefs, and preferences. In organizations, individuals can, through their various roles, affiliations, and team memberships, belong to several institutional practices, creating internal conflict and confusion and generating seemingly irrational behaviour. The value of seeing group dynamics in terms of thought-style is that the behavioural practices cultivating them can be seen and studied as institutional or social entities in their own right.

This casts a different light on group-as-a-whole dynamics identified by Bion (1961) and Rice (1965). Focusing on the basic assumption pattern and mechanisms of defence may miss the social operation and consequence-generating effects that groups can have. This is especially the case in the wider contexts that groups perform in, are influenced by, and in turn influence through their goals and desires. Prioritizing attention on the primary processes in group dynamics can miss the organizing logic and guiding social values operating within them. How a group uses its secondary processes or task focus was a central feature of Bion's group theory and practice, which he crystallized during the Northfield experiments. In recent times these have tended to be downplayed within the paradigm (Armstrong, 2012a). The secondary processes, it is argued, should also include how individuals use their political beliefs and values to influence each other and the groups they belong to.

Cultural theory, through an institutional perspective on groups and social defences, can offer one such additional perspective. For diagnostic purposes, a social or institutional lens, for example, can be incorporated into Wells's (1995) systemic, five-levels framework. The framework utilizes five systemic categories—intra-psychic, interpersonal, group-as-a-whole, inter-group, and organizational—to identify and place where unconscious psychological dynamics may be emerging and be better understood. It is a variation on Lewin's (1997) alternating "figure-ground" perspective. While it offers a systemic view of psychological dynamics, it remains a psychological perspective on behaviour. This is not the same as a distinctly social perspective. The importance of this is that where a more psychological perspective may direct intervention toward individuals and teams as a way to understand and "work through" the emotions and dynamics they are caught up in, an institutional or social perspective will direct intervention on the nature and organizing logic of the context itself and how this is triggering and influencing behaviour. These address the organizational systems, structures, and working practices that Menzies Lyth's innovation directed attention to as where social defences operate. A social perspective can analyse the social nature and operation of both the social defences and the context in which they arise.

The contributions of Emery, Trist, and Jaques

The work of Emery, Trist, and Jaques provided the opening of the theoretical space to include a more sociological perspective alongside psychoanalytic insight and method. It helped to identify the under-developed and under-utilized social side of social defence theory and to provide the clues of how to bolster it. It drew attention to the regulative, political or values-based and cultural–cognitive influences on behaviour. Together their works highlight how internal structural conditions and external organizational environments are not only the context in which psychological dynamics such as social defences appear, but frequently their causal drivers. It helped focus attention on what is required to bring about organizational-level vs. individual and team change. This requires inverting causality from psychological to social factors and treating social defences or the psychological dynamics on display, in the first instance, as symptomatic rather than causal. They are something that needs to be explained and not what is doing the explaining. This was Jaques's rationale for abandoning his social defence hypothesis (1995, 1998)[3] and, like Emery and Trist, for focusing instead on the social variables influencing behaviour and developing research and intervention methodology that can provide viable causal explanations of the social causes, the social processes and consequences set in train by social defences. Arguably providing such feasible causal accounts can assist organizational leaders and the consultants to better respond.

Cultural theory exhibits much of the logic inherent in the latter works of Emery, Trist, and Jaques. It also builds on Menzies Lyth's innovation to the theory through reconceptualizing the nature and functioning of social defences as social systems in their own right that generate their own social consequences. With its roots in anthropology and political science, the strength of cultural theory lies as a social, political, and institutional theory of sociocultural conflict, viability, and change. It is used here to assist in explaining how social stability and change occur and to provide a true social perspective[4]—one that sits alongside psychoanalytic ones when using multiple systemic perspectives as different levels of analysis or diagnostic lenses as advocated in the paradigm (Wells, 1995), and alongside methods facilitating the in-depth study of emotional experience in organizations (Armstrong, 2005a).

Cultural theory: formal and informal institutions and thought-style

Cultural theory offers a viable and missing theory of *how* social environments, and the formal and informal institutional practices found within them, generate their own social dynamics. Unlike many social theories, it gives a clear role to individuals and their agency in co-creating, challenging, and transforming their social environments (Douglas, 1982),[5] while emphasizing the social causation of behaviour and of the consequences generated in social organizations. The causal emphasis is placed on the social environment and institutions as the independent variables, or something that can better do the explaining (6, 2011), and not on psychological dynamics. Causal priority is given both to "thought-style" (Douglas, 1986) and informal institutions in generating outcomes in social organizations (6, 2011), especially those outcomes that are unintended, conflict with espoused purposes or principles, appear to come from nowhere, or are subterfuge or undermine organizational functioning in subtle ways. These are the internally generated outcomes within organizations that are difficult to spot and mostly operate beneath the level of conscious awareness.

For example, organizations, networks, and groups, large or small, formally constituted or informal, are both nested within larger social environments and also generate their own distinctive or more immediate social environments or cultures. Seen this way, each social environment, group, or organization will draw upon existing or established behavioural practices or institutions as well as creating its own. Defined most simply as conventions to achieve a purpose or to solve problems (Douglas, 1986, p. 46), institutions are behavioural practices that cultivate their own distinctive "thought-style", or ways of thinking about and doing things. Once cultivated, institutional thought-styles will influence their members to think and behave along similar lines, whether or not they agree with these in principle. Douglas (1982) suggests that how an institution or culture is created is through a series of ongoing contributions and negotiations between members of a group in which everyone contributes—actively, passively, or even anonymously—but does not necessarily agree with the specific results or the outcome. This outcome generates a "collective consciousness [that] manifests . . . by making penalty-carrying rules and justifying them" (p. 190). In this way, institutions provide for the coordination of behaviour, but also "establish order and regulate" it, providing for the patterning of social relationships. Institutions not only make "the rules of the game, they structure the incentives of players" (Douglas, 1996, pp. 411–415). Perri 6, building on these ideas, further differentiates between the "style" of thought from its "content". While institutions will cultivate distinctive thought-styles or a manner in which ideas, beliefs, and feelings are framed and used, its actual content consists of its specific ideas and beliefs, which may be accepted or not. In this way, "people with diametrically opposed ideologies [or world views] may exhibit similar thought-styles [and] ideological allies may think in contrasting styles" (6, 2011, p. 1).

Seeing the social defences that manifest as informal institutions arising in reaction to particular events and/or other practices or institutions, and cultivating distinctive "thought-styles", which may be conflicting, can better account for both their social operation and their consequent impact on the organization.

Douglas suggests that all thinking and hence behaviour is to some degree institutionally influenced. This is in keeping with mainstream theorizing about how institutions exert their own "regulative, normative and cognitive" influences on people and behaviour (Scott, 2008). This is also in keeping with more recent theorizing that suggests how it is tacitly or loosely held informal institutional practices that in particular exert a causally critical influence on behaviour and organizational outcomes, frequently making it possible for formal institutions to achieve the leverage they do (6, 2011, p. 59). This is because they are better able to work around the more formal and often cumbersome procedures, channels, and structures to get things done. Equally so and exactly because informal institutional practices are tacitly, loosely, and albeit unconsciously held, their regulative, normative, or cognitive contours can be sufficiently ambiguous to "provide opportunities" for actors to use their "creativity and agency" to "exploit" or manipulate conditions for change, or for "endogenous developments" reflecting "gradual and piecemeal changes" to "show up or register" as changes especially if we consider longer time-frames (Mahoney & Thelen, 2010, p. 12). Moreover, because these practices are tacitly held, informal institutions can be triggered by and in turn trigger their own psychological reactions in people, but they can also allow the influence of both conscious and unconscious human agency that contains both a deliberative and choosing quality while allowing for both resistance to existing conditions and the creativity to do something different (e.g., see DiMaggio, 1988; Emirbayer & Mische, 1998; Wilsford, 2010).

The cultural theory typology and the elementary forms of social organization

Douglas starts from the assumption that all forms of social organization, like the people in them, are never static but are continuously being built and challenged through an ongoing process of bargaining and negotiation between people. From Durkheim, she takes two key ideas. The first is his social origin of thought—the idea that "classifications, logical operations and guiding metaphors are given to the individual by society" (Douglas, 1986, p. 10), and from this she develops institutional thought-styles. For Durkheim, it is not beliefs that explain society, which in their diversity contribute to differing forms of solidarity and conflict, but society that provides the individual with a menu of social, political, moral, and philosophical beliefs and tools for thinking. It is such a menu of assumptions, beliefs, and tools for thinking and (psychologically) reacting that breathes life into her cultural theory and from which her elementary forms of social organization draw.

The second of Durkheim's ideas is his two dimensions of sociality—social regulation and social integration. These represent two distinctive ways in which any social environment is shaped and will, in turn, influence people's thought, behaviour, and pattern of social relationships. These are the degree to which any human environment, large or small, is socially regulated (where rules and regulations constrain behaviour) and the degree to which it is socially integrated (where group membership or affiliation influences behaviour and choice and contributes to a shared world-view). What Douglas did was to cross-tabulate them, revealing four distinctive elementary forms of social environment. Each contains a distinctive way of organizing social relations, along with an underlying ethic, set of values, and cultural bias. Figures 6.1 and 6.2, respectively, capture the two social dimensions and the four elementary forms. Figure 6.3 explores the underlying values and behavioural dynamics embedded in each of the elementary forms. Figures 6.4 explores the types of organizational designs that may be found in an organization's environments, institutional practices, and cultures, reflecting particular elementary forms. These figures summarize the

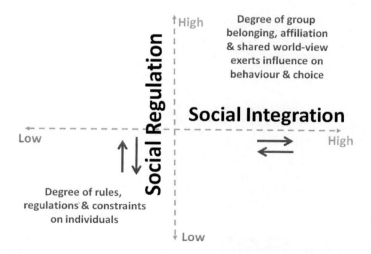

Figure 6.1. Durkheim's two dimensions of sociality or social organization (cross-tabulated by Douglas)

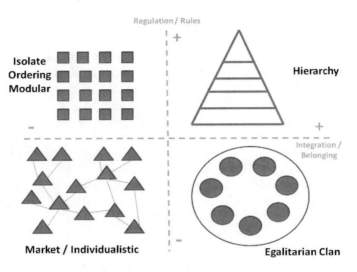

Figure 6.2. Douglas's four elementary forms of social organization. (Adapted from Mars, 2008)

Figure 6.3. Underlying values and behavioural dynamics of elementary forms

Isolate Ordering

Power is despotic or experienced as
controlling & arbitrary

Thought style: eclectic & fatalistic

Behaviour: coping, opportunistic,
shortage of trust & cooperation

Leadership: controlling or absent

Anomalies: tolerated as inevitable, survived

Ethic & Norms:

survival, looking out for oneself

Hierarchy

Power (& status) vary according to rank

Thought-style: order,
Authoritative, stability

Behaviour: rule-bound, duty, respect

Leadership: aligned, top-down
bureaucratic, authorised

Anomalies: adjustments made to accommodate

Ethic & Norms:

social order, duty & obligation

Markets / Individualism

Status varies with power =
control over resources

Thought-style: freedom, flexibility, innovation

Behaviour: strategic & self-interest

Leadership: behind-the-scenes,
adventurous, taking calculated risks

Anomalies: are opportunities to gain from

Ethic & Norms:

liberty, choice, initiative, flexibility

Egalitarian Clans

Power is collective but fragile

Thought-style: internal equality, fairness

Behaviour: camaraderie, collaborative

Leadership: charismatic, principled

Anomalies: are threats & rejected

Ethic & Norms:

equality & social justice

Figure 6.4. Organizing strengths, weakness. and tendencies to disorganization within the elementary forms

literature that describe the elementary forms and how they operate within institutions and social environments (see Douglas, 1982, 1986; 6, 2011; 6 & Mars, 2008; Thompson, 2008; Thompson, Ellis, & Wildavsky, 1990).

The cultural theory typology and the elementary forms as a social map for organizational diagnosis

The elementary forms are best approached as theoretical types (Coyle, 1994). They rarely if ever exist in their pure form but in some combination of weighted mix or hybrid (6, 2011) within institutions, groups, networks, organizations, and societies, or whatever configuration of groupings people are to be found in. Because of the overlap of people's memberships to such groupings, individuals can be exposed to a conflicting variety of influences and pressures depending on the groupings they belong to and the institutional practices they have developed preferences for, or subscribed to, or spent most of their time within. These influences ultimately reflect the nature of the elementary forms underpinning their immediate and wider contexts in which they circulate, and the external and internal pressures operating upon and within them.

In this way, there is rarely ever one culture in organizations of any size, but several, often competing for both adherents or offering their own best solutions to pressing problems. Because different cultures, in the same way that individuals prefer some more than others, reflect competing underlying values, beliefs, and assumptions,[6] this offers an alternative conceptualization of conflict and competition with social groupings based on competing socio-political values, assumptions, and preferences held by individuals or coalitions.[7] Like the people in them, these hybrids can remain relatively stable over time or, in response to changing circumstances, crises, or internal conflicts, quickly change their relative weighting. But this is never a simple or straightforward process. If a hybrid shifts or changes, so too will the pattern of social relations and the underlying values buttressing it. This leads to tension, conflict, and dislocation until some relative pattern is reached, settled upon, or emerges through default.

For example, change either the organizational pattern or design of a group's social relations and this will affect, undermine, or dislodge the existing values supporting it. This, in turn, through individuals' resistance or indignation, may assert a countervailing opposition. Likewise, fiddle with existing organizational values, as leaders are prone to do to achieve some end or means, and this will affect, undermine, or change the design or pattern of relations (see Thompson, 2008). The thrust for such change can come from either external sources that exert pressure upon systems, or internal influences such as brooding debates or conflicts, making the existing design or values of a social organization less viable. This reflects the theory's dynamism in accounting for both relative social stability and quick or slow change. It does this through casting light on two underlying social factors: the social-political values and the pattern of social relations that together buttress social systems and will initiate change if either is affected or manipulated.

Figure 6.5 represents the typology as a blank social map on to which various groups, organizational initiatives, and policies or individuals' social, political, or moral philosophical assumptions and social defences can be approximately plotted. I have used this in the research phase of a consultation to roughly map where the organization had been, where it currently was, and where its policies, politics, people, and social defences were likely to be taking it.

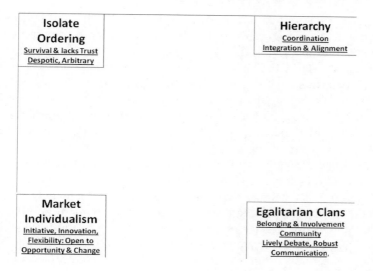

Isolate	**Hierarchy**
Ordering	Coordination
Survival & lacks Trust	Integration & Alignment
Despotic, Arbitrary	
Market	**Egalitarian Clans**
Individualism	Belonging & Involvement
Initiative, Innovation,	Community
Flexibility: Open to	Lively Debate, Robust
Opportunity & Change	Communication,

Figure 6.5. A cultural theory social map without the boxes and as theoretical extremes allowing for hybridity (6, 2011) and for incremental movement between the elementary forms. (Adapted from Coyle, 1994, and Boyle & Coughlin, 1994.)

The utility of cultural theory as a social map allows, first, for gauging the social nature of social defences, which are external to or independent of their individual contributors and are guided by an organizing logic and social values of an elementary form of social organization or hybrid. Second, it can gauge to what in the environment—such as policies, initiatives, external influences, each also containing their own internal organizing logic—the social defences were a reaction. From here, the third step is to identify and trace what in the social environment the social defences as consolidated social entities in their own right will, in turn, likely affect.

Thought-style as lynch-pin and causal engine generating the social consequences of social defences

One of the important ways in which social defences operate like informal institutions is in the thought-style they are likely to cultivate in people—how through common behavioural practices individuals come to think and act along similar lines. Douglas (1986) places the causal influence of behaviour within institutions on the thought-style they cultivate. In Menzies Lyth's terms, this is how "members become like the institution in significant ways . . . sharing [its] common attitudes" (1989, pp. 40–41). With Fenichel's ideas, she strives beyond her emphasis on "socio-therapy" and working through (1988, 1990) to a conceptualization of what organizational change involves when she states that "institutions, once established, may be extremely difficult to change . . . they modify the personality structure of their members, temporarily or permanently . . . [but] *to change the members one may first need to change the institution*" (Menzies Lyth, 1989, p. 26, emphasis added), but again she does not develop this idea.

Organizational change requires such a focus. In this way the causal influence attributed to thought-style on behaviour in institutions generated by underlying elementary forms of social organizations (Douglas, 1986; 6, 2011) helps to traverse the roles played between psychological and social factors in organizations and action research projects (Trist, 1950).

Thought-style also closely relates to what Menzies Lyth defines as "work culture". It is the analysis of culture, she suggests, following Alistair Bain's influence, that is one of the three kinds of analysis, along with role analysis and structural analysis, that organizational consultants must be concerned with. Work culture, which she suggests is the "most closely related to psychoanalysis", considers such things as "attitudes and beliefs, patterns of relationships, traditions, the psycho-social context in which is done and how people collaborate in doing it" (Menzies Lyth, 1990, pp. 466–467). For Douglas, it is the "thought-style" cultivated within institutions that "set[s] the preconditions of any cognition". "Its essential nature", she suggests, is "hidden from members of the thought-collective" (Douglas, 1986, p. 13). It "encodes information" and contributes to "making routine decisions, solving routine problems and doing a lot of regular thinking on behalf of individuals" (p. 47).

What may seem like the operation of unconscious psychological dynamics underlying collective anxiety and social defences, while not exactly the same as, may in fact be better approached as the thought-style collectively cultivated and generating its own separate or social influence on behaviour and the organization. In this way, we not only *theoretically better capture* the social operation of social defences as informal institutions, operating and generating feedback within larger institutional wholes, but can also, through cultural theory and the values and organizing logic encoded in its elementary forms of social organization, *better predict* in terms of the underlying elementary form embedded within social defences what they may be a reaction to in the organization and what possible social consequences they are likely to generate.

The concept of "thought-style" is here used as a lynch-pin to theoretically reach into the social and internal nature and contributions of individuals, as well as into the underlying psychological reactions and dynamics that have been activated. Socially it can capture the political and moral assumptions and values-orientation driving the institution and hence behaviour. Such sociological dimensions are mostly absent from psychology.

Menzies Lyth's case study through another lens

Through the lens of cultural theory, social defences as informal institutions can operate according to their own guiding social logic, which in turn gives shape to a distinctive thought-style that influences the ways people collectively think and act. This can capture the social nature and operation of social defences or to what in the wider environment they are a reaction.

If we look at Menzies Lyth's nursing study, the wider hospital environment was organized around a single and dominant organizational form: hierarchy. The excessive pressures of a dominant and domineering organizing hierarchy, especially between doctors and nurses, left nurses with little or no discretion to use their initiative, let alone their thought and insight, in caring for patients. This was despite their considerable medical knowledge, compared to that of junior doctors, in the treatment of patients and especially in care and rehabilitation. The dominance of the hierarchical form left little room for alternative ways of organizing to develop, or to be facilitated or championed. It exerted considerable pressure upon nurses to conform to its demands. As a result, the social defences that manifested in the nursing service took on the social character of a defensive adaption to hierarchy, or, in Bion's terms, basic assumption "dependency". Within a dominating hierarchical form, dependency is frequently the most viable and only defensive manoeuvre open to people. Those nurses who could tolerate the dependency were arguably more likely to stay, whereas those who resisted voted with their feet and left—what in Bion's terms is basic assumption "flight". In this case, the "flight" manifested through nurses leaving and junior nurses dropping out of their training, a major reason for the consultancy request in the first place. This "flight" did not manifest along with "fight" nor was it utilized to push forth an alternative way of organizing the nursing service and the hospital that could still achieve the hospital's primary task within its current budgetary limitations. The social defences that Menzies Lyth so adeptly described were symptoms of this organizational backdrop.

From a cultural theory perspective, the nurses' dependency can be seen as displaying an isolate form of organizing. In going along with their constraints, they behaved more as isolated individuals in ways that reinforced their marginalized and disenfranchized role within the organizational hierarchy. If, instead, their social defence system displayed elements of egalitarian or market organizing, we may have seen, respectively, more coordinated protest and supportive camaraderie or the initiative to find alternative ways of doing their work within the constraints placed on them. The dominating hierarchical form promoting "dependency" subverted competing organizational forms from being mobilized.

Compared to the dependency found in response to dominating hierarchy, in market or egalitarian organizing we could expect to see variations of basic assumption fight/flight as the most viable forms of defence, as well as both basic assumption "me" in market forms and "oneness" in egalitarian along with the logical consequences that these could generate. In hybrid forms, which are mostly found in empirical settings, different institutional practices, departments, organizational levels, and leader's initiatives may be organized under the sway of different and competing elementary forms. This better accounts for the psycho-social dynamics and political manoeuvring that is found in many organizations, which in turn exert competing pressures towards either stability, seeking to reinforce the dominant elementary form within the mix or hybrid, or change, represented by the challenge and alternative offered by one of the less dominant forms that may act as an attractor or rallying-point of resistance within organizations. In these situations, the social defences are likely to be organized according to a less dominant and competing elementary form to that of the dominant one.

In her study, Menzies Lyth's started by analysing many of the structural elements exerting an influence upon nurses' behaviour. This was through the various working practices and systems that were put in place guiding what nurses ought to do. Although she clearly saw how the wider structural elements operating within the hospital system and the hierarchy between doctors and nurses exerted pressure on the local design of the nursing service and the social defences that became built into the work practices, we can see from her later work that her preference (Menzies Lyth, 1990) was to focus on how the nature of work itself evoked primitive psychological reactions, anxiety, and defences within individuals and helped them deal with their emotional reactions (Pecotic, 2002). While this represents one important aspect of overall intervention, and perhaps the only avenue open to consultants working within the lower organizational layers of monolithic public-sector or human service organizations, this is not the same as organizational-level change. Menzies Lyth was mostly likely aware, if only implicitly, of such distinctions of the types or levels of change, but she was not working with the organization's leaders and was discouraged by the matron to go beyond her mission. Nevertheless, where she implicitly placed the causal emphasis on the nature of the work evoking the anxiety-defences, she side-stepped the larger challenge of seeing how the wider hospital structure was itself contributing to the design and organization of the nursing service and contributing to the high rate of nursing turnover and younger nurses dropping out of their training, and how the social defences were themselves a reaction to the wider pressures acting upon the nursing service.

Focusing on how the nature of the work was evoking the social defences made it more difficult to assess how the organizational forces and pressures were acting upon the service and, in turn, upon the nurses' work, or how subtle changes to these forces in turn affected the service. Instead, these contextual influences were treated as a given that could not be changed, despite the difficulties and countervailing pressures they posed. This was one of Emery's criticisms of how open systems theory was utilized within the paradigm, since it mistakenly held that once inputs and outputs were taken into account, the system under observation could still be treated as a closed system. This did not allow seeing how the external environment and internal organizational design were themselves exerting more of an influence on individuals' thought, behaviour, and endeavours, more so than their own intentions. This was limiting the options and agency open to individuals within these settings (see Emery, 1997). In such situations, if leaders could be shown how the consequences of organizational design or influences from the external environment were undermining primary task, and they were then facilitated to explore alternative designs or adaptations with the input of staff most affected, this could lead to organizational-level change within the boundaries of existing fiscal and technological constraints.

Conclusion

Cultural theory offers a separate lens through which to view the influence and role of the social context or environment on behaviour that is not reduced to but used alongside the more psychological accounts and contributions that within the socio-analytic paradigm are held as shaping the immediate environment or social field under study. Cultural theory can provide an alternative lens on how socio-political–cultural conflict, viability, and change can occur. This is done by inverting the causality of behaviour from psychological to social factors and seeing social defences in the first instance as symptoms that need explanation rather than as causes. As symptoms, social defences become the starting points to further organizational diagnosis and analysis. The underlying elementary form postulated as driving social defences systems can then be studied as a reaction—positive or negative—to the elementary forms operating within other institutions—formal or informal—and within the larger organizational whole or its external environment. Utilizing cultural theory also allows us to better infer the possible causes and social processes through which social defences operate and the likely consequences they may generate upon the organization or social context.

Notes

1. These ideas developed from retrospective research of a four-year coaching and consulting project within a medium-sized multinational manufacturing company. Social defences had only developed well after an external organizational crisis, but also well before real organizational problems. It was as if the social defences were forewarning of the impending crisis, but a traditional-style action-research intervention of presenting evidence, working hypotheses, and facilitating problem-solving discussion did not lead to change. This was in spite of the relative accuracy of the working hypotheses in pinpointing the likely causes of the social defence to the consequences of the actions taken by the senior team in response to the earlier crisis. Nevertheless, the true and diagnostic value of the appearance of social defence for the consulting was their forewarning. But focusing on the anxiety and defence dynamics, and inviting the senior team to explore their own dynamics, undermined the intervention, as did the lack of a causal explanation linking the senior team's actions first to the social defences and second to viable predictions of likely consequences if not attended to. The findings of this case will be set out in a later publication.

2. Three analytic models were useful in developing the social side: feedback loops; the counter-posing of agency and structure as two types of causality (Mouzelis, 2008); and adopting a broad institutional framework that differentiates between the formal and informal organization and captures the regulative, normative, and

cognitive (Scott, 2008) influences on behaviour. Social defences operate within the informal organization as task-enhancing or task-undermining informal institutions that generate their own feedback and consequences.

3. His belligerent statement that psychoanalysis is dysfunctional in organizations, and that "it is badly organised social systems that arouse psychotic anxieties" and not people "concocting" organizations for their psychological needs (Jaques, 1995, p. 343), detracts from his important insight and prods a defensive confrontation from psychoanalytically informed consultants (see Amado, 1995). His debates with Amado (Jaques, 1995) have polarized the two perspectives rather than brought them together, as argued here. I have argued elsewhere that Jaques would not have arrived at many of his latter insights without his earlier immersion in psychoanalysis. He erroneously did not differentiate psychoanalysis as a theory from psychoanalysis as method, as Amado suggested, but turned his psychoanalytic insights into the dependent variable or something that needs to be explained (Papadopoulos, 2010).

4. A true social perspective is one that is not built up from psychological insights but relies mainly on "social facts" or explanations to account for other social facts. This was Durkheim's innovation to the sociological method in the 1890s and is a distinguishing contribution of sociological analysis in social science (see Keat & Urry, 1975). With Menzies Lyth's innovation, social defences can be seen as "social facts" that could and should also be explained by other social facts.

5. For a broader discussion advocating the importance of finding a role for both people's or "actor" agency and social structure in explaining both stability and change in social theory and the social sciences more broadly, see Mouzelis (1995, 2008).

6. Be it about how the world works or different assumptions of human nature or the best solution to pressing problems, each underlying elementary form within various social contexts cultivates a distinctive "bounded rationality" or world-view.

7. Wood (1987) found that the basis for sub-grouping, splits, and coalitions found in small groups was better explained on the basis for preference for socio-political values and beliefs, such as political beliefs or affiliations, than on other factors such as race or gender and arguably psychological dynamics alone. Moreover, the underlying elementary forms evident within groups, more so through individuals' competing preferences and through their negotiations, arguments, and disagreements, contribute to the creation of group dynamics and to a more conflict-prone thought-style that is subsequently cultivated and in turn generates its own feedback influence back on members. Such thinking also provides an alternative view of the conflict and competition of group dynamics based on competing values and beliefs rather than on psychological group-as-a-whole dynamics alone.

PART II

Health and nursing

CHAPTER SEVEN

Reflections on Isabel Menzies Lyth in the light of developments in nursing care

Liz Tutton & Debbie Langstaff

Menzies Lyth's (1960) study of hospital life provided a clear and challenging view of the nature of nursing work, a view that is still of relevance today. It informed a stream of work that focused on developing therapeutic intent incorporating relational aspects of care, knowing the person, understanding their needs, and directing care in ways that benefit them. This work has developed alongside significant changes in the way nurses are educated and in healthcare demand and provision. In the last 50 years a lot has changed, and there have been many influences on healthcare. This chapter considers Menzies Lyth's work in light of the influence it had on developing nursing practice and ways of organizing care that facilitate patient-centred care. This is demonstrated through the evolution of Nursing Development Units, relationship-focused care, and the concept of emotional labour. The discussion here also considers current concerns regarding managerial pressures impacting on health environments. The conclusion suggests that Menzies Lyth's work still has relevance when reflecting on current healthcare and the provision of care within scarce resources.

Menzies Lyth's influence

Historically Menzies Lyth's work has been influential within a changing landscape of how nursing work has been defined and enacted
over time. Her work came at a time when most basic nursing work
was undertaken by student nurses, who were left to run the wards at
night and had very little teaching from ward sisters, mainly learning
from each other (Goddard Report, 1953). Prior to this the Wood Report
(1947) had noted the poor conditions of service, long working hours,
overly disciplined practices, and lack of care for nurses' health, leading to an inability to keep nurses in the service. They recommended a
form of training that separated nurses from the provision of service.
This concern continued into the 1960s when Menzies Lyth was asked to
undertake work to explore the low morale of nurses and high attrition
rates during training.

Menzies Lyth's (1960) study included 70 interviews (some individual and some as small groups) with nursing staff; senior medical
and lay staff were also included. The observation was undertaken in
a London teaching hospital that included "three small specialist hospitals and a convalescent home" (p. 95). This work became influential
as a critique of the way in which nursing practice was organized at
that time. Menzies Lyth was embedded in the work of the Tavistock
Institute, and the theoretical framework for her study drew on Freudian and Kleinian perspectives. From her findings she identified nursing
as dirty, intimate, and emotional work that generated a high degree of
anxiety, with nurses at constant risk of being overwhelmed by "intense
and unmanageable anxiety". She notes, "we found it hard to understand how nurses could tolerate so much anxiety and, indeed found
much evidence that they could not" (1960/1988, p. 97), with a third of
nurses not completing their training and with high levels of sickness. In
Menzies Lyth's view, by avoiding confrontation of anxiety and learning
to deal effectively with it, staff lived in a "constant state of impending
crisis", "fear of failure", and "no sense of satisfaction". To manage
their work and limit the impact of anxiety, Menzies Lyth argues that
nurses used socially constructed defence mechanisms such as splitting
up of the nurse–patient relationship through task allocation, depersonalization, detachment from feelings, ritualistic task performance,
reduced individual and lack of direct lines of responsibility, delegation
of responsibility up the hierarchy, underestimation of individuals'
responsibility, and avoidance of change.

Menzies Lyth's work was not qualitative research undertaken

within the current theoretical frameworks that guide good-quality research, and she did not place the work within the current socio-political and cultural norms of the time. However, the findings reso-nated with nurses; there was a feeling of familiarity with the findings that has endured over time, with many references to her work, such as Barnes (1963), Smith (1986), Mackintosh (2000), Titchen (2000), and Evans, Traynor, and Glass (2013). The theoretical underpinnings of her work in relation to the perspective from Freud and Klein are largely ignored in nursing literature. This is also the case within service provi-sion: "Those who are currently managing or designing organizations to carry out health and welfare work do not seem to take into account the impact of anxiety on staff functioning" (Lawlor, 2009, p. 527). Menzies Lyth suggests that the experience of caring for people who are suffering creates strong emotions that link back to childhood: "The work situa-tion arouses very strong and mixed feelings in the nurse: pity, compas-sion and love; guilt and anxiety; hatred and resentment of the patients who arouse these strong feelings; envy of the care given to the patient" (1960/1988, p. 98). As a result, "The nurse projects infantile phantasy situations into current work situations and experiences the objective situations as a mixture of objective reality and phantasy. She then re-experiences painfully and vividly, in relation to current objective reality, many of the feelings appropriate to the phantasies" (p. 99).

The strong feelings of anxiety created in the nurse presumably require processing through therapy, although Menzies Lyth does not indicate how this should be managed. Lawlor (2009) highlights the link between emotions and "containment" as "the ways in which emotion is experienced or avoided, managed or denied, kept in or passed on, so that its effects are either mitigated or amplified" (p. 525). This aspect of emotional support for nurses has been largely lost in discussions of nursing developments, although more recently clinical supervision and coaching or mentoring are trends that aim to help work stress to improve aspects of work. What was taken on board was the need to change and develop a stronger patient-focused relational dimension within nursing. This encompassed refocusing care on the patient and away from tasks and routines.

Nursing developments

From the 1960s onwards, there was a professionalizing move within nursing to develop the knowledge and skills base for practice in order to keep pace with an increasingly sophisticated and technological healthcare system. This occurred throughout education, research, and practice. Education evolved with the rationalization of Schools of Nursing and development of the curriculum, with a focus on patients as opposed to tasks (Briggs, 1972). This trend continued with an increasing number of degree courses run alongside traditional courses until the introduction of Project 2000 (UKCC, 1986), a diploma-level course, and subsequently a move to degree-level entry into nursing by 2013 (NHS Careers).[1] Alongside this was an increasing focus on generating knowledge through research and practice to develop further the evidence base for healthcare (Rycroft-Malone et al., 2004). Against this backdrop, developments in practice also moved forward.

Developments included moving away from traditional ways of organizing care towards new ways of working incorporating clear lines of decision-making and increased continuity of care, as advocated by Menzies Lyth (1960). Developments included structured decision-making for patients through the nursing process (goal-directed decision-making) (Kratz, 1979); individualized patient care (looking after and knowing a group of patients rather than the whole ward) (Redfern, 1996); progressively increasing the degree of continuity of patient contact through methods of organizing care such as patient allocation (looking after the same group of patients for a number of days), team nursing (a group of nurses looking after a group of patients), and primary nursing (one nurse looking after a group of patients for the duration of their stay) (Ersser & Tutton, 1991); and nursing models for practice to help nurses make sense of the different areas of knowledge used in practice (Pearson, Vaughan, & Fitzgerald, 1996). Underlying these developments were values and beliefs that moved away from task orientation, ritualistic care, depersonalization, and lack of responsibility identified by Menzies Lyth. The focus of care moved toward patient-centred care, continuity of care, and clear lines of accountability and responsibility for decision-making to one nurse or a team of nurses.

Understanding the process of changing practice to incorporate the values and beliefs, ways of working, knowledge, and skills required for modernizing nursing was crucial for achieving sustainable change. Research was focused on how to change practice, notably Alan Pearson's work at Burford Community Hospital (Pearson, 1985). This led to the birth of the Nursing Development Units as a way of diffusing change across the health service (Black, 1993; Pearson, 1988; Pearson, Punton, & Durant, 1992; Salvage & Wright, 1995). The thoughtful way in which care can be provided when based on patient-centred principles is outlined in Binnie and Titchen's (1999) action-research project, which documented the change from traditional-based care to patient-centred nursing through the organizational, cultural, leadership, and practice journeys. The complex and often subtle changes in practice from "doing for" to "being with", valuing apparently simple tasks like washing as part of understanding more about the person's progress to recovery, were often learnt through experiential learning and role modelling. A critical part of the process of change in this study was active facilitation. Titchen (2000) developed a model of "critical companionship" to guide the process of developing professional craft knowledge for patient-centred care through facilitation. The study highlights the importance of experiential learning; reflecting on the art of decision-making and the balance between intuition and rational thinking; and the use of storytelling and dialogue to enable patients to recover and staff to develop expertise.

A core feature of the new way of nursing was the "nurse–patient relationship" and the way a nurse could use herself as a therapeutic tool to enhance patient recovery. Ersser (1997) explored this using ethnography and identified the presentation of the nurse—her personality, manner, attitudes, and emotional state—as crucial, alongside her "presence"—the ability to develop a psychological and physical closeness, which was important for patient well-being. In addition, the nurse's ability to relate to patients conveyed the emotional quality of the interaction, and specific actions of the nurse were often ascribed therapeutic significance largely due to expressive actions. The ways in which nurses used presence and created different environments in order to enable patient-centred care is further explored in a study of nursing intimacy by Savage (1995). She identifies how posture, intent, and control of the environment aimed at patient benefit can create a relaxed home-like environment despite staff being busy. Focus on relational aspects of care continue to be highly valued and clearly evident in Dewar and Nolan's (2013) model of compassionate relationship-centred care. The core constructs are "appreciative caring conversations", "who people are and what matters to them", "how people feel about their experience", and participation through "work together to shape the way things are done" (p. 1247).

The research demonstrates how focusing on changing cultures (the way it is done around here), creating opportunities for nurses to develop their expertise or craft knowledge and focus on relational aspects, can change the environment of care away from the patterns of care identified by Menzies Lyth. This, alongside improved education and research knowledge, created rich opportunities for good practice.

Emotional labour

Menzies Lyth's focus on the nature of nursing work as intimate, physical, emotional work that engenders an emotional response in nurses continues to be valuable. A range of work has evolved to explore emotional labour, a term coined by Arlie Hochschild (1983) to identify the paid work employees do to "induce or suppress feeling in order to sustain the outward countenance that produces the proper state of mind in others—in this case, the sense of being cared for in a convivial and safe place" (p. 7). In a study of care in a hospice, James (1992) identified dilemmas between physical care and less well understood or supported emotional care. She noted the gendered, invisible nature of emotional labour, which was not regarded as real work (unlike physical work), and the difficulty of balancing patient needs for support within the broader needs of the patient group. Smith (1992, 2012) demonstrated how an explicit emotional management style of the ward sister/charge nurse was influential in creating an environment in which student nurses felt safe to emotionally care for patients. Alternatively, a hierarchical management style, where students felt anxious or worried, developed opportunities for stereotyping and labelling of patients. If students were exposed to this too often, it became their preferred style when qualified. It was noted that ward sisters with an explicit emotional style drew on the principles underlying the nursing process and primary nursing to direct their practice towards sensitive patient-centred care. A framework for emotional labour in nursing was identified by Theodosius (2008), with three domains of emotional labour: therapeutic (focused on the patient's recovery), instrumental (focused on facilitating a patient through an event), and collegial elements (focused on facilitating the team). Within these she suggests that nurses need to acknowledge and understand the impact of their own emotions in order to help others, and they should be developed and supported to enable them to become mature and reflective emotional workers.

Research in the area of trauma and stroke highlighted patients' suffering and the work staff do to process their emotions. Tutton et al. (2008) explored staff and patient experiences of traumatic injury and identified that "closeness" remains an important concept for patients and staff. Both groups felt close to injury, suffering, and death. Patients identified the near-death experiences when they told the story of the event that brought them into hospital, and they struggled to cope emotionally and physically with their changed bodies. Patients in a study of hope in stroke care (Tutton, Seers, Langstaff, & Westwood, 2011) watched helplessly as their feet flopped about totally out of their control; they worried that the next stroke would kill them, and they fought against the constant feelings of despair that threatened to overwhelm them. Suffering was in full view, and staff felt close to patients, emotionally and physically. When exploring closeness with staff in the trauma study, Tutton et al. (2008) found that the staff felt they had to "let go" of their emotions—if they held onto them they would just "go down". The staff identified times when they felt "detached", "emotionless", but often felt that this was when they had run out of energy and had become emotionally fatigued. In general, the supportive nature of the environment enabled staff to work closely with patients, although it was recognized that some staff were worn out and had to move on to other areas where interactions with patients were less intense. The method of organizing care—primary nursing—was evident in the findings that identified proactive care, continuity of care, and knowing the patient through providing direct care as positively beneficial for patients and staff.

> S6 . . . With the patients I look after here, not only do I wash them, wipe their bottom, check their pressure area, but I also go and deal with all the occupational therapists, the physios, you know, the dieticians, the consultants because I know that patient so well that they can ask me a question about them and I'll be able to tell them. [Tutton et al., 2008, p.150]

There was a real pride in knowing patients, and knowledge gained from continuous care of a patient made care easier for staff and patients.

In this study, staff actively took on board the emotional labour of the unit, enabling patients to move forward in their recovery. This was also identified in a further study (Tutton, Seers, & Langstaff, 2012) exploring the concept of hope in stroke care and traumatic injury, where staff identified the use of "realistic hopefulness" as a means of actively facilitating patients' physical and emotional recovery. Here the staff aimed to balance the ups and downs of emotional recovery by trying to "keep it real" to help patients cope with the present and facilitate patients' feelings regarding their hopes for the future.

Staff were actively engaged in managing patients' emotional and physical recovery, and there was an acceptance that the work was physically and emotionally exhausting, but they were enthused by the nature of the work and appeared to have well-developed informal systems of coping. The amount of work that was undertaken to actively manage the organization was alluded to in the category "making things work" (Tutton, Seers, & Langstaff, 2008). Research is required to explore how these environments are sustained over time and what supportive structures are required to keep staff functioning in this way. Changes in current healthcare processes suggest there are real challenges.

The current culture of healthcare

Since the time of Menzies Lyth's work we have a history of attending to developments in relational and patient-centred care, obtaining an increased understanding of the knowledge, skills, expertise required, and types of facilitation necessary to change and develop practice. However, current reports suggest that practice is not consistently good across the health service, with some examples of really poor, dangerous care (Francis, 2013). This suggests that despite the current knowledge base and historical development, the knowledge/practice divide remains an issue, with ideals that are difficult to attain consistently within the reality of daily clinical practice.

Savage (1995) warned us—now two decades ago—that within the current culture of the NHS with a focus on cost-effectiveness, giving fundamental care over to untrained personnel, and taking on medical tasks, a return to task allocation is likely and "close" nurse–patient relationships may not be possible.

> In the present political and economic climate, widespread adoption of the principles of the "new nursing" such as close nurse–patient relationships, may just not be viable, despite the rhetoric of policy initiatives. [p. 128]

Nursing roles have changed, with increasing documentation of patient safety issues, performance targets, and extended roles to cover reduced working hours for doctors; the European Working Time Directive for doctors in training (Pickersgill, 2001) reduced the number of working hours down to 58 hours in 2004 and 48 hours in 2009 (Health and Safety Executive).[2] Traynor, Stone, Cook, Gould, and Maben (2014) argue that "new public management" introduced in the 1990s has increased the degree of bureaucratization of professionals, reducing professional power and increasing managerial control over professional activities and the quality of their performance. This, combined with increasing focus on patient safety, standardization, and the introduction of performance ratings based on targets, has changed the context in which healthcare is provided. Maben, Latter, and Macleod Clark (2007) have shown that student nurses are unable to maintain their ideals and values once they are in the reality of NHS ward life unless they are in well-resourced areas. A longitudinal study of newly qualified nurses over a period of three years post-qualifying was undertaken. All nurses started out with strong ideals and values based on using evidence in practice, providing high-quality, holistic patient-centred care. However, they increasingly despaired because they were unable to maintain these ideals within the intense, routinized reality of daily practice. The nurses experienced four covert rules, most often identified in challenging environments: "hurried physical care prevails", "no shirking", "don't get involved with patients", "fit in and don't rock the boat" (p. 103). They felt they had little time to think, talk with patients, or physically care for them; their time was spent managing and coordinating and administering drugs. The study categorized the nurses into three groups: "sustained", "compromised", and "crushed" idealists. Sustained idealists found places within the system, such as intensive care areas, where there was a high level of support for development, good role models, and good staffing. Compromised idealists were frustrated by environments with poor staff, few role models, and lack of support; they tended to move jobs frequently but kept optimistic that they might be able to change things in the future. Crushed idealists felt they had been unrealistic and there was little hope of change and considered leaving the profession. The authors' view was that education is instilling ideals that are not realistic in practice, and a change of focus is required to ensure staff are equipped to manage and lead what is essentially an unqualified work force who provide the majority of direct hands-on care.

The suggestion that providing a good-enough service within scarce resources is all qualified nurses can hope for, regardless of their high ideals, is indicative of bigger challenges. In discussions with experienced nurses in a range of forums, they identified concerns based on (1) increasing surveillance alongside limited autonomy; (2) increasing complexity alongside lack of expertise; and (3) increasing emotional labour alongside a need to be increasingly resilient.

1. Increasing surveillance reflects an increasingly target-driven culture that requires continual auditing, action plans, and feedback

mechanisms. Gilbert (2005) suggests that this increased managerial control over professional activities, through targets and audits, is based on distrust, whereas previously trust had been based within social interactions. Staff experience this as overload, where they are constantly measuring activities in ways that they feel do not reflect the true nature of their work. In addition, staff constantly respond to top-down NHS initiatives such as the productive ward/improving efficiency; 15 steps/a quality initiative; safety thermometer/keeping a harm-free environment; think pink/infection prevention.[3] All of these require assessment and action plans, with new activities added on top of existing priorities.

2.   Patients admitted to hospitals are older, with increasingly complex co-morbidities (Darzi, 2008). These patients require skilled expert nurses, yet senior staff struggle to find the appropriate levels of expertise for their teams (RCN, 2014). Developing staff requires intense periods of time and effort that they feel is often not valued or supported by organizations. There is also a sense of a reduction in autonomy (freedom to act) with centralized top-down micro-management, where staff are directed how to manage care regardless of existing processes or standards. An example is intentional rounding (Hutchings, Ward, & Bloodworth, 2013) where staff visit patients every hour or two hours with a script directed at their comfort. This may be introduced as a tick-box process or alongside a set of beliefs and values that include leadership with a focus on supporting and developing staff and the provision of high-quality care. Rounding as an entity may be appropriate in areas where staffing levels or skill mix is low and patients have little direct contact with staff. However, routinization of care can lead to unthinking task allocation, as described by Menzies Lyth. It may therefore reduce the quality of care in environments where there are sophisticated forms of decision-making, strong leadership, and high levels of expertise.

3.   There is a sense that the demands placed on staff to manage a service within scarce resources, where they are unable to provide the standard of care they would like, creates stress (RCN, 2013) which requires an increasing degree of emotional labour. M. J. Rustin (2013) argues that the move towards market-driven, target-orientated healthcare leaves workers feeling that "the prin-

ciple value and meaning of what they do goes unrecognized, disparaged and even abused by policy-makers and the managements that are made to serve as their instruments" (pp. 26–27). Resilience or the ability to sustain emotional labour over time despite constant change becomes crucial. Staff felt they could only go on for so long and then everything becomes overwhelming. Drawing on Jackson, Firtko, and Edenborough's (2007) definition, resilience is "the ability of an individual to adjust to adversity, maintain equilibrium, retain some sense of control over their environment, and continue to move forward in a positive manner" (p. 3). There is a sense that conditions required to sustain the physical and emotional demands of the work are not sufficiently strong to allow equilibrium to be maintained. Sometimes compassion is "bled out of people", and often a fresh start in a new job is required, where people "turn back into the person they were before". It is suggested that being compassionate is required alongside a "hard core of steel" in order to survive in healthcare environments over a sustained period of time.

There is a sense now that management cultures contain elements of what Patterson, Nolan, Rick, Brown, and Adams (2011) identify as a "Perform or Perish" culture of change that leads to an impoverished environment where the focus is on a quick fix; short-term top-down change; punitive transactional leadership; and superficial metrics as indicators of success. They suggest that an enriched environment is more likely to be achieved through a "Relational and Responsive" cultural model of change where complexity is recognized; change is tailored to individual situations; there is transformational leadership; all stakeholders are included; and meaningful relationships and quality indicators are used as measurements of success. While these two models are presented as ideal types, they provide a framework for understanding the current "tick-box" culture that aims to act quickly and have a visible effect (red trays, green tape). Reflecting on Menzies Lyth, the perform-or-perish culture could be influenced by anxiety generated by increased surveillance of NHS services by patients, the government, and the media. The Francis Report (2013) may well be adding another level of top-down change as a response to poor standards of care at Stafford. Causal factors were identified as poor staffing levels, poor leadership, and a management culture of fear, secrecy, and bullying, yet a range of generic measures for nursing were suggested.

Nurse selection should include a test of compassion, a concept that is limited, under-researched, and implies that compassion is innate and cannot be learnt or moulded by education and practice. Experience of hands-on care (untrained) prior to nurse education is now considered essential, regardless of the quality of the experience or any evidence of its educational value. A focus on the role of the ward sister/charge nurse to reclaim the clinical aspect of this role would be a move in the right direction; however, recommendations that they should at all times know the care of all the patients on the ward and carry out all the ward rounds takes us back to the 1960s and 1970s and the inherent anxieties within this type of role identified by Menzies Lyth (1960). Underlying these recommendations are values that suggest things were better in the past, yet analysis of past methods of organization as presented in her paper would suggest otherwise.

To conclude, the work of Menzies Lyth provided supporting evidence for developments in nursing practice towards patient-centred care. Although our understanding of emotional labour in nursing has increased, the underpinning theoretical framework of anxiety has not been assumed into nursing developments. Nursing encompasses a high level of emotional work, and there are many stressors in caring for people who are experiencing traumatic injury or illness or are dying. While we know much about the process of supporting patients' physical and emotional recovery, staff seem to just get on with it and expect little formal access to support. Wallbank (2013) suggests that restorative strategies such as clinical supervision may help the processing of emotions, but, in general, support for managing anxiety as identified by Menzies Lyth (1960) remains absent. Anxiety itself was not a term readily used by staff or patients, which may reflect its common usage as a diagnostic term rather than an expression of current emotions. Current tensions expressed by senior staff identified a lack of professional autonomy in relation to choosing proven ways of providing patient-centred care. This, combined with the increasing pace of healthcare and priority on cost effectiveness that is creating increasing tensions within practice areas, feels very much like the anxiety identified by Menzies Lyth when she described nurses as being in a "constant state of impending crisis" and "risk of being overwhelmed". The question raised by Savage (1995) therefore needs to be revisited for our current time: Is nursing based on close nurse–patient relationships viable and, if it isn't, will nurses still want to nurse and will patients be happy with their healthcare experience?

Notes

1. www.nhscareers.nhs.uk/explore-by-career/nursing/nurses-to-have-degrees-from-2013
2. www.hse.gov.uk/contact/faqs/workingtimedirective.htm
3. NHS initiatives:

   www.institute.nhs.uk/quality_and_value/productivity_series/productive_ward.html

   www.institute.nhs.uk/productives/15stepschallenge/15stepschallenge.html

   www.safetythermometer.nhs.uk

   www.jpaget.nhs.uk/section.php?id=12169

CHAPTER EIGHT

"I'm beyond caring": a response to the Francis Report

Marcus Evans

T he Francis Report (2013) outlined the way a group of staff had systemically become detached, cruel, and disengaged from their responsibilities. The report highlighted the lack of compassion from nursing staff for their patients. Since then there has been a cacophony of cries for compassionate treatment, courses in compassion, and even compassion therapy. I find myself wondering what has gone so wrong that a high court judge has to write a report emphasizing the need for compassion in nursing when this should be taken as a given.

In my role as a clinician, teacher, manager, and supervisor of nurses and other clinical staff at the Tavistock and Portman National Health Service (NHS) Foundation Trust over the past twenty years, I have been able to observe the quality of clinical engagement demonstrated across a wide range of NHS settings. I believe this has also put me in a position to assess the relationship between standards of care, the quality of training, and staff morale, as well as the management and support of front-line clinical staff. In this chapter I describe a fragmented management system that fails to authorize and support clinical staff. The target culture and NHS Trusts' anxieties about survival have created a top-down management system that pushes anxieties about survival down the hierarchy into front-line clinical staff.

This persecutory environment can undermine the thoughtful relationship between management and clinical staff necessary for good clinical care to thrive.

These problems have been compounded by problems in the way nurses are selected and trained. The current training still emphasizes the importance of the nurse's theoretical knowledge at the expense of learning through experience. Although there have been many attempts to bridge the gap between theory and practice, many nurses continue to leave training with deficits in their practical knowledge or experience of what it is to be a nurse.

In his letter to the secretary of state, Lord Francis says;

> Building on the report of the first inquiry, the story it tells is first and foremost of appalling suffering of many patients. This was primarily caused by a serious failure on the part of a provider Trust Board. It did not listen sufficiently to its patients and staff or ensure the correction of deficiencies brought to the Trust's attention. [Francis, 2013, p. 3]

Proper healthcare has to go beyond the physical care of the patient. Crucially, it has to help the patients and their relatives manage the profound anxieties associated with illness, dependency, death, and psychological disturbance. In order to provide appropriate care for their patients, staff need to feel they are supported and valued by a management structure that understands the nature of their work. They also need clinical and managerial structures that help them contain the inevitable anxieties inherent in their work. Unfortunately in the current climate this is not the case in parts of the NHS, and as a consequence morale is low in many areas.

There will have been specific issues and conditions in Mid Staffordshire NHS Foundation Trust, which are important to understand. However, many of us in the nursing profession have been concerned about the direction of travel for some time. If Mid Staffs is treated as an isolated problem, requiring special explanation, rather than an episode that reveals a chronic systemic crisis in the nursing profession, then a vital opportunity for learning will be lost.[1]

In this chapter, I outline some theory that I have found useful when thinking about clinical care and clinical institutions, before going on to examine some of the features of the current system. I then focus on the fragmentation of the authority and support for staff in front-line clinical posts and problems in training that leave nurse without a sufficiently robust professional identity.

The therapeutic setting

Melanie Klein described the healthy infant's dependence upon the mother for sustenance care and love in order to support the development of a strong ego and sense of self. When the infant feels safe, he feels he is in the presence of a "good" loving mother and has loving feelings towards her. The "good" mother is internalized by the infant in a loving way and forms the basis of the infant's ego. However, when the infant feels anxious in pain or neglected, he feels he is in the presence of a "bad" threatening mother who fails to provide protection and care. Aggressive feelings towards this uncaring "bad" figure then further threaten the infant's ego and sense of security. In order to protect the ego and any residual good feeling, the infant projects these aggressive feelings towards the "bad" mother out into the external world. These aggressive feelings are then felt to reside outside the object in the external world and are always threatening to return. Klein described this as the paranoid-schizoid position, and its psychic defences are based on primitive mental mechanisms such as splitting, projection, denial, and idealization (Klein, 1935). Over time the infant begins to lessen the split between the "good" mother he loves and the "bad" mother he hates. Indeed, the infant starts to recognize that his aggressive and loving feelings are both directed towards the same mother. This causes feelings of depression and guilt as the infant is faced with the anxiety of realizing that he may have aggressive impulses towards the same mother he depends upon for sustenance and life. Good objects that have been attacked or damaged form part of the internal world. Klein called this state of mind the depressive position, and it may lead some people to pursue an adult career based on reparation, such as nursing or medicine. Klein (1940) also recognized that guilt and depression can lead to a regression into a manic state of mind in which the infant tries to deny his dependence upon the object by denigrating the object and employing mechanisms of triumph.

Bion (1962b) described the infant's dependence upon the mother for his emotional and psychological development as well as his physical development. He outlined the way the infant's ego is overwhelmed by raw psychic experiences that are unavailable for thought. Bion outlined the way the infant evacuates and communicates these raw experiences through noises, looks, and bodily movements. The mother takes in these raw experiences before using her capacity to empathize and think about the infant's state of mind. Bion described this as the mother's capacity for reverie. In order for this process to work, the mother needs to be able to be affected by the communication without being overwhelmed. Thus the mother's ability to "contain" the infant's raw emotions helps turn raw emotional experience into food for thought. In addition to taking in the communication, the infant takes in the feeling that he is being cared for by a figure that understands his feelings.

Implicit in the role of the nurse's relationship with the patient is the capacity to empathize and contain the patient's suffering. This involves a process of taking in the patient's states of mind and projections through observations and contact with the patient's emotional and physical state (Fabricius, 1991). Using his or her own internal experience of suffering and anxieties about illness and damage, the nurse forms an identification with the patient. The nurse conveys understanding of the patient's anxiety and pain through a compassionate and thoughtful attitude. This is conveyed by his or her manner and behaviour in carrying out these clinical tasks. Thus the nurse contains the patient's emotional states and in the same way as Bion described the mother does for her baby.

Segal (1957, 1991) also built on these ideas by describing the difference between a symbolic representation and a symbolic equation. In the case of a symbolic representation, there is an acknowledgment of the difference between the symbol and the object being symbolized. However, in the case of a symbolic equation there is no differentiation between the object and symbol. In a symbolic equation there is a complete identity between the object and the symbol. This gives rise to what we mean by concrete thinking—using words as if they were the thing itself. Thus in a symbolic equation the statement "give me a minute" is literally interpreted as 60 seconds rather than the meaning of the symbolic representation of the idea "give me some time". In order to maintain the difference between a symbolic equation and symbolic representation, the subject needs to be supported in establishing a psychic separation from the concrete object.

When things are going well, this identification with the patient is based on the patient being a symbolic representative of the nurse's own damaged objects but not wholly identified with them in a concrete way. A separation is maintained between the patient's state of mind and damaged figures from the nurse's internal world. The capacity to move between empathic identification for the patient's suffering and objective professionalism is an essential process in maintaining a mature and healthy clinical approach. However, this process requires the nurse to take in and "contain" the patient's pain, vulnerability, and anxiety without being overwhelmed, leading to the danger of an unbalanced symbolic equation in which the nurse can no longer distinguish her own internal damaged objects from the patient she is nursing. In order to develop and maintain a balanced approach, nursing staff need settings and structures that help them digest the anxieties and pain involved in their work. Support needs to be provided through clinical discussion, reflective practice, and good management. On the one hand, these opportunities can help the nurse separate from the effect of the patient and restore an objective clinical approach, while on the other, staff who have become hardened are helped to reflect more on the emotional impact of the clinical contact. These organizational reflective structures act like Bion's maternal reverie and support the nurse through a process of containment, followed by separation and thought. Thus, reflective practice helps the nurse maintain the difference between the patient as a symbolic representation of the nurse's own damaged figures and a concrete equation with them.

When the nurse loses the capacity to separate his or her personal anxieties, thus forming a symbolic equation in which the patient becomes concretely identified with his or her own damaged objects, confusion arises. This confusion of the internal world with the external world can either lead to manic and/or heroic attempts on behalf of the nurse to cure the patient or the nurse becomes defeated by the impossibility of their task. The nurse may develop a hard external skin that gives the impression of cruel indifference as a way of keeping the patient and his or her difficulties at a distance. Time and resources for reflection on the clinical work should not be seen as a luxury, but, rather, as an essential part of good clinical (and nursing) practice. Well-led and well-managed teams use these structures as opportunities to examine and think about their clinical practice.

Britton (1989) describes the importance of the oedipal situation in supporting thought and the development of symbolic thinking. He emphasized the importance of the third object (psychically the father) in supporting the mother–infant couple while also providing room for separation and thought. The triangular situation provides a structure for thinking and helps prevent the collapse into concrete thinking or enactments.

Teams that treat patients whose clinical condition is accompanied by disturbing psychological states of mind often need the help of an external supervisor. For example, patients in mental health settings with a diagnosis of borderline personality disorder often get under the skin of staff, while those with a diagnosis of anti-social personality disorder can induce sadistic responses from staff. These patient groups can have a profound impact upon staff, which can undermine the team's capacity to contain patients. Clinical supervision run by an external supervisor, who acts as a third object in the way described by Britton, can help to restore the container. By acting as the third point in the nurse–patient–supervisor triangle, the supervisor can provide an appropriate space for thinking about the psychological impact of the work and reduce the pull toward re-enactments (Evans, 2011).

Leadership and institutional support

The nurse–patient relationship takes place within a clinical team structure, which can help to contain the anxieties inherent in clinical work. The team contains individuals' work with patients by providing a clear structure that supports this task. Good leadership is an essential ingredient in any well-run team, as the leader is responsible for establishing an environment in which high-quality clinical care can take place. This leadership provides teams with clear lines of accountability, realistic goals, effective communication, high standards in relation to recruitment of staff, appropriate training, adequate staffing levels, and good relationships with ancillary support. The team's capacity to provide good care is also affected by many factors outside the ward or team, including the quality of managerial support and containment provided by senior clinical managers external to them. Teams need senior clinical managers who are engaged in helping them to resolve the conflicts and dilemmas involved in managing difficult clinical issues. Senior clinical managers also need to help clinical managers to review staff performance and issues concerning recruitment and development. Once again the senior clinical manager can act as a "third object" that helps the ward manager restore his/her capacity to contain the clinical area.

A study from history

Menzies Lyth was invited into King's College Hospital in order to examine a problem in relation to the allocation of trainees within the hospital. She looked upon the problem as a symptom of underlying difficulties within the institution, which she began to explore. At the time of the study (in 1959), the Matron was ultimately responsible for the running of the hospital as a clinical service, and she had extensive authority over all clinical matters, from standards of care to cleaning, catering, laundry supplies, etc. This kind of authority was also reflected throughout the hospital and so the Charge Nurse/Ward Sister (as they were called at that time) was responsible for all aspects of ward life, including who came into the ward and with what purpose. The Matron (and the Nursing Officers who supported her) would "walk the wards" on a daily basis. This maintained a personal and ongoing link between the wider hospital management system and each individual clinical area. Thus Ward Sisters/Charge Nurses were able to talk to senior nursing management and keep in touch with the clinical situation on the ward. The managerial relationship was designed to address ongoing problems as well as to help with handling immediate crises. The Matron of the hospital was also responsible for the school of nursing and so embodied the organic relationship between clinical practice and training.

Although this system had many positive attributes, there were also negative aspects, which undermined the benefits of this integrated system. In her 1960 paper Menzies Lyth outlined the way the system encouraged an over-reliance on nursing officers and matron to make decisions. She described an obsessional institutional defence, which involved pushing responsibility for decisions up the hierarchy in unnecessary and risk-averse ways, which undermined the decision-making capacity at ward level. Thus legitimate and necessary anxiety associated with the management of the clinical area and the standard of clinical care was projected away from the clinical setting, creating a passive–dependent relationship between the sister/charge nurse and nursing officers/matron. This system encouraged the projection of capacity and ability up the hierarchy into the matron, while incompetence and lack of trust were projected down the hierarchy and into sisters/charge nurses. This system undermined sisters/charge nurses' confidence in their ability to do their work and contain their clinical area. It was as if, rather than support the function of the ward sister/charge nurse, the matron "third object" was seen to undermine their confidence and the containing function of the ward.

The fragmentation of authority for clinical areas

The clear lines of accountability and integration that are necessary for good morale and good team functioning have been eroded away over time in the NHS. As a response to negative attributes of the system, the authority of the matron was removed in the late 1960s. In addition, the clinical managers' authority for many important areas of care such as cleaning, catering, and laundry have been outsourced in order to reduce costs. These changes have had their own negative consequences as they have weakened the clinical nurse managers' control over key areas of the setting. Also the responsibility for training has been removed from the clinical area and now resides with the universities. Clinical nurse managers (as they are now called) are left with the responsibility and anxieties about the quality of care available in the clinical setting, but without much of the authority they need in order to execute these responsibilities.

Consequently many nurses are reluctant to take positions of authority and prefer to stay on the nursing bank and/or work as an agency nurse. It is my experience that many nursing staff do not feel they have either the necessary authority or the required support from those in senior management roles.

"... Assumptions that monitoring, performance management or intervention was the responsibility of someone else."

Francis Report, 2013

Nurses feel that the containing structures are no longer there and the management is seen as distant and persecutory rather than supportive and helpful. The vacuum in clinical leadership was recognized in the early 1980s with the introduction of Nurse Development Units (NDUs) but these did not survive the managerial changes of the late 1980s. The new style Modern Matron in 2000 was tasked with arresting the falling standards of clinical care.

"... A failure to tackle challenges to the building-up of a positive culture, in nursing in particular but also within the medical profession."

Francis Report, 2013

However, the problems are systemic and so cannot be solved by the reintroduction of a post that bears the name but lacks the authority and wide-ranging responsibility that characterized the old-style Matron. It is like trying to re-invent the wheel but providing no road for it to run on, and serious concerns about standards of cleanliness and the quality of food provided in hospitals remain. Hence the lack of clear lines of accountability and authority present an ongoing problem.

The effect of survival anxiety on the healthcare system

". . . A culture focused on doing the system's business—not that of the patients."

Francis Report, 2013

The system that manages the NHS is driven by a belief that competition and targets drive up quality and provide the best guarantee of getting value for money for the taxpayer. It is widely known that only strong NHS Trusts will survive in this new market and that failing Trusts will be taken over. The three main sources of survival anxiety are the internal market, the effects of cuts, and the target culture.

The internal market

The internal market, introduced early in the 1990s, has created an increasingly fragmented healthcare system as different parts of the system are encouraged to compete for patient contracts, rather than work together in the interests of the patient. Competition can be seen as healthy and representing an important source of motivation for improvement and progress. However, unhealthy aspects of competition may also affect relationships between colleagues or services when destructive rivalry based on triumph and survival starts to infect thinking.

The market is always in danger of disintegrating into a fragmented world in which there is an attempt to deny the interdependence between individuals, disciplines, and clinical areas. Manic defences are employed in order to triumph over feelings of vulnerability, inadequacy, and failure. These states of mind are then projected around the social system. The world starts to be divided between survivors and casualties, winners and losers, in a paranoid-schizoid position. This superior and defensive state of mind undermines the attitude required for reverie and learning through experience. In a paper called "Primitive Mind of State", Bell (1996) outlined the way the "market" is seen to represent a system free of waste, efficient, and lean where only the fittest survive. In reality, market forces in healthcare systems often appeal to parts of the personality that wish to triumph over feelings of inadequacy, vulnerability, and/or dependency.

The introduction of PBR (Payment by Results) has seen the introduction of a tool for evaluating the level of the patient's difficulties and accompanying packages of care appropriate to the patient's needs. A price for the package of care is then identified, and commissioners pay for a certain number of packages. This system encourages the clinical services to think of the patient as suffering from a condition that will be dealt with by the appropriate package of care during an identifiable length of time. Patients with long-term, complex needs requiring inter-ventions from different parts of the health or social care system pose a particular problem for the "package of care" system. Long-term care is expensive; this group of patients has the additional burden of having to fight their way through layers of regulation and red tape in order to get the care they need. Services have lists of eligibility and exclusion crite-ria, designed to protect them from expensive or demanding cases with complex or long-term clinical conditions. This is pertinent in relation to mental healthcare, where many services view the patient as someone who suffers from a list of symptoms that need to be removed rather than as a person with a particular psychological structure and person-ality. Increasingly commonplace is the "provision" of short treatment programmes that may be temporarily helpful but bear no relationship to the long-term and complex nature of patients' clinical conditions. Consequently, patients are often passed from one service to another, as they search for a service that will look at the long-term nature of their difficulties.

The effects of cuts

". . . The report has identified numerous warning signs which cumula-tively, or in some cases singly, could and should have alerted the system to the problems developing at the Trust."

Francis Report, 2013

As financial constraints have increased, economic pressure has forced a downgrading of clinical staff and of the skill mix required by the team. Nurses frequently have to reapply for their jobs and accept lower sala-ries, and large numbers of experienced staff have taken either voluntary redundancy or retirement. These changes also mean that healthcare assistants are increasingly left on the front line of clinical care while qualified nurses become more and more responsible for management. Morale among nurses is at an all-time low in many areas, and experi-enced staff are retiring early. Forensic staff working in a high-secure setting recently informed me that they were only allowed one qualified member of staff for each ward at night. A change in shift patterns in many areas means that nurses are working 12-hour shifts, with very little handover time. The loss of this overlap time between shifts is a serious threat to the crucial teaching sessions: supervisions or reflective practice groups, which are an essential part of ongoing clinical practice and should not be perceived as a luxury (Evans, 2007).

These changes can make front-line staff feel as if they are on a tread-mill, with very little respite. They may develop an unexpressed resent-ment of both the organization and the patients they care for, as they are uncared for themselves. It should be no surprise, then, that "burn out" and clinical "mistakes" are on the increase. However, such failures are too often blamed on the individual, with nurses being referred for stress counselling, thereby diverting attention from the systemic causes. In this anxiety-fuelled environment, it is commonplace for clinical staff to develop defensive practices designed to avoid criticism rather than to care for or treat the patient. Staff are also frightened to speak out.

". . . An institutional culture which ascribed more weight to positive information about the service than to information capable of implying cause for concern."

Francis Report, 2013

Financial pressures and the demands of the target culture mean that senior managers are often unable to really listen to concerns about lack of resources for patient care. Clinical managers who are responsible for meeting their targets and staying within their budget may be tempted to stop cooperating with neighbouring services over resources as they become preoccupied with the financial health of their own area. Once again, this paranoid-schizoid state of mind undermines the need for services and staff in different areas to work together in the interest of their patients.

The target culture

". . . This failure was in part the consequence of allowing a focus on reaching national access targets, achieving financial balance and seeking foundation trust status to be at the cost of delivering acceptable standards of care"

Francis Report, 2013

Over the past twenty years, there has been a substantial shift in the clinician–patient relationship, and the authority of the clinician is no longer accepted as a guarantee of good-quality care. Instead, NHS regulatory authorities, commissioners, and patients look for "objective measurable outcomes" to provide an assurance of quality and good care (DoH, 1999). The information gathered can be helpful as it may provide objective information about one aspect of the system's functioning. The information provided needs to be fed into the managerial system in a way that adds to the overall picture. Then the senior clinical manager in conjunction with the clinical nurse manager can think about the meaning of the information and decide on appropriate action.

However, information often comes back at the clinical area in the form of an anxious directive—"your service is failing to hit this target and you need to improve this area of performance". This sort of directive has the impact of an instruction from an authority external to the ward that overrides any local authority or requirement to think about either the meaning of the figures or the priorities of the local situation. I have also noticed that the communication sometimes contains a moralistic tone: "aren't you interested in improving the service to your patients?" or "don't you care about the trust's Monitor rating?" In these communications, which are designed to induce guilt, there is no recognition of inadequate staffing levels or front-line clinical realities. This form of communicating can increase the clinical nurse managers' feeling that people outside the immediate clinical area erode his or her sense of authority and control. It is also in danger of causing a paranoid-schizoid split between front-line clinical staff and managers external to the clinical area.

> ". . . In introducing the first report, I said that it should be patients—not numbers—which counted. That remains my view."
>
> Francis Report, 2013

Although objective measures can be helpful, they provide no more guarantee of good treatment than the clinician's opinion. Our preoccupation with measuring everything can become a defensive distraction from the task of caring for the patient (Procter, Wallbank, & Dhaliwall, 2013).

The fear of failing to hit the various targets set by the Care Quality Commission, Monitor, NHS Litigation Authority, and Care Commissioning Groups, and failing to maintain a balanced budget, persecute Trusts. Responsibility for targets is located with the senior managers running central services such as Human Resources, Clinical Governance, Risk Management, Contracts, and Information Governance. The senior managers running these departments are accountable for overseeing the Trust's performance against targets, and there are real financial penalties that may threaten a Trust's future if the required standards are not met. Performance is measured against a series of targets monitoring different aspects of the Trust's work. Thus the clinical area is required to provide figures and information that contribute towards reports on patient turnover, length of stay, the number of patient complaints, performance against clinical contracts, patient satisfaction, ward cleanliness, standards of information governance, staff sickness, outcome monitoring data, disability data, ethnicity data, case note standards, payment by results figures, outcome measures, mandatory staff training, and many others. The risk of failing to reach a target provokes a directive (often by email) demanding an increased effort in the area concerned. Senior managers emphasize the importance of their own targets, and anxiety is often conveyed through the tone of the communication, which takes no account of the clinical team's capacity. Pressure builds as the demand for immediate action and resolution of a specific problem often ignores the fact that the clinical nurse manager and his or her staff have to continue running the entire service effectively so that patients receive the attention they require. The clinical team's resources are pulled in different directions as the clinical nurse manager tries to meet the demand to hit targets from different parts of the managerial system. Thus staff teams are exposed to unrealistic expectations, which have a damaging effect on morale.

This sort of environment also increases the likelihood of clinical priorities becoming secondary to the needs of the institution to achieve targets in an attempt to deal with its survival anxieties. Perverse outcomes often arise when this happens, and it is a case of the tail wagging the dog. For example, accident and emergency (A&E) departments are under immense pressure to see patients within certain time-constraints, and there are financial penalties for their Trust if they fail to meet these targets. This pressure can result in patients either being admitted to inappropriate wards or even being sent home when in reality they need admitting. The danger is that the target culture encourages a "blame game" where no one wants to be left holding responsibility for the failure to hit the target. You can sometimes see in the email trail (in which seeming half the Trust is copied) how individuals deny responsibility and push the blame elsewhere. Thus targets have undermined clinical judgment.

In his chapter in this volume, William Halton notes the presence in the defensive structure outlined by Menzies Lyth of obsessional defences designed to keep the patient and his or her anxiety at a distance. At the time she wrote, the primary concern was for patient care. By contrast, the current system is confronted by two anxieties coming from different directions. Up from the clinical work come the anxieties related to fears of managing illness, psychological disturbance, and dying, while down from the management come institutional anxieties about survival. There is a danger that this system creates a split between management and front-line clinical staff. Far from the system containing front-line staff, there is a tendency for management to push their anxieties into them via shards of survival anxiety. The danger is that this leaves clinical staff feeling blamed, overwhelmed, and unsupported. This in turn can lead to loss of morale and poor patient care as clinical staff feel that they are constantly failing on all fronts. Revans (1959) showed that there was a direct link between the morale of nursing teams and patient recovery. The split can also mean that misunderstanding abounds as management filled with their own anxieties about survival turn a deaf ear to the clinical staff's concerns. The primary purpose of targets has been subverted from the improvement of patient care to the survival of the hospital or clinical unit.

The effect of the survival anxiety on the healthcare system resulting from the internal market, financial cuts, and targets is that senior management are so anxious and insecure that they are not able to provide the containment and "reverie" that clinical managers need. The resulting lack of empathy from senior managers for clinical staff is one of the factors that leads to the nurses' lack of empathy for patients.

The training of nurses

". . . The complaints heard at both the first inquiry and this one testified not only to inadequate staffing levels, but poor leadership, recruitment and training."

Francis Report, 2013

Nurse training institutions have the task of helping their trainees develop their professional identity in addition to their students' academic knowledge and technical ability. This identity is developed through contact with good role models on clinical placements. Over time, students can internalize the qualities of good role models while on placement as they work alongside senior clinical colleagues on clinical placements. As mentioned in the opening paragraphs of this chapter, trainees must be receptive to their patient's psychological state, while also being able to separate themselves from their patients and maintain professional objectivity. Menzies Lyth outlined the way the patients and relatives transmit their anxieties about illness—and, furthermore, mortality—to the nursing staff. The staff in turn have to manage their own fears around this, as well as any feelings of disgust and vulnerability related to their patients' physical and psychological condition. The social system surrounding the nurses needs to support both the individuals and the clinical area as a whole in managing this process.

As previously discussed, in her 1960 paper Menzies Lyth described the way the social system within a training hospital created a defensive social system that fragmented the nurse–patient relationship and turned the patient into a diagnosis rather than a fellow human. This was done through a process of fragmenting the nurse–patient contact into task-orientated nursing—for example, Nurse A takes the patient's temperature; Nurse B makes the bed. Nurses would also refer to patients using diagnostic terms—"the liver in bed number 25"—in an attempt to distance themselves from the patient as a person. This fragmentation meant that patients were deprived of a nurse to relate to as a human being with feelings and a capacity for empathy. There was no practice of individual supervision for nurses, and they were not helped to deal with the emotional impact of the work. Nurses were also treated like objects with no individual characteristics or feelings of their own. as Nurse A was sent to surgical and Nurse B to medical with no thought about their individual skills, knowledge, or ability to complete the task. This undermined the crucial element of identifying and acknowledging individual interests and abilities.

By the 1990s, Project 2000 moved responsibility for nurse training from the schools of nursing, which were attached to the hospital, to the universities. Accompanying this physical move was a shift in the centre of gravity from the "hands-on" learning of the apprenticeship model to academic learning in the classroom. There was also a shift in emphasis in student nurse selection, from an aptitude for the vocation of nursing to a preoccupation with academic ability.

In the current model, trainees are often supernumerary and spend time observing clinical practice or attending clinical placements for short periods of time. Hard-pressed staff are sometimes reluctant to invest time in transient students, who are not part of the clinical numbers. Crucially, it is the quality of engagement between the student nurse and the clinical team that supports the student nurse's identification with clinical colleagues. If the student is committed to the clinical team, she or he will receive commitment in return. If the involvement with the team is half-hearted or fragmented, the student will not get the support or engagement from the clinical team she or he need in order to learn (Evans, 2009). Nurse tutors used to support placements by visiting the clinical placement regularly and by holding teaching sessions on the ward, observing and assessing clinical practice. The link tutor was also crucial in supporting the student nurse's ability to manage the emotional demands of direct patient contact. In another paper, "Psychoanalytic Understanding and Nursing a Supervisory Workshop with Nurse Tutors", Fabricius (1995) described her experience of running supervisory groups for student nurses, which aimed to help them digest and then learn from their experiences in clinical placements. This approach helps the student face painful aspects of the work as well as develop the self-critical objectivity necessary for high-quality clinical practice.

The "evidence base" and theory behind medicine and nursing provide a vital pillar of clinical training. However, I believe we threw the "baby out with the bathwater" when Project 2000 was introduced, widening the gap that exists between theory and practice, and, despite numerous attempts, this gap has yet to be bridged (Hewison & Wildman 1996). In her paper "Running on the Spot, or Can Nursing Really Change?" Fabricius (1991) outlined her belief that the movement from the emotionally charged experience of "hands-on" nursing, which involved being with the patient, to the academic and abstract environment of the classroom represented a wish to retreat from the disturbing aspects of physical and emotional contact with the patient who is ill or dying. Fabricius argued that this represented an attack on the nurse's maternal function and would ultimately undermine the nurse's identity as a caring figure from which he or she derives so much professional authority.

Financial pressure on universities has meant that many university link tutors are trying to oversee too many students and can neither give the necessary tutorial time nor make the regular hospital visits to support students or their clinical placements in a meaningful way (DoH, 2006). A weak or distant relationship between the tutor and the student can mean that the student drifts or fails to make proper use of the experience gained during training. Lack of time to visit the clinical placements means that qualified staff managing these placements do not get to discuss the student with the tutor. Thus clinical staff, tutors, and students struggle to find the time necessary to triangulate their picture of the individual's development. A recent report suggested that there was an ambiguity in the current system regarding who is responsible for failing student nurses who persistently fall short of acceptable standards. This means that some students who have been identified as having persistent problems in attitude and/or ability often continue on into their third year and beyond, despite the fact that there are ongoing questions about their level of functioning. Once again, the defensive nature of the system creates a fragmented social structure that breaks up the relationships necessary to support development.

> ". . . Too great a degree of tolerance of poor standards and of risk to patients."
>
> Francis Report, 2013

As a consequence of the failings in this system, many nurse directors and managers have recognized that recently qualified staff are often unable to complete basic nursing procedures (DoH, 2006). An additional problem is that many universities have had contracts (with financial targets attached) to fill a certain number of student nurse places, and thus the quality and aptitude of students recruited may have been less of a priority than the contractual need to fill training places.

We need to ensure that student nurses are interested in caring for people and shift the centre of gravity for training back to the clinical settings. Nursing students need to learn best practice from working alongside qualified nurses in live clinical situations. All clinical areas are potentially learning environments, and the teaching function of clinical areas needs to be supported. This system in turn needs to be supported by nurse tutors who have the time to genuinely support the student in learning through their experience. In this way, the trainee nurse's capacity for empathy can be supported, monitored, and developed *in situ*.

Conclusion

Things have never been perfect in the healthcare system, and ideas of a "golden age" are in themselves defensive and represent a denial of reality. Defences against psychic pain and anxiety are ubiquitous, universal, and necessary. However, there are significant differences between primitive defences designed to avoid reality and more mature psychological defences. In the current structure, we have supplanted the rather obsessive institutional defence of the 1950s and 1960s with an even more primitive defensive structure. This defensive structure has to deal with the patient's anxieties about illness, death, and fragmentation on the one hand and the Trust's or clinical service's concerns about survival on the other. Anxiety and blame are pushed around the system like a pinball bouncing back and forth between the different areas of responsibility. This is reminiscent of defences that emanate from the paranoid-schizoid position, as the institution employs defences based on splitting, projection, denial, idealization, denigration, and manic triumph. At the same time, there has been an erosion of the sorts of structures and relationships that help contain anxiety.

The squeeze on the time available for teaching supervision and/or case discussion undermines the time and structures necessary to support the reflective capacity of individuals and teams. Hence the structures that support the clinician's capacity to digest experience have been removed in an attempt to reduce costs. Instead, we are creating a system that increasingly distances the patient, and his or her suffering, from the nurse. There is also a danger that this system undermines the authority of the clinical nurse manager for the clinical setting, as the survival anxiety can create a split between front-line clinical managers who have the responsibility of managing resources in their clinical area and the managers of the central services who carry responsibility for targets. The target and regulatory system also dictates that much authority is located external to the clinical area. Clinical leadership roles are vital containers of anxiety within the healthcare system. However, anxieties about survival and fear of persecution can erode the confidence and authority of the clinical nurse manager. Clinical nurse managers are also often left with their anxieties about how they are going to manage the gap between senior managerial expectations and the capacity of their unit to deliver the clinical standards necessary. The persecutory environment increases the sense of the clinical area being policed by a raft of senior managers rather than supported by senior management colleagues who understand what it takes to manage a clinical area. When this happens, it undermines the important function that senior managers can have in acting as the third object that helps clinical nurse managers think through the conflicts, difficulties, and anxieties that need to be managed in their clinical area.

Over fifty years ago, Menzies Lyth was invited in to consult on a failing hospital system. However, we still have not learnt the lessons she outlined in her paper. Clinical nursing staff need to be supported by an authoritative managerial and clinical structure, which helps the nurse bear the anxieties inherent in the work. In order to achieve this, it is essential that clinical nursing and medical authority is at the heart of the managerial system. Menzies Lyth emphasized her belief that the most effective form of staff support was provided by good clinical managers. She also outlined the need for clinical areas to be managed by authoritative figures who would take full responsibility for the quality of clinical care provided to their patients (Menzies Lyth, 1999). While financial constraints represent important realities about the limit of resources, their influence has to be balanced against authority derived from clinical realities about care and treatment. Clinical services need experienced staff who are familiar with the realities of clinical practice and have the necessary authority and experience to know when corners are being cut, standards are being compromised, and/or risks are being taken in a damaging way.

Teams also need senior clinical managers who assist them in their difficult job via regular and supportive contact, rather than directives and surveillance. Senior managers also need to have the authority and confidence to communicate difficulties back up the hierarchy as well as communicate important issues down the hierarchy, and they must be prepared to stand up to senior colleagues in order to protect standards of care in front-line services.

Central to the Francis Report is the conclusion that the patient and clinical voice is not being heard. The current top-down management system driven by a target-based and finance-orientated culture has a tendency to push clinical staff's concerns down the hierarchy and away from the upper tiers of management (Cunnane & Warwick, 2013). The voice that carries knowledge about the effect of cuts and lack of resources, and which expresses anxiety about patient care, is often treated as if it is the carrier of a disease and needs to be barrier-nursed. In reality, it is often the voice of experience and needs to be listened to.

All healthcare systems have problems, and these are, by their nature, multifaceted. However, when the problems outlined here are combined with the current austerity measures, the scene is set for the eruption of more toxic situations like that exposed at Mid Staffs. It is surprising that similar events are not reported more often. However listening to nurses present their clinical work has convinced me that, despite the system's tendency towards fragmentation and the lack of support for front-line clinical staff, there are still large numbers of nurses who remain extremely committed to their patients and endeavour to do the best they can within the existing healthcare system (Evans, 2008). My worry is that we have reached a tipping point in this system and can no longer rely on individuals' valency towards care and responsibility. The persecution inherent in the system is creating an environment that is antithetical to thoughtful care. The consequence is that only exceptional clinical managers can juggle the demands between the persecution of the "target culture" while keeping the care of the patients at the heart of their thinking. This is not a sustainable position. In theatres that deal with matters of "life and death", you need leaders with experience who can manage the anxieties in the work and can support their front-line staff. These clinical leaders, in turn, need support from senior managers who can help front-line clinical managers contain anxiety and reduce the temptation towards blame, fragmentation, and splitting. As Lord Francis said in his report, we need to put the clinical care and nurturing of our patients back at the heart of the NHS. In order to do so, we need to start addressing the current moralistic and persecutory culture of the NHS. Exhorting nursing staff to work harder, be more empathic, and feel guilty for shortcomings in clinical services while depriving them of adequate training, managerial support, time, or status within the system is a recipe for disaster. The NHS needs to establish a clinical training system that supports trainees through an apprenticeship training, repair damage done to the authority of nurses and nursing in the system, and develop structures that really support and listen to staff.

Notes

This chapter is adapted from "I'm Beyond Caring": A Response to the Francis Report: The Failure of Social Systems in Health Care to Adequately Support Nurses and Nursing in the Clinical Care of Their Patients", by Marcus Evans, published in *Psychoanalytic Psychotherapy*, 2014, Vol. 28, No. 2, pp. 45–61. Taylor & Francis Ltd, www.tandfonline.com reprinted by permission of the publisher.

1. In 1999, the Tavistock and Portman ran a conference called "Facing the Crisis in Nursing". Three of the main papers presented (Evans, 2009; Fabricius, 1999; Menzies Lyth, 1999) outlined problems in the training of nurses and the fragmentation of authority in clinical areas.

CHAPTER NINE

Anxiety at the front line

Sebastian Kraemer

"If you don't talk about it, you don't know it's bad."

Intensive care nurse

It is an axiom of attachment theory that you give what you have received. To be attentive one has to be attended to. In any kind of danger, support close by is needed. Being resilient in one's work—as opposed to compulsively self-reliant[1]—depends on a lively sense that help is at hand, perhaps at the end of a telephone or at the end of the shift, but there nonetheless.

This is not well understood in public services. The nurse cited above conveys the dilemma precisely. It may be better not to know, and just keep working. The prevailing culture of front-line services—education, health, social, and emergency—is based implicitly on a military notion that once trained, you can do the job, if necessary by following instructions from a protocol. The latter are orders that are given in the absence of one who has authority. When there are new skills to learn, new instructions can be issued. Authority then exists only in the management, not in the worker.

The nature of urgent work is that it is exciting, which is not to say entertaining. Adrenaline suppresses tiredness, pain, fear, even thought. Slowing down enough to reflect on what has happened may be quite disturbing. Attempts to get junior doctors, social workers, teachers, family centre workers, and others to stop what they are doing and attend a work discussion group are routinely resisted. Once encouraged to do so, neonatal nurses noted how being on duty suppressed their bodily needs, even to the extent of not needing to pee. The addictive quality of work, together with the satisfaction of keeping a still-great enterprise such as the NHS going, is a powerful drug.

Staff group support is a "soft" process. There is no official advice on how to do it, and no suggestion that a resource that may seem self-evidently a good thing may, once set up, be undermined. Together with a colleague, I convened a group of clinical professionals who had asked for a meeting. This was well attended and produced floods of eloquent and moving narrative about the stresses—and physical dangers—of the work and the lack of support from management, even though one of the managers attended and spoke up bravely. The meeting was timed to coincide with an hour-long handover between shifts. Within a few weeks, the handover period had been reduced to fifteen minutes. The group could no longer take place. Was this deliberate sabotage? Our impression was that it was not, but that we had experienced a brutal unconscious attack on reflective practice, as if management had sensed the dangers of free speech. And who knows, if the meetings had been permitted to continue, might members themselves have found their own ways to stifle thoughtfulness?

The role of managers in staff groups is crucial. Citing examples from their work, Bolton and Roberts (1994) caution against meetings set up for the wrong reasons: "Support groups are unlikely to be appropriate for dealing with crises, or with the consequences of absent or inadequate management" (p. 164). A recent text on the politics of care says that "the NHS gives little thought to group dynamics and how to get the best out of teams. Too often, structure and culture impede rather than enable good team working. Rare tokenistic gestures such as training events and team 'away days' are not usually followed through and are often undermined by management initiatives that have not considered the effects on the team dynamic" (Ballatt & Campling, 2011, pp. 81–82). Milton and Davison's (1997) observational study of staff support groups in psychiatric services notes an irony in their use: "Action often occurred in place of thinking. In fact it seems that rather than being a space for thinking, the group was used as a repository for unbearable states of mind. Perhaps the very existence of the staff group represented an institutional defence in Menzies Lyth's terms" (p. 143).

The legacy of Isabel Menzies Lyth's 1960 study of hospital nurses is a principal stimulus for this book. Summarizing her view, she later wrote that social defences against anxiety "include the denial of feelings, evasion of significant issues . . . concentration on service and neglect of attachment functions [and] inappropriate delegation of authority" (Menzies Lyth, 1988, p. 188). In the 65 years since then much has changed, yet not nearly as much as our newer knowledge of attachment and of organizations would suggest. There seems to be an inherent fragility about meetings whose purpose is to reflect rather than to produce.

Even when groups are established with some care, an obstacle to reflection comes from the staff themselves. After a few sessions they begin to discover their own lack of authority. They come face to face with differences among themselves. A readily available defence against this discomfort is to unite in self-righteous grievance against managers who "never understand what we have to go through". This bolsters their self-esteem, but not their capacity for reflection. Identification with such an attitude has almost universal appeal, as in thrillers where the hero is a police officer who is undermined and even humiliated by his or her risk-averse seniors. This defiant adolescent theme is exploited both in Hollywood blockbusters such as *Die Hard* and *Dirty Harry*, but also in more sophisticated European TV dramas such as *The Killing* [*Forbrydelsen*], *Spiral* [*Engrenage*], and *Salamander*. The rogue officer is the hero, while the deskbound senior is a fool.

In this mood a staff group can avoid conflict but at the cost of their own sense of agency, achieving, as Wilfred Bion put it in 1948, "an equilibrium of insincerity" (p. 81).[2] Stuckness in human groups is familiar to anyone, such as readers of this book, who has studied them from inside and out. At the front line there is an even greater incentive not to take emotional risks. It is not obviously helpful to discover how badly one's physical and mental health is affected by the job or that there are fundamental flaws in the wider organization that one can do nothing about. Bion's basic assumptions (1961) are often recruited to explain this restraint—that group members are either waiting for one of their number to take the lead (which may well happen) or have simply lost track of why they were there in the first place. Yet this does not seem quite sufficient. I wonder if there is an even more fundamental human quality that can keep a group in cautious suspense, not thinking but waiting; not exploring differences, but suppressing them. When deprived of their day-to-day business, what is it that makes a group of people left to their own devices so oppressive? I will return to this question after a detour into mid-twentieth-century history.

The discovery of authority

As a young woman, Isabel Menzies Lyth had studied economics and experimental psychology at St Andrew's University, becoming a lecturer there in 1939. During her vacations the acting head of department, the brilliant social psychologist Eric Trist, invited her to join him in a new project to identify potential army officers, the War Office Selection Board (WOSB). Its procedure was based on the leaderless group method: "a learning community, which improved collective capacity through the sharing of common here-and-now experiences of the candidates" (Trist, 1985, p. 7). Men had to work and live together for three days and were given military problems to discuss and a practical group task to perform, such as building a temporary bridge together. The psychiatrists, psychologists, and military testing officers, among them Isabel Menzies Lyth, did not intervene but observed and took notes. What emerged from this remarkable exercise was the realization that social class, education, and athletic ability were less important for leadership than the capacity of the individual to attend to others in the group. Instead of a traditional authoritarian with an impressive voice and moustache, the better officers were sensitive to social process: "the conflict for each individual candidate was that he could demonstrate his abilities only through the medium of others" (Murray, 1990, p. 55). Up to that time the concept of authority had been implicitly associated with patriarchal notions of hierarchy and class. These pioneering social scientists had discovered that an exploration of differences within a peer group can lead to emotional learning about one's own part in it. This has to include a sense of attentive concern—a maternal function, perhaps. Authority then becomes a power within oneself to relate to others, rather than to control them. Individuals who had to direct fighting men at the front line were selected on the basis of their capacity to manage *themselves* in this role.

Along with Eric Trist and Jock Sutherland, Wilfred Bion (later Menzies Lyth's analyst) is regarded as the principal innovator of WOSB, but there were many others actively involved, including Ronald Hargreaves, A. T. M. "Tommy" Wilson, John Rickman, and Pierre Turquet. Next to Isabel Menzies Lyth in the photograph of the board (Figure 9.1) is John Bowlby, better known for his much later work on attachment theory, but who at the time did a follow-up evaluation of No. 2 WOSB. This showed greatly improved retention of officers, reducing the failure rate from 45% to 15% (Dicks, 1970, p. 107). In the front row of the group is Menzies Lyth's mentor Eric Trist[3] and behind her the Canadian

Figure 9.1. (*Front left*) Eric Trist, Raitt Kerr, Unknown, Unknown, Unknown, Fergusson Rodger. (*Back left*) Unknown, Unknown, Ben Morris, Elliott Jaques. (*Behind*) Isabel Menzies, John Bowlby, Jock Sutherland.

Summer 1943, 25th War Officer Selection Board, Headquarters, Hampstead, London. Courtesy Mrs Beulah Trist.

social scientist Elliott Jaques, the first to use the phrase "social defences against anxiety" in a scholarly publication (Bain, 1998). These fiercely egalitarian men and women were committed to the social applications of psychoanalysis. They became known as "the invisible college" that formed the basis of the post-war Tavistock Clinic and Institute. Here, for both Menzies Lyth and Jaques, were formative collective experiences of social psychology, both as observed in the group exercises and as experienced among themselves. "Our first experiment with group methods was on ourselves" (Trist & Murray, 1990a, p. 7).

These wartime explorations of leadership were taking place at precisely the same time as the new welfare state was being defined, when for the first time in the war there was hope in Britain for a better future, rather than fear of defeat. William Beveridge's best-selling report on *Social Insurance and Allied Services* was published in December 1942, less than three weeks after Winston Churchill's famous speech declaring that the allies had reached "the end of the beginning".[4] In those revolutionary times, everything seemed possible. The concept of socialism had not yet been contaminated by irrefutable revelations of the murderous dictatorship of our wartime ally Stalin, or by the later drift to the right[5] of the centre ground in Western politics. In 1946 the Tavistock Clinic's grand vision of a social psychiatry would engage the population from the beginning of life in "Infant Welfare Clinics, Obstetric Units, as well as . . . such organizations as a Nursery School and a Juvenile Employment Agency" (Dicks, 1970, p. 143). At the same time, within the clinic there was a radical commitment to horizontal collective relationships: "staff lists were printed without any distinction of seniority; the professional staff, the secretarial staff, the administrative staff and the refectory staff were all in the same type and with the same degree of emphasis" (Dicks, 1970, p. 162). The clinic at that time paid "identical salaries for medical and non-medical full time staff" (Dicks, 1970, p. 162). Derived from WOSB and other group innovations during the war,[6] the notion that everyone in the organization has an equal say was a serious aspiration.

The shift from vertical to horizontal relationships changed the Tavistock staff's consciousness of relatedness in groups, but others were less affected. There was greater social cohesion during and shortly after the war than at any time since, but the psychological or anthropological basis of this was not understood by political leaders or their advisers. In spite of the sheer scale and courage of the nationalization programme of the 1945–50 UK government—of which only a wounded National Health Service remains[7]—the group relations revolution in public services did not happen. Even today repeated government exhortations to service agencies to "work together" are uttered without any grasp of the powerful forces that prevent it.

There is evidence from contemporary accounts of a post-war waning in enthusiasm for group work. In 1947 Bion gathered at his consulting room a group of analytically minded colleagues, but he made it plain by his manner that he did not want to lead it. Trist, who was present, writes:

> He was subdued; Rickman was embarrassed; no one else knew what to say. . . . Those present were all people [Bion] trusted. He seemed to be asking something of us. . . . He wanted to be with us as a group. To use terms Rickman had used in a presentation to the London Psychoanalytical Society on the Creative Process, he wanted a "Pentecostal group" in which everyone could speak with tongues and would be accepted on an equal level with everyone else. Such a group would be neither a therapy group nor a seminar but would represent a new

mode—a mutually supporting nexus of "selectively interdependent" individuals. . . .

The consulting-room meetings petered out, partly for lack of conceptual clarity, partly because the unification of the social and psychological fields which had characterized the war period was beginning to break up and the society was moving away from a persisting ba F [basic assumption Fight] towards ba D [basic assumption Dependency]. [Trist, 1985, p. 27]

Trist is making the point that, in wartime, people are pressed into a collaborative and egalitarian struggle against a common enemy. Once that pressure is removed, so is the obligation to suppress our differences. Trist goes on to account for the group's failure to develop: "at that time we did not have concepts of domain (Trist, 1977), of selective interdependence, of appreciation of searching; neither had we recognized the special role of social networks (Bott, 1955), as distinct from holistic organizations, in fostering innovation" (Trist, 1985, p. 27).

The Tavistock innovation that did flourish after the war was selection for leadership. In 1990, Murray wrote: "More than 40 years later multiple assessment methods . . . traceable to wartime methods used in WOSB, continue in use for the appraisal of individual potential" (Murray, 1990, p. 65). In what are now known as assessment centres, exercises derived from wartime are still, in the twenty-first century, used to pick out leadership qualities in big corporations and organizations. Even if applicants become anxious during the group process, those ambitious enough to want senior posts are motivated to go through with it. Yet as a basis for consultancy and staff learning, the Tavistock's discoveries did not thrive.

The concept of social defences against anxiety became celebrated in academic circles, but applications in the workplace were few. Elliott Jaques complained that while his book *The Changing Culture of a Factory* (1951) was widely read and reprinted many times, he was not invited to repeat the exercise anywhere else. Citing his disappointment, Trist and Murray write: "no requests were received to continue this kind of work. As Jaques said at the time, 'the answer from the field was silence'" (Trist & Murray, 1990a, p. 9). Resistance to Menzies Lyth's 1960 study of hospital nursing was fierce, her findings rapidly dismissed as the fault of poor management. A review of her paper by a Registered Mental Nurse (1960) stated confidently that "My solution for the difficulties of the hospital would be to appoint a matron of known competence whom the nurses knew and trusted, who could restore their self-confidence by re-establishing order in the nursing service" (cited in Menzies Lyth,

1988, p. 94). This now classic study was published fifteen years after the war had ended, by which time cultural space for horizontal innovation had diminished even further. The power of the peer group had been harnessed in war and was to be developed by charismatic individuals in the therapeutic community movement, and in scattered enthusiastic efforts to get mental health staff groups going, but less so at the front line in social and health services. Krantz writes in a special review of Isabel Menzies Lyth's influence that

> there is also a bittersweet quality to the arc of her work. The great transformative potential of social defence analysis went largely unful-filled in the course of her work (Spillius, 1990). Few of her projects produced the deep, transformative change that seemed within the scope of her thinking. The nursing study, for example, largely fell on deaf ears. [Krantz, 2010, p. 195]

The reforming zeal of the invisible college, even as it became visible as the Tavistock Clinic, a founder member of the NHS in 1948, and as the Tavistock Institute of Human Relations, could not change its environment. The flaw in the Tavistock's concept of social intervention ("sociatry") was that society is like a patient; however, society does not ask for help as a patient does. When trying to effect change in an organization, a consultant is rarely able to get hold of the whole of it.[8]

The focus of this chapter is not so much on changing organizations as mobilizing the power of a peer group to learn from each other to promote staff development. At the shop-floor level, what do workers want from a support group? Even if they have asked for it themselves, enthusiasm for sitting in a circle of chairs every week reflecting on their experiences can quickly evaporate. Once pent-up discontents have been aired, what is the perceived gain of such emotional risk taking? Having had time to size each other up, members of the group may then discover from one another the truth of what they already sensed, which is that the organization is not able to carry out its primary task properly. Their preoccupations are ignored by senior managers who have other concerns, such as balancing the books. Group approaches to staff development haver never gained a critical mass in front-line services. Hartley and Kennard (2009) report a significant minority (around a quarter) of mental health agencies using staff support groups and fewer (less than a fifth) in social services, nowhere enough to make this routine practice.

Are systemic anxieties sufficient to explain the lack of reflective practice in front-line services? There is little doubt that supervision under the "new managerialism" (Lees, Meyer, & Rafferty, 2013) is more focused on recording and regulating risk than on containing it through reflection.[9] Child protection policy has been driven by the fear that yet more children will be murdered by their parents, but it has not prevented these deaths. It is a common complaint among statutory professions that they have to spend too much time ticking boxes instead of working with clients or patients. Yet this frustration may well conceal the greater anxiety of being left alone with a disturbed, possibly danger-ous, client. It is safer at the computer, where the ritual of entering data, in an ironic echo of Menzies Lyth's observation of nurses at work, offers reassurance and relief from anxiety (Taylor, Beckett, & McKeigue, 2008; Waterhouse & McGhee, 2009).

A basic condition of human groups?

Besides the crushing effects of micro-management, a valid explanation for the paucity of reflective practice at the front line is provided by the nurse cited at the beginning of this chapter. Urgent work generates anxiety, which is not only a mental process but a biological one, in that stress hormones (Sapolsky, 2000) facilitate action, not thought. When death is a possible outcome, it may be preferable to concentrate only on the technical task in hand. At the military front line a century ago, the 19-year-old Wilfred Bion was out of his mind with despair: "the fact remains that life had now reached such a pitch that horrible mutila-tions or death could not conceivably be worse. I found myself looking forward to getting killed . . ." (Bion, 1997, p. 94).

A more fundamental obstacle to free discussion in human groups is identified by anthropologists who have studied the hunter-gatherer way of life. Before the invention of agriculture around ten thousand years ago this was the only form of human social organization. Observing twentieth century hunter-gatherers, Woodburn describes fluid group-ings in which no adult will depend on another. Conflict between indi-viduals is dealt with by moving away, if necessary to another group, or by direct violence, including murder. Success is recognized but not privileged: "successful individual hunters are specifically denied the opportunity to make effective use of their kills to build wealth and prestige" (Woodburn, 1982, p. 440). No one is in charge. "Such arrange-ments are subversive for the development of authority" (p. 432). On the basis of similar observations of contemporary foraging people in many parts of the world, the anthropologist Christopher Boehm argues that prehistoric hunter-gatherers would have maintained similar levels of egalitarianism, because it was vitally necessary in a hostile environment. The survival of early human groups depended on a compelling obligation to share, especially the carcasses of great beasts whose meat could not be preserved for long. Foragers do not store food, and they live in larger bands than non-human primates. Boehm (who had earlier also studied chimpanzees with the ethologist Jane Goodall) notes a significant and puzzling difference between groups of humans and non-human primates. The latter are always led by a silver-backed alpha male, an individual who has fought his way to the top where he can then reserve females for his exclusive use and get the first and best choice of food. Hunter gatherers typically do not tolerate such domination, from which Boehm deduces that early humans evolved a different social system:

> As members of bands or tribes, humans can be quite egalitarian.
> . . . Individuals who otherwise would be subordinated are clever
> enough to form a large and united political coalition. . . . Because the
> united subordinates are constantly putting down the more assertive
> alpha types in their midst, egalitarianism is in effect a bizarre type of
> political hierarchy: the weak combine forces to actively dominate the
> strong. [Boehm, 1999, p. 3]

While ganging up against a more powerful individual is common in apes too, the outcome is invariably different:

> when a pair of rival [apes] manages to unseat an incumbent alpha,
> only one of the two will assume the alpha position as a new set of
> competitive alliances comes into play. [Boehm, 2012, p. 844]

How could this kind of hierarchical organization have been suppressed by their human descendants? Boehm's answer is that in order to survive in larger groups, we evolved a capacity to restrain the impulse to help ourselves at the expense of others—indeed, *to desist from taking a lead in any obvious way*. Like other anthropologists, Boehm has observed in many modern foraging societies that anyone who persistently tries to take over, or to have more than his share, is systematically mocked and if necessary ostracized by the group. He cites the anthropologist Jean Briggs's account of her exclusion by a small nomadic band of Inuit Eskimos, the Utku, with whom she had lived happily for many months in arctic Canada in the 1960s. She was impressed by a man named Innutiaq, who "kept strict control of his feelings . . . the effort was caught in the flash of an eye, quickly subdued, in the careful length of a pause, or the painstaking neutrality of a reply" (Briggs, 1970, pp. 41–42). Innutiaq never lost his temper, but he beat his dog "with a fury that was unusual" (Boehm, 1999, p. 53). Local white sportsmen began to borrow the Utku's two valuable and fragile canoes for fishing. The Utku did not like this but did not complain. When one of the canoes was damaged beyond repair, Briggs protested to the Canadians. Soon after, it became clear that the Utku no longer wanted her around. Boehm's understanding of this ostracism, which lasted for months, is that they would not tolerate someone who *"arbitrarily tried to make a decision that involved the entire group"* (Briggs, 1970, p. 59; emphasis in original). Briggs notes that amongst the Utku "people tend to look askance at anyone who seems to aspire to tell them what to do" (p. 42). Such individuals are identified by Boehm as "upstarts": "typical behaviours that are reasonably well controlled by the egalitarian band would seem to be: bullying behaviours; cheating or shirking in the context of co-operative efforts; serious degrees of deception or theft; and 'sexual crimes' like adultery, incest, and rape" (Boehm, 2000, p. 85).

But Boehm includes a greater sanction to enforce the foragers' egalitarianism. When mockery and ostracism fail to subdue an upstart, execution may be necessary: "hunter-gatherers live in intentionally reversed dominance orders, and . . . these muted hierarchies involve political tensions so strong that they sometimes require capital punishment to maintain them" (Boehm, 1999, p. 227). A paradoxical statistic supports this startling view. Providing detailed figures from a variety of communities, Boehm shows that among most foraging societies rates of interpersonal violence are far lower than in settled agricultural communities, while murder rates are higher. "Foragers do have very high homicide rates, but they also exhibit relatively low levels of lesser conflict, and are heavily preoccupied with the maintenance of social harmony" (p. 227). "The homicide rate per capita for egalitarian foragers is as high as in large American cities" (Boehm, 2012, p. 846). On this view, the original human condition does not allow much space for individualism. Egalitarianism of this kind is a potentially oppressive— a "profoundly conservative"—social system (Woodburn, 1982, p. 447). You would not want to set yourself up as a leader, or even express too discordant an opinion, if the group then ganged up on you or tried to kill you.

With this abbreviated account of human evolutionary and cultural development in mind, it becomes clearer why putting a group of professional adults in a room to discuss their relationships with each other is an alarming thing to do. Having been selected[10] to restrain upstarts over hundreds of millennia—and despite the flourishing of very different political arrangements since the invention of agriculture (Service, 1975)—human beings remain conservative socialists.[11] Anyone who has participated in a Tavistock–Leicester conference study group will recall the intense anxiety of their first moments with mostly unknown others. How are we to get on? Do I have to be nice to everyone, or can I risk having a go at saying what I actually think? My point here is that the anxiety in such gatherings is created *by the setting itself*, one that generates a remarkable paralysis of decision-making.[12] Any attempt to take over the group is both welcomed and undermined. Relief at having someone in the lead is accompanied by veiled attacks on assumed authority. A request, say, to visit another group elsewhere in the conference is slowed down by others who provide a variety of reasons for this not to happen: that "we must all stay together because there is some work to do first", that "we should be clearer about the reason for the visit", that the selected person is "not the right person" to go, and so on.

A hundred years ago, Freud first described his hypothesis about the origins of totemism and religion:

> In 1912 I took up a conjecture of Darwin's to the effect that the primitive form of human society was that of a horde ruled over despotically by a powerful male. I attempted to show that the fortunes of this horde have left indestructible traces upon the history of human descent; and, especially, that the development of totemism, which comprises in itself the beginnings of religion, morality, and social organization, is connected with the killing of the chief by violence and the transformation of the paternal horde into a community of brothers. . . . We must conclude that the psychology of the group is the oldest human psychology.13 [Freud, 1921c, p. 122]

Freud's mythical description of the primal horde's murder of the father may have prehistoric validity after all.

This narrative adds something to the psychoanalytic concept of primitive anxieties in groups. From the ethological point of view, it is the actual death of the group that is being defended against, rather than an infantile terror of disintegration.[14] Eric Miller (1998) notes an ambiguity in Bion's formulation of basic assumptions as involuntary and unconscious "proto-mental states" that are always affecting a group. He asks whether these are primarily instinctive—inherited—traits, or desires and anxieties acquired through experience after birth.[15] He proposes that during the later 1950s Bion shifted his view towards the latter, both under the influence of his final training analysis with Melanie Klein and also following the death in 1951 of his first training analyst and mentor, John Rickman (Torres, 2013, p. 18). Miller (like

Trist before him, and Armstrong[16] after) sees this as a reductionist view, underplaying the primal power of social life on all of us. He argues in favour of Bion's original, tentative, formulation of an "instinctive groupishness" that is common in other species such as bees, birds, and cattle. Curiously, though himself trained in anthropology, Miller does not speculate about its human origins, relying instead on his own "amateur" observation made decades earlier of a group of langur monkeys reacting "as if they were a single organism" to an external threat (Miller, 1998, p. 1501). By focusing on primate evolution, Boehm's hypothesis fills a gap in group theory. Apes do not behave like swarms or flocks—they defer to status. This primate tendency was suppressed in humans by a compulsive egalitarianism that reduced conflict:

> 100,000 years ago, humans, aided by much larger brains and by an advanced form of communication, created communities that could hold down not only domination behaviours by alpha individuals, but any other behaviour they identified as being directly or potentially deleterious to members of the group—or deleterious to the group's functioning as they saw it. [Boehm, 2000, p. 98]

The dangers of speaking your mind

Despite ten thousand years of predominantly settled agricultural and civic social organization, an instinctive pressure to conform in human groups still holds sway. It is not often observed, because groups usually have an external task such as working, learning, or playing. But when they do not, such as in support groups, the underlying regulation of initiative is exposed. There are anecdotes among service staff of meetings that they had to go to where "nobody spoke", where the facilitator was experienced as a Tavistock study group consultant sometimes is—as an inscrutable and frustrating person who ought to be taking over but refuses to do so. Such groups are soon abandoned, at least by those made most anxious by the silence. While sophisticated mental health staff in therapeutic settings can usually manage this, the majority may not. My own experience of reflective work with hospital front-line staff[17] is that in the absence of a formal didactic task or other programme, it is necessary to create a "change of gear" to get the group started. Though participants are usually keen enough to attend, their heads are full of things—urgent or mundane—that need doing, from which it is very difficult to drag them away. Any question about recent problems or stresses is met with a mixture of frowns and raised eyebrows and vague remarks to the effect that everything is fine. Given that there are almost always problematic patients who have been seen in the department since we last met, I don't believe this, yet saying so does not promote anything but further defensiveness. And waiting in silence at the start is the surest way of putting busy colleagues off any future meeting of this kind.

While trying hard to preserve the principle of peer group learning—that everyone has an equal voice—it is necessary to modify the method to get to there. I have found that my anxiety at the beginning of a meeting is best put to work by talking about current preoccupations in the department, such as a worrying patient (whom some of the staff will also know) or some administrative frustration I experienced earlier in the day, exploiting the fact that I have also, decades earlier, been in their position as a junior doctor in paediatrics. This kind of opener can get discussions going, to the point where participants are genuinely surprised to discover a whole range of topics that they rarely discuss—for example, the intellectual, ethnic, sexual, religious, social-class, political, professional, physical, and financial differences between them. The taboo of exploring rivalry among a group of highly successful (and mainly female) graduates is most striking. Yet, once loosened from that restraint, they are capable of emotional courage and generosity in exploring and sharing their clinical, training, and personal experiences.

While the modern public service setting does not seem fertile soil for reflection, there are promising developments. The structured methodology of Schwartz rounds (Goodrich & Cornwell, 2012), in which hospital staff are gathered for a monthly lunchtime meeting to discuss selected case presentations, may seem inflexible compared to psychoanalytic approaches, yet the anxieties I am describing are contained by this method sufficiently to keep the process going. It is regulated and facilitated by individuals who have been trained in it. In effect it is a manualized form of work discussion, and it is widely praised by participants. The text by Hartley and Kennard, *Staff Support Groups in the Helping Professions* (2009), though much less prescriptive, can be read as a handbook for group facilitators, offering practical yet sophisticated guidance for many of the familiar challenges of this work. A reflective method of teaching medical students to think about narratives of serious childhood illness has been running successfully in London for several years (Macaulay & Hirons, in press). A randomized controlled trial (Maratos et al., 2014) of staff support groups in mental health yielded promising results. The continued use, and effectiveness (Yakeley, Schoenberg, Morris, Sturgeon, & Majid, 2011), of Balint groups in GP and psychiatry training is evidence of a commitment to horizontal learning in preparation for front-line service. In social services, an innovative method of peer support—dubbed "the pod"—has been operating in the London Borough of Hillingdon with encouraging effect:

> groups of between six and eight practitioners, each responsible for an individual caseload . . . meet weekly to discuss their cases and provide support to each other. Whereas, in the past, staff were responsible for either the initial assessment process or longer-term care, now each member takes on a case from the start and sees it through to the point when it is closed. [Cole, 2013]

Conclusion: conflicting sources of power

Horizontal work relationships are fragile and easily overcome by the prevailing paradigm of corporatized public services, where using your authority can too readily be taken as an abuse of someone else's. Yet if staff feel secure enough, they can relax their guard and find their voices. However it is to be achieved, that security is promoted by a model of attentive leadership rooted in the systemic discoveries of seventy years ago, working at the intersection between the vertical and the horizontal, where conflicting sources of power meet: "to keep alive in one's experience the reality of the person, the group, the organization and the wider society" (Trist & Murray, 1990b, p. 37).

There is renewed interest in the dynamics of peer relationships from street-level political action such as in Madrid in 2011 and later all over the world in the Occupy movement. This alerted a new generation to the excitement but also the sheer stubbornness of a freely associated group, reliving our prehistoric struggle to bypass the power of individuals.

> It's impossible to switch off, I dream about it at night. It was hard work learning how to conduct the assemblies, especially the big one. . . . We learn something new every day.[18] [Anonymous, in *Le Monde Diplomatique* 12 July 2011]

Recent history has shown how much hope for political change from mass action, particularly in North Africa, has been dashed, but not all of it (Mason, 2013). Trist's explanation of the failure of the 1947 "Pentecostal group" was that they did not at the time have an understanding of the "domain", as he called it. His 1977 paper on that subject describes his hopes that the new social movements and methods of communication that arose in the 1960s would change political process fundamentally (Trist, 1977). The fact that they did not is sobering.

Notes

1. "A pattern of attachment behaviour related to compulsive self-reliance is that of compulsive care-giving. A person showing it may engage in many close relationships but always in the role of giving care, never that of receiving it" (Bowlby, 1977, p. 207). This pattern is over-represented in the helping professions: "being the caregiver, with the fantasy of being invincible and having no thoughts about one's own needs" (Garelick, 2012, p. 81).

2. A paper in which Bion himself adopts a tone of wounded innocence when referring to the closure of the experimental and very brief project since known as Northfield I: "The experiment was brought to a close by the authorities, and since it has not proved possible to investigate their state of mind I cannot suggest a cause of failure" (Bion, 1948, p. 81).

3. In the 1930s, Trist had been quite taken by Marxism and was engaged during that decade in investigating of the effects of unemployment in Dundee. See www.moderntimesworkplace.com/archives/ericbio/ericbiobody/ericbiobody.html

4. "Now this is not the end. It is not even the beginning of the end. But it is, perhaps, the end of the beginning." Churchill's speech at Mansion House, London on 10 November 1942, following the allied victory over Rommel's forces at El Alamein in Egypt.

5. Thatcher/Reagan; Clinton/Blair, the latter being leaders after the fall of communism, which may have been a counterbalance to capitalism, then unleashed (Glyn, 2006).

6. In particular, in the first Northfield experiment, "Northfield I", where the Quaker psychoanalyst John Rickman's influence was most marked (Kraemer, 2011)

7. "The current government views the NHS as a failing bank or business. This stance is one of the most cynical, and at the same time cunning, ways by which the government abdicates all responsibility for running a health care system" (*Lancet*, 2013).

8. At the Northfield Hospital in 1942/3, Bion and Rickman were not trying to change the army, but because they did not include senior officers in their radical therapeutic experiment, as soon as there was a crisis they closed it down (Bridger, 1990; Thalassis, 2007).

9. Just as "security" has contrasting meanings depending on whether it is a depressive or paranoid concept, so also "containment" can mean something thoughtful or repressive. Except in scattered experiments (see Cole, 2013), there is little sign of reflective practice being taken on as a matter of routine as encouraged by a recent UK national report into social services (Munro, 2011b). "The Standards for Employers and Supervision Framework set out a list of elements that employers should put in place to support practitioners, including welfare services, mechanisms for reporting concerns, regular supervision, supervision training for supervisors and continuous learning through case reflections" (Lees, Meyer, & Rafferty, 2013, p. 555).

10. Though epigenetic change is frequent, in the relatively short time since settled life became the norm, little change in the human genome is likely to have taken place.

11. Systematic conflict-avoidance in settled agricultural groups was carefully observed in rural Russia by John Rickman a hundred years ago: ". . . the village formed *a leaderless group*, and the bond which held the members together was that

they shared a common ideal. . . . When a topic came up for discussion someone would begin speaking in a guarded, vague and rather long-winded way. . . . By constant repetition of argument and many contradictory assertions made by nearly everyone present, the members of the group, after several evenings' talk, arrived at a fair guess at which way the wind was blowing. Personally, I never saw a vote taken. Everyone's 'face' was saved by this method. There was no minority, no one in particular had carried the meeting, no one was defeated" (Rickman, 1938, p. 162).

12. Because most of the those attending these events are professional people, it is tempting to assume that some kind of middle-class overpoliteness takes over, each member falling over him/herself to defer to others ("after you; no please, after *you*"). We can now see how this may be misleading. The anthropological observations cited are made in traditional societies where modern notions of social class could not apply; indeed, there is no class at all.

13. Including the following phrase in a footnote: ". . . there was only a common will, there were no single ones" (Freud, 1921c, p. 122).

14. Though, of course, infant terrors are related to anxieties of abandonment and death.

15. This theme has preoccupied group relations scholars for decades. Bion's ambivalence about his mentor and hero at medical school, Wilfred Trotter, plays a significant part in his view of the origin of basic assumptions (Torres, 2013). Despite the fact that several distinguished group relations practitioners and writers have been anthropologists, there is surprisingly little reference to this branch of knowledge in the literature.

16. "In his original and earlier series of papers, brought together in *Experiences in Groups*, Bion's focus is on the tension between the individual and the group, seen as built in to all mental functioning and involving an interplay between distinct but interdependent and interacting factors or forces. However, in the Review chapter, written subsequent to his training analysis with Melanie Klein, he can seem to read group mentality as if it were simply generated from within, an outcrop from very early primitive anxieties associated with part object relations. This reductionist reading, in my view, though not the only way of interpreting Bion's text, has played a major part in obscuring the significance of Bion's perspective within psychoanalysis and the corresponding tendency to read group and social phenomena simply as the outworking of individual pathology (cf. Elliott Jaques's formulation of social systems as a defence against anxiety, as against that of Isabel Menzies Lyth). From such a position it can become dangerously easy to extrapolate from psychoanalytic insight, without having as it were to take on either the discipline or the burden of a change of perspective, a different modality of engagement" (Armstrong, 2012, p. 6).

17. This illustration is primarily based on fortnightly work discussion with junior paediatric staff. Because of the shift system based on the European Working Time Directive, the membership of the group is never constant.

18. This quotation is from an unnamed young woman who had spent every day occupying Puerta del Sol in Madrid. The Indignados had been the first to be inspired by the North African Arab Spring, before Occupy got going. See also Mason, 2013.

CHAPTER TEN

A partnership of policing and health systems: containing the dynamics of sexual violence

Mannie Sher

This chapter describes the relevance of the "social systems as a defence against anxiety" theory (Menzies Lyth, 1960) in a complex organizational development consultancy to a Sexual Assault Referral Centre (SARC) and the wider systemic problems that appeared to flow from improvements in the SARC's management team's leadership capability. The chapter explores the see-saw effects of improvements in one part of the healthcare system leading to crisis in other parts as a consequence of not comprehending a "social systems" concept that could have provided the requisite containment for the functioning of the service. The chapter describes an organizational acting-out (Freud, 1914g, pp. 150–153; Kernberg, 1973) process at several levels, which ultimately forced the SARC management team and its consultants out of their respective roles into advocacy roles in order to protect themselves, their jobs, and their reputations from catastrophic attacks by the employing organization.

Background

In the autumn of 2009 the Tavistock Institute of Human Relations was approached by an NHS Trust to address interpersonal relationship problems at an SARC—"to sort out the senior management team". An SARC provides specialist forensic medical and counselling services for anyone who has been raped or sexually assaulted (http://www.rape-crisis.org.uk/Referralcentres2.php). The SARC aims to be a one-stop service, providing medical care, forensic examination, and psychological counselling following sexual assault. SARCs are funded and run in partnership, usually between the NHS, the police, and the voluntary sector.

Since the problem was defined as "difficulties at the top", the Tavistock team of three consultants, in the first instance, decided to work jointly and individually with the SARC's three internal managers—the Lead Clinician, the Clinical Nurse Specialist, and the Service Manager. Other SARC staff—administrators, psychologists, and sexual health advisers—were included in the schedule of interviews as part of the evaluation process during which they expressed their frustration with their managers, who, they said, seemed unable to work together effectively to coordinate strategic objectives and operational practices. The staff had complained to senior Trust managers over the heads of their own managers.

Following the initial assessment of the SARC situation, the Tavistock team reported:

> As a result of in-depth, diagnostic interviews, the Tavistock Institute consulting team concluded that interpersonal rivalries, inter-disciplinary tensions and challenges, were in part an enactment of broader dynamics at the partnership and inter-organizational levels—in other words, the issues occurring between individuals in the SARCs were also occurring at several levels across the health and policing organizational systems. As is common in multi-disciplinary work, conflicting aims and processes are compounded by the nature of the core work—that of treating the consequences of violence against women which is suffused with pain and is potentially overwhelming.
>
> Two questions that concerned the Tavistock consulting team were:
> - How do professionals work with the impact on them of daily encounters with victims of sexual violence?
> - How do those professionals defend themselves against the anxieties manifest in the work?

The administrative staff at the SARC, as the point of first contact, are potentially the people most exposed to staff and patient tensions as they come into the SARC space. The nursing staff deal intimately with patients, helping them through the first stages of the crisis, addressing the initial practical and emotional impact of the violence experienced by them. The doctors have responsibility for making clinical decisions, and they keep an emotional distance from the patients. They hold a "forensic stance", in order not to lose the opportunity to prosecute the perpetrators. The counselling team is confronted with the mid- and longer-term impact of the offence, as well as with mental health issues for which they cannot always offer adequate support, making them feel guilty. Some patients' mental health needs are beyond the scope of the SARC.

A consequence of the nature of the work for staff is their identification with the clients' feeling of being violated and aggressed. One result of this identification is that the staff themselves often feel helpless and victimized. In order to be able to cope with what is experienced as an unbearable sense of helplessness (without understanding where this feeling may come from), individual staff members take it out on each other, often aggressively. In the SARC we saw this through the enactment of a "cold war" or in indirect attacks on each other, or more directly blaming each other or their managers for their feelings of hopelessness, for not "doing their job", or blaming the broader organizational bureaucracies, at the same time as looking to them for protection from being overwhelmed.

Work-related anxieties (Jaques, 1951, 1955) were also manifest in the considerable role confusion among SARC staff and their inability to address this and through following various unnecessary routines, such as agreeing to work after hours to complete and deliver medical statements to the police. Underlying their interactions with each other and with the police was the staff's considerable anxiety about "getting it right" for the victim/patient. This anxiety, which had no place for expression and working through, was not acknowledged, and tensions accumulated.

Strategic partnership stakeholders—the police and the Health Trust—add to the complicated dynamics inside the SARC. On the one hand, the SARCs are constantly observed by the stakeholders, making the SARC staff feeling criticized, while on the other, strategic role confusion between the major stakeholders is not scrutinized but, instead, gets translated into operational role confusion within the SARCs.

The SARC, jointly commissioned by the NHS Sexual Health Services and the police, is structurally embedded in a Health Trust, and its employees are employees of that Trust. To manage the joint commissioning, representatives of the NHS Trust and the police come together under a Strategic Board, which is chaired by a police officer. In 2008, there had been an investigation into salary overpayments to one of the SARC doctors. The investigation was managed by the human resources department of the Trust, and the matter was in hand.

As a matter of course, the SARC Service Manager, as the SARC budget holder, reported the case of the overpayments to the Strategic Board. The (police) Chair of the Board independently acted on this information and requested the police fraud investigators to intervene in the Trust's investigation. This unilateral act by the chair of the Strategic Board had huge consequences at all levels—from the front-line SARC workers and their operational colleagues in the police specialist rape investigation unit, through to the Commissioners' loss of trust in the Trust's administration. The Chair of the Strategic Board was never challenged on his decision, and a connection was never made between his action and the unfolding interpersonal animosities in the SARC. Role confusion, betraying one set of commitments for another, and the corruption of relationships that resulted appeared to stem from a single act of individual power rather than an act of collective authority (Bion, 1961).

The work of the Tavistock consulting team was directed at reinstating the collective authority and decision-making of the three SARC managers by, first, improving their interpersonal relationships and then working with them on issues of their collective leadership. By February 2012, the three managers had achieved a satisfactory level of integrated leadership capability, and we ended our contract confident that they were working well together. They had agreed a number of significant changes that would improve the SARC service.

Staff support

Soon after the Tavistock team's engagement with the SARC senior leadership team was concluded, the Tavistock was notified by the Trust that a new crisis had erupted. During the last joint meeting with the three managers, the Clinical Nurse Specialist's behaviour appeared erratic and destabilized. We were told that the Lead Clinician and Service Manager, in their senior management roles, had referred the matter of the Clinical Nurse Specialist's instability to her line manager, and she was signed off sick. During her absence from work a number of patients' DNA samples were discovered lying unattended in her cupboard, and this led to the new crisis. The Tavistock consultants were called back to the SARC to provide support to the staff group.

The Tavistock team visited the SARC staff on several occasions during April and May and witnessed Trust officials closing the SARC and removing the Lead Clinician and the Service Manager. There was no communication to staff about the sudden removal of their leaders.

Trust security officers, with gloves, appeared and without explanation searched every drawer and cupboard in the building looking for misplaced DNA samples. Acceptance of new clinical cases and all teaching activities were suspended indefinitely.

The SARC staff discussed their difficulties of coping with vague Trust management pronouncements and the rudeness of the unknown investigators. The staff were stunned by the dramatic removal of the SARC leadership, and they were unclear how to proceed with their day-to-day clinical work. The Tavistock team's work with the SARC staff included strengthening them in their work roles and encouraging them to work closely together as a team and to seek help from their professional associations. After only four weeks of regular weekly staff support meetings, the Trust terminated the work of the Tavistock Institute.

The job

Work at an SARC—treating and managing dozens of traumatized patients each week, mostly women and child victims of sexual violence—is stressful. Matters are made worse by virtue of the patients' social, cultural, and ethnic backgrounds and their status as refugees and asylum seekers, people without basic rights and resources and living on the margins of society. The emotional toll on staff working all day with traumatized patients is huge and results in the deployment of various defensive manoeuvres to help them stay engaged with their patients' emotional states and remaining sufficiently professional for clinical investigation, prescription, and legal actions necessary to apprehend the perpetrators. Normally, in high-stress units of the NHS, the provision of regular support for staff through regular business and case discussion meetings, supervisions, consultations, and so on is given a high priority, and there is usually a significant budget for this type of support; however, in this case, support had been minimal. As far as the Trust managers were concerned, the SARC was said to be a case of "out of sight, out of mind". Trust managers seldom visited the centre or stayed long enough to find out about the work there. The Trust managers did not seem to notice a decline in morale and rising tensions in the SARC until junior staff took it upon themselves to go over the heads of their managers and write to the Trust managers. By being located off-site, the physical isolation of the SARC from the Trust became entrenched, leading to a damaging separation between

Trust managers and the managers at the SARC and a disincentive for the senior Trust management to proactively provide support for and supervision of the SARC activities.

Individual staff support

This author was deputed by the consulting team to provide coaching support to the Service Manager, Veronica (not her real name), who had been sent home on sick leave and told that she could not return to work at the SARC. Veronica had said that the senior SARC managers had for a long time reported difficulties in the structure and functioning of the SARC to their line managers in the Trust. After the crisis of the mislaid DNA samples, the Lead Clinician and Veronica were deemed to have mismanaged the SARC service and were excluded from the SARC pending a full investigation. In our view, the roots of the SARC difficulties lay in the complex relationships between the Trust, the Commissioning Board, and the police. It was never clear, for instance, why the Trust did not make a management charge for costs of services rendered (management time, finance support, HR, buildings safety and maintenance) as was the case with other UK SARCs and their respective Trusts. This was an issue that Veronica had alerted the Trust managers to and had advised them on the process that had to be followed to submit the charge, but the Trust did nothing. Sorting out the financial arrangements could have led to the Trust's feeling it was a beneficiary of the SARC; instead, not claiming income due to it seemed to have been part of the Trust's neglect of the SARC—administrative careless-ness later grew into an organizational crisis.

The tripartite management structure of the SARC—police, Com-missioning Board, and Trust—seemed to us to lie at the heart of the problems experienced at the SARC. Split responsibilities, lack of a clear unified strategic vision, the absence of monitoring mechanisms, the odd personalized arrangements for selecting SARC staff to sit on joint boards, the absence of any board evaluation process—all contributed to the systemic failure of the SARC. Behind these standard rational organizational reasons for failure lay other less obvious, hidden, and sometimes unconscious reasons for failing to sustain the SARC func-tions. (Miller & Rice, 1967). These lay in the competing tasks of care and compassion of vulnerable female patients—the primary purpose of the Trust—and pursuit, apprehension, and conviction of male perpetra-tors—the primary purpose of the police. The "partnership" between Health Trust and police that produced the SARC initially had care and

compassion of patients as its primary purpose, but, over time, privileg-
ing policing procedures superseded as the new unconscious primary
purpose. Another view of the Trust's disregard of the SARC may have
been the Trust's perplexity of where to place the rape service, since
rape falls beyond the traditional categories requiring health service
intervention—rape is neither an illness nor an accident. Rape is not
random; rape is a deliberate act of violently asserting male supremacy,
domination, and control over defenceless women. Those who attended
the SARC included a number who were from ethnic minorities, illegal
immigrants, or asylum seekers. These women attended the SARC
regularly because they were routinely raped by the same group of
men who were exploiting their fear of coming to the attention of the
police. Not understanding rape, or the social factors that support the
rape of women, it was not surprising the Trust turned away from the
SARC. Rape, unlike other clinical situations, invites turning a blind eye
towards it. Fraught dynamics, absent management, lack of communication, sensitivity, and appreciation of the SARC and the challenges it was
set up to deal with led to its collapse, turning the SARC, like the patients
it served, into a defenceless and uncontained victim.

The Tavistock Institute's brief was to work on "inter-personal relations". Knowing that working to this narrow focus would be unproduc-
tive, the consulting approach extended to diagnosing and treating the
interpersonal issues in the context of the SARC's position in the Trust,
the Commissioning Board, and the police. We believed this approach
to be the most efficient way of understanding and remedying the
organizational challenges, given the SARC managers' earlier struggles
to have their accounts of structural flaws and omissions and poor communications heard.

Later, an independent investigation into the services provided at
the SARC reported that it could find no evidence that the Trust took
action to review and implement the necessary actions following the
2008 audit. The SARC service was regarded by the Trust and Commissioners as a high-profile one which was reported as being a successful
service that met the complex needs of the individuals who required its
services; client feedback was overwhelmingly positive. The SARC was
never raised as a struggling service on the Trust's Independent Investigation Report into the SARC Service, nor was it considered a service
that needed reviewing, with the exception of the working-relationship
review undertaken by the Tavistock Institute. Senior management was
aware of underlying concerns relating to staff as it was reported "as a
volume of unhappiness and noise coming out of the department".

Some staff described being actively discouraged from following up their concerns. Escalating concerns to senior members of the Trust did not appear to resolve these issues as there appeared to be a lack of understanding of what the service entailed. When concerns were voiced to the Trust regarding the impact of the dysfunctional relationship between the three service managers, the action the Trust took was to commission the Tavistock Institute to provide coaching and mentoring. An investigation of the underlying service and broader systemic reasons behind the relationship difficulties were not carried out or considered when these concerns were raised by the Tavistock Institute. Improvements were noted after the Tavistock Institute's intensive contact with all staff and particularly with the three senior managers and their collective leadership. The Tavistock Institute's work ended, but following the Serious Incident (misplaced DNA samples) the Tavistock Institute was recalled to work with the whole staff group at the SARC and to provide regular support.

How useful was the concept of social systems as a defence against anxiety in this work?

A recommendation of the internal management review of the SARC following the crisis of the mislaid DNA samples and suspension of the three SARC managers was that the Service Manager and Lead Clinician should continue receiving support from the Tavistock Institute. The following is an account of the coaching provided to the Service Manager, Veronica, by this author that illustrates the need to keep in mind the *social systems as a defence against anxiety* concept to counter traditional cause-and-effect rationalist explanations. An understanding of *social systems*, it is argued, might have avoided a catastrophic organizational "acting out" of the violence-towards-women dynamic. It seemed as if a predominantly male leadership was driven unconsciously to enact this dynamic—*some woman, somewhere, had to be beaten up*. Stress on the two surviving SARC managers, both female and both strongly committed to the care of victimized women, resulted in their physical and mental breakdown. This organizational "enactment" mirrored precisely the violence-against-women dynamic that the SARC service was originally set up to address—to help women victims of sexual violence and to prosecute the perpetrators of that violence. That goal was reversed; the Trust and Commissioning Board unconsciously replicated the violence perpetrated against the SARC's female patients in their behaviour towards the three female managers, whose rights were denied, who were made "stateless" (as many of the SARC patients were), and who were extruded (deported) from the system.

By repeatedly interpreting the "social systems" dynamic in which my client and the Tavistock Institute were caught up, we were able to make sense of the terrifying unfolding dramas over the next 12 months of suspension, exclusion, internal management reviews, disciplinary hearings, sackings, appeals, upholding decisions to sack, independent reviews, and finally an employment tribunal. In addition to these harrowing ordeals, Veronica had to endure rumours about an alleged affair she was purported to have had with the police chair of the Commissioning Board, the loss of her sickness certificates by the administration, and other acts of mismanagement.

At the beginning of our coaching work, Veronica and I agreed that it would be beneficial to work on understanding (1) the interpersonal relationships in the SARC management (which is what the Trust management had requested) and (2) the inter-institutional relationships of the Commissioners, the Trust, and the SARC service. Why, for instance, had the Trust forfeited its management charge of £100,000 p.a. that could have had a positive impact on Trust funds? Did the Trust forfeit these funds because it wished to keep the SARC at arm's length?

An early contributor to Trust–SARC tensions was an administrative error that led to a doctor being overpaid 10 times more than the agreed salary. (0.1 WTE was interpreted by the Finance Department as 1.0 WTE). Veronica, as SARC budget-holder, was caught in acrimonious communications between the stakeholder organizations, which turned her into a "hate figure" in the Trust administration. Veronica was accused of neglecting her responsibilities and was designated "not fit for work". We compared the possible metaphoric meaning of the DNA samples being mislaid in a cupboard with the way the Trust management defined the problem and referred the matter to the Tavistock Institute—"stashing the SARC in the Tavistock cupboard" and forgetting about it, thus denying the core problems in the sponsoring organizational structures of the SARCs. Defining the difficulties in the SARC as interpersonal conflict meant the problem and its solution could be out-sourced. The employers could continue avoiding facing the issues of the non-payment of costs, the difficulties inherent in the inter-institutional collaboration between the police and the Trust, the nature of the SARC's business, and its uniquely disturbing problems presented by its patient population of violated and traumatized women. When problems came to a head, Veronica was made the scapegoat—she was the only person mentioned by name in the report of the investigation— another case, we thought, of a woman violated.

Six months later, Veronica's grievance against her manager for management neglect had been partially upheld—that is, the Trust now accepted that it could have done more to help her. With this deci- sion, Veronica was confident that instead of being sacked, she would be offered a job elsewhere in the Trust, if there was one available, or else be offered redundancy and a pay-out. Nevertheless, the Trust still maintained that Veronica had failed to carry out her responsibilities to ensure that policies and practices were in place in the SARC. It decided to proceed with a disciplinary enquiry against her, which it did, and promptly sacked her. At this point, Veronica found it difficult to hold on to *social systems* thinking, and she blamed herself for the failure of the mislaid DNA samples. She needed reminding that (1) she had said sev- eral times that she had complied with her responsibilities and ensured that policies and practices were in place and that she had no reason to doubt her co-managers; (2) they had told her that they had complied with policy requirements, and, additionally, she had no authority to investigate them; and (3) historically, the Trust appeared never to have wanted the SARC in its jurisdiction. Veronica had become identified as the iconic abused woman and treated in the same way as the client population that the Trust unconsciously wished to have no business with. Also unconsciously, it treated Veronica in the way that the women served by the SARC are treated as a group—without rights, without defences, abused and ejected. Veronica decided she would not allow that—she would fight this, no matter how painful.

Non-police referrals

The issue of non-police referrals was an indication of wider systemic problems between Police Commissioners, Trusts, and SARCs. Although forming only a small percentage of referrals, non-police referrals appear to have played a role in the saga of the mislaid DNA samples that led to the crisis in the SARC. It appeared that some samples of non-police referrals had not been collected for analysis by the police in line with their usual procedures, or, where they had been collected, details of the resulting analyses had not been returned to the SARCs for onward reporting to patients. This practice of non-collection and non-reporting appeared to have been happening since 2004 in several SARCs in the country. Veronica said that the police ignored non-police referrals (1) because the referral, by not coming through the police, was not logged as a crime. The arriving samples from the SARC's non-police referrals would now have to be logged as a crime, with a risk that the victim might decide not to press charges against the perpetrator, meaning that the police would have to enter a number of unsolved crimes into their statistics (*The Times*, 20 November 2013, "Police Lied about Crime Statistics"); (2) because the police were not keen to acquire more work from unlogged cases turning into logged cases. Other SARCs had similar problems with the samples of non-police referrals. When these SARCs reported their difficulties with non-police referrals to their Commissioners, *the Commissioners did not share that information with "our" SARC*. Had the Commissioners done so, "our" SARC would have been apprised of the problem and could have taken steps to investigate their own records of non-police referrals and do something about them. The problem *was systemic across all the SARCs*, but "our" SARC was kept in the dark until the crisis erupted and the service was halted, probably in order to avoid an investigation into police practices.

Working with Veronica

The sudden notice of suspension, accusations of shirked responsibilities, and being designated "not fit for work" were shocking and led to a period of sick leave and attention by Occupational Health. As often happens with rape victims, Veronica had internalized her experiences of rejection, abuse, and blame, and this had become a conviction that she was indeed solely and entirely responsible for the debacle, a feeling that was reinforced when the Trust sacked her.

At this time . . .

For the purposes of this chapter, Veronica wrote the following postscript:

> I now have a permanent post in another NHS Trust. The union solicitors, who had been advising me that my case was likely to succeed at an employment tribunal, withdrew their support on learning that the Clinical Nurse Specialist had also been dismissed. The Trust refused to settle before the Tribunal date and, instead, proposed that I withdrew my case to avoid facing a claim for costs from them.

After much deliberation, I agreed to withdraw my claim. The Trust forwarded an agreement that would bind me not to disclose the terms of the settlement and not to communicate in any form about the events that had led up to the filing of the claim, in return for which I would not be pursued for legal costs. I declined to sign such a controlling agreement and stated, instead, that I would continue the case without union support. Only then were all confidentiality clauses removed and an agreement finally reached the week before the scheduled tribunal. The metaphor of the Trust wanting to hide problems away in a cupboard seemed to reach its peak here, as if the Trust wanted to "lock the cupboard" permanently.

It had taken fourteen months from the point of dismissal to reach the tribunal date. During this time, some of the broader system failures within the Trust were brought into the light by a journalist who made good use of the Freedom of Information (FOI) Act. This permitted access to information that the Trust had tried to hide; the external report that had identified the systemic failures within the Trust's senior management was published online and in the national press eight months after the Trust had received it. The ensuing media attention focused entirely on the Trust's cover up of the events at the SARC and its failure to disclose the report until legally obliged to do so. The Trust's response pointed out that staff had been sacked and the service taken over by another Trust. It overlooked its own role in creating and maintaining the impotent structure that had allowed such events to happen.

John Steiner's (1985) work on Oedipus seems pertinent here. He considered the story of Oedipus as one example "in which we seem to have access to reality but chose to ignore it because it proves convenient to do so" and refers to this as "turning a blind eye" (p. 161). Similarly, the Trust was aware of the flaws within the SARC structure but appeared to find it convenient not to move to rectify this. The three managers at the SARC had repeatedly informed the Trust senior managers that the structure and systems at the service were not fit for purpose and that intervention was needed to avoid a major failure. Steiner considers the conscious and unconscious levels of knowledge and remarks that "At one extreme we are dealing with simple fraud where all the facts are not only accessible but have led to a conclusion which is then knowingly evaded" (p. 161). The external review had access to the same information as the Trust and did not hesitate to conclude that the failures were systemic rather than individual.

The role of the police in the unfolding of this failure could be likened to what Steiner (1985) describes as the second factor in "the creation of such illusory worlds where we believe something against the evidence of our senses because it suits us to do so, and that is the factor of collusion. *A cover-up requires conspirators who agree either covertly or tacitly to collaborate*" (p. 170; emphasis added). It is my hypothesis that just as the Trust found it convenient to ignore its responsibility for the systemic flaws in the SARC service, so did the police find advantages in overlooking the SARC's difficulty in managing the non-police forensic samples. The same journalist used FOI requests to reveal a significant decrease in the number of rape allegations put forward to the CPS for a charging decision, while a report by Her Majesty's Inspectorate of Constabulary (HMIC) uncovered a number of rape allegations that the police had chosen not to record as crimes at all. While both of these issues covered police forces across the country, they were particularly prevalent in the city where the SARC was located. My hypothesis is that an emphasis on performance metrics within police culture fostered an environment where officers sought to sidestep the challenging reality of supporting a rape victim through the lengthy process of reporting and, instead, created an illusory option of "non-police referrals" which shifted responsibility for victim management from the police to SARC staff. Since publication of the external report would bring into the open the police failure to collect forensic samples or to report on forensic results, it can be argued that it suited the police force to collude with the Trust in "turning a blind eye" to it and covering up the report.

The final decision to withdraw from the Employment Tribunal owed much to a deeper understanding of what had motivated the claim in the first place. Grosz (2014) writes "Anyone can become paranoid, that is, develop an irrational fantasy of being betrayed, mocked, exploited or harmed—but we are more likely to become paranoid if we are insecure, disconnected, alone. Above all, paranoid fantasies are a response to the feeling that we are being treated with indifference" (p. 82). Having been off work for an extended period of time, I had become isolated and disconnected, which made me struggle to recognize the Trust's behaviour towards me as indifference. Reconnecting through my involvement with the

Tavistock Institute and finally returning to work allowed me to develop a new perspective in which it was possible to acknowledge indifference without losing myself.

Conclusion

Our main point of theoretical importance, and of relevance for the *social systems as a defence against anxiety* construct, is our understanding of the treatment of the SARC, of the SARC managers and the Tavistock Institute as a projection of the anxieties evoked by the primary task (Shapiro & Carr, 1991) of the organization (coping with the effects of sexual violence), and the failure to contain or process these primary issues and anxieties within the social system. By accepting the SARC within its jurisdiction, the Trust should have been aware of an inherent risk to the organization of this task and, in particular, of the potential for management failures.

Our work with the SARC managers and the managers of the Trust was to set out and demonstrate the relevance of the "anxiety" thesis and to show how powerfully it explained an evolving catastrophic development. We urged a greater focus on the role of unconscious defences and their enactment, and we demonstrated that the latter were indeed going on and that these ideas captured the meaning of it in beneficial ways. We focused on the particularity of the anxieties that aroused the specific defences that are relied on to cope with them, such as suppression, denial, and projection, when working with the consequences of sexual violence upon weak and unprotected members of society. Sexual scapegoating of female patients had become translated unconsciously into sexual scapegoating of the SARC's all-female leadership and all-female staff. It seemed that women had to be made into victims socially, institutionally, and individually.

This chapter has a more obviously central theoretical purpose and tries to set out its understanding in a way that might help all the parties better understand what had taken place. In the events that unfolded, it should have been important to downplay the implications of blame, even if blame might have seemed to be justified. We need to acknowledge that inevitably partisan feelings do get stimulated in an environment of acts of violence and injustice, as a consequence of the emotions that this work involves, but we need to try to get beyond these and try to understand the situation and its passions as a whole, explaining what was happening to everyone involved. An element of critique can hardly be avoided, given what happened, but our emphasis is upon understanding the unconscious effects of working in situations of violence and retribution.

Acknowledgements

The work with the SARC was a team effort. I am grateful to my two colleagues, Eliat Aram and Camilla Child, for their compassion and insight into the unfolding drama of an organizational implosion and its effects on the people in it. It is almost impossible to appreciate the on-going trauma that my client, Veronica, and her colleagues suffered during that time. I was impressed with her resilience, honesty, and professionalism as she fought her way through the nightmare and stayed the course.

CHAPTER ELEVEN

Running the gauntlet of institutional defence: from the prison gate to the hospital wing

Anne Zachary

very institution builds its own characteristic defences. This is, of course, well documented by Isabel Menzies Lyth, whose work is the basis of our book, in her selected essays, *Containing Anxiety in Institutions* (1988). She undertook this ground-breaking work in hospitals, focused on the work of the nurses, having been brought in to investigate why they were leaving the profession soon after training (1960).

Menzies Lyth understood the particular stress on nurses of being so close up to the patient. In their day-to-day work, they can expect to have extremely close physical contact with the patients (washing and dressing) and to encounter severe illness, major suffering, and subsequent disturbed or regressed behaviour. This situation undermines their own defences in the same way that mothers caring for small children are put in touch with their own infantile defences and yet have to maintain their adult position.

There are many ways in which, in order to carry on, these defences—many of them unhealthy in themselves—are strengthened. This includes institutional defences as well as individual ones, and Menzies Lyth approached her work diagnostically, picking out "the problem of student-nurse allocation as a presenting symptom" (1960/1988, p. 45). The student nurses, as in the other professions such as medicine, or even involving those not yet embarked upon training (nowadays known as

Health Care Assistants), are thrust into the frontline in mental health, often locked into the intensive care with very disturbed patients for hours on end. The most disturbed are looked after by the least trained. Meanwhile, the senior staff remain office-bound, metaphorically locked to their computers, "organizing" things. This, together with reduced staff numbers, was part of the tragedy of Stafford Hospital (Francis, 2013) when 1,200 patients died, seemingly of neglect (for more on this, see chapter 8, this volume). Menzies Lyth could diagnose and understand the problem, but it can still happen. Reflective practice with staff groups is offered widely now but is not always taken up. There is resistance to change, which only reinforces the defences.

Menzies Lyth takes her ideas about hospitals from social organizations in general. She says that,

> In developing a structure, culture and mode of functioning, a social organisation is influenced by . . . the primary task. . . . The technologies available for performing that task; and the needs of the members of the organisation for social and psychological satisfaction and above all, for support in the task of dealing with anxiety. . . . [This] leads to the development of socially structured defence mechanisms which appear as elements in the organisation's structure, culture and mode of functioning. [1960/1988, p. 50]

She acknowledges Jaques (1955) for first using the term "social defences" in industrial organizations.

Menzies Lyth's conclusion was that

> the social defence system represented the institutionalisation of very primitive psychic defence mechanisms, a main characteristic of which is that they facilitate the evasion of anxiety but contribute little to its true modification and reduction. [1960/1988, p. 77]

In this chapter I describe two visits to a prison in order to carry out assessments for the court. I want to explore in these descriptions how I think both the settings I was visiting and my own response to them were affected by the context of severe mental illness as well as a perverse element, which I believe is liable to pervade many aspects of these environments. I try to show how the environment of mental ill-health, especially when it also has the additional dimension of violence and perversion associated with forensic psychiatry, can impact on all those involved with it, including oneself. I hope to show that it can be difficult to retain a clear orientation, and to know what is happening, in apparently simple situations in which no explosive incidents take place. I also hope to show from my experience that the process of reflection and understanding, as practised by Menzies Lyth (and others), can make a difference and offer much support.

But first I want to give some background to how I gained my particular experience of this field and learned a way of working, which then informs the way in which I would go about even such an apparently limited task as making two assessment visits to patients. I realize that someone else going to do assessments like these might not notice all the things I found myself aware of and now feel compelled to write about. But I was schooled in a certain method advocated by Menzies Lyth and developed to the full, originally and in his own way, by Tom Main (1957) at the Cassel Hospital. This was where later I did my NHS training in psychotherapy concurrently with training at the Institute of Psychoanalysis. This method is formally documented by Hinshelwood and Skogstad in *Observing Organizations* (2000). I worked at the Cassel for three and a half years during the 1980s (mostly on the Families Unit[1] with Roger Kennedy). The enduring impact of this experience makes it seem as if it had been for a lot longer. Young adults and families who had broken down were admitted to different units and nursed and observed, with a focus on the relationships that developed between patients and staff. What was seen to be really important was the effect of these relationships with patients on those between the staff members themselves. It was seen that staff responses tended to "mirror" the patients' pathology. All these relationships were then studied with the help of individual and group therapy, individual and group supervision, and a variety of other formal and informal structures, notably nurse–therapist supervision (Tischler & Heymans, 1986). The aim was to eventually modify the conflicts that had arisen in staff relationships, with the aim of then indirectly resolving the patients' breakdowns that had brought them into hospital. Our experience was that if the staff could work through their differences, then the patients tended to improve. All this was based centrally on an awareness of the countertransference and a commitment to make use of it as a resource for understanding.

I became so immersed in this model of working at the Cassel that it felt as if I could stay there forever. I took my chances in the highly competitive round of consultant job-appointment committees. But to my knowledge, the Cassel had never had a female consultant, and only now in 2014, nearly 30 years later, has it appointed one.[2] Is this some recompense? Was I set free? These are questions to which there are no real answers. Life occurs as it does. My training analyst said to me, "You would have sold your soul . . .".

Instead of staying at the Cassel, I spent my consultant career at the Portman Clinic, which is renowned for treating violence and perversion. Equally fascinating and equally privileged psychoanalytically, the Portman is an outpatient clinic and therefore very different from the Cassel Hospital. Unfortunately, the study of the effect of the patients' dynamics on staff relationships, which I had learned at the Cassel and had sought to introduce as an approach at the Portman, was not felt to be a very welcome idea. My wanting to continue to think in these terms, which led to my putting forward suggestions, was met with defensive responses. These included, "You can't blame the patients", although, of course, the idea that the patients' states of mind might be having profound effects on those of the staff was not an attribution of blame, merely a description of psychological reality. I found that staff relationships were often very very difficult, and it is only now, having retired from the NHS, that it has felt possible for me to acknowledge in personal terms at an individual level the sadness about the damage that the pervasive atmosphere of perversion could do to working relationships. An example of what could happen is the sadomasochistic timing of communications, verbal or especially written, which could occur just before the weekend and therefore had to be carried home to smoulder or fuel anxiety until the following week. (Living south of the river, I learned to take a deep breath on the bridge and try to leave all thought of whatever the latest crisis of feeling was on the northern bank. That, followed by a stiff gin and tonic on arrival home could often do the trick.) I remember the late Harry Karnac coming into the Clinic for a period of time to help with some research after he retired. He named the Clinic "The Slaveship". This captured helpfully how hard everyone worked but also how badly people could treat each other. At one stage, further influenced by anxiety-provoking managerial changes, relationships among the staff became so difficult that Isobel Menzies Lyth herself was asked to come and conduct a consultation. One important helpful thing that emerged was that we had to face up to the reality that there were not "good" and "bad" members of staff, but that we were all in the same quagmire of violence and perversion together.

There was naturally a strong forensic context to much of the work carried out at the Portman, and there was always a pull away from the psychoanalytic framework of perversion to the more practical label of "forensic". The pull was from the "reality third", the Law, which inevitably skewed the transference–countertransference couple. Obviously, violence, much perversion, and, in those days before the new Millennium, some aspects of homosexuality were against the law, so there was a constant political/ideological tension. But on the other hand, a psychoanalytic approach was valued in the wider field, and so throughout my career at the Portman I was seconded at different times to various more secure institutions, two medium-secure hospital units,[3] and one of the three high-secure Special Hospitals. This was important, too, in terms of professional development, to gain experience in the whole spectrum of intensity of crime, violence, and perversion and not just where these things could be managed at an outpatient level. Also, assessments were often requested by prisons, usually assessment of prisoners who were, or who had become, mentally ill on remand. So I come now to the two prison assessments I want to describe, which took place at the same prison nearly four years apart. (This prison had a category A wing, so security was very high.)

I have noticed that within the secure system the intensity of the institutional defences is noticeably different at each increasing level of security. This is not surprising, given that the level of pathology and disturbance and the risk of acting out of the inmates is also generally increased. In the way I have already described in the hospital setting, the level of pathology in prison frames and then emotionally affects the quality of the relationships between staff, including with visiting staff. There are nursing staff in both secure hospital and prison settings. Secure hospitals are an integrated part of the NHS, but the prisons are still in the endless process of becoming incorporated into the NHS and are managed by the separate and more disparate system of the Prison Medical Service. Current good practice is that there are seconded individuals with NHS appointments who consult to the Prison Medical Service. More used to high-security hospital care myself, I describe below the impact upon me of a visit to a top-security prison. My focus here is on the journey from the prison gate to a patient on the hospital wing, rather than on the interview with the patient.

The experience of going to work in a secure hospital rather spoilt my experience of that prelude to a holiday abroad when the passage through airport security has to be endured, but when one is relaxed and has positive feelings of excitement and expectancy. Instead, going through not-dissimilar security procedures at work now made going on holiday feel like going to work until later in the process. At work,

depending on the degree of alert prevailing at the time, there was camaraderie and no need usually to remove one's shoes. No mobile phones,
no knives (which staff might like to bring with their lunch), were
allowed—the usual thing. I could never quite understand why, when
it rained, staff were simply allowed to keep umbrellas of every shape
and pointedness with them. Although this was practically understandable, since the hospital buildings were spread out and staff had to walk
distances between them, unconsciously, it completely undermined the
whole security system.

Visit 1

A patient who was attending a therapy group at the Portman Clinic
then reoffended and was held on remand at the prison with the category A wing. Though he was on the local wing, the highest levels
of security were maintained for all visitors. He was not my patient,
but I was the case manager at the Portman and so knew his case. I
had met him outside the group for assessment on several occasions.
In this capacity I was required to prepare his court report, so one
Wednesday afternoon I went to visit him. He was brought from his
own wing to the hospital wing for the assessment.

We are all accustomed to the transformation from one's day-to-day
life into one's professional persona. This often begins with a check-
list before leaving home—watch, keys, money, ticket, phone, and so
on. It is disconcerting to have all these (apart from a pen and paper
and essential paperwork) removed at the "airport-like" security
entrance of a category A prison. (Another anomaly surrounded the
wearing of belts, which men are asked to remove at the airport. In
hospital and prison, all permanent staff are issued with keys and a
regulation thick leather belt if they don't have one.) One's belong-
ings are all stowed away securely in a personal locker, rather like at
a visit to the swimming pool.

On the day I visited maybe it was a bad day or a "high alert" day,
but before this "professional undressing" happened I was kept
waiting for more than half an hour, receiving absolutely no eye
contact from the desk even if I went to remind them of my presence. I noticed that there was also no eye contact taking place
between the staff. This situation persisted throughout my eventual
passage through the system until at last I arrived at the hospital

wing to which the patient had also been brought. Stripped and "deprofessionalized" of my usual aids but especially of my watch (and the clock on the wall in the hospital room had stopped), I felt completely disarmed, disorientated. On the way through various locked doors, the prison officer who had finally come to collect me would meet other members of staff and stop to exchange information. Even in that almost social setting, there was no eye contact between them, or with me. This mutual avoidance was between men and women alike. (Perhaps I thought the women would be more empathic?) This was then taken to the extreme at one of the internal gates where we had to report to a room through a window that was at waist level so that the gatekeeper could not see who we were, nor we them. There was just a paper to be marked. I have only ever seen this system before in a highly reactionary religious institution. There, women served meals to the men, from an adjoining building, through a waist-high hatch; this way, they could not see each other's faces, the aim being, presumably, to attempt to reduce sexual temptation. In the prison, sexualized behaviour in the part-object act of cottaging comes to mind. At the prison, it was as if the institution required such a perverse system of relating in order to maintain enough resilience for staff to tolerate being there. The other dynamic is that in hospital the staff are there to help. While this is also to a degree the case in prison, the latter is primarily a penal institution, and "helping" is not its main function or purpose. I was there to try to establish mitigating circumstances around the patient's wrongdoing, to emphasize that though he had re-offended he was currently in treatment which might at this stage inadvertently undermine his defences and lead to another misdemeanour (he was an exhibitionist). I felt punished even for having the idea that I could help. I was being inaugurated in depersonalization, kept waiting, deprived of knowing the time, only my notes and a pen left to enable me to function. (A pen is the implement commonly used as a weapon in prison, probably because it is all that prisoners have left to use.) Then the biggest challenge was for me not to finally greet the patient as a familiar face in a hostile environment—as if I were no longer the doctor and he the patient, that all-important professional boundary in the group, at the Clinic, but now violated as we found ourselves thrown together elsewhere. And, of course, he greeted me, obviously relieved to see me but just a little too warmly, knowing that wrong-footing me was an option, because I was less adjusted than he was to the system, and he was always looking for another opportunity to pervert the appropriate relationship with the object.

Visit 2

After I had decided to write about that visit which took place four years ago, as an illustration of institutional defence, I was by chance asked to go back to the same prison recently to see another patient, this time someone I had not met before. I can add a contrasting experience that may in some ways seem to undermine the significance of my previous experience but, because it says something positive about the institution, is nevertheless worth describing.

Of course, I had been there before, and such familiarity with a setting always makes for a 95% improvement. On this occasion, rather than an ordinary kind of day it was a particularly beautiful day. I felt apprehensive and, to enhance my morale, I took a taxi from the station instead of the local bus, which I knew from my previous visit meandered through a sink estate. I had some difficulty finding the correct entrance from the car park where I was dropped and, seeing signs of life through a window, went to ask where it was. A group of women were preparing food. They opened the door and invited me in. I had happened upon the visitors' café and had entered through the kitchen! There was time to have a cup of tea before they directed me to the main gate. This time, staff were friendly throughout, and there was no longer a problem of lack of eye contact. I was kept at a halfway house during my journey to the patient, and the prison officer on duty on that gate, who seemed vulnerable himself in that he had something like cerebral palsy, was friendly and spontaneously kept in touch with me during the wait. His clock was functioning.

While I was waiting, I reflected on the difference between my experiences. Perhaps the level of alert on this particular day was lower. But then, so much has to do with projection. How much of my previous experience was to do with me? I realized that perhaps I had changed. I had retired from the system, was no longer such a part of the extended system. I could be more objective, less affected by the institution. I was not visiting a man with a perversion whom I already knew. In fact, this patient was a man whose perversion appeared to have broken down into an acute psychosis, something that can happen when someone is kept in detention when his or her previously perverse and defensive practices have had to be given up or have become more difficult to maintain. This patient was in no condition to seek gratification out of my disorientation (less this time) and visitor status. He was being nursed on the hospital wing and needed to be transferred to hospital, needing my help to bring this about. Alternatively, as I had to include as a possibility in my report, did the particularly conscientious efforts of the staff to consult with me about how ill they thought the mute and food-refusing patient was mean that no one wanted to care for him (as a massive drain on scarce resources and a threat to staff psychic equilibrium) and that a collusive transfer out of the prison now suited them as much as him? In fact, I heard later that he was indeed transferred to my own high-secure hospital a month or so later after he had received formal Mental Health Act assessment and sectioning (Section 48).

How can one explain the differences between these two experiences of apparently quite similar visits to the same secure prison environment? I encountered some real differences in the setting, comparing the degree of incivility and cut-offness during the first experience with the much friendlier atmosphere of the second. My greater orientation once inside having been there before and the fact that I had entered benignly via the kitchen of the visitors' café on the second occasion explains some of this, but not all, since even the routine passages through security were less hostile and negative. I did not simply imagine these differences, or project my own anxious states of mind on to the environment. But on the other hand, it might not be stretching a point to suggest that I was in a different state of mind too. The theory of observing institutions allows for the possibility that my observations in the intervening time had made a difference to me and to those with whom I came into contact. My being able to reflect on the defensiveness of the staff as their way of dealing with the intensity of the pathology of the inmates may have enabled a shift to occur between one visit and another. This was not one of those changes that arises from deliberately shared observations and their processing, as within the Cassel structures. If a shift had occurred, it was at a more unconscious level where, if someone understands a difficult situation, then some improvement can come about, which is very much a Winnicottian idea. I would even dare to think that, at this same level, my training at the Cassel had contributed to some attenuation of the Portman's difficulties in its staff relationships.

I would also like to think, though, that perhaps in the four-year interval between my two visits the character of the penal institution had shifted, that youth, better training, and a change in politics meant that relating could now be more direct, more positive, more humane. Menzies Lyth's work lives on but requires constant attention.

Notes

1. The Families Unit at the Cassel is discussed in Heymans, Kennedy, & Tischler (1986).

2. Jennifer Johns (personal communication) said that in the very early days Tom Main had a most competent female deputy.

3. There is one of these in each geographical region (Butler Report, 1975).

PART III

The private sector

CHAPTER TWELVE

Extreme work environments: beyond anxiety and social defence

Larry Hirschhorn & Sharon Horowitz

"The secret for harvesting from existence the greatest fruitfulness and greatest enjoyment is—to live dangerously."

Nietzsche

The Tavistock framework

We have inherited a generative framework from our Tavistock predecessors for understanding the psychology of work. Thinking within this framework we can say that any work worth its salt—which means it entails significant risk—stimulates anxiety. For example, when a person works alone, the anxiety may be a prod to good performance. Consider, for example, the stage fright a person feels before she is about to address a large audience. This feeling can induce a state of high arousal, enabling her to be attentive to all the signals in her surroundings. If, however, at the moment she begins her talk, she remains anxious, her performance may be impaired—for example, she will forget her opening lines. But there is a third alternative. She may feel sufficiently anxious days before she is supposed to speak and, if unable to contain her anxiety, may rehearse carelessly by ignoring the difficult spots in her speech. In this last case, we say that she has developed a defence against the anticipatory anxiety. The defence takes the form of a detrimental practice: ignoring difficult spots.

Isabel Menzies Lyth suggested, however, that if people worked together to execute a shared task, they could develop a group-level defence that operates in just the same way. Thus, for example, if a group of executives use a "concurrence chain" to make decisions, so that no decision is made until everyone signs off on it, this frees up each executive from having to make the decision alone. In this way, each executive avoids the anxiety associated with making high-risk decisions for which he or she would be singularly accountable. But just as individual defences can impair performance, the concurrence chain will slow down decision-making or result in unimaginative decisions.

Using this framework, we can work backwards from a symptom of poor performance to ferret out the underlying risk that creates the uncontained anxiety. This becomes a method for diagnosing poor performance. We can then ask how the experience of risk can be managed more effectively—for example, do people need more training, better tools, a more conducive organizational structure, or a more effective leader?

This is a powerful diagnostic framework, but is it adequate to understanding much of the work experience today? What if we posited that people at work enjoy risk, that they willingly approach situations of psychological danger (for example, when their reputation or money is on the line), and that these high arousal experiences are pleasurable. How would we—and, in fact, should we—amend our framework?

These are not simply theoretical questions. Decades ago Eric Trist and Fred Emery, also from the Tavistock, suggested that the advanced economies of the Western world were entering a period of what they called "turbulence". The executives of organizations facing turbulent settings could not rely on inherited assumptions or practices that once made their organizations successful. They had to lean into risk. Does, perhaps, the resurgence of entrepreneurship in the economy and its salience as a cultural symbol mean that we are building a business culture that embraces risk and values danger?

This hypothesis is the basis for our chapter.

A consulting case

Consider the following case. An investment firm that owned and invested in a hedge fund, among other ventures, called upon co-author of this chapter Sharon Horowitz (henceforth S.H.), to provide consultation. The co-leads and portfolio managers of the fund, Bob and Jim, were at an impasse. Started in 2005, the fund was very successful for its first five years, and at one point had just under a billion dollars of assets under management. But starting in mid-2009, its performance faltered and investors were unhappy.

Bob and Jim could barely sit in the same room together and had no vehicle through which they could resolve their differences. At one critical meeting prior to S.H.'s introduction to the fund, Bob, who was the junior in terms of age and investing experience, proposed to Jim that he [Bob] take over the fund for a temporary period in order to rescue it. In support of his argument, he presented some data to indicate that his performance had been superior to Jim's over the last few years. As Jim reports it, Bob told him, "I think I have earned the right to run this business. I will run it for a few months and turn it around and then you can have it back." Jim was shocked and, as he termed it, he felt "betrayed", since in the past they had never dissected each other's performance. "Bob comes in with a stack of paper. He says, 'This is my performance.' I was shocked. My reaction was not to take it (the stack). I knew it was over. That is a cardinal sin in a partnership. To come in and say, 'this is my performance.' We never ran the portfolio like that."

In describing this same set of events, Bob recalls the urgency he felt. "I was crawling out of my skin. I felt like I was trying to shake people. 'What we are doing does not work. I will show you the numbers. Here are the numbers. Here is where they were prior to March of '09, here is what worked and is not working for the last couple of years.'" But he felt no one was listening.

The fund ultimately shut down, ironically in part because Don, the head of the investment firm, had called upon S.H. for consultation. She interviewed Bob and Jim and made many attempts to find a workable solution. But Bob believed strongly in his own new investment thesis— "I have never been more certain than anything in my life"—while Jim could not possibly agree to let him implement it.

Don and S.H. together realized how serious the impasse was. As a result, Don wanted to withdraw his own capital from the fund. This now meant that the co-leads' impasse was in legal terms a "disclosable event", which all investors were entitled to know about. And, once informed, they too would most probably withdraw their money. So to prevent a run on the fund and damage to the investment firm's reputation, as well as to preserve his own capital, Don shut the hedge fund down. As S.H. describes it, "I too felt under extreme pressure— there was no time. My ability as a professional to help was handcuffed because of these other interdependent variables. It was a perfect storm. And I kept thinking, both partners are right, and they both represent a piece of wisdom of the marketplace and if only there had been time to work it through . . . "

We can think of this story as the familiar one of an organization that breaks apart under the stress of poor performance. But we propose considering this story in a different, if complementary, light. We posit that hedge-fund owners and managers work in "extreme environments" where danger and threats are both exciting and nerve-wracking. Extreme work environments, we suggest, are an adaptive response to turbulence. In this chapter, we suggest that we can gain additional insight and develop more effective consultation methods if we understand the psychodynamics of such extreme settings—what makes them tick, and when and why they break down. Our case study indicates that our inherited framework for thinking about the psycho-dynamics of organizations—the interplay between work, anxiety, and social defence—is not adequate for an age of turbulence. Instead, we should build one based on the interplay of danger, excitement, and protective frames.

This chapter is divided into seven sections. In the first, we define an extreme work environment and link this definition to the rise of extreme sports. In the second, we examine the links between extreme sports, feelings of excitement, and the concept of the "sublime". In the third, we describe the process of the fund's failure and the ensuing rup-ture between Bob and Jim. In the fourth, we examine Michael Apter's (1992) idea of "protective frames", which enable people to experience danger as exciting rather than as threatening. We highlight three protec-tive frames that Bob and Jim drew upon: the market as a game, process over results, and the magical pair. In the fifth, we describe the collapse of the fund in terms of the loss of these protective frames. We suggest that with the frames lost, anxiety replaced excitement and, as a result, both Bob and Jim may have acted out. In the sixth, we propose a new model for linking risk, excitement, and protective frames. In the last section, we summarize our argument.

Extreme work and extreme sports

We define an extreme work environment as a setting in which the stakes are great, the velocity of decisions and their consequences are high, bad decisions are often irreversible, and regularities that govern a market or setting are short-lived. Indeed, this could be one definition of a "turbulent market", a setting that many believe shapes the rhythm of enterprise in a wide range of industries. Hedge-fund owners often face this kind of setting and also confront circumstances that intensify the experience of extremes. We suggest that such settings are becoming more common.

For example, while passive investors, such as those who invest in index funds, gain or lose money based on the rise and fall of the market overall, hedge-fund owners also want to make money in bad markets while extracting extra profits in good ones. In the parlance of Wall Street, they are after "alpha" returns— that is, returns in excess of what a passive investor would normally earn. Moreover, they want *absolute* returns—that is, returns that are their own yardstick, rather than relative to the performance of some index or average, like the S&P 500 or Down Jones. While everyone can profit simultaneously from a rising market, getting what are called, "beta" returns, securing "alpha" means essentially taking money from another trader or inves- tor. Investing becomes a zero-sum game and is thus more harsh and unforgiving. As Jim notes, "By and large, you find smarter guys in the hedge-fund world, because you have to deal with multiple variables. The requirement to be both long and short gives you a counterfactual perspective in everything you are doing. You have to keep in mind different variables . . . you are going to attract people who are going to kill to make the money." This is one reason that investors and traders are so tempted to look for short-cuts by drawing on inside information, even if it means violating the law.

Describing the experience of extremes, Jim notes that hedge-fund trading can be "a lightning bolt to your stress response mechanisms. Because every day you get a cortisol shot. There is all this looking at screens and getting this feedback stuff. You get into that stress—you no longer control your day. The screen determines your day. You are looking at the screen rather than doing your work." Bob, by contrast, highlights the pleasure of working in such an extreme setting: "What is fun and intrinsically rewarding is when you are right on a short. It is the best feeling, because of what all these other people were saying. And then you can say, 'I was right and you were wrong' and that is a great high. It is very addictive."

We are drawn to this concept of the extreme work environment for another reason. Paralleling the rise of turbulent markets, extreme sports, such as skydiving, rock climbing, extreme biking, hang-gliding, base- jumping, skateboarding, and surf-boarding, have all grown in popu- larity. As one author notes, "Over the past two decades, participation rates in extreme sports have grown exponentially, far outstripping the growth rates of any other sporting activity" (Brymer, 2010, p. 219).

Another notes that this increase "has been shown not to be just a 'flash in the pan', but a 'sign of the times'" (Brymer & Gray, 2009, p. 136). One common proposition is that extreme sports have grown in popularity because day-to-day life is increasingly safe. As one researcher writes, "Life in modern society is too predictable, too civil and too safe. Sports and especially risk sports present us with manufactured risks that are actually designed in such a way as to preserve natural dangers or build new ones" (Breivik, 2007a, p. 20).

We want to propose a different explanation. Sports and games express aspects of the wider culture that compel our attention. They provide venues within which wider cultural challenges can be "played with" and where experiments are possible. In this sense, extreme sports, we propose, are a sign of the times insofar as they share features of the turbulent environment. After all, extreme-sport participants face significant risks, surprise is likely, speed is at a premium, and obstacles are not always predictable. The culture of participation in extreme sports in this sense provides some clues about how the wider society is responding to turbulence.

Following this line of thought, it is striking that researchers who study extreme sports emphasize the experience of freedom they create, and the manner in which participants often cultivate their image as deviants. One researcher reports that climbers say that "climbing provides an opportunity to escape from the perceived mundaneness and petty rules of day to day life. It offers a degree of freedom from the externally imposed duties and expectations that constrain us in societal life, freedom to pursue our own personal projects in a way unfettered by those constraints" (Ebert & Robertson, 2007, p. 59). Similarly, one researcher who interviewed extreme bikers noted that "one of the most passionate points that riders stated, regarding their ownership of their own ramps and jumps on a vacant lot, was that they were in charge of themselves, and that adult intrusions were not present. Skaters of all kinds, snowboarders, riders . . . adhere to these philosophical tenets at one time or another" (Ilundain-Agurruza, 2007, p. 129). Another scholar noted that "Law is an especially salient example of what summiteers seek to escape in climbing. Lawyers and law bring complex entanglements with conflicts of interest and with authorities. Mountains are attractive because they call on people to act directly rather than through the law and because they appear to be relatively unregulated spaces", something, the author notes, "that is becoming far less true"(Simon, 2002, p. 191).

We suggest that extreme sports in this sense represent a kind of entrepreneurialism in which risk is embraced and freedom of manoeuvre is valued. People reject cautiousness, as if an alien authority had imposed it. It is in this sense anti-bureaucratic. Indeed, it emerged historically as a cultural polemic against organized sports and games, through which adults supervised young people. In this way, it shares some similarity with painting graffiti on walls and buildings.

Lacan's idea of "jouissance" bears a family resemblance to this idea. In contesting an argument that the philosopher Immanuel Kant made, Lacan suggests that, if given the chance, a man may very well have sex with a woman he desires the most, even if it meant sure death.[1] In other words, jouissance suggests that sometimes we may reject the rational calculus of pleasure and pain and, instead, live dangerously by throwing caution to the wind. Since many people believe, reasonably, that entrepreneurial conduct is one adaptive response to turbulence, it is sensible to suppose that extreme sports is sustained partly because it has become a model, a psychosocial zone of preparation, for the world of work. Of course, we recognize that there are limits to this analogy. Most importantly, many extreme sports are not team sports, in contrast to work settings, where people work in groups. But despite this limitation, we think the psychology of extreme sports can provide us with needed insight into extreme work settings.

Extreme sports, excitement, and the sublime

One factor that makes extremes sports compelling is that they are exciting. Participants are not just in it for the thrills, but excitement certainly ranks high as a reason to participate. In a survey of extreme sport participants, a researcher reports that 56% cited its thrill, 51% its immediate fun, and 45% the experience of serious achievement it provides (survey participants could give multiple motives) (Kerr & Mackenzie, 2012, p. 650). This may seem obvious, but to some degree it goes against the grain of our typical psychodynamic theorizing, wherein we privilege the concept of defences against anxiety. Extreme sports can be dangerous; indeed, danger is the price one pays to feel excited. So within our customary frame of thinking, the idea that people court danger to feel excitement seems contradictory.

There are two routes out of this quandary. The traditional psychoanalytic explanation is to discount the excitement and emphasize instead the sense of mastery the sport provides. This brings us closer to Freud's idea that people will often entertain significant pain if they can relive and therefore master the situation that gave rise to the pain in the first place (Freud, 1920g). This is why he suggested people might relive a trauma in their own minds. In this sense, we could say that the extreme sports participant is doing nothing but mastering a prior sense of injury or trauma and is repeatedly doing so. She confronts the danger in order to conquer it. But because the danger may have psychosocial origins—for example, she was traumatized as an infant as a result of a long hospital stay—she can never really undo the past. But she will continue to try. Balint in his book *Thrills and Regressions* (1959), which has many novel ideas, nonetheless takes just this approach; hence his focus on regression.

But we posit that this approach violates the essential common-sense meaning of excitement and may block us from understanding the widest range of human emotions. For example, researchers who looked at scientists living in camps in the Antarctica found that they simply could not understand the scientists' motives using what they called a "negative psychology". Such a psychology "does not address the dedication to making all the needed preparations that lead to the tired but confident state of some polar crew members even before their mission begins, or the similar dedication to the mission that leads crew members to sacrifice free time or sleep time in order to put in extra work" (Suedfeld, 2001, p. 23).

"Approaching the study of behavior from a positive orientation", the author proposes that

> researchers could measure the degree to which crew members find in their own sojourn an opportunity to stretch themselves, to be all that they can be; to enjoy the close camaraderie of like-minded others; to feel the exhilaration of looking out at a vast Antarctic ice field, to lose themselves in the beauty of the landscape or the rhythm of their work; to enjoy both the novelty of the situation and its increasing familiarity; to structure and decorate the inside environment so as to make it homelike and cozy, not just cramped and crowded; to improvise creatively in solving unforeseen problems or in improving adequate features and making them superior; to work together in achieving something new and important, which none could achieve alone; to contemplate and reflect, and to come out with a new appreciation of values previously overlooked in the hurly- burly of modern technological society. [Suedfeld, 2001, p. 23]

In this regard Michael Apter, who presents an alternative conception in his book *The Dangerous Edge: The Psychology of Excitement* (1992), has

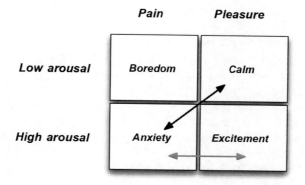

Figure 12.1.   Psychological states matrix (after Apter, 1992).

influenced our thinking. Like Freud, Apter highlights a pleasure–pain calculus to understand experience, but he adds a second independent dimension, which he calls arousal. This schema creates four psychological states, as shown by the 2 × 2 matrix in Figure 12.1

Anxiety and excitement are thus both states of high arousal. In traditional psychoanalytic thinking, we focus on the transformation of anxiety into calm, and vice versa. That is what we mean by the "containment of anxiety". But Apter invites us to focus on the transformation of anxiety into excitement, and vice versa. Accordingly, just as we use the concept of social defence to talk about containment, Apter presents the concept of a "protective frame", which in the face of danger prevents excitement from turning into anxiety. He likens the protective frame to a cage of a tiger. The tiger at first provokes anxiety, but if assured that it will be held in its cage, the vinegar of our anxiety—to use one of Freud's metaphors—is transformed into the wine of our excitement (Chamberlain, 2001, p. 106).

It is important to understand the phenomena of such excitement, for in the world of extreme sports we cannot reduce it to thrill. Thrill adequately describes the experience we might have on a roller-coaster. The simple act of falling, a feature many extreme sports induce, is sufficient. But in most extreme sports, with perhaps the exception of base-jumping, a sports person confronts danger and overcomes it by exercising discipline, developing skills and using good tools. The result might be termed a "sublimated" thrill, which opens up onto a range of other experiences—for example, awe at the power of the natural world, particularly the force of gravity, the appreciation of nature's beauty, the experience of sustained rhythm, and the total immersion in an experience.

One windsurfer, describing his experience, writes that, "I think everything is blocked out at that point, you're very single minded. Everything is happening so fast, but at the same it's kind of like slow motion, you're dropping down and there are so many situations coming at you, it seems like time has expanded. Time gets expanded and you're noticing little bits of kelp floating up the wave or people on the side of you. You tend to notice small things that seem to take a long time and you're adjusting to the situation all the time, you're changing the track of your board or setting an edge a little harder, to do the things that are going to take you out of that situation again" (Anderson, 2007, p. 73)

One researcher studying rock climbers argued that, "As a group they should not be seen so much as thrill seekers but as truth seekers. They climb not just for the adrenaline or exercise but also for the opportunity to gain insight into themselves and the world around them" (Breivik, 2007b, p. 173).

A hang-glider writes on a blog that, "for me hang gliding is the ultimate in achieving union with the forces of nature, immersion within them. Gravity, wind, lift, sink, these are all invisible and exploiting them to savor for a few minutes requires understanding of physics, sensory acuity, and various types of reasoning. . . . Unfettered movement in three dimension with only the sound of wind in the ears is fantastic. Flying close to hawks and eagles, flying with them, is beyond description."[2]

Indeed, researchers who studied the physiology of parachutists found that participants are most aroused before and after the jump and most calm during the jump. By displacing arousal, which is experienced as some combination of anxiety and excitement, to the beginning and the end, the skilled parachutist is calm when he most needs to be, during the jump itself (Epstein & Fenz, 1965). In this sense, the skilled parachutist foregoes some thrill, but in the exchange he gains other feelings, not only of mastery but, as we have seen in the case of the windsurfer and hang-glider, a sense of awe and an appreciation of beauty.

Sports psychologists reference the eighteenth- and nineteenth century concept of the "sublime" to understand these reports. The common-sense meaning of sublime today is something wonderful. But the eighteenth-century term evoked the idea of finding pleasure in something terrifying or dangerous. This idea is reflected in the concept of gothic fiction, with its mix of horror and romance: "The effect of Gothic fiction feeds on a pleasing sort of terror."[3]

Freud's concept of "sublimation" also bears some relationship to this idea as well. Because the sexual impulse is dangerous—it may lead to punishment—a person sublimates it. As a result, he re-finds its pleasure in something beautiful or awe-inspiring, such as a work of art. Thinking about extreme sports we say that a participant displaces and expresses thrill by experiencing beauty and awe. In either case, a person does not seek quiescence but, rather, arousal. Perhaps it is a measure of the difficulty we have today in parsing out excitement from anxiety that sports psychologists have drawn upon a three-century-old term.

J. Rande Howell, a psychologist of stock trading who posts articles on his website, writes that, "You can be passionate *about* trading, but you cannot be passionate *while* trading."[4] This is because the mind interprets uncertainty as fear, and fear overwhelms thoughtfulness. A trader in this way of thinking regulates emotions in order to convert feelings of uncertainty into thoughts about probability. As behavioural economists have demonstrated, thinking about and deciding with probabilities in mind is a highly unnatural state and requires training, discipline, and experience (Kahneman, 2013).

One result is that the pleasure gained from trading activity derives partly from gains in self-knowledge, truths about oneself—much as the researcher we quoted described rock climbers as people seeking insights into their own characters.

Howell in another lovely quote says that the, "Speed of life is much slower than the speed of trading", because, "you can sit in self-deception for a lifetime before the consequences show up and catch you. In trading, you have to face your dragons because they're now stalking you. You can't get away from them."[5]

Another client of S.H.'s described trading in this way in an email: "I love what it's like when you cut away all the layers of insulation, and just be in a less conscious and at the same time more conscious state. After all you don't know what's down deep unless you are willing to dig to the bottom of yourself. How many people ever get to see what's at the bottom of themselves?"

We can recognize in this rendering of experience the description of a state of mind in which a person feels more fully alive and real, precisely because they are walking up to fear and then regulating it with thought. This experience establishes the passion for trading much as, for example, a group relations aficionado experiences a passion for conferences precisely because they are painful.

There is also evidence that traders and investors experience something akin to the "sublime" when they talk about the "beauty of the market", a phrase one can search for readily and find on the web on numerous pages. Leo Melamed, one of the architects of the Chicago Mercantile Exchange, writes near the end of his autobiography the following:

> But the important effect of trading is that it keeps me linked to reality and truth. The beauty of markets, and for me their quintessential characteristic, is that they are the final determinant of veracity.
>
> Washington policy makers, Tokyo or Berlin ministers, officials of governments the world over can try to tell the world whatever they want, but the markets tell the world the truth . . . their opinion doesn't count a tinker's dam unless or until it is endorsed by the market. [Melamed, 1996, p. 436]

Another writer examining the rise and fall of the hedge fund Long Term Capital Management, writes, "There is no point in blaming the market if it is acting irrationally. The market is the sum total of everyone else in the world. Isn't it unlikely that everyone else in the world is irrational, and you are rational? And even if it is acting irrationally, there is nothing you can do about it. The market will do whatever it wants to do. It will not respect reality, knowledge, economics, ability, genius or anything. That is the beauty of the market."[6]

A trader discussing interest rate volatility wrote to S.H., "That's why I love the Market. It's always changing and you change with it or you get run over. It's as simple as that."

These quotes highlight the idea that the market is something apart, and something inexorable, and this is what makes it beautiful, even "when it hurts".

Falling apart

One important question is, when does a trader's or investor's relationship to the market as a sublime instrument break down, when does the market simply become dangerous? The case of Jim and Bob and the failure of their fund provide us with some insight. Before joining Jim, Bob was a political science professor with tenure at a prestigious university, but he found life in academia to be unchallenging and irritating. At the same time, his wife was very unhappy in her work and wanted to stay at home raising their children. In fact, she ultimately home-schooled them. So he quit academia and moved with his family to New York City, taking considerable risks. As he notes, "We became stress junkies to move up here sight unseen with the kids and no bank account—without a net." As we have noted, he joined Jim as a junior partner, in 2005, in a hedge fund owned by a larger investment firm. Jim himself had had a career in investing, but had taken off several years in mid-life to get a master's degree in philosophy.

They complemented each other well, Bob had a good grasp of macro-trends, and Jim was a master of the mechanics of trading and was an experienced stock-picker with an impressive track record. But as their shared interest in the world of theorizing suggests, they developed a special chemistry, based on their thoughtfulness and their capacity to connect the market with wider issues in politics and economics. In addition, Bob, a self-taught software programmer, understood the world of information technology. Don, the owner of the investment firm that housed the fund, loved talking with the two of them as they assessed market trends. They had exciting and thought-provoking conversations.

S.H. recalls how Don would find any occasion to join them in a discussion, even though their fund was one small part of the overall firm.

Bob, an astute reader of the intersection between markets, politics, and social policy, anticipated, as a few others did, the housing crash and in particular focused on the difficulty politicians and financiers would face in trying to recover from a financial meltdown. He notes, "I went from this secure job working as an idea person with Jim, to seeing how the world is coming unglued and how much money you could make with it ungluing. Now the risk genes kicked in. In fact I had zero experience. But I said 'Paris is burning' and let's make money! It was exciting. I thought I had figured out a puzzle."

They executed trades following Bob's insights and despite the crash in March of 2008 they were actually up 20% for the year. To succeed when so many others were failing was telling. Investors wanted in. By March of 2009, their assets under management grew close to a billion. With a management fee of 2%, typical for the industry, this meant that they were pulling in close to $20 million in fees.

Yet starting in March and continuing through to 2011 they faltered. As Jim reports, "We lost over half of our assets in six months in 2011." Two factors played a role. First, paradoxically, they suffered in what we might call the "soft" bull market that succeeded the crash. As Figure 12.2 shows,[7] the stock market has been rising since the crash and had nearly reached its pre-crash peak by the end of 2012.

This was the result of an unusual "one-off" situation. To save banks and prevent corporate bankruptcies, the Federal Reserve Bank flooded the markets with money, driving interest rates so far down that the stock market became one of the few vehicles through which

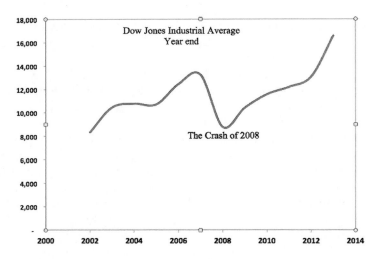

Figure 12.2.   Stock market trends, 2001 to 2012.

the investors could make money. In addition, this increase in price was based on unusually low volumes, indicating that many investors were willing to hold cash or very low interest bonds rather than risk trading in stocks.

As a result, as Jim pointed out, stock-picking became a futile exercise, because all stocks were going up and, as Jim adds, "the correlations went to 1 across asset classes". If assets move in the same direction, shorting becomes less profitable. In other words, it was no use being clever in such a beneficent market. A hedge fund could certainly profit from a rising market, but so could an index fund. Why would investors pay extra fees for a level of performance they could get by simply investing passively? As Jim notes, "What happened after 2008, what people did is they moved from one side of the boat to the other saying that there is no more fundamentals and stock-picking does not work."

An outcome, as Figure 12.3 shows,[8] was that between 2010 and 2012, long/short equity funds earned some of the lowest rates of return.

Jim experienced this development as oppressive, feeling that he was being called upon to achieve impossible performance targets: "There was an automatic tension that arose between how I thought I could make money and how I was being measured. If your performance turns down, the time period collapses on you. You are on the phone with clients and they are saying 'last month' and you already thinking,

I need to have an up month. Who runs money like that? I never did, it is stupid." While Jim characterizes the hedge-fund business in general as a "fast money business", he believes that investors traded using an even more compressed time horizon after 2008. "Everyone wants liquidity, no one wants to get caught in 2008. Investors are always ready to run. Everyone is managing money accordingly; the returns from managing money collapse."

Bob believes that in March of 2009 it was "as if someone flipped a switch in terms of our stock-picking. The stocks that Jim clung to diverged in a lot of characteristics from what our clients wanted. Jim stopped talking to clients for well over a year. And so the tension between believing in the long haul and therefore holding on to the stocks that you know well, versus responding to clients, grew. I too was getting pressure from the clients." Bob argued for a new strategy based on "macro" developments and the intersection of politics and economics. Jim reports that Bob said, "'I can trade the macro.' And we all said, 'You cannot. George Soros okay, he could do it, but it is too hard to do so consistently.' Bob would send emails quoting Steve Jobs. He really thought he was like Steve Jobs. That was weird stuff."

The growing conflict between Jim and Bob over strategy set the stage for their meeting in which Bob, describing his better performance,

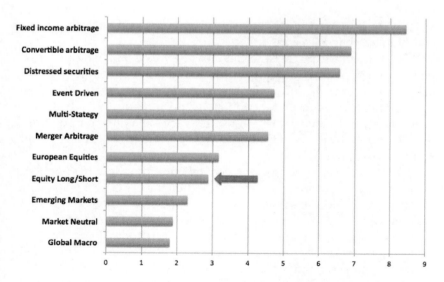

Figure 12.3.   Returns to different hedge-fund strategies, 2010 to 2012.

asked that he be allowed to run the fund. As we have seen, Jim felt betrayed. They faced an impasse, and as a result Don closed down the fund.

The three protective frames

As discussed, Apter suggests that people construct a protective frame in order to experience danger as excitement. They are drawn to danger, it is what makes them feel alive, but they need to be protected from it as well. A useful question to ask is, what protective frames do hedge-fund traders use, and what happens when these protective frames break down? We identify three frames that we think were operative in this case: the market as a puzzle or game; the reliance on process; and Bob and Jim as a magical pair.

The market as a game

Describing trading, Bob notes that, "What I think I am good at is figuring out the rules and playing the game at a micro level. The market is a puzzle and I am really good at it. It is all game play. It is very addictive. Whether you are long or short you are never proved completely wrong. You can always be right. One day you are feeling low and the next day you get that high. I think one of the parts about this is that you are staying in the game for the next. The market will open tomorrow and I have a chance to win."

He likens this experience to the pleasure he gets playing poker. "I played a lot of poker in college. Thank God internet-poker did not exist back then, because my life could have gone down a bad path if that had been available. It is absolutely addictive and it requires the same sort of on-the-fly risk management and numeracy—making computations quickly in your head—that trading does. If you are wired to enjoy poker you are wired to enjoy investing."

Bob likens losing one's perspective when trading to what happens in poker when a player "goes on tilt". "When the cards go against you, you bet crazy, and the same thing can happen with the market. That is what you have to watch out for." Indeed, one of the pleasures of trading, he argues, is that just as in a game, "You know if you are right or wrong every day." Consistent with Howell's notion that the speed of trading is faster than the speed of life, this is one explanation as to why Bob found academia frustrating. "One reason I could never stand academia is that you are never wrong and you're never right. And to be even kind of right, means your work is repeated enough and you're cited enough and that takes freaken years!"

Bob is also an aficionado of "game theory"—the mathematical description of how agents interact when each is advancing its own interests and cannot fully understand the motives of others. When he taught political science he developed a method for engaging students by having them play political "games" like "war games". Describing his teaching experience, he notes that, "It is difficult to describe the dynamics of nuclear deterrence by writing it up on the blackboard. But if you place people in the roles—you are the U.S. president, you are the Soviet premier, etc.—give the rules of the game, and play it—then students get it so quickly. The behaviour emerges from the structure of the game. I loved communicating these dynamics to students."

The "game" can also be considered as a transitional object between fantasy and reality. In this way of thinking, the game of markets—just like that video games and poker—is arousing and creates stakes, but in the end its does not implicate one's life chances, unless, of course, one becomes addicted to them. It is exciting because while dangerous, it is not completely real, and in this sense the game is like the cage of the tiger. Indeed, Ray Dalio, the head of Bridgewater, one of the most successful hedge funds in the world, writes that he "loves the game of markets". He even goes on to suggest that his subordinates and mentees think of life as a game: "To help you stay centered and effective, rather than stressed and thrown off by your emotions, try this technique for reducing the pressure: treat your life like a game or a martial art. Your mission is to figure out how to get around your challenges to get to your goals" (Dalio, 2011, p. 25). While extreme, it signals how successful traders use the idea of a game as a way to sustain their excitement and pleasure in the face of danger.

Processes and tools

In describing the fund's downfall and his own failure, Jim notes that, "I had always focused on the process not the results. And every decision was put through that process. It was a buy or sell and a look at the portfolio. I always focused on the process not on the performance. And then I got flipped around. I just started focusing on performance." Jim is emphasizing a common-sense strategy for managing risk in high-arousal settings: focus on the steps in the journey not the goal. If you are golfer or baseball player, you don't think about your batting average or points below par but try to produce the best swing possible. Since states of high arousal can undermine discipline, you achieve excellence when you focus on your swing rather than on your standing or reputation. You can control your swing, but you can't control many of the factors that affect the outcome, such as the pitcher's skills, or the wind blowing across the golf course.

Similarly, Ray Dalio believes that you need a process and the tools that support it in order to drive out emotion and eliminate arousal all together. In contrast to George Soros, he does not make his money by making outsized bets based on intuition. Instead, he makes small but persistent gains on a large number of positions that he holds. He does this by focusing on macro-trends in the global economy, investing in a wide array of instruments, from Japanese bonds to copper futures, and by calculating the correlations between many different securities. His trading style is dogged, disciplined, and based on quantitative models of the world economy. As he noted to a reporter, "Rather than just make a decision that I should buy the U.S. dollar and short the Euro because U.S. productivity is strong in relationship to European productivity, I could study all the different productivity differences and relationships, develop the strategy, develop a rule, and build track record" (Derivatives Strategy, 2000). He, too, predicted correctly that the boom in property prices would end badly.

Sometimes tools function less as frames and more as defences. Karl Weick has discussed the puzzle of why people in dangerous situations don't drop their tools when an emergency calls for it (Weick, 1996). "Navy seamen sometimes refuse orders to remove their heavy steel-toed shoes when they are forced to abandon a sinking ship, and they drown or punch holes in life rafts as a result. Fighter pilots in a disabled aircraft sometimes refuse orders to eject, preferring instead the 'cocoon of oxygen' still present in the cockpit. Karl Wallenda the world-renowned high-wire artist, fell to his death still clutching his balance pole, when his hands could have grabbed the wire below him" (p. 306).

As the last example suggests, under normal circumstances the balance pole creates the protective frame that stands between danger and catastrophe. But when for Wallenda the circumstances changed radically, he clung to the pole instead of letting go. In theorizing about the psychodynamics of thrills, Balint likens this to the child who clings to rather than holds onto mother. When holding, mother becomes a home base for exploring the world. When clinging, mother is the world.

Jim's report that he focused on results rather than process is surely part of the story of why the fund failed. But it is not clear that focusing on process would have been sufficient either. If Bob was right, he needed to see the situation entirely differently. As Bob told us, "I felt like the strategy of our fund was to find these company-specific cata-lysts that over a short period of time would result in a stock price going up or down into the next 3 or 4 months. THAT WAS BULLSHIT!" In short, you could no longer make an absolute return by stock-picking. As Bob adds, he felt that he was in effect saying to Jim, "Are you kid-ding? Do you not see that the sofa is on fire!"

The magic of the pair

There is little doubt that when Bob and Jim first joined up they felt like and appeared to be perfect complements and therefore an exciting duo. S.H. believes that when they were at the top of their game they were "yin and yang", bigger than the sum of the parts. As she notes, "their partnership was creative, and the two had a love of ideas". During our interview with Bob, S.H., in describing the pair, said that, "Most trad-ers are very micro-focused, they grow up in the markets; they are one-dimensional. Bob and Jim as individuals were compelling people, who loved to read, loved building on ideas, had a *joy de vivre*. And together, they were magic."

As we noted above, Don, who owned the investment firm, would spend a disproportionate amount of time with them because he found their conversation and thinking process exciting. Both Jim and Bob thought about trades and markets in a larger frame of reference, link-ing the market to wider social and political issues. In addition, Bob had seductive qualities: a blend of genius and passion, along with a capac-ity to express complex ideas sharply—he is an excellent writer—that drew people to him. It helped, of course, that the two made money in 2008, when everyone else was losing money. Clients could see them has having a secret sauce, a magic that protected them and the money they managed from the angry market gods. John Paulson, the famed hedge-fund manager who shorted credit-default swaps during the housing crash and made an unfathomable $3.5 billion in one year, projected this same quality as well.

Jim also believed that they complemented each other. "Bob is incred-ibly creative he would see some big trends and I would operationalize them. Not having any experience in stock-picking he used to call me his 'Obe Wan Kanobe' and I was his mentor." Bob described Jim as the nuts-and-bolts portfolio manager while "I would come up with the ideas". Ironically, after the fund folded and Bob set up his own fund, he acknowledged that he had undervalued Jim's day-to-day contribution. "I thought that portfolio management was not making us money. I now realize that if you are not on top of it in that focused way, you lose money with a thousand little cuts."

It is tempting to see the pair as simply the expression of a basic assumption, in Bion's terms. But perhaps it is better to think of this pair as representing what Bion termed the sophisticated use of a basic assumption to do real work. As an exciting pair they attracted people and investors to them, but they also experienced themselves as special. One hypothesis is that their sense of being special gave them confidence, which in turn allowed them to think in contrarian ways and enabled them to make money when everyone else was losing. This gives added meaning to Jim's experience of Bob's behaviour as a betrayal. It was not simply that Bob was being unreasonable or was denigrating Jim's contributions. Rather, he was puncturing the helpful myth that they were a unit and therefore were special.

The frames collapse

Bob and Jim's failure can be understood as the collapse of the three protective frames. As discussed, Jim lost the protective frame provided by a focus on process, and, of course, when Bob asked for the helm he undermined their shared experience as a magical pair.

In describing how the game as a frame slipped away, Bob noted that, "the extreme jumped the gap from the business to the personal", affecting his family life. Perhaps most telling was the realization that he might be acting illegally—for example, if he colluded with others to conceal the breach between himself and Jim. He describes this moment as a moment of physical quivering when "you were no longer playing the game of making money". He had a similar feeling when, at the apogee of the financial crisis, he thought Goldman Sachs would go under. "That is when it stopped being a game, because the Meta game really quivered." He believes this experience, this mood, casts a pall on the markets today. Today you do not simply "risk your commercial reputation. You have criminal and civil liability."

The use of the word "quiver" is telling. It describes the bodily feeling that accompanies that moment when we prepare to flee or fight. The quivering means we are already in motion. The body interprets quivering as anxiety, but since anxiety, as Freud notes, is a signal of danger, quivering also brings to the fore the threat one faces. There can be no denying it. This suggests that when Bob and Jim were left with no protective frames, danger, which could once have been experienced as exciting and compelling, became instead an out-and-out threat, resulting in significant anxiety.

When Bob betrayed Jim, the latter experienced the moment as implicating issues of identity and character, issues far removed from the mechanics of daily trading. "The first thing I said to Sharon (when she started to consult to us) was, 'The most important thing is for you to stop me from doing something I will regret later.' And she was great. I do not regret the decisions I made. I now feel—I ask myself—whether or not I missed things. Was there a deeper personality issue for me in the way I deal with people? Do I give up power too easily? Do I have a need to please? These things are real. There is a lot of time and effort of thinking about stuff like that." He then exclaims during the interview, "*I am getting tense!*" as if he were reliving the moment.

One common response to anxiety, particularly if it is sustained, is to "act out". In other words, instead of responding to the danger rationally, we retreat back to fantasy, enacting roles that are gratifying even as they are unrealistic and unhelpful. These are the times when we can, "shoot ourselves in the foot". We can speculate that Bob's proposal that he take over the fund was just such a moment and that he was enacting the role of hero, out of a sense of grandiosity. On the other hand, we cannot be sure that he had any alternative. Perhaps he accurately assessed Jim's recalcitrance, who after all did not believe that the "sofa was on fire". Bob started his own fund some months after their fund closed. But this effort failed when he bet against the likelihood that the Euro would remain stable. On the one hand, this may suggest that he had been grandiose. On the other, though, perhaps his failure was due in part to the fact that he was no longer linked with Jim, who linked his bold ideas to the practicalities of trading.

Perhaps Jim, too, acted out. While his comments suggest that he worried about giving up power too easily, perhaps his feeling of betrayal reflected an unwillingness to subordinate himself to someone who was more imaginative, just when it took imagination to see through the riddle of a stock market and go beyond traditional long/short strategies that no longer worked.

Toward a new model

This case suggests that we can map two distinct group-psychological processes, each of which highlights a different response to risk. In the classical framework, risk creates anxiety, which in turn stimulates a social defence. In the framework we are considering, risk creates excitement, which stimulates, by contrast, a protective frame (see Figurer 12.4).

Since, as Apter's 2 × 2 matrix suggests, excitement and anxiety represents two alternative ways of coding a state of high arousal, one as pleasure and the other as pain, one question we can ask is, under what conditions do we experience risk as pleasurable? Let us propose the following hypothesis, which merits further exploration.

The key is the nature of the fantasies that risk stimulates. Consider the start-up venture, which is saturated with both risk and excitement. It is reasonable to assume that people working in the start-up are motivated by fantasies of future success, which at times they can almost "taste". People's version of success will, of course differ. For some, success is represented by money, for others by recognition, though probably all the fantasies contain an underlying belief that the world will be beneficent and loving. These fantasies, we suggest, are for the most part consciously engaged and experienced, in much the way that sexual fantasies are. Indeed, like sexual fantasies, the success fantasy is itself a source of excitement. By contrast, upon experiencing anxiety, people are more likely to repress the thoughts associated with danger by engaging in various psychological operations—for example, blaming "bad" co-workers for the situation, or looking upon the setting ironically and with detachment. In this case, the *fantasies* become, in Melanie Klein's rendering, *"phantasies"*—the transformation of those hateful feelings induced by danger into unconscious ideas about the sources, meaning, and consequences of danger (Melanie Klein Trust, 2014). In this frame of mind, people code the present unrealistically,

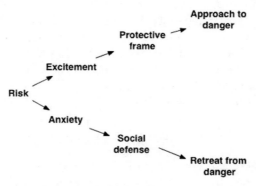

Figure 12.4.   Group-psychological processes generated by risk

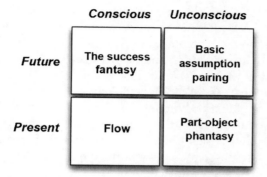

Figure 12.5.   The coding of present experiences in light of past experience.

stimulated partly by past experiences of being threatened by parents and siblings, or what Klein called a person's "part-objects".

This hypothesis points to the 2 × 2 matrix in Figure 12.5, which we hope merits further consideration.

People can be in a conscious or an unconscious relationship to their work setting. In addition, they can be attending to their images and thoughts about the present or about the future. As Figure 12.5 indicates, this scheme establishes four different frames of mind. Thus, for example, when the experience of risk creates excitement, many people entertain a conscious "success" fantasy in which they imagine all the good things—for example, wealth, admiration—they will experience in the future. But when the experience of risk induces anxiety, they are likely to resort to what Bion described as the unconscious "pairing fantasy": the idea that some couple in the group will, without one's own help, give birth to a beneficent future. When the risk is contained—in other words, when it is experienced as a normal demand for work and effort—people can arrive at a state of "flow", or total absorption in the present, unmediated by either fantasy or phantasy. When the risks are not contained, people project out their anxiety onto others, who are then experienced as part-objects—that is, as unmitigated sources of danger.

In sum

Hedge-fund trading can be seen as an extreme work environment, and such environments increasingly characterize a world of turbulence. The rise of extreme sports is one indicator of this development.

Using Michael Apter's conceptual scheme, we argue that in extreme settings people get pleasure by approaching danger. The pleasure is experienced both as excitement and as high-arousal states associated with feelings of awe, wonder, and beauty, pleasures that can be linked to the concept of the sublime. In the case of Bob and Jim, they had at their disposal what Apter calls psychological "protective frames" that transformed the danger of the markets into excitement. These frames are "the market as a game", the focus on "process and tools", and the "magic of the pair". When, as a result of their failing trading strategies and their impasse, these protective frames collapsed, both Bob and Jim were exposed to anxiety and acted out.

We propose that our chapter offers some new points of departure for understanding the psychodynamics of work. Instead of looking at just work, anxiety, and social defence, which was a conceptual scheme adequate to an earlier period of economic development, we should develop a theory appropriate to turbulence—a setting of great uncertainty and unpredictability. Such a theory, we suggest, can be based on the links between danger, excitement, and protective frames.

Notes

1. Adrian Johnson: www.lacan.com/forced.htm
2. www.hanggliding.org/viewtopic.php?t=15838
3. https://en.wikipedia.org/wiki/Gothic_fiction
4. www.tradersstateofmind.com
5. www.tradersstateofmind.com
6. http://research.stlouisfed.org/fred2/series/DJIA/downloaddata
7. Data from: http://measuringworth.com/DJA
8. Data from: www.bloodhoundsystem.com/blog/index.php/2013/05/year-hedge-fund-returns

CHAPTER THIRTEEN

Corporate cultures and inner conflicts

Aideen Lucey

The study of social defences systems in organizations has tended to focus on task-related anxiety. What I want to explore in this chapter is the way in which anxiety to do with the wider societal context contributes to social defence systems in organizations. The issues raised may be relevant across different sectors, but the discussion here is based on the experience of working with large corporate organizations.

The shortcomings of corporate organizations have not gone unnoticed in recent years. The global banking crisis has been the catalyst for a critical appraisal of corporate activity. Casino banking, toxic debts, tax evasion, sweatshops, damage to the environment, and disproportionate rewards for senior executives have all been the subject of media attention. Some of the excesses have been reigned in, but nothing has fundamentally changed about the way that business is done across the global economy. The majority of executives I meet in my work want their work to make a positive contribution to the world. Why, then, do work practices that undermine human well-being continue to be so pervasive? This is a question that social defence theory can help us understand.

Social defence systems

We know that the main problem with unconscious defences against anxiety is that not only do they not protect people from the anxiety they are attempting to avoid, but they also prevent them from knowing about the nature and source of that anxiety. The anxiety that could be a source of intelligence (Armstrong, 2004) is not therefore available for understanding, and the issues pertaining to it are not addressed. What Menzies Lyth's 1960 work highlighted was the way in which defences operate within and across a whole system, leading to a kind of systemic blindness. Bain (1998) added to this the idea of domain-level defences that operate across a whole group of organizations with a similar primary task. Krantz and Gilmore (1990) argue that social defence systems in organizations are also generated by wider societal factors. In their paper about the splitting of leadership and management they say

> . . . certain pervasive social themes and emergent trends in the wider society are imported into organizations in such a way as to serve as social defences. [p.187]

It is this aspect of social defence systems that I am interested in here. In my work with different global organizations, I am struck as much by the similarities between them as the differences to do with task. What these organizations have in common, in my experience, is a performance culture that cuts across differences in task and is, to a greater or lesser extent, mobilized to form part of a social defence system.

It is not that task-related anxiety and defences are not significant, but in a globalized, technological age societal influences have a profound impact in and across organizations. With fewer boundaries to support containment and fewer structures to support traditional defence systems, anxiety is more infused in the culture of organizations and diffused in the individuals within them.

Hinshelwood and Skogstad (2000) in their book about anxiety and defences in healthcare highlight the role of culture in social defence systems, which they define as "unconscious assumptions, attitudes and beliefs about the work task and how to perform it" and a "collectively generated sustained atmosphere into which people come" (p. 9). They point out that that culture bridges the individual and the social:

> The social defence system is [thus], in Trist's sense, a psychosocial process—sets of cultural attitudes, which reach down to the depths of the individual personalities. [p. 9]

I am proposing that the performance culture of large corporate organizations carries unconscious anxiety and defences, which are connected to the wider social context and serve the purpose of attempting to protect people from inner conflicts related to the societal context of work. What I am suggesting is that it is the attempt to avoid these conflicts that causes a kind of systemic blindness that results in the perpetration of work practices that do not, in the end, serve the interests of most people.

In the leadership development work that I am engaged in, I encounter executives who are very caught up in a performance approach to work and, at the same time, seem to be longing for meaning that has been lost as a result of that approach. The leadership development work often becomes the work of containment (Petriglieri & Petriglieri, 2010). It involves helping people to articulate and make sense of feelings and experiences that, it appears, there is little room for in the performance culture of contemporary organizations. In socio-technical terms, it entails restoring sentience to the system. The participants are often very grateful to have an experience where human needs as well as the needs of the task are acknowledged and worked with. If these people, many of them senior leaders in large organizations, are so keen to give attention to human needs, why, then, does a reductionist performance culture remain so pervasive?

Lip service is given, for example, to work–life balance, but in reality the balance is tipped hugely on the side of work. Aggressive targets, global travel, and managing large complex organizations leave little room for the "life" side of the balance. Advances in technology and globalization mean that people are expected to be available for work 24/7. Corporate life involves a great deal of activity and little space for reflection. In this context, targets can replace thinking and have a defensive quality along the lines of "all will be well as long as we meet these targets". This way of thinking leaves little room for meaningful engagement with the wider context of work. Initiatives such as corporate social responsibility and sustainable development exist, but there are limits to how far these go when they are not allowed to present too much of a challenge to the performance imperative and the status quo.

Instrumental vs. substantive ways of functioning

In a recent paper (Lucey, 2013) drawing on Paul Hoggett's work, I have argued that instrumental thinking and ways of functioning have been privileged over more substantive ways of thinking in contemporary

organizations. Instrumental thinking is concerned with technical efficiency and outcomes, and it tends towards superficial ways of relating
and functioning. Substantive thinking, on the other hand, is concerned
with ethical, aesthetic, and spiritual motivations for action and puts an
emphasis on meaning and purpose (the kinds of things the executives
I mentioned often feel they are missing in corporate life). Humans are
driven by both instrumental and substantive needs, but, as critical theo-
rists have pointed out, instrumentality has taken precedence as a way
of thinking and functioning under global capitalism, and this is what
is at the heart of the performance culture.

Hoggett (1992) wrote about this more than 20 years ago in his book
Partisans in an Uncertain World. In this work he argues that under the
instrumentality of late capitalism, purpose becomes drained of its
meaning, leaving organizations lacking the binding function necessary
for containment. Because of failures of containment, organizations
develop a defensive, superficial way of functioning akin to Bick's (1968)
second-skin defences in infants. Hoggett goes on to say that this way
of functioning has resulted in an institutionalization of shallowness
in organizations. This resonates strongly with my work experience.
The superficiality of the performance culture robs people of a deeply
felt sense of meaning and purpose, and this is what they look to have
restored in the leadership development work. The leadership development work can help restore meaning to some extent by allowing people
to engage with the lived experience of their work, but it does not usually address the underlying issues to do with context.

One example Hoggett gives of second-skin-type functioning in corporate organizations is what he calls "simulated moral communities".
He maintains that superficial ways of functioning lead to a simulation
of morality which denies rather than creates meaning, making it difficult to know what is real or what is not. Because anxieties and concerns
related to the wider societal context of the work are not fully engaged
with, attempts to address those concerns through different initiatives
do not get to the core of the problem and so are more like a simulation
than a real response.

Second-skin defences

Esther Bick (1968), in her work on infant observation, identified what
she called second-skin defences in infants. In early life, parts of the personality are felt to have no binding force and are experienced as being
held together passively by the skin. The skin is the boundary between

mother and infant which provides a sense of both contact and separation. When containment works, the skin is felt as a symbolic boundary through which communication takes place (painful sensations can be understood and made tolerable). When containment fails, infants feel as if there is no boundary or psychic skin holding them together. Instead, they feel as if they are falling apart or falling through space. In order to deal with this terrifying feeling, they create a pseudo-protective layer: a brittle outer shell that gives the feeling of being held together. This is the second skin, which can manifest as physical rigidity, clinging to people or things, clamping the eyes on an object, and hyperactive or ritualistic behaviour.

In an organizational setting, a similar kind of protective layer or brittle outer shell can be constructed in response to failures of containment and manifest in similar ways of functioning—for example, rigidity in procedures, obsessional behaviour, and manic activity. The second skin may provide some limited protection from anxiety, but it also interferes with communication as it involves the covering up of underlying anxieties, which are not then available to be understood and related to. One of the consequences of second-skin-type functioning is that relating takes place at a superficial level rather than in depth.

Second-skin-type functioning has the following characteristics:

» Relating takes place at a surface level.
» This surface-level relating does not allow for a real exchange (projection and introjection, in psychoanalytic terms), which inhibits psychic growth and development.
» It involves a reliance on the self rather than on others, limiting one's capacity for attachment.
» The second skin may make the person look strong on the outside, but he or she is actually fragile within.
» When the second skin breaks down, there is a sudden collapse, like the rupture of a boundary.
» The second skin masks real issues, which leads to distortions that, in turn, interfere with the capacity for containment.

What is particularly important and relevant to the discussion here is the way of relating when second-skin defences are at play. Second-skin-type functioning involves an adhesive form of identification which is a superficial way of relating, as opposed to the more in-depth three-dimensional way characteristic of containing relationships. It is this phenomenon that strongly resonates with my experience of working with executives. Very often I feel I encounter people who act in a way that they think is expected of them rather than based on their real experience. This I put down to the performance culture, which produces a kind of "can do" and fake positive attitude.

I recently worked with a group of young executives who were up for promotion within the company. On first meeting, they were very upbeat and positive about their jobs and future prospects. After a few days working with them, it became clear that their situation was much more complex than how it first appeared. The company had an "up or out" promotion structure, which meant that if they were not successful in the promotion process they effectively had no choice but to leave the company. Promotion was so highly valued within the company that not to achieve it was tantamount to professional failure, and it would be enormously difficult to shake off the stigma if one stayed with the company. This had the impact of turning promotion into a win-or-lose game. Such was the pressure to succeed that some people had never taken the time or mental space to consider properly what this next step involved, what the impact on their lives and families would be, and even whether it was what they wanted. It was if they were on a fast-moving conveyor belt that they couldn't get off. Others who had experienced some setbacks in the gruelling process were so fearful of not successfully jumping over the next hurdle that they were paralysed. What was evident in all, at least initially, was an inability to relate in any other way than that which they thought was expected of them. This pseudo way of relating is typical, I think, of the second-skin defence of the performance culture.

The leadership development work became about providing a space for thinking about these experiences. It involved helping them to connect to their own agency and authority so that they could make better judgements about what they did or did not want, rather than feeling like pawns in a game. For others, it was helping them realize that they could, in fact, have more genuine conversations at work about their place in the process. In this way, the consultants were able to provide containment and model something about relating based on real experience rather than on what individuals think is expected. This intervention, though, has limited impact as it only deals with the symptoms not the cause of the problem.

The "up or out" promotion structure goes hand in hand with a hard-nosed approach to business that some corporate organizations feel they have to adopt to remain competitive in an aggressive global market.

One can see how, with such a promotion policy, the performance imperative penetrates deep into individuals as well as into the work culture. Once individuals get into the promotion race they have to perform and succeed almost at any cost, as if they were machines. On the other hand, these executives are also expected to be emotionally intelligent and authentic, in line with contemporary ideas about leadership. This puts them in a double-bind that makes it very difficult to speak out against such processes. As a result, little space or opportunity exists for thinking about the context of such stresses. To do so would call into question the *raison d'être* of the organization. Growth and consumption, even if couched in other terms, have become the purpose of such organizations, and the performance culture is the vehicle through it works. The "up or out" promotion structure supports the needs of the market and, at the same time, silences any dissenting voices. The manic activity that it generates feeds the performance culture and simultaneously stops people from engaging with what is really going on and the context in which it arises. This is not unlike some of the processes Menzies Lyth described in her hospital study. The difference here is that the anxieties defended against are linked to consumer capitalism rather than the nursing task, and the defences are institutionalized within the culture of the organization rather than in particular organizational structures. Power interests, for sure, elevate economic performance above all else, but these kinds of psychosocial processes help to keep it in place. What specific kinds of anxieties, then, might the defence system of the performance culture be defending against? I am suggesting that they are linked to the wider societal context.

The context of contemporary organizations

Globalization and new technology have broken down geographic and other boundaries across the world. The neoliberal policies of the last three decades have removed controls and regulations, thereby extending the power of market forces, as pointed out by M. J. Rustin (2011) in his paper on the psychology of neoliberalism. With this we have seen the rise of the corporation and the decline of the nation state and, simultaneously, an increase in the pursuit of individual interests and a decrease in collective projects. The collapse of communism has left no opposition to counter the failings of capitalism, as highlighted by Stein (2011) in his paper on the credit crisis. This has given rise to a widespread sense that there is no alternative to the current way of doing things.

The unregulated global market has resulted in what Sjoholm (2013) has described as the "aggressive commodification of society all the way down". Or, as Sandel (2013) has said in an *Observer* interview: "we have moved from a market economy to living in a market society in which just about everything is up for sale". More than a century and a half ago, Marx wrote about the way in which, under capitalism, profit comes before people and market forces pervade every aspect of our lives. In the past it was labour that was exploited for commercial purposes, but now it is the individual's subjectivity itself. This is materially expressed, for instance, in what has been called "big data": the mass of data that we inescapably produce and is mined just as profitably as are minerals and oil. I am talking about the way our thinking, our feelings, our leisure interests, our family lives, and so forth are all now exploited for commercial purposes through the monitoring of internet activity and patterns of consumption. This means that the forces of production have penetrated to the very deepest level of the individual, and it is difficult to escape this condition. It also means that it is very difficult to think independently or critically, because we are all inextricably caught up in the processes of production and consumption.

Meanwhile, executives (and others) are concerned about the cost of this to their lives, families, and communities. And as Cooper and Dartington (2004) have pointed out in their paper about containment in a networked world, there is an increasing preoccupation with risk and trust in society and organizations. Quoting Giddens (1990) and Beck (1992), they link this to a societal shift in focus from concern about scarcity and redistribution to concern about survival. These provide a hint of the anxieties underlying the performance culture of organizations.

Globalization, new technology, and modern science reveal to us not only the wonders of the world but also the limits of the world. We now know more than ever about the finite nature of planetary resources. We know about the damage done to the environment by climate change. We know that despite the benefits of development in poorer parts of the world, prosperity has also brought greater inequality (Wilkinson & Pickett, 2009). We know that with the rise of markets in Asia, Africa, and South America there is economic decline in the West and an associated threat to its power base. This has left previously powerful nations with a growing sense of insecurity about their place in the world.

Our response to the issues of scarcity and precarity seems to be to seek to generate more growth. Judt (2010) pointed out in his book *Ill Fares the Land* that unregulated capitalism is based on a delusion of endless growth. Anxieties relating to our limits and the finitude of the planet are what I think we are turning away from, and the delusion of endless growth is the distortion that feeds the defence system. The performance culture therefore serves the function of wiping out anxieties associated with scarcity and precarity, and it provides the false reassurance that all will be well as long as we continue to perform and produce. The performance culture could be seen, therefore, to be both driven by and in flight from these anxieties.

Conclusion

In short, the argument I have sketched here claims that anxieties related to our human limits and the limited resources of the planet in the context of globalization and neoliberalism are fuelling defence systems in organizations. I am suggesting that the performance culture produces superficial ways of functioning similar to second-skin-type defences that distort reality. This gets in the way of thinking and containment and the possibility of responding differently. The superficiality of the performance culture is a significant aspect of social defence systems in contemporary organizations, creating a kind of systemic blindness. I do not, however, believe that there is an absence of concern beneath the superficiality. I have suggested that there is persecutory anxiety that needs to be contained and depressive anxiety that needs to be liberated. This leaves managers, leaders, and consultants with a significant challenge. It is not enough to fill the emotional gaps created by the performance culture. The question demanding urgent attention, I have argued here, concerns how organizations can work beyond the superficiality of second-skin-type social defences in order to connect with the societal context of work.

CHAPTER FOURTEEN

Defences against anxiety in the law

Jon Stokes

The nature of work

Work provides a sense of self-efficacy and self-worth, but it also entails anxiety. The anxiety may be personal, with roots in past personal experiences or in the personality. It may be collective, with its source in group dynamics or emotional contagion. Frustrations, which work (the tie to reality, as Freud described it) necessarily entail, generates anxiety. The work itself arouses feelings and may stimulate anxieties through contact with frightening experiences—for example, in nursing, contact with physically damaged individuals, or, in the police, contact with physically dangerous individuals, as a toxic element and against which defence is appropriate. All work entails some anxiety in the sense of something incomplete that needs to be completed and the exercise of decision and discretion in achieving this (Stokes, 1999). Even a task as simple as sweeping the floor involves choices. We each sweep a floor in our own way, expressing attitudes to cleanliness, order, and aesthetics.

Working effectively is also an opportunity to master and repair the imagined or actual damage we have caused in our relations with others to our internal objects, or to ourselves. As a consequence, becoming unemployed deprives one of a significant opportunity for reparation and hence can be a central element in depressive breakdown.

Organizations and work

Organizations are designed to reduce uncertainty and anxiety and create predictability by structuring tasks, boundaries, authority, and relationships. The psychoanalyst Otto Fenichel (1946) described how membership of an institution affects the personality structure of its members. Membership requires identifying with the organization's values, and members become like the institution in significant ways—by introjecting and operating its characteristic defence mechanisms, sharing common attitudes, carrying on the conventional modes of relationship, and so forth. If an individual is unable or unwilling to conform in these ways, he or she is unlikely to remain a member. Thus organizations, as well as rejecting individuals who are not suitable for the work, will also tend to reject individuals who are independent minded and creative and in various ways unwilling to submit to the organization's defensive structures.

Elliott Jaques (1955) went on to develop the specific hypothesis that "one of the primary cohesive elements binding individuals into institutionalized human association is that of defence against psychotic anxiety". In other words, rather than organizations causing psychotic anxiety (what Melanie Klein, 1948, describes as paranoid-schizoid anxiety and which is found in all of us), they are human creations designed to contain them; when they fail to do so, psychotic anxiety is expressed more openly. This is an important point since the argument advanced in group relations thinking has often been made the other way around—that is, that organizations cause their members problems and are somehow a malign influence—rather than Jaques's suggestion that we use our organizations as vehicles for both containing and expressing psychotic anxieties. It is when this function breaks down that we see psychotic anxiety erupting—for example, during times of organizational change.

Isabel Menzies Lyth in her 1960 paper on social systems as a defence against anxiety writes that

> the need of the members of the organization to use it in the struggle against anxiety leads to the development of socially structured defence mechanisms, which appear as elements in the organization's structure, culture and mode of functioning. An important aspect

of such socially structured defence mechanisms is an attempt by individuals to externalize and give substance in objective reality to their characteristic psychic defence mechanisms. A social defence system developed over time is the result of collusive interaction and agreement, often unconscious, between members of the organization as to what form it shall take. The socially structured defence mechanisms then tend to become an aspect of external reality with which old and new members of the institution must come to terms. [1960/1988, pp. 50–51]

For the past seven years I have consulted to a number of City law firms in London, providing organizational role consultancy to those in senior leadership roles, such as senior or managing partners or group heads, and also providing assistance with selection decisions such as promotion to partner or, at times of significant career transition, with promotions to leadership roles, promotion to partner, or the on-boarding of lateral hires. These firms provide legal services to commercial and government organizations rather than to individuals. I shall also draw upon experiences that my colleague Richard Jolly and I have had designing and delivering management development programmes for a number of law firms, as well as workshops in which lawyers and their clients work together on their relationships. In this chapter, I want to reflect on and consider these experiences using Isabel Menzies Lyth's concept of defensive social structures, drawing also on the work of Elliott Jaques, who first described the phenomenon (Jaques, 1955).

There has arisen an artificial divide between those who look at an organization from the perspective of the individual and his or her individual defences and psychopathology (psychoanalysis), and those who look at an organization from the perspective of the social system (systems psychodynamics). This has resulted in a futile chicken-and-egg debate as to whether it is the social system that predominates and causes the pathological behaviour of the individuals in it, or whether it is the individuals' defensive structure and psychopathology that is at the root of the problem. In fact, both are involved in a process of mutual cause-and-effect. Individuals create organizations in part in order to assist them with reinforcing mechanisms of defence against anxieties, which these organizations then, in turn, both provide superficial containment for but may also exacerbate. The group relations tradition of work, which explicitly disavows the analysis of individual motivations, has become rather split off from the psychoanalytic tradition of understanding organizational events solely from the perspective of the internal world of the individual. This, to my mind, has been one of the causes of the stagnation and lack of influence of either tradition on organizational consultation and on the field of organizational behaviour in general.

The unconscious structure of organizations

Organizations are created in order to get work done through collective effort, the structuring of which impacts the relationships and psychological state of those working in the organization. They also have a more unconscious function, which is to contain anxiety associated with the work by creating containing structures. Over-structuring, a form of obsessional defence often seen in financial services, produces a silo mentality, which creates the opportunity for splitting and projection of unwanted parts of the self or the group into others, with a consequent weakening of the sense of effectiveness, accountability, and self, leading in turn to the sense of victimhood so prevalent in the workplace. Under-structuring, a form of narcissistic defence often seen in advertising and other creative industries, on the other hand, can result in some members becoming overwhelmed by a lack of clarity and boundary, with consequent acting out of anxiety in extreme forms of behaviour.

Working in a large organization provides a means of containing anxiety through the redistribution of bad internal objects and "bad" impulses among the members of the organization—"them" who are bad in some way, and "us" who are essentially good. What has to be contained is a combination of anxieties arising out of feelings evoked by the work, the attitudes of the various sub-groups towards each other, and the sort of personalities attracted to this work and this organization. Together, these influence the culture of the organization, which is also affected by the existential anxiety of the organization concerning what may be required for its survival, its primary task, with a final and significant factor being the context and environment in which the organization operates. The way that most workplaces are structured in these split and splintered ways is more conducive to paranoid-schizoid mental states, where the primary concern is for personal survival, with a resulting predominance of destructive rivalry over productive competition. This is in contrast to a depressive mental state, in which there is the acceptance of a need for others, and for their well-being, and for both collaboration and healthy competition. The resulting deprivation of experiences of positive contact with others results in a longing for camaraderie and togetherness, which are provided by the creation of meetings of often dubious value, beyond their social purpose of bringing people together, and the cause of much frustration because of their lack of sense of purpose.

To the extent that we choose our work and the organization we work in, we do so in order to express ourselves both constructively and destructively; we also do so in order to help us manage our concerns and anxieties, to repair real or phantasy damage done to others or to ourselves. Certain personality types are drawn to some work and organizations more than others. I have written elsewhere (Stokes, 1994) of how at a deep level effective work mobilizes the sophisticated use of Bion's (1961) three basic assumptions. For example, medicine and hospitals utilize dependency, social work flight–fight, and therapists pairing—or a basic assumption of hope, as I prefer to describe it. Of course, actual work entails using various degrees of each of these, but understanding the predominant basic assumption drawing people to a profession and motivating them provides a useful framework for understanding the breakdown of working relationships into the corrupt forms of basic-assumption activity—bullying, paranoia, and collusive relationships, respectively.

In summary, any work situation is likely to be influenced by some or all of a series of underlying anxieties:

» in the person (personal anxiety)
» anxieties associated with the necessary exercise of discretion required by the work (role anxiety)
» anxieties generated by the work itself (task anxiety)
» anxieties generated by the structural arrangements of the organization (group and system anxiety)
» existential anxiety concerning organizational survival and its relationship to its environment (organizational anxiety).

In working with organizations, it is useful to distinguish between these various levels in the way in which one diagnoses a problem. As a consultant, one needs to be alert to the ways in which these different levels of anxiety affect one another and underlie the presenting request, whether this be a desire for learning or help with a problematic individual. Any and all of these levels of anxiety can be relevant to a better understanding of problems in the workplace. Effective leadership entails some capacity to identify and understand both the nature and the location of anxiety in the system.

The choice of work:
the professionalization of drive and defence

All professions could be said to offer a "professionalization" of the task of managing personal anxiety. This is at the heart of the unconscious elements in the choice of profession and the reparative opportunities it affords. The concept of profession entails the notion of a vocation, or calling. The term "occupation" is often used implying a pre-occupation, a sense of being occupied with and by something. While not applicable to all, it is most likely to be applicable to those who make such a decision at a relatively early age, as many of the best lawyers do.

Occupations provide opportunities for the discharge and gratification of drives, from which derives the motivation, as well as opportunities, for reducing internal conflict over the expression of these drives in a socially sanctioned manner. Put simply, work needs to provide avenues of expression for the energies of both aggressive and libidinal instincts. When it stops doing this, it becomes drudgery; when it absorbs these instincts, it becomes an instrument of gratification. Just as importantly, it offers the opportunity for the symbolic reparation of the damage that the expression of these impulses is feared to result in. When this opportunity breaks down or is not available, the individual has to face his or her anxieties and frustrated needs more directly, often resulting in a violent attack on the object that is felt to be frustrating the desire to repair—for example, the "shocking" treatment of hard-to-help elderly or patients who fail to get better. Current attempts to improve the quality of care mistakenly scapegoat the errant professional, whose removal, perhaps justified, is felt to be a solution to the problem. While a temporary solution, it fails to deal with the heart of the problem—that is, that such events are an inevitable "dark side" of the "caring" professions. The patient or client is hated as the source of a potential "return of the repressed" feeling of helplessness and dependency which the professional finds it difficult to own. As the mental mechanism embedded in the professional role of helper which has in general successfully projected these needs onto others threatens to break down, the hatred of these feelings is violently directed against the recalcitrant patient or client who "refuses" or "will not" get better.

While professions are conscious management systems for both standards of behaviour and the quality of service, they also operate as unconscious management systems for the inevitable anxieties that work generates. The psychological structure of the workplace can be usefully viewed in terms of what I have called the emotional process of the organization (Stokes, 1999)—that is, the emotional processes required by the transformational process of the institution, turning something (inputs) into something of greater value (outputs). So, in educational establishments, where the transformation process is that of learning, one then finds the staff room stratified between the "cleverest" and the "most stupid" teacher, who is the scapegoat and recipient for the stupid feelings of the group. In psychiatric institutions, there is established in a similar and inevitable way the "mad" staff member into whom the staff collectively get rid of fears about their own individual sanity; in the police, the same process is represented by the search for the "crooked" police officer. In other words, social institutions are in part structured by the anxiety of failure in relation to the primary task.

Different professions are akin to different societies, each addressing different values and applying different educational measures, resulting in different forms of dealing with the conflict between desires and reality. Again akin to societal differences, different professions can be characterized by the way in which they deal with conflicts between impulses and social acceptability. Different professions result in different professional superegos. "Social institutions influence the instinctual structure of the people living under them through temptations and frustrations, through shaping desires and antipathies" (Fenichel, 1946, p. 488). The external institution and the internal institution of psychological structures are thus co-created by the members of the organization as they pursue their work.

The detachment and denial of feelings

A necessary psychological task for the entrant into any profession is the development of adequate professional detachment. The novice professional must learn, for example, to control his or her feelings, refrain from excessive involvement, avoid disturbing identifications, and maintain his or her professional independence against manipulation and demands for unprofessional behaviour. This detached stance often invites the repression of feelings and the building of a defensive denial against them; the corollary is that there is a constant unconscious concern at their potential eruption. The lack of women in senior roles in law firms is, in my view, partly caused by the discomfort that their male colleagues anticipate their presence in the firm at senior levels will provoke in terms of sexual arousal, competitiveness, and rivalry.

An element of affect phobia—for example, hatred of helplessness, dependency, feeling foolish, and so on—is at the root of the unconscious aspect of professional defensive structures and the reason for the choice of profession. A profession offers the young person considering a career an opportunity both to express certain needs—for example, to care for others, or to win an argument—but also to contain the anxiety associated with the shadow side of these needs—the expression of aggression towards others, against which the choice of a caring profession, for example, is a form of defence. In other words, they offer an opportunity to master the affect phobia from which the young professional suffers—for example, in young doctors the fear of dependency on others is expressed through seeking a relationship of dependency from others. Professions are forms of social institutions that have been sanctioned to manage what Bion terms "basic assumptions". In this way, professionals can maintain "professional" unconscious contact with a feared emotion in a vicarious way in clients who are struggling with the same problem, but consciously. In my experience, one should not underestimate the impact of traumatizing experiences that have led an individual, and often the best practitioners, to seek a certain line of work: traumatic helplessness in the case of doctors, and a traumatic sense of being excluded or ostracized in the case of lawyers; traumatic and humiliating experiences of foolishness in the case of teachers when they were children at school, and traumatic feelings of powerlessness in their family during childhood in the case of politicians. All these are professions with which I have worked in various ways over the years.

One purpose of a professional role is therefore to provide a container for the emotions both brought to and evoked by the task. For example, lawyers are typical of individuals with a high need for achievement and are concerned with the possibility of failure as much as success. As a consequence, owning up to failure is often so painful to the self-image of the professional that he or she prefers to blame clients for the failure to be able to help them. Rationalization is used as a defence to argue that the client brings failure upon him/herself. This is one source of the professional's drive to achieve high levels of performance, sometimes leading to addictive over-working. They are generally individualistic in orientation and disparaging of management, which is perceived as a potential threat to their individual freedom with consequent difficulties in sharing, cooperating, and working with others. Success is perceived predominantly to be an individual matter rather than a group achievement. Consequently management can easily become the receptacle for the projection of unwanted fears and anxieties, which cause internal tension such as the threatening sense of potential failure in relation to excessively high, often perfectionistic standards. These unrealistic and sometimes guiltily motivated excessively high standards are projected elsewhere onto clients, who are felt to be unreasonable, or onto management, who are felt as constraining and restricting. The concept of management as helpful is virtually unrecognized except in its more acceptable administrative form—that is, a sort of "mother" whose job is to make sure that the needs of the busy professional "child" are met. A further twist to this process is that the neediness of the professional is projected into the so-called support services, who are viewed as needing the professionals more than vice versa, with a resulting feeling of inferiority in the individuals who operate the various business services a law firm requires. These staff then retaliate, at least unconsciously or in their private attitudes, in ways that are unhelpful to the building of constructive relationships with the lawyers. The attitude of professionals towards management is essentially to see them as restrictive, really an expression of their own unconscious identification with a punishing authority, which will be unforgiving towards their own limitations and dependency.

The resulting atmosphere in a law firm is often what a former colleague Bob Gosling described as the boarding-house state of mind, in which the view was held that the professional should be provided with a room in which to work but without expectation that he or she contribute much to the overall upkeep of the place. The task of looking after the organization is left up to management, viewed unconsciously as parents, whose purpose should be to serve the interests of the individual members over the primary task of the organization. Individuals are prepared only for minor participation in so far as it affects one's self or group interest. Busyness with clients and matters are given as surface reasons while obscuring the deeper dislike, even fear, of social interaction. Typically little responsibility is taken for the overall venture and generally without much enthusiasm for it. The model of the organization in the mind of lawyers sometimes seems more one that should serve their needs, without consideration of the competing calls on available resources that this necessitates. The risk inherent in making judgements about one sectional interest versus the responsibility for the overall organization is delegated to senior management, resulting in a splitting process and disowning of personal responsibility for the overall good of the organization. Consensus management under the guise of "democracy" is preferred since it always enables the power of veto, sometimes to represent sectional interests, sometimes in the service of resistance to change, often to the detriment of the enterprise overall. The resulting schizoid and suspicious atmosphere is one in which it is very difficult to do productive collaborative work.

Defences can be useful or they may be anti-developmental. They can shield the professional from the otherwise unbearable impact of daily contact with highly disturbing situations in ways that enable the efficient carrying out of the professional task. Or they can be limiting and disabling. Menzies Lyth did not include an analysis of the personalities of those drawn to the nursing profession, an understanding of which is, to my mind, crucial in being able to consult effectively with any psychological depth. In other words, one needs both the psychoanalytic perspective from the internal world of the individual as well as the social systems' perspective of group and institutional processes. The premature attempt to remove defences generates a fear of regression in the individual, leading to defensiveness and ultimately rejection of the consultant. Individuals vary enormously in their capacity to modify or relinquish defensive attitudes, and consequently expectations that this can happen solely through the modification of the organizational structure or through group relations events are unrealistic. Alternatively, increasing self-awareness of employees without structural change is unlikely to lead to real change.

Those drawn to the law: the lawyer's personality

As in any other profession, many of the best of those who have chosen the profession of law do so while still at school. The childhood of these individuals is often characterized by a sense of personal insecurity and uncertainty, sometimes a sense of being an outsider or excluded, leading to a preoccupation with fairness and injustice which the choice of profession provides an avenue for working on. They are frequently highly risk-averse outside their area of expertise and knowledge and have a strong aversion to feeling foolish or looking stupid, which makes acknowledging difficulties and the process of learning difficult. The skills of arguing and argument are developed, as they provide a means of defence and self-soothing against distressing experiences. Arguing can become a way of being that provides a shield against emotional pain. If developed at an early age, the defence can become habitual. I have learned that the offering of a new idea to a group of lawyers will almost certainly be met not by interest but by argument, finding fault or exception however that idea is presented. Once one realizes that this is how they deal with new experiences of any kind, it is easier to restrain oneself from becoming too defensive. In a sense, the lawyer's mode of being is one of continuous argument with the unsatisfactory state of things, as a defence against feelings of helplessness, though with a tendency to disabling victim mindset. When this is expressed against their own organization, it results in a despairing vicious cycle of criticism and defence expressed against each other.

Research on the personality profile of lawyers using various personality questionnaires carried out by ourselves and others suggests that lawyers are:

» typically more pessimistic than the average, perhaps requisitely so, since the task is to be hyper-vigilant to error
» as trainees, often mildly to moderately depressed, becoming more so as the training progresses
» extreme in their high need for achievement (which when driven by a fear of failure leads to the relations of paranoid-schizoid rivalry in their suspicious relations with each other)
» prone to scapegoating and ostracizing—for example, of older members, who are seen as past their sell-by date—as a way of spitting off and projecting feelings of inadequacy and vulnerability
» frequently low in the desire for personal development
» low on the need for power, so that it becomes a difficult task to find anyone prepared to take up leadership roles

All of this combines with an often heightened need for affirmation since this is often not met by the culture of a law firm as it is viewed as a weakness. Consequently individuals who have pre-existing concerns about intimacy and feel reluctant to express emotion, as well as being individuals who find it hard both to recognize their own need for affirmation and to seek it from others, are left with a sense of emotional deprivation. A result of this is that feelings about the value of one's contribution to the partnership are projected into debates and into complicated systems of adjudicating reward systems with often quite byzantine structures that no one other than one or two individuals fully understand; the result is that they are less effective in their conscious intention to reward high performance, since no one knows or agrees what this constitutes.

A necessary professional healthy sense of mistrust and a predisposition to carefulness and caution enables the lawyer to turn these dispositions to advantage. A high need for control and a tendency to mistrust seems to the lawyer to have produced good results so far, and thus it comes to be believed that through these means a magical omnipotent ability to control the situation has been developed. The more this apparently produces the desired results, the more the unconscious fantasy is reinforced. This is part of the professional self-image of the lawyer as the knight in shining armour who comes to rescue his or her unfortunate and needy client.

The emotional structure of law firms

To understand better the culture of a legal firm, it is helpful to understand the unconscious influences on the social structure. In Bion's terms, they are a specialized institution, like the Army, which is used by society to deal with the basic assumption of fight–flight or prosecution–defence in the language of the lawyer. Menzies Lyth's work, in contrast, was with the dependency needs that are handled by hospitals.

In a comparable way that Menzies Lyth describes nurses in a hospital, lawyers allocate responsibility and irresponsibility between partners and associates. It would seem that the worst thing for a lawyer is to look "stupid" or "silly"—certainly it has been my experience in workshops with lawyers that a fear of foolishness can be an impediment to productive discussion and learning, and anyone who makes a foolish remark may be subjected to teasing, derision, and scorn, more so than in other professions. It is the common experience of associates that they are treated as less responsible and more stupid and silly than they really are. Their work in the early years is little more than administrative or less. The function of the social structure would seem to be to allow the partners to divest themselves and project unwanted anxiety about the success of a case, expressed as concerns about inaccuracy, which, of course, can be a costly affair, into their juniors, whose work is gone over in meticulous detail. It is not difficult for the partner to justify such behaviour, as inevitably juniors will make mistakes; the problem is that that is also how they learn. I once worked with a newly promoted partner who had never been allowed to send an email to a client that had not been checked beforehand by her supervising partner.

Trainee lawyers are not permitted to make deep relationships with the client, for good professional reasons ("they're not experienced enough"), but also because the client is deemed to be owned by the partner, who jealously guards anyone who attempts to work with the client even though this may be to the disadvantage of his colleagues and the firm as a whole. So it is economically useful to maintain the view of juniors as incompetent and in need of close supervision. Trainee lawyers are kept in a highly dependent relationship with collusive social redistribution of responsibility and irresponsibility. The partner maintains overall responsibility and often finds it hard to delegate to associates.

The profession is characterized by a frequent failure to develop age-appropriate maturity and relationship skills due to a defensive retreat into focus on detail and expertise. Insufficient effort is made positively to help the individual confront the anxiety-provoking experiences and, by so doing, to develop the capacity to tolerate and deal more effectively with the anxiety. In the case of law, the anxieties are of incompetence, of failure, of being attacked. Associates are not helped with these experiences but are expected to master them without discussion. They then emerge as "partners", with often a striking degree of immaturity compared to others of the same age—for example, in corporate managerial roles. One result is, just as Menzies Lyth described in nursing, that paradoxically it is sometimes the better and more independent individual who leaves the firm.

There is a further complication in that the expectation of stupidity so infects the juniors that they can under-function, through an introjected identification of a diminished self-image, frustration with which then takes the form of a sullen stupidity-inducing response to the way in which they are treated. As Menzies Lyth described in relation to nurses, irresponsibility is delegated downwards and responsibility upwards. Concerns about failure are denied and are projected into a management or the business services staff, who are seen as the cause of potential and actual failures. Alternatively the firm's strategy is blamed, all in the service of preserving the fragility of the professional's self-image, which the prospect of change threatens. Elliott Jaques writes that

> effective social change is likely to require analysis of the common anxieties and unconscious collisions underlying the social defences which determine the phantasy social relationships. The resistance to social change is greater where the social defence systems are dominated by primitive psychic defence mechanisms, collectively described as the paranoid-schizoid defences. The nature of paranoid-schizoid defences is such as to prevent insight into the true nature of problems and a realistic appreciation of their seriousness, with the consequence that action is generally only taken when a crisis occurs. [Jaques, 1955, p. 498]

This is what is happening with the commoditization of low value-added legal work in City law firms.

The lot of the business services (finance, HR, IT, marketing, etc.) is also not an easy one. They are often referred to as "non-fee-generating" or as "support staff", clearly indicating their expensive and inferior status, with no recognition that it is the partners themselves who are the original source of cost in their need for support. And this is support that any self-respecting lawyer really doesn't need in the first place, with their phobia of dependent feelings being expressed in the view of themselves as "independent" practitioners.

The consequences for clients are often no better. Lawyers' fear of intimacy, and a need to find fault with others when anxious, result in a mechanical approach to problem-solving, with a fear of taking responsibility, which makes the client feel distanced and regard the lawyer as merely an expert to be called only for technical advice rather than for discussion of the wider aims and direction of the client's business, from which more valued work might be derived. Because of the extended dependency of their training, lawyers have in many cases not developed the mature social skills that are required in order to interact with their more senior clients, or sometimes even, indeed, with each other. The resulting defensive emphasis on knowledge, longevity in the job, and expertise, as against understanding the client and relating to the client, does neither side any favours.

Postscript

I am aware that all of this may read as an unjustifiably negative view of a profession that offers an essential service to society, as well as opportunities for individuals to achieve great satisfaction in the work. Working with law firms and lawyers has been one of the most satisfying experiences of my career as a consultant and coach. Needless to say, any profession could be submitted to the same sort of analysis with equally apparently critical conclusions. This has not been my intention; rather, it has been to analyse some of the underlying factors in the difficulties of managing law firms and, hopefully, to shed some light in ways that are helpful in understanding some of the more difficult problems that have to be managed. As the reader might imagine, neither psychologists nor coaches when placed under similar scrutiny would come out any better!

PART IV

Social welfare and education

CHAPTER FIFTEEN

Spotlit: defences against anxiety in contemporary human service organizations

Andrew Cooper & Amanda Lees

Organizational formations and cultures in the twenty-first century are in rapid and radical evolution. However, trajectories of change differ according to political, social, and cultural contexts. In British public sector contexts, the influence of neoliberal market ideologies and practices, encapsulated by New Public Management theory, may be a dominant transnational force intersecting with other local and national traditions and trends. Isabel Menzies Lyth's (1960) original thesis about the functioning of social systems as a defence against anxiety was itself developed under specific professional and historical circumstances, and it is also imbued with particular psychoanalytic theoretical presuppositions.

In this chapter, we propose that the meaningful application of her ideas to contemporary human and public service organizations requires considerable development of the precepts shaping the founding thesis. First, in summary, the nature and sources of the anxieties with which front-line staff and human service managers must contend have evolved to include a powerful range of extra-organizational forces and pressures. Second, the anxieties arising from these new sources are typically different from the familiar task-related anxieties that were Menzies Lyth's main preoccupation, but they are also often congruent with the latter in important ways. We suggest it is helpful to think of task-related anxieties as predominantly depressive in their

nature, and those emanating from the managerial and political environment as predominantly persecutory. Both varieties of anxiety give
rise to socially structured defences, and both also generate "secondary
anxieties", which are the unintended consequences of these defences.
A nuanced capacity to disentangle these different processes, and their
effects on organizational experience, is required. So, third, the contemporary state of affairs requires a more fully psycho-social framework
of understanding than Menzies Lyth offers, in which there is (at least)
a two-way direction of influence acting on operatives to produce their
"lived experience" of the work and its organizational context. The total
situation results in a distinctive "structure of feeling" characterized by
"fear and dread" in modern British human services. This overall way
of thinking indicates a need for case-study-based research programmes
that capture the particularities of specific organizational/cultural formations. Thus, we report and draw upon the findings of a small-scale
ethnographic empirical study of front-line child protection services to
elaborate and illustrate the wider thesis we are proposing.

The transformation of human service organizations

In an earlier paper about the contemporary relevance of Menzies Lyth's
ideas, Cooper (2010) suggested that since the 1980s British public sector
organizations have been the object of successive but also cumulative
waves of external pressure associated with the neoliberal political project and its determination to variously "transform", shrink, marketize,
or reposition the welfare state as a whole in its relation to wider economic and state–civil society boundaries. "Modernization" is often
the catch-all phrase for these trends, although this term may disguise
as much as it reveals about the deep structure of the transformations
concerned. Resource rationing, performance management and target
cultures, inspection and audit regimes associated with a "value-for-
money" public transparency and choice ethic, interagency and cross-
sector collaboration ("joined-up working") all combine to create a
distinctive and new network of organizational demands, accompanied
by new forms of professional anxiety. In many ways, these contextual
forces constitute the phenomenon of public sector "governance", itself
a telling neologism denoting a variety of social order and discipline
unsteadily located on the boundary between traditional government
and new forms of regulation and social surveillance.

Hoggett (2010) and others suggest that the distorting impact of
these forces in relation to the traditionally conceived "primary tasks"

of health and care services constitutes a kind of systematic perversion of those tasks. Krantz (2010) points to the influence of new technologies and digital information and communication systems as further transformative forces shaping organizational life, mobilizing new and unfamiliar forms of anxiety. To date, however, there has been little empirical study of whether and how professional anxieties have actually been modified by these developments, or whether we can confidently assert the emergence of new forms of defence against such anxieties. Anecdotal and experiential accounts abound, but the danger here is that we narrate and hear only those anecdotes that confirm our fears and anxieties about social change, so that the important project of describing and conceptualizing change processes becomes confused with a "narrative of loss".

The research project described below was undertaken by Amanda Lees [hereafter A.L.], and in part it set out to test the validity of Andrew Cooper's and others' formulations about modern organizational anxieties (Lees, 2014). However, the two authors did not collaborate on this project, and they only met one another after it had been written up. This work describes in detail organizational structures and systems, behaviours, practices, rituals, and affective states that will seem very familiar to anyone who has a working relationship with modern British health or statutory care settings. Alongside our necessarily summary account of this work, we do offer some additional anecdotal accounts of direct experiences of the contemporary "structure of feeling" in these settings, because it is important to grasp just how extreme these can be, and thus how important it is to achieve a more coherent and convincing understanding of what is being enacted in the name of "care" or "welfare" in our society—and what part "defences against anxiety" play in all this.

Cases and contexts

This chapter might usefully be read in conjunction with others in this volume that engage with similar questions—for example, the contributions of Hoggett (chapter 3), Halton (chapter 1), and Boxer (chapter 5). We are in sympathy with the broad position that Paul Hoggett outlines in his chapter concerning the need for a more fully psychosocial account of organizational defences and a less reductionist and more "binocular" psychoanalytic account of the origins and nature of both organizational anxieties and defences, and the strong case he makes for the existence of an autonomous sphere of group and societal defences. The theoretical ambivalence of Menzies Lyth, Jaques, and others towards the ontological autonomy of defensive systems at the organizational or cultural levels is more fully explored in Cooper (1996). William Halton's suggestion that the defences against anxiety reported by Menzies Lyth in her original study are obsessional in nature also resonates with our experience, with earlier theorizations by Andrew Cooper (Cooper & Lousada, 2005, chap. 3), and with A.L.s' new findings. Like Halton we think it important to be able to specify the anxieties that might be shaping any particular organizational culture, and we have some propositions to advance about the differential nature of task-related anxieties in the care and health sector, and the societal ones that intersect with these.

Our allusions to the specificities of context-shaping organizational cultures and anxieties, allied to the differential nature of organizational primary tasks that are assumed to mobilize anxieties, suggest that a rigorous case-study approach is required for the development of both more refined theory and useful models to inform consultancy or other practical interventions. As Obholzer (1989) notes, Menzies Lyth's key propositions include that "there is innate psychic pain inherent in all institutions (and) that the nature of the pain is specific to the primary task of the institutions" (p. 63). Given the additional variable of social-political context, what holds for a financial services organization in Hong Kong will probably not hold for a hospice in Harlem. Differential organizational forms, the characteristic anxieties their tasks generate, the societal pressures and demands shaping their evolution, distinctive professional cultures within a society, and so on, all combine to create particular organizational "cases" that must be understood psycho-socially as "complex particulars" (Cooper, 2009b). Different organizational cases may manifest considerable similarities with one another, but complex particularity means that these will take the form of stronger or weaker "family resemblances", rather than simply identity or difference .

The case of English child protection work

A.L.'s study was undertaken in three systemically linked front-line child protection teams in an English local authority, with a focus on information-sharing practices. We suggest that English child protection organizations, policies, and practices over the last decade provide unusually instructive examples of how task-related anxieties and internally generated organizational responses to these have intersected in complex and unpredictable ways with powerful political, cultural, and societal processes to produce organizational "states of mind" consistent with those described by Menzies Lyth, but not actually explicable solely in terms of the mechanisms she postulates.

Rigidly protocolized information-sharing practices are a salient feature of this picture. Overtly, these new procedures and practices derive from the repeated findings of Public Inquiries, Serious Case Reviews, and other analyses of "failures to protect" children at risk, which suggests that ineffective information sharing among agencies and between intra-agency subsystems made a significant contribution to the ultimate fate of children at risk. However, the organizational mind states and behaviours associated with these practices bear all the hallmarks of a socially constructed system of defences, with the "obsessional" features noted by Halton very much in evidence. But what accounts for what in this picture? Do profound task-related anxieties associated with professional responsibility for "safeguarding" vulnerable and at-risk children from harm, and ultimately death, dispose front-line and first-line managerial staff to erect organizational systems of defence? Or do public, judicial, and media allegations against individuals, organizations, and at times entire professions, of "failure" to protect children dispose policymakers towards excessively rationalistic, proceduralized policy solutions that are themselves infused with anxiety and hence particular varieties of defence against anxiety? In effect, policymakers have mandated "ritualized task performance" as a solution to perceived "performance failures". However, policy prescriptions never fully determine the implementation process, and they are always available for mediation, interpretation, and resistance on the part of organizational and professional leaders and management. But if the form in which public policy "solutions" to profound periods of social anxiety about our capacity to protect children from harm are congruent and intersecting with the "solutions" to task-related anxiety arising from the psychic pain and anxiety of the primary task, then we are looking at an over-determined state of affairs in which internal and external dynamics are reinforcing each other in complex ways.

Menzies Lyth and modern policy processes: from depressive to persecutory anxiety

Lees, Meyer, and Rafferty (2013) discuss the striking parallels between Menzies Lyth's typology of defensive behaviours and practices found in the hospital setting, including the secondary anxieties these defences generated, and the defensive character of policy-driven "solutions" to the succession of public and professional crises that have afflicted child care and protection work in Britain. *The Munro Review of Child Protection* (Munro, 2010, 2011a, 2011b), which aimed to dismantle the rigid, proceduralized organizational and practice culture of child protection work, may represent the most powerful example of Menzies Lyth's influence on public policy, although Munro also draws on a number of other theoretical and research traditions. However, we think there are important theoretical and practical distinctions to be articulated with respect to the origins and nature of defensive processes generated at the task and the public policy levels.

Central to Menzies Lyth's analysis is the idea that it is anxiety about potential harm to patients that drives the individual and collective need to erect defences—to offload decision-making responsibility, generate obsessional rituals around decision-making, maintain emotional distance from patients, project harsh and critical voices onto junior staff, and so on. Menzies Lyth directs attention to how close contact with suffering, loss, injury, anxieties about death and dying, as well as the libidinal impulses aroused by close contact with patients' bodies, may mirror and mobilize early infantile anxiety states in staff. These core anxiety states conform mostly to what Kleinian theory denotes as "depressive anxieties", in which fears about harm done to the "other", and the consequent fear of guilt about such harm, predominate.

Lees et al. are right to point to the congruence between the varieties of defence that arise at the task level and at the public policy level, but are the underlying anxieties the same? We suggest not. Rather, the dominant source of anxiety inhering in, and deriving from, the public sphere is of allegations and accusations of failure, of the potential for public humiliation and scapegoating of individuals, of entire organizations, and even of professions, with many well-publicized real-world instances to reinforce such fears. In a performance culture, the consequences of organizational "failure" are real and rapid. Heads roll, careers are destroyed, organizations shamed and put into "special measures" and so on. Here the paramount anxieties concern threats to the self, not to the other—that is, to "persecutory anxiety" in Kleinian terms. Hence the familiar and oft-repeated observations about contemporary defensive organizational practices being directed towards "covering your back". What is implicitly lamented here is precisely the replacement of concern (albeit anxious concern) for the patient or service user by a dominant anxiety for the survival of the professional self.

We think this is an important and useful distinction to recognize, but of course it is also not as neat as the above formulation suggests.

First, we can see in the Menzies Lyth thesis how projections or displace-
ments of anxiety into superiors, or onto junior staff, dynamically position them as potential "persecutors", who via processes of projective
identification may then indeed enact exactly this role. In post-Kleinian
clinical thought, the oscillations and dynamic interplay between persecutory and depressive states have been well theorized and illustrated
(e.g., Britton, 1998a). But the key point remains. Where persecutory
anxiety predominates, the vulnerable or suffering other is obliterated.
Where depressive anxieties predominate, there is at least the possibility
of retaining emotional contact and concern for others.

So, second, when we describe policy prescriptions and the cultures
of practice emanating from them as "defensive", what are we suggesting they are defending against? Is it the same kinds of anxiety that Menzies Lyth identified, or something different? It is not clear to us that the
anxiety states driving policy processes are "depressive" in nature, but
more that they are efforts to quell anxieties about allegations of "failure" by governments, ministerial departments, professional leader-
ships, and so on, as well as the political and professional repercussions
of blame becoming attached to any of these. Cooper (2005) and others
(Reder & Duncan, 2004) have noted how public enquiry and media
preoccupations are marked by the absence of any conscious or explicit
sense of mourning, or depressive reflection in relation to the tortured,
dead, or severely injured children who are their supposed object of concern. Equally, these political and public processes have been emptied of
any reference to the idea of tragedy or accident. Instead, a discourse of
perfectability and failure or disillusion in relation to a shattered ideal
predominates—"This must never be allowed to happen again, and
today I am announcing measures that will ensure this."

Thus, our contention would be that when human services become
the object of intense critical public scrutiny, then the likelihood is that a
social dynamic will ensue that entails an escalation of generalized persecutory anxiety, organized by idealized fantasies, with accompanying
defences against such anxieties that translate into an overdetermined
anxiety situation at the level of front-line service provision. Cooper
(2011, 2014) has conceptualized the history of child protection policy in
Britain as a story of successive episodes in which the containing boundary of the formal child protection system has been breached at points
of crisis, resulting in the need for some form of arbitration or "settlement" in the judicial or public sphere, before some semblance of social
containment is re-established. The Francis Inquiry into Mid Staffs NHS
Trust, successive public scandals in the wider social care domain, and

the trail of crises afflicting the police service suggest that the analysis advanced here is probably applicable well beyond the particular professional case with which we are primarily concerned.

But what might all this mean for the "lived experience" of staff working within services afflicted by these complex processes, and for the vulnerable children and adults who depend upon them? How have anxieties developed since Menzies Lyth's study? Given the recognition of an increasing burden of policy prescription and performance management, have persecutory anxieties replaced depressive task-related anxieties or do the two coexist? And in response to these, how do socially structured defences manifest and to what end? This has received less attention than it deserves, and its study requires a closer, experience-near, or ethnographic form of enquiry.

A psycho-socially informed case study

The small-scale empirical study reported here (Lees, 2014) comprised a psycho-socially informed case study. The study employed ethnographic methods of observation, interviews, and documentary analysis and was theoretically informed by the work of Menzies Lyth and that of Woodhouse and Pengelly (1991), Cooper (2010), Krantz (2010), and Hinshelwood and Skogstad (2000). Research questions related to social workers' experiences of information sharing in the context of multi-agency working to safeguard children. Underlying the research was the recognition of the problematic nature of information sharing and a belief that it is an area of practice likely to be influenced by anxiety and defensiveness.

The cases were three social work teams within the same Local Authority Children's Services directorate. The teams were a Referral Screening Team (RST), an Initial Assessment Team (IAT) and a Longer Term Team (LTT). Practitioners in all teams were open about the anxiety-provoking and emotionally intense nature of their work that, in many ways, is unlike any other. As one senior practitioner in the LTT expressed it:

> You're very often taking the weight of the world on your shoulders, I mean where else, I sat back . . . one day and listened to the phone calls that were going on around me, I had one young boy of 12 that was in a sexual relationship with a family dog, I'd got another one who it was her father, and you can go round the table and you've got Mr A knocking absolute skittles of shit out of his wife, every night,

night after night after night, the children are caught up in it all, you've got another baby over there that's just eaten a huge lump of cannabis and has been rushed to hospital. Where else can you actually get up, shower, come to work in the morning and it's full on?

A great deal of anxiety, and other powerful emotions such as sadness and anger, were generated by the nature of these cases and by contact with vulnerable children and adults. (Powerful emotions in many forms were present in the workplace, and we agree with Paul Hoggett that anxiety is not the only emotion that needs defending against. Social workers often reported using humour, for example, as an antidote to the sad and upsetting nature of the cases they dealt with.) Social workers also spoke about dreading visits with particular service users and of being threatened and even physically attacked. This was not unexpected terrain—such issues have received attention within the academic literature (e.g., Ferguson, 2005; Taylor, Beckett, & McKeigue, 2008; Waterhouse & McGhee, 2009). These powerful emotional states resonate with the primitive anxieties aroused within nurses in pursuit of the caring task in Menzies Lyth's study.

Perhaps somewhat surprisingly, then, given the nature of the cases described in the quotation above, most day-to-day worry and anxiety for social work practitioners within the research site was caused by the demands of heavy workloads and competing priorities, within contexts of high demand and scarce resources.

You're kind of almost always catching up with yourself and you're almost always doing just enough. Which is why they get into this cycle of case open, little bit of signposting, case closed, referral, case opened, signposting, you know. You just kind of get into the circle. And time and time again you see families coming round and round and round . . . I think that's probably the worst part, is that if the case loads were lower and the timescales weren't so prominent I think we'd all do a much better job than what we do, even though we all do the best we can with the time we've got. (Social Worker, IAT)

Reflecting the increasingly "informational" nature of social work (Parton, 2008), it now appears that "managerial" anxieties are inherent in the working lives of social workers, as much as exposure to abuse, distress, and hostile clients. Menzies Lyth identified a number of these "managerial"-type anxieties in her study, but she described them as being secondary consequences of the adoption of socially structured defences against the primary, primitive anxieties of the nursing task. For example, she suggested that fears about operational breakdown (or inability to cope with the work) resulted from the defensive adoption of rigid and inflexible processes. Frustrations about the lack of opportunity to use professional judgement was described as another secondary anxiety of this rigid organization of work. In this study however, it is clear that external pressures of high demand for services and policy blueprints for work organization have given these anxieties a life of their own. They bear down on social work teams from outside and are as powerful, if not more so, on a day-to-day basis than anxieties about caring for vulnerable children.

Reflecting this, Cooper (2010) suggested that the political and policy context of twenty-first-century organizations was likely to have created a new set of anxieties, related to the prevailing conditions of market economy. These he named as:

» rationing anxiety (relating to the scarcity of resources)
» performance anxiety (relating to performance management and audit)
» partnership anxiety (working in networks and multi-agency arrangements over which no one has central control).

Anxieties expressed by participants across the three teams strongly resonated with the broad categories that Cooper defined. "Rationing" anxieties commonly expressed included staff and service cuts, pay freezes, staff turnover, and outdated/unsuitable office space. "Performance" anxieties related to heavy workloads, high administrative burden, competing priorities, performance management, and being able to do work well enough in pressured environments exacerbated by cases that are ambiguous and complex. While social workers' concerns about their own ability to function well and to keep children safe were depressive in nature, persecutory anxieties abounded as well. These related, in particular, to the monitoring by senior managers, of social workers' adherence to case timescales. Although social workers often did not feel this to be a fair reflection of the work they were doing, they were nevertheless susceptible to feelings of shame when they were flagged as falling behind.

> When we get work allocated to us that's late, Day 1 starts on the day of the referral regardless of when it's allocated to us. So we all have periods of time where all of our initial assessments are red because

> they're over 10 days, so then you're like I'm crap, I don't do my job
> . . . So you then do the monitoring report avoidance: I'm not looking
> at it because I know I haven't done it so you don't need to remind
> me every day. (Social worker, IAT)

For social workers within the LTT, the court environment added a
tranche of anxieties about their ability to present evidence that was
clear enough to stand up to cross examination and to allow the best
judgements to be made for children. In such adversarial environments,
persecutory anxieties did not seem to be misplaced.

> Especially when you're in court, you're going to have to give evi-
> dence in court, court proceedings are a bit of a blood bath. You get
> cross- examined, you need to be very thorough in your work . . .
> (Social worker, LTT)

"Partnership" anxieties were often forcefully expressed and related
to the lack of willingness by some other agencies to engage fully with
the child protection process, with social workers feeling that they were
sometimes literally, as well as figuratively, left "holding the baby".

Socially structured defences against anxiety

How, then, did defences manifest in response to the anxieties outlined
above? In this study, socially structured defences were taken to be
working processes that appeared to be disproportionate responses to
the situations encountered (Trevithick, 2011) and that were linked to
secondary consequences such as delays, frustration, and despondency.
These were identified tentatively by the researcher during observations
and checked out in interview with research participants. As a result of
this process, a new socially structured defence was identified, which
took the form of "spotlight" practice to clarify and justify the focus
of professional attention in the context of limitless demands, under-
resourcing, complex cases, and rigid performance management. This
took a variety of forms—in particular, attempts to make sure that over-
worked teams were doing the right work in the first place (manifest in
boundary and threshold disputes), to make facts and proposed courses
of action as explicit and clear as possible, and to rehearse and repeatedly check actions and decisions to ensure that mistakes are not made.
    Boundary disputes between agencies and the careful checking of
referrals by social workers have previously been identified as defensive

features of practice related to heavy workloads (Broadhurst et al., 2010) and feelings of being under siege (Woodhouse & Pengelly, 1991). Within the research site, boundary disputes were most evident at the internal boundary between the RST and the IAT. Despite the existence of a detailed local authority threshold document within the research site, interactions between the two teams were characterized by disputes over the nature of cases and whether they warranted social services intervention. Within the IAT, there was criticism of the RST's ability to filter cases "correctly". The IAT would sometimes immediately close cases that had been referred to them by the RST or would send them back with requests for further information. In turn, there was a perception among the RST team that their decisions were being scrutinized and unfairly criticized by the IAT. Within both these teams, there was also frequent criticism of the inability of some other agencies to make appropriate or detailed enough referrals. As the team leader of the IAT explained, the careful manning of in-boundaries represented a defence against taking on the "wrong" work, when they already have too much of the "right" work to do. If this happens, nothing can be carried out to a high enough standard.

> If we took that premise we'd be inundated and we're already too busy as it is. So if we are doing all the wrong work we can't get to the right work . . . I'm like "STOP! Don't do anything!" because we have a principle here that we must challenge this. We have to challenge this, because if we start taking things . . . I think has been part of our problem why we've been so inundated, because we can't just be a "yes" team.

Prominent in the LTTs, elaborate processes for clarifying and checking facts and decisions had developed. Social workers' tasks were often laid out, and reported back, on a step-by-step basis—with seniors setting out specific tasks for social workers to complete, who would then complete the task and return straight away to the senior to provide feedback. Involvement of a number of levels of management in discussions about casework were also frequently observed. Practitioners described multi-layered systems for the approval or sign-off of documentation—in particular, court paperwork. While the involvement of seniors/team manager in the day-to-day details of cases was perceived as supportive by some more junior members of staff in need of reassurance, it could cause frustration for those with more experience who identified associated consequences of delay and role overlap.

Why is that system in place that 3 people need to check it? I don't understand. Isn't someone competent enough to be able to check that report once, sign it and send it off? Because otherwise it's making the whole process even longer than what it needs to be, because ideally you'd want your court work done a week before. It's impossible. (Social worker, LTT)

These defences resonated with a number of those identified by Menzies Lyth regarding decision-making and checking with seniors. They also had an obsessional aspect to them, as Halton suggests. Taken together they represented socially structured defences against anxieties about carrying out important and risky work in contexts characterized by lack of time, resource, complexity, and ambiguity but, importantly, also in the shadow of an omnipresent inspectorial "management system in the mind" that was not the sole product of task-related anxieties or defences against these.

Spotlighting was used to shed light on complex and ambiguous cases, to illuminate decision-making, and to sift out any of the "wrong" work. While a spotlight is powerful for illuminating the details of dark and murky contexts, it is less able to provide a wider view, and therein lies the problem for inter-agency information-sharing and collaboration. Important issues may be lost in the shadows outside the concentrated but narrowly focused spotlight of professional attention. Information that is lost in the shadows cannot be shared. To allow a more diffused view to be taken, there is a need for enhanced "holding" of professionals through an increased sense of role clarity and containment within the organizational and inter-organizational contexts.

The professional "self"
and modern organizational anxieties

Our own experience of intensive post-qualifying training work with social workers and healthcare staff strongly suggests that the state of affairs we are describing has profound impacts on the lived experience of the workforce at all levels. Most people enter human service work with a primary, if sometimes naïve, desire to "help others", to provide care, and to engage humanely with complex human predicaments. Whatever else their roles and task demand, they want to be able to work in a relationship-based fashion and to use their professional self as a central resource in doing the work. Menzies Lyth's great contribution was to show us how complex and disturbing this simple aspiration actually transpires to be, as we encounter the reality of suffering, injury, mental pain, internal and relational conflict, fears of death and dying, and strong libidinal impulses in both others and ourselves in the ordinary course of such work. However, the hopeful dimension of her work was to show that if organizational boundary conditions are attuned to these realities, allowing space for continual non-judgemental reflection upon working experience, then the satisfactions and rewards of the work may far exceed any detrimental impact of the anxieties it generates.

Equally, the hopeful dimension to the case study described above is that *despite* carrying the weight of persecutory and depressive anxieties, practitioners nevertheless expressed much joy and satisfaction in their work with their service users. The respondent below surprised the researcher with this comment—as most of the conversations they had shared in the office were to do with his stress concerning the magnitude of his workload and performance management reports:

> . . . we all are, I think, making some difference somewhere, some positive impact somewhere. Um, you know, not all the clients would be happy with us in terms of like the parents or dads and mums, um, but I think we are working for the children. They may not even be able kind of, . . . share their views when it's really like, um, you know a teeny tiny child, um, but I, I am glad I'm doing it and I feel good by the end of the day. Most of the days (*laughs*). Not all the days, most of the days! I feel good that at least, you know, we have done something about that situation, about the child.

Thus, in the research process, A.L. was arguably subject to something analogous to a negative transference from her subjects. Given an opportunity for open-ended narrative disclosure, it is the weight of frustration, anger, and despair that is first communicated to a receptive listener, because these feelings and thoughts have no proper organizational outlet. This is a frequent experience for psychoanalytically attuned researchers, and it facilitates access to the complexities and subtleties of the lived experience of subjects, much as a good organizational consultancy would aim to do. The thinking and research advanced in this chapter suggests that negative, externally generated "boundary conditions" have become much more prominent in shaping the context of service delivery and that the anxieties and defences involved typically invade organizational "space" and, beyond this, the mental space that is the self of the worker. An account of lived organizational and personal experience by a child protection worker, written some years ago now and reported in Cooper (2009a) illustrates this vividly:

> I am working in a factory. I have been working there for the last five years. When I started working there I did not think it was a factory. It didn't look like a factory, not from the outside and not from the inside.
>
> We produce initial and core assessments in our factory. Our management counts the assessments completed on a weekly basis, and informs the workers of the results in team meetings and by emails. The workers don't seem to care about these numbers but they preoccupy the management.
>
> There have been many changes in our factory in the past five years, due to demands from above and competition from other factories. The management has been replaced, the teams were reconstructed, the machinery (workers, forms, IT systems) also saw great changes.
>
> I am quite confused about who is my master and who do I need to serve. Is it the customer or is it the government and do they have conflicting interests? I am thinking of running away from this factory to look for another job . . . in another factory.

Later she writes of how:

> The management measures (in percentages) the reports of initial and core assessments completed on time, and compare these to other teams. When the team manager reports these statistics in team meetings, I can recognise how my body becomes tense and my heart rate increases, and I get very angry . . . I have voiced my resentment about to this ritual but it was ignored by managers and other colleagues.
>
> In order to adjust practice to inspection standards our organization has become:
>
> > Obsessive about records
> > Obsessive about statistics
> > Manipulative of the statistics.
>
> > [Cooper, 2009a, pp. 174–175]

Our experience of receiving experienced, well-qualified practitioners like the one who wrote these passages into post-qualifying "continuing professional development" trainings is that they are often, in effect, depressed by their working lives. However, they do not usually know this, but gradual exposure to both the experience of reflective "work discussion" spaces (M. E. Rustin & Bradley, 2008) and also experientially inclined seminars on contemporary policy processes enables them to begin to feel and know about their depression and the frustration and anger that underlies it, and to rediscover a "lost" or buried sense of professional vocation rooted in the desire to engage with other people—a professional self that has gone into hiding. But crucially, *both* forms of training experience are required. Reflective case discussion that does not engage with the baleful impact of the organizational and policy environment goes only so far. Recognizing, naming, and recovering some sense of personal agency in relation to the different, intersecting, and frequently congruent forms and sources of anxiety delineated in this chapter—those that are located primarily in the difficult nature of the primary task, and those that flow from the organizational, managerial, and policy environment—becomes possible and, to a degree, liberating.

Fear and dread: a contemporary "structure of feeling"

In a much-cited but not very well developed or articulated passage, Raymond Williams introduced the idea of a "structure of feeling" to suggest that particular social epochs or formations are characterized by pervasive, organized, but not cognitively very "legible" collective emotional experiences. A structure of feeling, he writes,

> is as firm and definite as "structure" suggests, yet it is based in the deepest and often least tangible elements of our experience. It is a way of responding to a particular world which in practice is not felt as one way among others—a conscious "way"—but is, in experience, the only way possible. Its means, its elements, are not propositions or techniques; they are embodied, related feelings. In the same sense, it is accessible to others—not by formal argument or by professional skills, on their own, but by direct experience . . . [Williams, 1993, p. 18]

Menzies Lyth's seminal thesis about the functioning of social systems as a defence against anxiety captured something of the same idea, but at the more specific, micro-level of organizational culture. The sense so many people have of finding in her work the articulation of something they have "always known" but for which they have had no language or concepts with which to make sense attests to its potency. For example, recently one of us (A.C.) encountered a senior professional and psychotherapist who had been his social work tutee twenty years earlier. She recalled, "I told you about my struggles in the agency where I was on placement. You said, 'Go and read Menzies Lyth'. I did and I never looked back."

The practitioner in A.L.s' study who described "taking the weight of the world on your shoulders" was referencing the astonishing variety, complexity, and emotional intensity of his team's encounters with individual suffering, family conflict, infantile vulnerability, and adult perversion and neglect—the demands of the primary task. The practitioner who expostulates, "Why is that system in place that 3 people need to check it? I don't understand. Isn't someone competent enough to be able to check that report once, sign it and send it off?", is referencing something different that in our view cannot be fully explained or understood with the conceptual resources Menzies Lyth bequeathed to us.

However, it is in the nature of defences, whether functional or dysfunctional (and most defences are sometimes or in part one and sometimes the other), that they successfully disguise or obscure the threats, feeling states, and fantasies to which they are an attempted solution. As a paradigm instance of good psychoanalytic work, Menzies Lyth's research allows us to see beyond certain kinds of apparent bureaucratic mindlessness to the literally "dreadful" sources of anxiety, located in the task, that generate defensive practices. There is much further work to be done in order to provide corresponding empirical support for the proposition that the pervasive obsessionality of modern managerialist practice arises—in part, at least—from a collective need to defend against equally pervasive fears of personal and organizational failure emanating from, and situated in, a public sphere organized by a competitive, risk-averse policy and political climate. The sociology of modern organizational development suggests that many forces other than just task anxiety are at work in producing the total picture we are describing, forces imbued with but not simply reducible to processes of projected anxiety or social ambivalence. In line with Halton's observations, we hold that we can only undertake this more fully psychosocial enquiry via a rigorous engagement with the experiences of social subjects inhabiting the live world of such psychosocial formations, and in these terms we believe that the work reported in this chapter is a beginning.

CHAPTER SIXTEEN

Still not good enough!
Must try harder: an exploration of
social defences in schools

Simon Tucker

In *The Future of an Illusion*, Freud states that "the path from the infant at the breast to the civilized man is a long one" (Freud, 1927c). He points to the role of education and, more specifically, religious education in supporting the child in navigating this pathway. Amid declining faith in other institutions—including the church—schools have inherited increasing responsibilities for their congregation and have the societal task of providing tools for their subjects to survive in civilized society. They thereby contain anxiety about rivalry, about competition, and about future failure and success. Schools are also charged with safeguarding and providing a return on the emotional investment of parents; in contemporary and individualized society, children may be the only relationship that can be counted on. Because of this dynamic, their education and care is also charged with tremendous anxiety.

It was of interest to me as a researcher and consultant to head teachers that 30% of newly qualified teachers drop out in the first year (Rozenholtz, 1989)—a close comparison to Menzies Lyth's (1988) student nurses. Wider reading revealed some shocking data: the Health & Safety Executive (HSE, 2000) rated teaching the most stressful profession in the UK—with 41% of teachers describing themselves as "highly stressed".

One of the most striking surveys was conducted by the National Association of Head Teachers (NAHT) in May 2000. The data from the survey suggested that stress levels in head teachers are rising, with more than a third of absent rates being due to work-related stress: 40% of respondents had visited their doctors with stress-related symptoms, 20% felt they drank too much, 15% believed they were alcoholics, and 25% experienced depression, hypertension, insomnia, depression, or gastrointestinal disorders (*The Guardian*, 13 July 2000).

The NAHT went on to suggest that four out of five head teachers were considering early retirement, and many were reporting burn-out in their forties.

As a consultant to head teachers, I had become aware that many appeared to be deeply troubled in their occupational roles; I was also aware of the complex origins of these states of mind. It became clear that the experiences of these individuals had both an internal and an external dimension: an internal dimension in the aspirations and anxieties they brought with them into their role and their work situations, an "external" dimension through the culture of the work environment itself.

Powerfully connected to both appeared to be a fear of failure, giving rise to violent and intense feelings in the head teachers I met as a consultant and researcher into leadership in schools. Apparent within my study of head teachers is that the individual defensive structures presented during interview—that is, working harder and harder to avoid anxieties associated with failure or fear of failure—could also be understood simultaneously as institutional defences at play: a collective defensive formation, as it were, operating within the school environment.

Despite being impressive individuals and professionals, many appeared to harbour underlying doubts about their abilities, and many had experienced difficult childhoods—feelings of failure, of being out of control, of not being good enough—which for some had been behind the choice of teaching as a career. Education was selected because it was a mid-way profession (e.g., not a solicitor or GP) and because it was an easily identifiable avenue to prove self and a means of taking control. This had provided a template and drive for later success and, for some, a quick rise to headship:

> But I had that real "*I have got to succeed*" and I particularly had that when I started working, wanting to be successful. And I think that stems from my early life where the fact that I hadn't, that I had failed something (my 11+ exam), was a big issue for my parents and therefore a big issue for me.

Failure at school appeared to be a recurring theme and a source of motivation to work in education. For participants, "failure" could be not doing well on the 11+ or not getting into Oxford.

> I got 10 A-grade GCSEs and 4 A levels, 3 As and a B. And the first thing my head of house said to me when I got my A-level results was "oh, what a shame about the B" (*laughs*). That was literally the first bit of feedback, I remember that (*laughs*). I was predicted an A and I got a B in French. It was like "oh god the world's gonna end", you know?

Many had experienced failure or a sense of shame early in life—experiences that had driven them to succeed and made it hard to stop. Indeed, the early defence in the face of anxiety of working harder—"must try harder"—would for some be a response to increasing pressure and stress as a head teacher. But this came at a great cost because it was also a key source of stress—the very drives that had been the motivation and impetus for professional progression and success took some to headship and others to the edge of breakdown. The fear of failure appeared to drive individuals to greater and greater efforts, even when these appeared unrealistic or damaging to the self.

> I just literally went to the doctors and broke down and she actually said to me is the only thing I can do, and I am going to do, this happened in the March, and she said I am going to sign you off until September. I said you can't do that I am back at work on Monday!

Head teachers in this study had largely progressed through a succession of educational experiences to their positions as leaders of schools. Many had no experience outside family or school of existing within other institutions. In this respect, they were products of a uniquely circular experience: from family to school to university back to school—a dynamic that had some benefit, giving them a deep empathetic understanding, but also intensified the identification with self and work and the potential emotional impact of the role.

Crumbling historical institutions appear to have left schools and head teachers picking up increasing responsibility for children who have fallen through gaps in the wider societal fabric. Many agencies have been eroded in recent years, and, with thresholds receding, schools and head teachers are left shouldering concerns and anxieties on behalf of the wider community and professional network.

Schools have been colonized by a whole series of functions that were previously assigned to other institutions, including families. Concerns raised in political discourse and in the media appear to become rapidly designated as problems that schools are expected to solve. This apparent delegation of responsibility for broad social ills enables the wider society to feel absolved of responsibility and leaves schools and head teachers' "holding the baby"—that is, anxieties—on behalf of all of us. Schools have become the proverbial chestnut tree, which has just kept spreading.

Anxiety arises from deep-rooted fears about future life-chances and survival, in a competitive and precarious social environment. This is especially the case as individual life-chances have come to depend so much on children's performance within the educational system. These anxieties generate a continued *"need to do better"*, a mantra that appears to dominate discourse in schools and, indeed, the earliest childhood memories and narratives of a number of the participants.

The failing school in this structure is seen not as a product of the whole system but, instead, merely as an individually flawed and dysfunctional unit requiring special attention, "special measures", or even closure. This institutional splitting allows others to be named as "super-heads" and their schools as outstanding. Obviously this is problematic—by nature super-heroes, whether supermen or super-woman, tend to be unusual. But this is what the system of education appears to require. Surely the strength of any system is how it provides an environment that allows the ordinary, the average, to reach their full potential, not how many super-heroes it creates.

Good news is only good news if it can be related to bad news in some way (Lousada & Cooper, 2005). In schools, the only place to put bad news is "special measures". As Obholzer (1994a) suggests, the task for schools is, at an unconscious level, daunting:

> At an unconscious level, what is hoped for from the education system is unreality: that all our children will be well equipped—ideally, equally equipped to meet all of life's challenges. [p. 172]

Truth appeared to be largely avoided, in an organizational sense. Many spoke openly about this. The technology pushed people into circumstances they knew were unreal. It was a burden for some.

To understand why this is we need to go to the study conducted by Rutter (1979). Rutter had demonstrated that, even taking into account differences at intake, schools had a significant impact through culture and ethos. This study was tremendously influential in the way schools (in particular, failing schools) have been viewed and supported over the last three decades.

Rutter's study shifted the previous emphasis on "structural" explanations (in particular, social-class intake) as the variable in determining success. On one level, it was a substantial and informative piece of research demonstrating the difference that organization, culture, and morale could make to outcomes. But it was misleading. The inference drawn by politicians from this research was that any school should be able to produce results irrespective of intake characteristics. It has become the "stick" that many schools and head teachers in socially disadvantaged communities have been beaten with in subsequent years where the average or less than average have been attacked by the example of the exceptional.

The principal conclusion drawn from this research, however, ignores one key aspect of the reality: social class, as a variable, still has the greatest impact on outcomes.

Participants chose their profession because of their personality characteristics—conscious and unconscious. This is the psychological skeleton we bring to work. But these characteristics are both fostered and fed by institutional, group, societal, economic, and political processes.

The status anxieties of teachers highlighted previously also reflect an external anxiety linked to a long-running uncertainty within the teaching profession in recent decades. Teaching has been described as a "semi-profession", and it has lacked some of the autonomy, control, and status of other, "full" professional groups (i.e., law and medicine). Its main representation has been through the trade union movement, not professional associations—trade union collectivism having been chosen, perhaps, because other professional avenues for recognition and expression were not available. Because of this, the relationship with successive governments over the last twenty years has been antagonistic, with the profession increasingly losing the authority to determine the curriculum and assessment system it is expected to deliver.

The removal of schools from local authority control was, on one level, a "solution" to perceived teacher collectivism and a difficulty in controlling what conservatives and free marketeers saw as the progressive establishment represented by teaching unions and their (at the time) left-wing allies in the university sector. This was dealt with by the reduction of the academic part of teacher training and the weakening of the supportive and insulating structure of local authorities. While empowering head teachers (albeit as administrators of more centralized forms of control—i.e., assessment and the national curriculum) and rewarding them, in terms of status, money, and power, it also exposed them to failure and a weakening of the support structure, including collaborative and collegial relationships with colleagues. This provided opportunities, but also greater risks—a loss of identity and support.

There was a shift, highlighted in interviews with head teachers who took part in this study, in a corporate direction allied with a changing perception of schools as businesses, leaving teachers as employees or hired hands. This shift has been complicated by traditional cultures, which in some respects run counter to the current direction of travel. These polarities were clearly apparent during interviews:

> I thought it de-skilled teachers to say we are going to do it by num-bers, this is how you will do it, then teachers lose their skills.
>
> The only thing that is consistent in school, it's *not the teachers, it's not the pupils*, it's *the systems* that you put in place.
>
> It's basically running a business and anyone who tells you differ-ently is wrong.
>
> A Head of a school as opposed to being a boss or a leader in busi-ness is different because there is that social and moral responsibility that goes with it.

Wider changes in society have created fracture lines within the pro-fession. The pressure for teachers and head teachers to provide for dependency needs are considerable, because of the nature of the work with children and the accompanying parental and community expec-tations about care and support (as well as education). However, the changing nature of the institution means that schools are becoming unavailable for these types of projections; the underlying psychological task is thereby obscured, resulting in disappointment and conflict at the boundary of the organization. This confusing and highly emotional situation generates increasing pressure and persecutory anxiety for those who work in schools.

The weakening of status and class differences in society, and the construction of more homogeneous lifestyles and consumer patterns, have exposed everyone to the same anxieties that give rise to the same question: How well will my children do at school? What will happen if they do not succeed?

As education becomes more important to children's life-chances, head teachers are expected to have the answers. They have a par-ticular symbolic role in school, in society, and in the communities in which they work, a role that acts as a conductor for the social anxieties described above.

However, when faced with difficulty, their position appeared to make it difficult for them to ask for help. On one level, these group projections were largely welcomed by them, inviting aspects of themselves with which they felt comfortable (professional success and competence), while denying the source of anxiety—the fear of failing—which kept them locked into realizing group expectations while denying their own needs and vulnerabilities. Some were, in this way, their own worst enemies and could not ask for support.

One major source of stress appeared for some to be the very drives that had been the original motivation and impetus for professional progression, which had allowed a sense of mastery over earlier anxieties. Great efforts had provided a potent model for professional success, but this had become problematic when participants were overwhelmed or were unable to "succeed". The objective situation was no longer a representation of an inner phantasy but was, instead, equated to it. The work situation of the school, which could have provided a legitimate avenue for coping and developing new skills, instead provoked in some a massive regression. Faced with potential "failure", they were thrown back to childhood—the site of early narcissistic wounds. In response, many pushed themselves even harder and learnt defensive strategies, which took some to the edge of breakdown.

> I would wake up in the middle of the night thinking about work, all my dreams were nightmares and they were all about work . . . Then suddenly I found myself at work . . . I couldn't make a decision, trivial trivial decisions (*laughs*) I couldn't make any. I would find myself wandering around the school, I wouldn't know what I was doing where I was going, I would occupy my time doing trivial things when there were important things that needed doing, and I suppose after being like that for well over a month, probably two months, I just knew that I wasn't safe any more.
>
> I came away from school in the middle of the day thinking I will just have some time off, I need some time off (*laughs*) and I never went back.

One hypothesis that emerges is that the professional experiences of teachers and head teachers have become inhabited by the anxieties of the children and communities for whom they provide a service.

Feelings aroused—fear of judgment, fear of failure, helplessness, pow-erlessness—can spawn increasing cycles of panic and distress, distur-bance that may be acted out by staff or are felt but not understood. These can be deflected onto others who are seen to be less able or capable, who then bear the shame, humiliations, and burdens for the system, which drives them to increasingly manic acts of reparation to try to "make good".

Education is a passport to future success and increased life-chances, but in a rapidly changing social environment where we have witnessed the collapse of entire industries and secure employment prospects, schools have perhaps taken on greater significance and have there-fore become more pressurized and loaded with anxieties of govern-ments, communities, and parents alike. Societal aspirations are, in some respects, dependent on the children of today. We are all on a blind march towards a future horizon that is increasingly unpredictable and for which schools are expected to prepare our children.

There have been heightened expectations placed in schools. This in part reflects changes of a social kind and, more specifically, in the labour market. Up to and including the 1960s, aspirations were limited for many people, and there were large fields of manual employment, some of it skilled, to absorb those who did not succeed educationally. Therefore, what happened in schools was not so indicative of later occupational chances or future economic well-being.

However, the reduction in manufacturing and rises in unemploy-ment have considerably shifted this position. Heralded by Tony Blair's mantra "Education, Education, Education" in 2001, schools have become the new route to economic success, while other routes have fallen by the wayside or become more restricted.

The key to a successful life lies in the labour market, and the key to success in the labour market lies in education. Education is therefore deeply linked with selection. It is a conclusion that emphasizes the anxiety that exists in schools, the core of which lies in fears about future life-chances and even survival—collectively we will all, one day, be dependent on the children of today.

We want schools to provide year-on-year improvements and to pro-vide us with good news and good results. However, this can become a collusive contract that is hard to question. Everyone wants successful schools. But schools only give an illusion of upward mobility for all through education. According to Ulrich Beck (1992), schools have never provided this and are never likely to. And yet we expect all children to meet the same standard, and schools are expected to deliver this "Amentia" (Freud, 1927c), a collective illusion in which we all invest. Interviews revealed that head teachers were trying to manage realities connected to the task which were hard to acknowledge and, in some respects, were completely denied in the wider system.

Many children are not going to be doctors or solicitors or teachers. To expect all children to meet the same standards is unachievable, and yet this is what we expect teachers and head teachers to deliver. The circumstances and limits of their work are not recognized by the defined task, and because of this many of them will continually fail or will distort practices to meet official targets.

The current definition of task is on one level obvious, on another far from clear. The current list of tasks schools should deliver does not appear to usefully convey to role-holders where their end and their beginning should be—either at work or outside it. It offers fertile ground for reparative omnipotence to ride rough-shod over reasonable expectation, militating against work being contained within manageable proportions, and preventing realistic evaluations of self and task.

The effect on head teachers is perhaps twofold. Omnipotence fuelled by individual and systemic projections creates unrealistic expectations and may result in attempts to enact societal fantasies. In recent years, there have been significant societal changes in home life and a blurring of boundaries between home and work, as people increasingly work long hours or work from home. Head teachers were no exception. Many worked at weekends and during the evening. In a life dominated by work (for some, school had become home, and home school), work appeared to be the only source of gratification.

The extension of computer technology was evident in my interviews, a vein that ran across the last two decades which made detailed assessment, examination, audit, and inspections possible. The technology has been used to increase the scrutiny of schools. It does not seem to take away anything and is adding to, rather than eroding, the workload. This created more pressure for some and was felt to undermine their authority, initiative, and judgment as they had to provide data that, even when positive, was not always felt to convey the reality of the work. This discrepancy between the real and the prescribed aspect of the work was again a significant source of stress. Truth and authenticity appeared to be the required sacrifice for the appeasement of authority figures—the superintendents of the inspectorial order increasingly placed in schools.

Policies, regulations, inspections, and targets were the organizational "support" that was offered to head teachers. Rigid prescription, itself an expression of social defences, gave rise to rigid task-performance and practices such as "teaching to the test". Unsurprisingly the overall effect was generally more persecutory than helpful—in some schools nothing appeared to be left to chance:

> The only thing that is consistent in school, it's not the teachers, it's not the pupils, it's the systems that you put in place and those systems have to run from nursery to year six otherwise you have no direct comparisons and you can't then implement them successfully.

Traditionally, anxiety is captured and held within the hierarchy of organizations. This can no longer be true of schools (or many other organizations that exist in modernity). Instead, what has become apparent is a position of aggregation, separation, and isolation. Responsibilities that are increasingly pushed into schools are monitored and inspected, providing relief for those higher up the organizational hierarchy but apparently leaving destructive impulses and associated anxieties wedged in the school itself. It has the net result of severing responsibility and ensuring contamination does not spread to the wider system. It is not, on the face of it, a model of containment; it is a type of quarantine.

Jaques (1955) demonstrated how bad impulses can be projected into different groups as a defence against paranoid anxiety. Some groups become viewed as sources of trouble and thereby become identified as objects of attack. Schools may hold this underlying role for government, appearing to be the targets for regulatory sadism where regulators have inflicted excessive burdens on schools in attempts to control them.

Education, apparently driven by the desire for individual "choice", is itself a product of social and societal discourse, which often articulates values of the corporate world—which schools and head teachers are expected to model, disseminate, and comply with. As such, they are also exposed to these processes of scrutiny and control themselves, which increase the levels of paranoid anxiety within the system. Underlying fears about social chaos represent powerful political drivers to establish and maintain systems of control through schools. We have a sense of them sitting on the edge of the class system, subject to the tensions and anxieties at the threshold.

Businesses are driven by competition to create profit. Increasingly, education is exposed to the same endless process of production, producing pupils for increasingly complex labour markets. The danger is that unlimited and unrealistic drives for educational improvement increase defences and expose teachers and head teachers to alienation, stress, and suicide.

Schools find themselves in a difficult position when the labour market contracts and secure and satisfying career opportunities diminish. The concept of the "squeezed middle" (Ed Miliband, 26 November 2010) applies to the labour market as well as to living standards (these things are obviously connected). An increase in top jobs (e.g., in the City, etc.) and lower paid and poorly rewarded work opportunities has occurred while professional and skilled opportunities in the mid-range have significantly declined (*Daily Telegraph*, 1 March 2014).[1] Schools are expected to maintain the aspirations (and frustrations) of students (and parents) when many opportunities outside are diminishing.

Headship in an area of high unemployment is, I suspect, a very different proposition compared to an area where employment opportunities are more available, identifiable, and accessible. Further research exploring headship and schools in these differing contextual situations would be invaluable.

At the turn of the century, a period of "collective upward mobility"—an expansion in white-collar and professional work—created a climate of relative optimism. This may have disguised the anomic anxieties as the middle arena became flooded and competition increased, as did the fear of and exposure to failure. The following economic contraction meant that opportunities went down and anxiety went up. League tables in schools signalled a shift externally as opportunities became scarce and competition became fierce. This became translated in schools, where increasingly any institutional failings were met with sanctions and disgrace.

These societal and institutional responses through schools are in part due to increasing economic pressures and stresses placed on parents through weakening community structures—unprocessed and un-contained by the wider system, these expectations and associated anxieties are placed in schools to manage, ultimately for head teachers to navigate and hold.

Pushed in terms of self, head teachers and teachers are also pushed in terms of role and pushed in terms of organization. This is a potent combination. It could result in a successful school. Or it could push role-holders beyond their limits, with both predictable and, at times, dire results. The converging power and force of these internal and external factors should not be underestimated—in my study, criticism or any failing at work appeared to be acutely felt and was defended against through working harder, even when participants recognized this was unrealistic. It did not make them effective, and, without a space for understanding, challenge, or thinking they were unable to consider or gain perspective on their own professional practice or even their own welfare. Instead, many appeared driven by a wider anxiety that had found its mark or resonance in the early experiences of many of the head teachers in this study. With no formal system of supervision, there was no organizationally sanctioned route for the emotional experience of work, nowhere to explore it without judgment or without intrusion. Not accounted for, emotions were left trapped in the individuals themselves.

Irene Hogg was a head teacher who a few years ago went missing and was later found dead, having killed herself less than a week after a visit from Her Majesty's Inspectorate of Education. Her trade union commented that "you *never quite know the individual circumstances*". Of course they were right, on one level: that they did not know. The question is, what is it that prevents us knowing? Sadly this is not the only example of suicide in schools: In 2007 two primary school teachers committed suicide as "a result of OFSTED induced stress".

More recently Helen Mann, in a headship post for just six months, was found dead: the coroner recently recorded a death of suicide following a poor Ofsted report. Those who worked with her said she was terrified of "failure".

A focus solely on technology, assessment, and inspection ultimately runs the risk of ignoring the fact that human well-being is fundamental to the health of any organization, and to any society. However obvious this may seem, the current system of education does not realize or support this. Anxiety about failure drives a system that is increasingly reductionist and mechanical in nature—where learning and the love of learning are sacrificed to targets and outputs and where those responsible for delivering the necessary results are persecuted by a wider system that is apparently determined not—or cannot bear—to hear about the realities of the work.

The wider climate of blame and shame, fostered in part by the rhetoric and preaching from those in central government, does not acknowledge in any way the complexity of the social systems in which schools are so deeply embedded. These denials give rise to fragmenting and part-solutions that keep anxieties locked in schools, with all the damage and despair this can mean for those who work within them.

The anxieties this chapter has attempted to trace are simultaneously located deep within the inner worlds of individuals, in the communities they serve, and in the sociopolitical systems within which modern day's schools exist. Profound anxieties arising in the face of globalized and increasingly complex markets have come home to roost in schools at a time when the breakdown of the supporting structure has severely damaged the capacity to tolerate extreme anxiety. Unless the systems of support for teachers and head teachers can be bolstered in some meaningful way, the organizational task as well as the health and well-being of individuals will always be threatened by the anxieties that underlie the education system.

Note

1. Research by the think-tank Resolution Foundation and the London School of Economics (Plunkett & Pessoa, 2013) found that the number of people in middle-paid roles fell by 170,000 to 14.61 million between 2008 and 2012; over the same period, the number of people in low-paid employment rose by 190,000 to 7.86 million and the number of best-remunerated jobs increased by 140,000 to 6.79 million.

CHAPTER SEVENTEEN

Work discussion groups as a container for sexual anxieties in schools

Emil Jackson

This chapter explores the use of work discussion groups, offered to teachers,[1] as one important method of helping teachers address, explore, and contain a range of anxieties within school settings. In particular, this chapter aims to illustrate the ways in which work discussion groups can provide teachers with a unique space—not usually offered elsewhere—to process intense anxieties evoked when the student–teacher relationship and learning environment is disturbed by matters relating to sexuality.

Anxiety as an ordinary feature in school life

At the most basic level, the very essence of any learning environment involves the management of effective levels of anxiety. When the level of challenge is set too low for a student or class group, they will soon "switch off" and become disengaged through under-stimulation and boredom. Equally, when the level of challenge is set too high, students can become flooded with anxiety in a way that has an adverse impact on what they are able to absorb. In contrast, outstanding teaching and learning usually involves teachers stretching students out of their comfort zone into new and unfamiliar territory, which, by its very nature, generates some anxiety—but in a way that feels safe and supportive—

engaging students in a way that keeps them alert, attentive, and stimu-lated (cf. Vygotsky, 1978).[2]

More broadly, the nature and trajectory of school life requires chil-dren, parents, and their teachers to develop the capacity to manage and contain a multitude of ordinary—and ordinarily intense—anxie-ties. Within secondary education, for example, these include anxieties relating to the transition from primary to secondary school; the painful process of separation from family towards greater independence and autonomy; discovering one's own identity amidst the development of peer-group relationships and pressures; managing the stress of exams; and leaving school and facing an uncertain future.

Anxieties often increase dramatically around puberty, when the pace of bodily and hormonal changes can leave adolescents feeling besieged by unfamiliar thoughts, feelings, and impulses. Some are left feeling like virtual strangers in their own body. Sexual and aggressive urges are felt to be especially threatening, particularly when they are experienced in relation to family members. Adolescents are then driven to export much of their energy away from their family and into the school environment, where it is discharged and transferred onto rela-tionships with fellow students and teachers.

Sexuality and sexual anxieties in schools

Given that the student population in secondary schools is almost entirely comprised of adolescents who are charged with burgeoning hormones, one would expect sparks of sexuality to be present nearly everywhere. And not just between the adolescents. It is, for example, completely normal—even healthy, within reason—for adolescent stu-dents to become infatuated with and have all sorts of sexual fantasies about their teachers. However, when the pace of change within their developing bodies and minds is at its peak, many young people struggle to differentiate between feelings of intimacy and sexuality—especially with those teachers to whom they have become attached.[3] While this process is essentially "normal" from a developmental perspective, it can nevertheless generate intense anxiety and confusion for all concerned.

What is striking here is not the rather ordinary phenomena and anxieties I have described above. Instead, what is striking is that despite the fact that these phenomena are common-place and although almost all teachers agree that the student–teacher relationship lies at the heart of effective learning, they receive almost no input whatsoever in this area within initial teacher training or subsequent professional development and in-service training (INSET). And if this area is overlooked, then the whole area of student–teacher crushes and fantasies is treated as virtually taboo. More often than not, for example, there seems to be some sort of half-conscious group process that ensures that teachers turn a blind eye to uncomfortable issues such as these, ignoring them or, at most, laughing them off as if they were some sort of joke. All of this tends to leave staff at greater risk of isolation and with little support or training in how to prevent, manage, and diffuse potentially problematic situations from arising. This can unfortunately result in situations arising that are indeed very serious—and anything but funny.

For these reasons, this chapter focuses on the potential for work discussion groups (WDGs) to provide teachers with a unique space in which they can be helped to process and contain sexual anxieties that are inevitably evoked in the ordinary course of school life.

The work discussion group model

Work discussion groups are one of the most central and highly valued models of training and supervision that have been developed at the Tavistock Centre over the past 60 years. The evolution of the work discussion methodology has been well described in the book by Rustin and Bradley (2008). The more specific application and evaluation of WDGs in educational settings has also been described in some detail by, for example, Jackson (2002, 2008) and Warman and Jackson (2007). To the best of my knowledge, the potential for WDGs to help teachers process and contain anxieties evoked by matters relating to sexuality in schools is not something that has been written about previously.

Put simply, WDGs in schools offer teachers a regular opportunity to share and think through any anxieties, dilemmas, or challenges that are preoccupying them in relation to their work with students and class groups. Each meeting would be likely to involve one or two teachers outlining a current concern, which would then be more fully explored and discussed with the group, facilitated by an external consultant—a bit like a group consultation. Rather than primarily seeking a specific solution or direction for the "presenter"[4] to take, WDGs aim to open up different ways of seeing and thinking so as to generate a deeper understanding of what might be happening beneath the surface. Within educational settings, WDGs would frequently involve discussions about students who are causing concern and whose academic or emotional development are at risk. Often, it is the students who manage to get under their teachers' skin, provoking the strongest feelings in others, who are most helpfully considered. As one teacher put it when introducing her concern to the group, "It is not what the student says or does that I find most difficult, but rather the way it makes me feel". Following the group discussion, while being extremely careful to protect confidentiality, the presenter and others in the group are then free to take (or leave) whatever insights or suggestions feel most useful and helpful.

School-based WDGs are usually facilitated by an external consultant, often a child and adolescent psychotherapist, whose thinking and approach is underpinned by a combination of core psychoanalytic, group dynamic, and organizational concepts. It is often an understanding of processes such as projection, splitting, transference, and countertransference that are experienced as most helpful by teachers—even revelatory—though the language used to explore them within the WDG would be straightforward and void of terminology to ensure that everyone's understanding is maximized. WDGs with more senior members of the school leadership team might involve two external consultants co-facilitating—for instance, a child psychotherapist working together with an organizational consultant.

WDG meetings usually take place anything between weekly and monthly. They can be effectively offered to staff at any level of an organization—though group membership would usually comprise staff with similar roles and responsibilities. WDGs are best suited to staff who voluntarily opt to attend because of their own wish for learning and development.

The examples that follow are drawn from my experience, over the past 16 years, of facilitating WDGs with qualified and unqualified teachers, middle and senior leaders, and headteachers.

WDG Example 1

Some years ago I worked with Peter,[5] an empathic and thoughtful young man who was newly qualified as a teacher and had recently taken up his first substantive position. In his tutor group was a vulnerable 13-year-old girl who, sensing Peter's compassionate demeanour, quickly engaged with her teacher and sought him out for additional supportive discussions about her difficulties. Then, one day within his first term of teaching, the student made an allegation that Peter had behaved inappropriately towards her—inferring that he had made some sort of sexual approach. The school, needing to follow established procedures, had to suspend Peter while the allegation was properly investigated. The investigation involved social services and continued for over a month before the student finally retracted her allegation about her teacher and reported that she was actually being sexually abused by her uncle. While Peter was relieved that his ordeal was finally over and he could return to school, he felt traumatized—all the more so because necessary protocols militated against the possibility of support or contact with colleagues—leaving him feeling horribly shamed, isolated, and helpless, with his sense of his credibility as a teacher and as a person feeling shredded, much as his student may well have been feeling.

Shortly after returning to work, Peter asked to join a fortnightly WDG set up to support teaching and support staff[6] in relation to their work with students. For some time, he contributed thoughtfully to presentations made by other members of staff but did not volunteer to share any of his own issues or concerns. Several months later, for the first time, Peter finally felt able to talk with his colleagues in the WDG about what had happened and how affected he was, and continued to be, by the experience. He described, for example, how "even now, when I see the student across the corridor, it impacts immediately on my whole physiology . . . making me tense up and feel anxious . . . I don't feel safe when I am anywhere near her". The sense of anguish he conveyed was palpable.

Peter then offered some more information about the original situation and how it had evolved from his perspective. He told us how he could sense that his student was having a tough time and had wanted to support her, but then he had started to develop a nagging concern that she was seeking him out more regularly and might be becoming overly attached and dependent. He didn't share this with colleagues or his line manager because he wasn't even sure there was anything to worry about, so he didn't want to waste their time. When this was further explored by group members, Peter also admitted his fear of being judged—for instance, in case his colleagues would think that her over-involvement was an indication that he had done something wrong.

There were a number of important elements to the discussion that followed. At one level, it was an enormous relief for Peter simply to be able to share what had happened more openly with his colleagues within a small-enough and safe-enough environment. He described, for example, how, until now, he had hardly felt able to look anyone in the eye—as if he feared his name and reputation had already been tainted forever. The capacity of the group to explore this in a receptive and non-judgemental manner left him feeling less ashamed within himself as well as less shamed in the mind of his peers. This already felt to him as though a heavy burden had been lifted.

Within the WDG, members acknowledged what an awful experience this must have been for Peter and were compassionate towards their colleague. Some anger was initially expressed towards the student for making the allegation and towards the "management" for suspending the teacher. "How can they let the student come back into school after what she has done?" With some help in thinking about what might be going on from different perspectives, these angry feelings soon gave way to a sense of concern and appreciation about what the girl might have been enduring within her home environment and how meting out a permanent exclusion as punishment would also not have been a fair or helpful solution. Linked to this was also a greater awareness about some of the impossible choices parents and other family members might find themselves having to make in situations such as these—where there is no such thing as an ideal solution.

One member picked up on what a loss it must have been for the student to have her teacher's support withdrawn, even though it was withdrawn because of her own actions. Another teacher commented on how guilty she must have felt and terrified of what people at school would now think about her: "It isn't just her tutor's reaction that might scare her . . . can you imagine what her peers would think if they knew she had caused them to be robbed of their much liked teacher?!" Group members were then helped to make important connections between what the student was experiencing within her personal life and how aspects of this were repeated within the "school family", in particular within her relationship with her tutor. A number of significant parallels were noted, including the feelings of isolation; the reluctance to act on one's gut feeling that something was not right, for fear of being judged; feelings of having been wrongly violated and robbed without a means of protecting oneself; and feelings of betrayal, abandonment, and loss. The group were also alerted to the way in which their own reactions within this very discussion might be symbolic of a significant dynamic—for instance, the connection between their initial outrage that the girl was allowed to remain in the school "without recourse" and the student's likely outrage that the alleged "abuser" (the uncle) was allowed to continue to visit the home without being "excluded" from the family.

In the latter part of the discussion, the group returned to the teacher's earlier comment about what it was like to see the student across the corridor and how it continued to affect him. Members identified with how difficult they would find it if they were in a similar position. The group also helped Peter to consider what, if anything, would help at this point—for example, whether a further facilitated meeting might be needed and, if so, what form this might take and whom it might involve.

By the end of the discussion, Peter looked quite different—as if an underlying sense of dread, rather like a dark cloud, was no longer hanging over his head. For the first time since he had returned to school, he said that he now felt a little less scared of walking the corridors and seeing the student. As much as benefiting from the insights gained from the *content* of what was discussed, Peter seemed to value the *experience* of sharing his experiences—and feeling heard—within the supportive setting of the WDG. To a large extent, this was also due to his understandable relief at discovering that his colleagues were concerned and accepting of him and validating of his experience without judgment. "Without judgement" in this context did not mean without robust exploration. For instance, it was important for both Peter and the group to acknowledge some of the hard but important lessons to be learnt— such as the reality that Peter had inadvertently underestimated the seriousness of this student's emotional state as well as his gut instinct that something wasn't quite right—and that this had prevented him seeking support at an earlier stage, leaving them both all the more isolated and at risk. In this respect, perhaps the most reparative element of the discussion for Peter was his sense of finally having been released from the solitary confinement of his experience and shame—something that he and others recognized might be a much longer and painful journey for the girl. The magnitude of this was evident some years later when I bumped into him in a social-like situation. On seeing me, he greeted me warmly and introduced me to his partner as the person who ran "the WDG that had literally saved his life".

WDG Example 2

First presentation

In a different WDG[7] offered to middle leaders[8] within a leadership training programme,[9] the absence of anyone having a specific issue they wanted to share created an opportunity for some free-flowing and exploratory discussion. I reminded the group that we now had an opportunity to think together about things that they never usually got a chance to discuss and wondered what this might include. There was an immediate flurry of responses. These included: "how to handle male students flirting with or leering at female staff"; "dealing with difficult parents"; "working with students where there are no parents involved or where parents behave like children themselves"; "working with students who have suffered experiences such as trauma or bereavement"; "what to do when you feel that nothing makes any difference or when the student even seems to sabotage your attempts to help them". While acknowledging the importance and validity of all these issues, I followed the consensus in the group, which was that they wanted to focus on how to manage sexuality and sexualized behaviour. As one teacher put it, "It's so in your face sometimes and yet we never speak about it!"

One teacher, Sally, then described her difficulties with a group of 15- to 16-year-old boys from a Middle Eastern country. She spoke about how they would stare at her in lessons and in the corridor while sniggering in their own language. It made her feel uncomfortable, and she didn't know how to handle it. Group members played this down at first, reassuring Sally that her description sounded ordinarily flirtatious, given that they were a bunch of adolescent boys testing out their prowess and alpha-male status—posturing with each other as much as with her. When Sally continued to speak about how apprehensive she felt about the prospect of being left in the classroom on her own with them, the group's attitude changed and people agreed she was right to take it seriously.

Sally's description generated a range of responses within the group discussion, including an emphatic reiteration about how rarely these issues are ever discussed in schools, despite their prevalence. After some (perhaps necessary) space to sound off about the rude behaviour of some students, the tone of the discussion soon settled down. Some members picked up on the cultural background of the boys and whether there were gender inequalities that might impact on the way they treated women. Others linked this with their own experiences of boys from other cultures where women were felt to have a more subservient place.

The initial discussion was infused with a hint of anger and judgment and perhaps a sense of "those boys deserve what's coming to them". However, the level of interest in and compassion towards the boys increased when the group were invited to consider what else might be going on for them. At this point, someone noted that they were all Year 11 boys, approaching their GCSEs with little hope of achieving the grades necessary to remain in sixth form. Others commented on how difficult it would be for them to get a place in another school or to secure paid work within a challenging job market, especially given that most of them apparently had limited support from their families.

The group then engaged in a thoughtful discussion about the range of insecurities these boys might be experiencing and how they were now potentially facing the loss of their "alpha-male status" within the school, along with all the protection it provided them from the realities and demands of life. One of the teachers wondered whether the boys themselves might secretly feel intimidated by what lay ahead. Another commented on how they might be the ones who really feel humiliated—connecting this to the way Sally had described herself feeling in relation to the boys. Sally agreed with this, noting how they always left her "feeling stupid . . . perhaps this is how they feel underneath".

With the benefit of some exploration and greater understanding, there was also some pragmatic and solution-focused discussion about the range of approaches that Sally (and others in a similar situation) might take. Members agreed that different approaches might be needed depending on how the boys and their behaviour were understood—for instance, whether they felt more like ordinary flirtations, which one might ignore or diffuse lightly, in contrast with something that felt more actively intimidating (whether conscious or unconscious), which may need to be addressed differently and more directly. Members shared, for example, their uncertainty about how to respond when the boys were talking in a foreign language. One teacher suggested that Sally might show them she wasn't threatened by simply stopping and looking at them firmly for a few moments without saying anything and then continuing on her way. On balance, though, members thought it was safer not to engage with them in moments like this, given that Sally was not sure what the boys were actually saying and that this might unnecessarily escalate tensions.

As the discussion progressed and became embedded in reflection rather than reaction, the atmosphere of underlying animosity towards the boys decreased markedly. In this respect, when consideration was given to whether Sally might need to share her concerns with and seek support from other staff (and managers) in the school, it was not fuelled by a wish to report the boys in the spirit of retribution (as it might have been at the start of the discussion) but, rather, to help Sally manage them, and herself, more effectively.

Sally was appreciative for the help the group had offered her. Even though she still felt a bit anxious about having to face them the following day, she said she felt much less threatened and more solid in her sense of herself and her own authority.

Second (brief) presentation

As this discussion ended, another female teacher, Rolene, asked for a "few minutes" to share her concerns about a young newly qualified teacher (NQT) she was mentoring as part of her role. "The woman is an absolute goddess . . . neither the boys nor the girls can take their eyes off her and it can be quite disruptive to their learning in lessons!" She went on to describe her mentee's looks in such glowing terms that one of the male members asked which school she was working in and which subject she taught so they could look her up! There was some excitable laughter as Rolene added, "I am happily married but even I fancy her!"

When the group settled, Rolene admitted that despite her years of experience as a teacher and middle leader and despite her specific responsibility towards her mentee, she had not yet felt able to broach the subject of her looks. She wasn't sure whether she should raise it and was concerned she would "say it all wrong and just end up upsetting her colleague".

In the brief but focused discussion that followed, group members agreed that it was important for Rolene to find a way to talk with her mentee, although they acknowledged her sense of awkwardness about the prospect of raising the subject. Although everyone could relate to the dilemma, it was striking that no one in the group had ever managed to have such a conversation. The group were then helped to explore a number of possible approaches. These included the possibility that Rolene might "simply" ask her mentee rather frankly how she was managing the students' responses to her inside and outside the classroom, and whether she wanted some help to think about it. Rolene and others were interested in this more straightforward approach and agreed that if she could put this to her mentee in a rather matter-of-fact and non-critical way, it might reduce the possibility of either Rolene or her mentee being consumed with discomfort. They might then be able to have a more ordinary conversation about it which would probably be a support to the mentee and a relief to them both. I commented on how it wasn't just Rolene and her mentee who might be relieved, and I noted that people in the group also seemed calmer at the prospect of a manageable way forward. "It's true," one teacher responded, ". . . it's amazing how uncomfortable some of these basic conversations can feel . . . and somehow in school they never get discussed."

Third presentation

After Rolene indicated she had got what she needed from the discussion, a male member of the group, Adam, asked whether he could use the last part of the meeting to talk about his forthcoming school trip to Africa with his lower-sixth year group (16- to 17-year-olds). He added that he had not planned on talking about this at all, but the previous discussions had made him realize that he really needed to. "The thing is, . . . I work in an all-girls school and although there is a whole team of teachers going on the trip, I am one of only two men."

Tensions in the group were slightly raised when another member retorted to his introduction rather sharply, asserting that "all-girl trips should be staffed by all-female staff". Others disagreed with this and seemed protective of their male colleague as they argued the importance of a mixed-gender staff group for all students. I tried to contain the tensions by acknowledging the importance of these different views and people's entitlement to different perspectives. However, I emphasized that whatever we thought, Adam would soon be going on this trip and our task now was to help him think through his concerns. The group settled and re-directed their interest to Adam.

Adam reiterated that the previous discussion had made him realize that there had been no discussion or support in his school about how to manage students or tricky situations on the trip. He then gave an example of a recent social event at the school—a bit like a disco—and how "one of the girls had pinched his bum". This produced some immediate gasps and hilarity from other group members. I, too, found myself smiling and being carried along with the giggles. I then stopped the group and said, "Let's hold on and think about what's going on for a moment". I wondered how Adam felt about this at the time. Adam linked the group's reaction to his own, telling us that outwardly, at the time, he also laughed it off, but actually he didn't like it and found it quite embarrassing. No one had said anything about it to him, apart from one colleague who made some sort of a joke. "It was uncomfortable though." I wondered why people felt it was OK for us to laugh when it happens with a female student and a male member of staff and asked what people thought the reaction might be if this was a male student pinching the bum of a female member of staff.

The tone of the group changed immediately and led to a more serious discussion about whether or not there was a difference. One teacher thought it was different "because men are stronger and could therefore protect themselves, whereas with a male student it has a different feel". Another added that "the social perception about men being a greater threat makes it feel different". Rather touchingly, someone else stressed that "we women need to back up our male colleagues and protect them!"

As the discussion progressed, there was a sense of interest and engagement from all members. The anxieties and hilarity evoked by the issue soon settled as group members shared thoughts in a more grounded and straightforward way. As the discussion (and meeting) drew to an end, Adam and others agreed on the value of suggesting a meeting with the other staff members on the trip to think about how they are going to manage potentially tricky situations like bedtimes, one-to-one discussions, or more specific physical and bodily issues such as periods. Adam said that the discussion clarified that he did need to do this, adding gratefully that he felt much less awkward about raising it now and was sure that some of his other colleagues (female as well as male) would also appreciate it.

Sexual anxieties in staff

Given that issues relating to adolescent sexuality and student fantasies about staff are so difficult to address, how can schools begin to contemplate the even more unspeakable reality that teachers themselves may sometimes feel besieged with uncomfortably intense feelings towards their students—including sexual feelings. By this, I am not referring to teachers who are actually at risk of acting on their feelings in a wholly inappropriate, boundary-less, or abusive way. Rather, I am referring to teachers who, through their passion and commitment to their students' learning and well-being, coupled with their capacity to develop engaging relationships with them, get involved with students in a way that can sometimes feel confusing, intoxicating, or disconcerting due to them having some sort of sexual edge.

It is important to emphasize—and remind teachers—that the dynamics and difficulties being described here transcend age, gender, and sexual orientation of student and staff member alike. Having said that, it is also important to be aware of certain factors that may increase the likelihood of them occurring—such as in work with physically developed and sexually provocative adolescents who behave in an actively seductive way towards their teachers (whether consciously or unconsciously). This was vividly illustrated on one occasion when I said something to this effect in a WDG. In response, a female teacher told the group about her acute embarrassment and discomfort when she was persuaded to join in a game with some of her sixth-form students[10] on a summer residential trip. She told the group how, one night after dinner, she had been sitting around the campfire with students who were playing a game where one person uses a finger to spell out a word on someone else's arm and the other person has to work out what has been written. At some point, some of the students coaxed one of the confident and self-assured boys to write something on the teacher's arm. Although the teacher felt instantly uncomfortable, she was taken by surprise and didn't feel able to say "no" within the informal and social atmosphere of the trip. On the inside of the teacher's forearm, the student then gently wrote "I like you"—after which he looked up and gave her a knowing smile. The teacher was left feeling stumped, silenced, and seduced, all at once.

Similarly, it is also important to be mindful of the reality that even the most mature and talented of teachers may not yet have had adequate experience in school or in life to accurately calibrate optimal levels of temperature and distance within the learning relationship. This was vividly conveyed by a learning mentor who had the courage to bring to a WDG his difficulty in making the transition from being an ex-student in his school the previous year to being a staff member that year, and how he now had to work with some students who were, quite literally, also his friends.

Although in some ways, talking about staff sexuality is less uncomfortable than student sexuality, it can still feel terribly anxiety-provoking for staff to raise issues that might risk themselves or their colleagues being exposed or compromised in any way. This was evident in a multi-school WDG for middle leaders when one person cautiously described the toxic dynamics in their school, which, they believed, were rooted in the "worst-kept secret"—that their (married) headteacher was having an affair with one of the teaching assistants. Although the teacher described the behaviour of their Head as being "outrageous", he also conveyed loyalty to the school and spoke of his fear of what other WDG members would think of the Head and their school.

When faced with highly sensitive issues such as these, it is especially important for group members to feel that the WDG consultant can take a lead in a way that feels firm, containing, and safe. In this instance, for example, WDG members needed the consultant to interject early on, to re-emphasize the need for absolute confidentiality among group members—including the consultant. The group also seemed relieved when the consultant re-emphasized the need to rein in any judgements we might have—however ordinary they may be—and to anchor ourselves instead in the spirit of thinking and trying to understand what might be going on, and how this situation might be affecting the presenters, and to explore how we might help them function as effectively as possible in the midst of it.

The need to provide support and containment for teachers

Within initial teacher training and subsequent professional development, there is a virtual absence of input relating to adolescent development. This gap in provision is especially striking given the centrality of the student–teacher relationship and the fact that disruptions to this relationship invariably result in disruptions to both teaching and learning. When the force of sexual development is felt to be overwhelming and aspects of sexuality intrude into the student–teacher relationship, anxieties are all the more acute and disruptions to the learning relationship are all the more likely. Paradoxically, schools often seem to turn a systemic blind eye to the difficulties emerging—perhaps because they do not feel equipped or confident about addressing it themselves. However, in certain situations, like some of those described in this chapter, it is dangerous—even potentially neglectful—to leave teachers inadequately supported or contained in their work. It is this lack of support and containment at a staff level which can later result in otherwise ordinary anxieties escalating into something more toxic within the student–teacher relationship.

WDGs are an effective method of addressing important gaps in professional development, support, and containment for teachers. The peer-group setting of the WDG, helped by the facilitation, contribution, and containment of an external consultant, provides teachers with regular opportunities to present and process their thinking about a range of issues, students, and concerns. This can feel like a unique and highly valued experience for all involved.

Over time, shared discussions of this nature will usually result in teachers experiencing a progressive level of understanding, tolerance, and confidence in containing and motivating challenging students. These benefits are further compounded by the group nature of the WDG, which increasingly enables group members to become a consultative resource for each other, independent of the external consultant. When WDGs are well established and well supported by management, the culture of consultation and containment between WDG members has the potential to extend into the wider culture of the school, triggering something akin to a cascade effect.

Teachers frequently report their relief on discovering that it is possible to explore anxiety-provoking issues non-judgementally within the WDG. In the case of uncomfortable and potentially exposing issues relating to sexuality and sexual development, the group discussion often leaves teachers feeling they have gained a renewed sense of clarity, control, and safety within themselves and their work relationships. The capacity for this to have a developmental, therapeutic, and even transformative impact on both teachers and students should not be underestimated.

Acknowledgement

I would like to express my appreciation to Andrea Berkeley for the support she first offered me to develop WDGs in schools over fifteen years ago and the on-going support and backing she has consistently offered ever since.

Notes

1. "Teacher" is used as a generic term in this chapter to denote any member of staff working with students.

2. Although it is not the specific focus of this chapter, the same might equally be said in relation to the management of effective levels of anxiety, pressure, and support with staff.

3. The confusion between intimacy and sexuality is often at its peak in early adolescence.

4. The term "presenter" here is used to describe the person who is sharing an issue or concern with the group. This sharing, or presenting, does not involve any formal presentation as such—but, rather, a talking through of the situation, often illustrated with some more specific interactions with the student concerned.

5. All names and identifying details throughout this chapter have been changed to protect confidentiality.

6. Support staff in this instance primarily included Teaching Assistants and Learning Support Assistants.

7. Within this two-hour WDG, there would usually be time to explore two or three "presentations" (issues).

8. A combination of Heads of Year and Heads of Department.

9. In this programme, WDGs were offered approximately once per half term for two hours. Participants work in a range of schools and usually do not work directly with each other outside the WDG.

10. Aged 16-17 years.

CHAPTER EIGHTEEN

Social defences in nurseries and the contemporary value of the concept

Peter Elfer

Menzies' original work in nurseries

Isabel Menzies Lyth spoke of applying the concept of social defence systems to an "enormous variety" of situations (1989, pp. vii–viii), and these included day nurseries. The original work took the form of detailed case studies of London day nurseries between 1970 and 1979, commissioned by the government and starting with a study of four local authority and three private nurseries (Menzies Lyth, Robertson, Scott, & Gwynne, 1971). These gave rise to an action-research study to develop an improved model of day care (Bain & Barnett, 1986). Menzies Lyth said that their findings seem "fully to justify the feelings of uneasiness which prompted this study" (Bain & Barnett, 1986, p. 1), an "uneasiness" shared too by nursery staff themselves, by nursery nurse training colleges, and by health professionals regarding the quality of day nurseries (Menzies Lyth, 1989, p. 215).

The basis of this uneasiness is described in more detail below, but essentially Menzies Lyth considered that the separation of young children from their mothers for most of each weekday was likely to undermine the mother's opportunities to develop a nurturing relationship with her child (1989, p. 217). This general factor was compounded by aspects of the nursery situation. These included the system then of allocating nursery places only to children where there were emotional or behavioural difficulties, lack of training of nursery staff on early emotional development, and little day-to-day psychological support for staff as they grappled with these difficulties.

The chapter first reviews the social context of nurseries fifty years ago and the experiences of children and staff. It then describes how nurseries have changed since Menzies Lyth's first research and discusses the different sources of stress now evident and the anxieties they provoke. Finally, it considers the relational dimensions of nursery policy and practice and how the workforce could be better valued and better supported to be more effective.

The social context of nurseries
fifty years ago

Since 1945 and certainly through to the time of Menzies Lyth's first nursery research (October 1970 to August 1971), the organization of nurseries fell roughly into three groupings. These comprised "nursery schools", with early education tasks; "day nurseries", with the primary task of protecting children and supporting families where there were particular difficulties (financial, social, or medical); and playgroups (now pre-schools), offering sessional opportunities for play and social interaction. In her investigations of day nurseries, Menzies Lyth was observing a particular group of children, most of whom had significant behavioural difficulties. High rates of problem behaviour in nurseries had been confirmed by McGuire and Richman (1986, p. 138).

At the time of Menzies Lyth's original work, social attitudes towards mothers' participation in the paid-labour market were beginning to change. In 1945 the government strongly advised that children under 2 years were best cared for at home by their mothers (MoH & MoE, 1945). Twenty-five years later, the demand of women for greater access to day care and equality of opportunity with men in the paid-labour market, coupled with the demand of industry for female labour in the burgeoning service sector replacing heavy industry, were both gaining momentum. However, governments were reluctant to commit to any national early years education and care policy, preferring to leave this to the discretion of local authorities. With very little day nursery provision available, young children needed to evoke considerable anxiety in order to be offered a nursery place.

The consequences of nursery life
and its social context for children, mothers, and staff

The most detailed and vivid descriptions of the children in the nurseries come from Bain and Barnett's abridged report of the London case-study nurseries to which Menzies Lyth acted as a consultant. The following is a description by a nursery nurse of children in her room:

> When Gary, aged 2.5y first came into the nursery, he used to shake and quiver all the time; he couldn't even hold his spoon. . . . Now he doesn't do that unless he hurts himself . . . he still rocks on his bed and when he sits in the big chair, he bashes his head on the back of it. . . . Guy 18m (a battered child), started in the nursery two weeks ago: "Now all he wants to do is sit on my lap all day". . . . John and David, brothers, who were suspected of being battered. Sally said she couldn't understand John and David was very quiet. . . . Another child who is "very mixed up" is Conrad. . . . His Mum usen't to look after him properly and he came in smelling awful, really nasty like stale urine, and his hair was filthy greasy. . . . [Bain & Barnett, 1986, p. 12]

At the beginning of Bain and Barnett's action-research intervention, an average of 53 days per staff member per year were lost due to sickness (1986, p. 8). Given the collective demands of the children and frequently being understaffed, the demands on staff were overwhelming. In the face of this, Menzies Lyth argued that staff tended to manage by finding ways to avoid or minimize the children's demands. She thought they did this partly physically, removing themselves through busy practical activity, and partly emotionally, cutting themselves off and avoiding thinking too much about the children.

The care of young children does involve a great many practical tasks, and thus physical activity supplies a legitimate and ready-made opportunity for avoidant busyness. This strategy is only useable if staff can also manage to turn a blind eye to the children's needs—physical avoidance requires emotional avoidance too and the loss of capacity to think about the children's behaviours and their possible meanings. Thus, Menzies Lyth described staff who seemed unable to distinguish between normal and abnormal distress. Demanding behaviour was treated as manipulative and firmly ignored or punitively controlled. If children became withdrawn and then detached, they seemed to become "not noticed". This is similar to the "not noticing" by nursing staff of children who were distressed when separated from their parents because of hospitalization in the 1950s (Robertson & Robertson, 1989).

While the children's needs in these circumstances cannot possibly be well met, there are consequences for parents too, particularly mothers. Menzies Lyth noted the pressure placed on mothers to use nursery either as their duty to supplement the family income or as a relief from the demands of their children. This relieved mothers living in particularly stressful circumstances of the daily demands of parenting but also removed its satisfactions. Menzies Lyth saw this as risking undermining mothers' own investment in parenting. This was in turn reinforced by the way some mothers alleviated guilt at sending their child to nursery by developing an attitude that the nursery provided a superior experience to home life (1989, p. 231). In her view, one consequence of nursery was therefore to risk further undermining and marginalizing the self-confidence of the mothers.

How nurseries and their social context have changed

Since Menzies Lyth's first report in 1971, there have been major changes in social values, patterns of family life, and the tasks and organization of nurseries. I focus here on six aspects of change.

Attitudes to maternal employment

Menzies Lyth commented on the combination of societal (duty to work), financial (income maintenance), and psychological (social isolation) pressures she felt led mothers to use nursery. She was commenting on a particular group of mothers often deemed by welfare authorities to be not managing parenting well. Today, maternal rates of paid employment are much higher, public attitudes towards mothers working have become more accepting and supportive, and nursery intakes are much more socially diverse (Stanley, Cooke, & Bellamy, 2006).

The primary tasks of nurseries

The historically sharply differentiated primary tasks of nurseries have now largely been removed. Nurseries are no longer referred to as "day nurseries" or "nursery schools" but as combined centres, integrated centres, or children's centres. Indeed, governments have become more ambitious about what nurseries can achieve, seeing them as instruments of social policy to address disadvantage through social intervention programmes (Brehony & Nawrotzki, 2010). They are required to be holistic in their approach and attentive to early education, family support, and the needs of working parents, often with community development tasks too.

The expansion of the nursery market

The strongest impetus for the now-widespread availability and use of nursery provision has come from the business community. This has been achieved through the development of a private nursery market. The corporate nursery sector, from being negligible in 1997, was providing 50,000 places ten years later (Penn, 2007, p. 199). Latest Ofsted data shows over 28,000 nurseries, pre-schools, and children's centres (Ofsted, 2014). The market has thus been successful in securing major expansion. However, Penn concludes that "considerations of profitability are now paramount" (2007, p. 204). Profit has thus become a new primary task of nurseries, with implications for the role and experience of the staff.

Standards and regulation

At the time of Menzies Lyth's work, inspection of nurseries was undertaken by local authority inspectors. Each local authority had its own standards, although there was broad national guidance on these. Authorities often combined inspection and developmental/advisory roles. In 2000, inspection of nurseries was transferred to Ofsted as a centralized system, with common national standards, including staff-to-child ratios,[1] minimum space per child, and vetting of staff. These, together with the practice of unannounced inspections and the internet availability of inspection reports, seem to have ensured nursery environments that are physically very safe. This is a significant improvement in the safety of nurseries compared to before 2000, when inspection and enforcement were much weaker (Elfer & Beasley, 1991). Alongside improvements in safety, regulation has also ensured that awareness of the importance of emotional well-being and the provision of a broad range of opportunities for play and learning is commonplace. I say more about this in the next section.

Relationships with children

Bain and Barnett (1986) used the phrase "multiple indiscriminate care" to describe the interactions they observed between nursery staff and children that were fleeting and interchangeable between staff (p. 16). Civil servants worked intensively during the late 1980s drafting the new guidance on nursery standards to be issued with the Children Act 1989. This was at the time of the publication of Bain and Barnett's work (1986) and of that by Hopkins (1988) showing the value of social defence systems as a way of understanding the avoidance of close and individual attention to children in nursery. Although present at many meetings, I do not recall civil servants making any reference to the Menzies Lyth/Bain and Barnett work, although it had been commissioned by the same government ministry. This may have been because the view of Menzies Lyth—that full-time day care was inappropriate for young children—would have been politically unwelcome. Nevertheless, since 1965 there has been a steady strengthening of attention in official guidance on nursery standards to the importance of consistent relationships between staff and children (MoH, 1965). By 2012, this expectation had moved beyond "guidance" to the status of statutory requirement that each child had a "key person" in order to encourage attachments (DfE, 2012).

How far can this attention to relationships with children be attributed to Menzies Lyth's work? My sense is that her work, if it was considered at all, was seen as advocacy for the value of consistent and individual staff attention to children. However, her concerns would have been seen as met by the new guidance issued with the Children Act 1989. Menzies Lyth's explanation of social defences as a means of protecting staff from the psychological stresses of the work would have been seen as having diminishing relevance as the child intakes of nurseries were becoming socially broader.

It is interesting, therefore, that despite the statutory underpinning for nursery attachments and good-enough staff-to-child ratios to enable them, implementation seems very patchy at best, with much confusion about the role of the key person. There is developing work on the emotional complexity of making intimate relationships with children in nurseries (I say more about this in the section below on the relational dimensions of nursery organization and practice). However, apart from my own published work (Elfer, 2013), there is very little use made of the social defence thesis in contemporary writing about the emotional dynamics of nursery. It seems as difficult today to achieve currency for social defences as a useful explanatory model as it did thirty years ago.

The training of nursery staff

Much has been achieved in the development of the workforce in terms of leadership training, the development of many early childhood studies degree programmes, and a big investment in continuing professional development. One of the concerns Menzies Lyth described about the day nursery system was the rather didactic form of training for nursery staff. She considered that staff lacked the opportunity for learning based on group discussions about observations and experiences, led by a skilled facilitator (1989, p. 226). Hopkins (1988) has described in detail the process and value of such a group.

In a recent review of early years qualifications, Nutbrown (2012) acknowledged the rapid growth in early years qualifications (para. 2.2) but also expressed the same concern as Menzies Lyth regarding the didactic or skills-based nature of much training and the need for attention to the processes of thinking and learning (para. 2.6). The present Coalition Government rejected Nutbrown's main recommendations. However, it has made it a requirement that early years staff should have access to regular supervision (DfE, 2012). This offers some possibility to meet the concern of Menzies Lyth about space for thoughtful and informed reflection, although the Ofsted criteria for evaluating supervision emphasizes audit rather than reflection (Ofsted, 2013).

Anxiety and defence in contemporary nurseries

How have these societal changes, the demand of economies for the skills of both women and men in the workforce, equal access for women and men to employment and careers, and social acceptance of mothers' employment influenced the provision and organization of nurseries? In turn, what has been the subjective impact of this much expanded role of nurseries in the upbringing of the next generation for those involved—babies and young children, families, professionals, and politicians? The particular patterns of stress and anxiety documented by Menzies Lyth seem less intense but more complex and diverse in nurseries today, some similar to those documented by Menzies Lyth, some new.

Social attitudes, the nursery market, and parental anxiety

Greater social acceptance of mothers' paid employment (Stanley, Cooke, & Bellamy, 2006) will have made it easier for mothers who wish to work or follow careers to do so. The prevalence of two-income families and the standards of living this enables may equally make it more difficult for mothers who wish to be at home with their young children during the day. Leach et al. (2006), investigating mothers' decisions and feelings about child care, showed how, generally, mothers valued the opportunity that nursery gave them to continue work and careers. However, these authors also found continuing conflicts for mothers. A fifth of mothers described feeling guilty about the use of day care (p. 493).

Menzies Lyth spoke of how parents frequently denigrated their own knowledge and expertise and elevated that of the nursery staff (1989, p. 231). Contemporary nursery staff have referred to a similar experience, speaking of their idealization by some parents (Elfer, 2009). However, this idealization often evaporates as soon as an even relatively minor difficulty occurs—for example, an unexpected change in timetable, a minor injury, or a mislaid item—and is replaced by harsh criticism. Not all or even a majority of parents appear to respond in this way. However, the episodes reported are powerful and evoke equally extreme responses in the staff, expressed disproportionately in terms of their own guilt and sense of failure. It contributes to a major emphasis in nursery management to ensuring faultless practical organization, rigorous safety procedures, and feelings of intimidation in young or less confident staff.

A different side to this is the way the continued development of the nursery market has strengthened parents' confidence, as customers and consumers, to expect and ask for information and to make judgements (Roberts, 2011). Menzies Lyth considered parents were "too easily satisfied" (1989, p. 231), so this shift in power between family and nursery may be helpful in some ways even if increasing anxiety for staff in others.

The economy, nursery cost, and political anxiety

The nurseries that Menzies Lyth investigated were publicly funded. The vast majority of today's nurseries are mainly funded through parent fees. With the pressure to reduce public expenditure and to encourage mothers off benefit and into paid employment, the Coalition has increasingly emphasized "affordability" (DfE, 2013) with proposals to trade off fewer staff and less space with better qualified staff. These proposals included increasing ratios, so that one member of staff could look after four babies rather than three as now, with savings to be used to raise salaries and lower fees. Although dropped after a campaign of protest, the proposal that one member of staff should look after four babies shows the degree of political anxiety about affordability.

Political anxiety about educational attainment

There is also much anxiety about education attainment and the evidence of a gap in attainment already well before statutory school age between children from low-income families (those receiving free school meals) and all others (Ofsted, 2014). Evidence of this attainment gap is not new (Allen, 2011; Field, 2010). What is striking is the role Ofsted argues it can play in addressing the gap by "much tougher arrangements" of regulation (2014, p. 12).

When inspection was centralized, away from individual local authorities, as a national function in Ofsted, local authorities retained a developmental role. That is now being seen as a duplication of the Ofsted role and is being cut (House of Commons Education Committee, 2013). "Tougher regulation" is exactly the outcome that Cooper and Lousada (2005) describe as a consequence of the political desire to transfer welfare services from government to liberalized market providers, to address the anxiety of failure or scandal (p. 66).

This is consistent with the way nursery managers speak of their preoccupation and anxiety about demonstrating learning outcomes (Elfer, 2012). Although Ofsted asserts that it wants to see better informed professional judgement, there is considerable anxiety about producing what Ofsted expects to see. In this scenario, the emotional complexities and conflicts of the work (Page & Elfer, 2013), and the anxieties they provoke, remain, but it is time-consuming and messy trying to think about them when there is so much pressure to produce "results".

Nurseries to address inequality: the anxiety of multiple tasks

Successive governments have seen nurseries as having a role in addressing social disadvantage, reducing social exclusion and gaps in educational attainment. The SureStart initiative was intended to provide a national network of local support nurseries (children's centres) for families with young children. This universal programme is gradually being replaced by a more targeted approach to those most disadvantaged. Two-year-olds in the 20% most disadvantaged wards were offered 15 hours of free nursery education from September 2013, to be extended to 40% in September 2014. Yet nursery tasks, as well as being more targeted, are also broadening in scope. In a recent conversation with a nursery head, I was told that the nursery had been asked by Ofsted what it had done to increase local rates of breastfeeding. The head was bewildered and demoralized by the escalation of expectations beyond the provision of high-quality nursery education for local children. Community development tasks are quite different in their implications for organization and practice, and it is not surprising that staff should express uncertainty and anxiety about their roles.

Nurseries as commercial enterprises: managers as anxious entrepreneurs

Now that the majority of nurseries are either small enterprises or parts of nursery chains in the "for-profit" sector, the role of nursery managers includes commercial priorities. This is a dominating anxiety, especially for nurseries (Elfer, 2012). Public grading of nurseries, with one of four possible grades (inadequate, satisfactory, good, and outstanding), give private nurseries, especially those operating at the margins of commercial survival, a key edge or critical disadvantage in the market. Commentators have described the stresses for leaders in nurseries and schools as their role shifts from focusing on standards of practice to one that includes entrepreneurial and business elements (Osgood, 2004; Tucker, 2010).

Nursery staff anxiety about safety and attachment

I have said above that the physical safety of children at day nursery has been a major achievement of centralized inspection. Nevertheless, staff still report that a child being injured on their shift is their greatest anxiety (Elfer, 2009). After this comes anxiety about physical contact with children, about accusations of abuse, and about the fear of children becoming too dependent (Piper & Smith, 2003). The following quotation from an interview with the leader of a toddler room is revealing:

> . . . it's nice to give them a cuddle but a quick cuddle's nice, not a 20 minute cuddle . . . when I was at college I was taught about not sitting children on your laps. . . . If a member of staff in my class was doing that I'd have to be worrying about the bonding they are having with that child . . . [Elfer, 2009, p. 89]

This person, who I came to know well over six months of fieldwork, was experienced, well qualified, sensitive, and dedicated, working in a highly resourced nursery. Yet her statement is clear in its emphasis on "worrying about bonding" and the use of time limits to avoid this. There is no indication in the quotation of the relevance of professional judgement, the exercise of observation and thought. This suspension of thinking by staff was noted by Menzies although it is less extreme and pervasive here.

The relational dimensions of nursery organization and practice

Nurseries are able to offer major benefits to families. They enable both parents to work and develop careers and provide rich opportunities for early learning and social interaction for children. Much has been achieved in their organization and practice since Menzies Lyth's first work. With very few exceptions, nurseries are safe, structural standards are better, research has deepened understanding of the processes of effective early learning, they are more holistic in approach to children and families, professional training at degree level is much more common, national guidance on good practice is detailed and emphasizes attachment, and inspection is rigorous.

Yet there are also concerns. The trend towards universal provision and socially broad intakes of children is slowing, with an increasing emphasis on targeting families in need (House of Commons Education Committee, 2013). The advisory and developmental role of local authorities is being greatly cut back (Mathers, Eisenstadt, Sylva, Soukakou, & Erkey-Stevens, 2014). Recommendations for wide-ranging improvements in the training of the early years workforce (Nutbrown, 2012) have been largely put on hold, the implementation of opportunities for babies and young children to experience attachments in nursery is variable and inconsistent (Elfer, 2013), and Ofsted has found that only a third of children from low-income backgrounds reach a good level of development (Ofsted, 2014).

Politicians are understandably anxious to improve educational attainment and emotional well-being for those children most at risk of disadvantage as the attainment gap opens so quickly. Although structural and workforce reform are unlikely in the foreseeable future because of public expenditure constraint, much could still be achieved, at much lower costs, by attention to enabling the workforce to be more

effective in their relationships with children. Three specifically relational areas stand out as in need of strengthening:

1. The need for much better partnership working with parents, espe-
    cially parents who have not had positive prior experiences with
    professionals or officialdom (Brooker, 2010; Greenfield, 2012).
2. Better support to staff to assist them manage their anxieties about
    allowing children to become attached and understand the differ-
    ence between attachments that facilitate children's explorations and
    those that restrict them (Elfer, 2006; Page & Elfer, 2013).
3. Staff also need support to see how children's involvement and
    thinking in activities is energized by adult's genuine interested
    attention, inquiry, and planning informed by detailed observation
    (Mathers, Sylva, & Joshi, 2007).

What weakens these practices? In my own research in nurseries, staff
often did not see what I saw as an observer. Babies' and children's
vitality in their play and thinking brought about by a staff member's
interest and attention (what Alvarez terms "reclamation"; 1992) often
collapsed when the staff member, thinking the child was well settled
into the activity, turned away to some other task. How might more
sustained and consistent attention be achieved?

The tendency of staff to distance themselves from the children
is sometimes understood as reflecting a lack of training. Training is
important, but it is not sufficient to enable sustained attention. Many
under- and postgraduate students, who are also working in nurseries,
will speak with sophistication and theoretical detail in the university
seminar room about the general importance of relationships in fostering attachments or early learning in nursery. However, when the
seminar turns to focus on their own interactions with children within
their own work setting, they seem to disconnect themselves from this
knowledge and reject the idea of consistent close individual attention
as impracticable or inappropriate.

Lack of training or weak regulation on its own does not explain
this avoidance of sustained individual attention. Menzies Lyth's great
contribution was to show the role of anxiety in professional interactions
with young children. Then, the anxiety was to do with being emotionally and thoughtfully close to children whose behaviour was disturbed
and whose home situations were painful to know about. Today, the
anxiety is of becoming too involved, of being sure to deter children's

attachments so they do not become too dependent nor evoke parents' envy. Worst of all is the anxiety of being suspected from a safeguarding perspective.

The complexities faced by nurseries charged with the care of the babies and young children of others for long periods of time are considerable. What are the primary tasks of a nursery acting in place of parents, and how are the stresses and anxieties of these tasks both more difficult and more manageable than for family members? Some distinction should perhaps be drawn here between babies under 2 years, and certainly under 1 year, and children who are in their third year and older.

All babies and young children have and need the capacity to stir up powerful feelings in the adults who care for them. However, in the first two years, these feelings are particular intense and can evoke, and are designed to do so, correspondingly intense feelings—love, hate, anxiety, and jealous protectiveness—in close adults. In responding to this, if the nursery practitioner is to be of value to the baby or young child, she must have some of the emotional receptiveness of a parent and the capacity to think about babies' emotional communications, their possible meanings, and how she should respond. She has to regulate her emotional responses, taking account of parental sensitivities and as a professional rather than a parent. A parent is expected to feel love, a nursery practitioner is expected not to—or at least not to acknowledge it. In addition to this, it is only gradually in their second year that babies begin to become more interested in peers, giving some respite to close adults as they turn their attention to playful interactions with friends and in groups.

The number of babies in nursery has begun to decline as parental-leave arrangements have improved, but it is still the case that most nurseries offering care in the full age range will have at least three babies under 1 year of age (Elfer & Page, 2014). The additional demands of babies and children under 2 years are recognized in better ratios for this age group (one staff to three children) so that a "baby room" may typically include twelve to fifteen under 2s with four to five staff. Despite the widely acknowledged importance of this earliest age phase, the work of the nursery "baby room" is still often seen as little more than feeding and changing, compared to work with older children. Managers are likely to deploy their youngest and least qualified staff members there (McDowall Clark & Baylis, 2012). This implicit denigration of the work may itself be a defence against recognizing its complexity.

While the primary tasks of nurseries in relation to babies and children under 2 might therefore be seen as somewhat different from those with 3- and 4-year-olds, the relational challenges facing the nursery practitioner are complex. In this context, what can be done to facilitate the relational aspects of nursery practice?

Enabling the early years workforce to be more effective: the contribution Menzies Lyth still has to make

Drawing now on twenty years of undertaking close observations in nursery rooms, I have a difficult-to-prove but strongly intuitive sense of how much the capacity of staff to give sustained and thoughtful individual attention to children is linked to how individual staff, in their turn, feel attended to and understood as they face the daily challenges of their work. I have shown in previous research (Elfer, 2009) the value of attention to staff experience arising from well-organized and -resourced nurseries that are clear about the tasks expected of staff and show a level of concern for staff well-being (breaks during the day, good pay and holidays, and opportunities for professional development)— implicit containment. Explicit attention to staff experience at work has a role to play, too. How is this to be implemented in nurseries?

The Coalition Government has made it a statutory requirement that all nursery staff have regular supervision. While supervision is a familiar concept in the psychological professionals, there is much misunderstanding of its meaning in early education and care contexts. However, Tickell (2011), who recommended supervision, was clear, seeing it as:

> an opportunity for practitioners to raise any concerns that they might have about children in their care, and to receive support to help them deal with difficult or challenging situations at work. [p. 46]

There are a number of models of supervision or professional reflection. One of these, specifically attentive to the emotion aspects of work experience, is work discussion (Rustin & Bradley, 2008). Here, a small group of staff, led by a skilled facilitator, give thoughtful scrutiny to the details of their day-to-day professional interactions, including attention to the influence of "beneath-the-surface" emotions and how they can be better managed. Jackson (2008) has shown the value of work discussion in primary schools, where teachers reported being more aware of the needs of their children and better able to manage the stresses of the work (see also chapter 17, this volume).

Work discussion provides an opportunity for a different kind of thinking and learning based on shared reflections on direct work experiences. Thinking about these experiences is facilitated by attention to the emotions that accompany complex professional interactions and which may otherwise become blocked by anxiety and defensiveness. Menzies Lyth referred to the general absence of these opportunities in the training of nursery staff, but she acknowledged that some tutors in colleges offered to be available to talk through with students how difficult work situations could be managed. In my own experience in nurseries, managers may offer the same "my door is always open" opportunity for individual staff to come and discuss a problem. Menzies Lyth saw this form of help as well intentioned but irrelevant:

> It twisted a potential and necessary learning opportunity into a somewhat irrelevant counselling relationship for the very distressed few who had to admit weakness and seek help from usually over pressed staff. [1989, p. 226]

I have been collaborating with child psychotherapists to develop through work discussion groups the practice of supervision in nursery. The aim is to facilitate thinking about the experience of individual staff in order that they can develop their own thinking about individual children and respond better on the basis of this (Elfer, 2012; Elfer & Dearnley, 2007). The contribution of such groups to positive outcomes for all the players in nurseries—more consistent attention to children, better engagement with parents, and increased job satisfaction for staff—has not been assessed in formal outcome studies. Yet there is the evidence of descriptions in shifts in staff practice, which we have given, and staff's own sense that the groups lead to changes.

Conclusion

Nurseries have come a long way in fifty years. However, the management and practice of making consistent, emotionally responsive, and intellectually stretching relationships with young children, especially babies, remains problematic. A convincing case can be made for understanding the difficulties in terms of the conflicting feelings the work entails and the anxieties and stresses these provoke. The work has parallels with parenting in the deep personal involvement it requires, but staff must also remember that the children are not their children and the relationship with them can be terminated at any time by parents and will, in most cases, last only a year. The chapter has sought to show

how anxiety about this and anxieties projected from the environment (demonstrating children's progress in early learning, safeguarding, and commercial stringencies) may be less intense but are more diverse than those shown by Menzies Lyth.

There are important ways in which this can be addressed. Caring work is systematically undervalued in society, and this may itself be a defence against acknowledging the painfulness of human need, whether for the young, the old, or the ill. It is difficult to see how, without greater public subsidy, staff can be paid adequately so that they are not under pressure to find better paid employment. Such public investment is unlikely in the short term because of cuts. However, there are much lower cost ways of better managing the emotional demands of the day-to-day work. One such model is work discussion groups, which have been shown in both nursery and school contexts (as well as in other areas of human relationship work) to be effective.

In nurseries, work discussion has resulted in better engagement with parents, and the risk (identified by Menzies Lyth) of parents feeling undermined by nursery is less. Nurseries can then be more attuned to parents' expectations about how the care of their child is managed while at nursery, so that the sense of partnership is stronger. It has also led to better support for children's early learning by enabling close attention to be given to the details and context of children's thinking and explorations. Perhaps most importantly of all, work discussion has been able to be attentive to the anxieties created by attachments in nursery so that these can be discussed less defensively. There is then less risk of staff either avoiding attachments altogether or of being too possessive of children so that the rich social-interaction opportunities of nursery (in friendships and groups) are restricted.

Note

1. At the time of Bain and Barnett's work, staff-to-child ratios were not set precisely. They were subsequently set in 1991 at one staff member to three children under the age of 2 years, one to four for 2- and 3-year-olds, and one to eight for children aged 3 years and above (DoH, 1991).

CHAPTER NINETEEN

Projective identification and unconscious defences against anxiety: social work education, practice learning, and the fear of failure

Jo Finch & Jason Schaub

S ocial work and social work education have long been subject to rapid change and reform, including organizational and legislative reform, often in response to highly publicized (and politicized) failures in child protection policy and practice. Public Inquiries and Serious Case Reviews into deaths of young children at the hands of their parents and carers, for example, frequently produce reports highly critical of social workers, and to a lesser extent other professionals, for the many missed opportunities that, with the benefit of hindsight, might have resulted in a less tragic outcome for the child concerned. Such reports often stress poor information-sharing and communication between professionals from different organizations, the need for appropriate supervision and scrutiny, and an inability to focus on the needs of the child.

In the wake of widely publicized child deaths—for example, Victoria Climbié and Peter Connelly (both in the London Borough of Haringey)—the last eleven years in England has seen major policy shifts in both social work provision and social work education, leading to what one social work academic aptly described to us as the "homogenization" of social work programmes across England. This process of homogenization has developed in an accompanying political climate of performance management, targets, inspection regimes, audit cultures, risk-averse practice, and a sanitizing technical-rational approach to the task of social work—what Cooper and Lees refer to in chapter 15 as the dominance and pervasiveness of "New Public Management" theory, which has had a profound effect on welfare organizations.

Within the context of a rapidly changing social work culture under threat by the neoliberal enterprise, this chapter centres on an important aspect of social work education in England: practice placements. The discussion explores the complex and challenging dynamics that are created between practice educators (social workers tasked with the job of assessing students on placement) and social work students. In our roles as social worker lecturers (formerly social workers in children and family settings), we were curious about why working with struggling or failing students appeared to prove such a difficult emotional experience for practice educators, particularly those working in children and family settings. We also noted how challenging it was for social work tutors. Additionally, we felt that the existing research base offered little in the way of a satisfactory explanation (for a thematic review of the literature, see Finch & Poletti, 2013; Finch & Taylor, 2013). Rather, the reasons proffered seemed defended in themselves, and the impact of affect was notably absent.

We were able to explore in an earlier discussion (Finch, Schaub, & Dalrymple, 2014) how far the concept of projective identification was useful in understanding why practice educators appeared to find the experience of failing a student so painful. We argued that these multifarious dynamics came sharply to the fore when students were underperforming or, indeed, failing their placements. One possible and very serious consequence of those complex dynamics, which appeared to powerfully invoke strong, uncomfortable, and intolerable emotions, was that practice educators may be reluctant, or indeed unable, to fail students when required.

We also noted in our empirical work potential concerns about variations in practice in different fields of social work. For example, practice educators within children and family settings appeared to have heightened levels of emotionality and difficulties around managing and reconciling the role of practice educator, and they seemed more reluctant to fail students in comparison with, for example, practice educators in mental health settings.

What we had not explored in the analysis was the dynamic between these individually felt projections and the organizational and societal context; as such, there was a missed opportunity to explore how far such projective-identification processes were symptomatic of wider organizational *and* societal defences against anxiety. This raises the question of the possible cause for this anxiety, which this chapter also explores.

We have the opportunity now, therefore, to consider these questions further to see if we can make a case to consider these powerful projective identifications that emerged so starkly in our research as:

1. a specific and powerful individual manifestation of an unconscious social defence against anxiety, which emerges most blatantly, we argue, when students are underperforming or indeed failing in practice learning settings;
2. persecutory psychic processes that induce anxiety states in practice educators;
3. the inducement, by the latter anxious states, of defensive practices that include being mobilized to not be able to think, reflect, and act appropriately.

We aim, therefore, to consider further the nature of these anxieties in social work, which, like Menzies Lyth's study, highlighted anxiety arising from the primary task—namely, the "continuous care for patients, day and night, all the year round" (1960, p. 97). It is possible that they emerge from the primary anxieties proffered by users of social work services. We suggest that these anxieties are also symptomatic of wider societal concerns and preoccupations about the often unbearable task of social work, one of which is the pervasive fear of failure. The exercise of further analysis and theorization of our research data therefore has the potential to build upon Menzies Lyth's original unconscious defences against anxiety proposition, by using contemporaneous research in a specific professional context—the social work practice placement.

The chapter begins with an overview of the changes and developments in social work and social work education, clearly very different from the context and culture of nurse training in the late 1950s—although yet sharing perhaps some of the complexities and emotional pain observed so acutely by Menzies Lyth. There is then a brief discussion of our previous empirical work in this area. The chapter next focuses on projective identification before going on to document how projective identificatory processes emerged in our research studies. There is then a discussion of the context of wider social work anxieties, which, we argue, impact upon and are played out by practice educators and social work students. The chapter finishes with a brief discussion about containment and, in light of our discussion, considers possible ways forward.

Social work education

The importance of practice learning on UK qualifying social work programmes, both undergraduate and postgraduate, has been emphasized by the plethora of reforms in both social work and social work education over the last 11 years. The introduction of the degree in social work in 2003, for example, increased the number of assessed days in practice from 130 to 200. Students were required to undertake two, sometimes three, placements in different settings and to have the opportunity to undertake statutory tasks and interventions. Students were assessed against newly implemented national occupational standards for social work. Social work became a protected professional title, and four regional care councils were set up to regulate social work and social work education. Programmes' suitability processes were strengthened, and students were required to demonstrate they were "fit for practice" before beginning their placement. The purported aim of these reforms was to increase public trust and confidence in the social work profession, to ensure parity with comparator professions (e.g., nursing), and to transform its status and image (DoH, 2002; Orme et al., 2009). These reforms can be seen as a consistently anxious policy response to the "problem" of social work, most notably its apparent constant failure to intervene appropriately in cases of child abuse.

More reform was enacted following the Social Work Taskforce (SWTF) report in 2009, set up in the wake of political, media, and public outcry at the death of a young child, Peter Connelly, who was killed by his carers (SWTF, 2009). The SWTF's later iteration, the Social Work Reform Board, continued the developmental work recommended, which included the setting up of a College of Social Work. Other changes included the abolition of the General Social Care Council, the regulatory body for social work in England, with the functions now being managed by the Health Care Professions Council (HCPC); the adoption of a professional-capability framework to assess practice learning; and a two-part qualification now required for practice educators assessing final-year students.

There have also been a number of reviews into the practice of social workers. The Laming Report focused on developments since

Victoria Climbié (Laming, 2009), and the Munro Review focused on children and family social work (Munro, 2011b). The Munro Review documented the unintended effects of the growing trend towards managerialism in social work, with the accompanying focus on targets having consequences in terms of professional judgement, autonomy, and practice wisdom. Most recently, Narey (2014) and Croisdale-Appleby (2014) have each recommended further changes to qualifying social work programmes. Croisdale-Appleby makes a number of recommendations, including moving training away from undergraduate level to postgraduate level and developing yet more stringent entry requirements and matching workforce development needs with the numbers of trainees. Narey adopts a more critical stance, advocating a move back to specialist routes in qualifying training away from the current generic model—completely at odds, of course, with the HCPC's and the College of Social Work's generic endorsement standards. Alongside these reviews (the former commissioned by the Department of Health and the latter by the Department for Education), a new children and families social work training scheme called "Frontline", similar in nature to the "Teach First" model, was rolled out in September 2014. It is notable that the programme is not seeking endorsement from the College of Social Work. At the time of writing, a similar scheme in mental health, termed "Think Ahead", has also been announced. Thus, the constant threat and culture of continuous change is still very potent within social work education, possibly impacting on academics, students, and other key stakeholders within local authorities. These different reviews take place in the context of a difficult economic climate, huge cuts to welfare expenditure, draconian housing policies (such as the "bedroom tax"), and the continued demonization of recipients of welfare.

Despite the flurry of reforms within social work education and reforms to practice learning, there have been persistent concerns raised about the placement component on social work programmes. Finch and Taylor (2013) identified historical and continuing concerns centred around three areas:

1.   the quantity and quality of placements;
2.   the low failure rate;
3.   the apparent reluctance of practice educators to fail students.

In terms of failure rates, for example, Menzies Lyth noted a high attrition rate for student nurses in the hospital under study, approximately one-third, and it is interesting to note that concerns about high attrition rates on nursing programmes remain a contemporary concern (Gidman, 2001). Indeed, the attrition rate in nursing education in 2003 was estimated to be 19% nationally (Glossop, 2002). This situation contrasts significantly with social work in England, as well as in other countries, which has relatively low failure and withdrawal rates (Finch & Taylor, 2013; Hussein, Moriarty, Manthorpe, & Huxley, 2008). Indeed, despite a number of changes to the qualification requirements over the years, as well as significant changes in entrance requirements, the failure rate has remained constant at around 2–3% (Finch & Taylor, 2013). The SWTF (2009) interim report, pertinently titled, *Facing Up to the Task*, stated ominously:

> Specific concerns have been raised about the . . . robustness and quality of assessment, with some students passing the social work degree who are not competent or suitable to practise on the frontline. [SWTF, 2009, p. 24]

Narey and Croisdale-Appleby also raised concerns about practice learning. Narey claims that placements are often poor quality and in non-statutory settings, and they do not prepare students adequately for the task of statutory children and families social work. Croisdale-Appleby noted that the quality of placements was inconsistent. From these different origins, it is clear that the placement element of social work training poses distinct challenges and contradictions. It lies at the intersection of social work's reality and the theoretical and abstract ideals of the academy, yet it remains a problematic site for many reasons.

In addition to these concerns, social work remains a contested activity. Therefore, assessing what is "good-enough" social work practice poses distinct challenges, not least in a culture where social work (and, by association, social work education) is often deemed to be "not good enough"; while low failure rates on their own do not necessarily indicate a failure to fail by the social work education system, they certainly are indicative of an anxiety around failing. Unlike the nursing education system of the 1950s, social work students are not voluntarily withdrawing.

Preceding studies

Our previously undertaken empirical work focused largely on practice educators' experiences of working with failing students. Finch's (2010) doctoral study examined why it seemed so hard for practice educators to fail social work students, and it highlighted the emotional pain associated with failing a student, which at times, it was argued, prevented practice educators from failing students when the evidence appeared to be unequivocal and was highly indicative of failure. Schaub and Dalrymple's study (2011, 2013), while initially aiming to consider the support needs of practice educators, nonetheless identified the significant emotional distress and acute anxiety experienced by practice educators when working with struggling or failing students.

Our work has since developed: first, through undertaking a comparative study with Italian practice educators, which gave us the opportunity, among other things, to consider more critically the English context, not least the unintended effect of the assessment framework and the particular culture of English social work (Finch & Poletti, 2014). Second, further empirical work was undertaken to consider other stakeholders, namely social work tutors (Finch, 2014) and important key sites of group decision-making about failing (and passing) social work students (Finch, 2014); and third, by extending our theoretical analyses further. For example, we considered how far the concept of projective identification was helpful in explaining these powerful feelings, which typically included, anger, rage, anxiety, and guilt and the subsequent ways in which practice educators were mobilized to act out or voice these projections (Finch, Schaub, & Dalrymple, 2014).

Projective identification

Building on the ideas of Freud, Klein developed the concept of projective identification. The concept was later taken up by Bion and others within the object relations tradition. Projective identification can be seen as an unconscious defensive strategy that aims to protect from psychological attack or harm. We argued elsewhere (Finch, Schaub, & Dalrymple, 2014) that given the heavily debated nature of the concept, projective identification can perhaps be least controversially conceptualized as a mode of unconscious communication of emotion. Projective identification, however, is more complex than a transference from one person to another; rather, it is often an expulsion of "unwanted or threatening ideas" (Frosh, 2012, p. 162), ranging from the relatively benign to the much more threatening and hostile. Projective-identification processes thus occur when a person cannot bear or tolerate certain aspects of him/herself and projects these deeply unwholesome and unsettling emotional states that cannot be borne into another person. These projections are often so powerful that they compel the object of the projections to mobilize those unconscious feelings into actions or behaviours and may impact on their ability to reflect, think, and act appropriately (Trevithick, 2011).

Projective-identification processes, then, are usually viewed as a dynamic between two people, occurring in all relational contexts, not just within a therapy room. We contended, therefore, that when confronted with the spectre of failing a placement—and often alongside that, failing the programme—a student is likely to be in distress and experiencing a range of conflicting emotions. Some of these will be conscious, but the fear of failure, of not being "good enough", and the accompanying feelings of guilt and shame, are likely to provoke deeply held unconscious feelings, emanating from infancy and childhood, that are intolerable for a student to bear. The practice educator becomes the object into which these deeply unsettling emotional states of mind are projected. There may also be envious feelings in the untenable and uncomfortable mix, such as an unconscious desire by the student to enter "the mind of the other in order to acquire the desired aspects of his psyche" (Spillius, Milton, Garvey, & Couve, 2011, p. 126). Indeed, Klein stated that projective-identification processes from the infant to the mother aimed not only at ridding himself of his bad parts but also intended to injure, take control of, and possess the mother (Klein, 1952). Klein later noted the envious nature of projective-identification processes (Klein, 1957), which we feel is of particular relevance to practice educator–social work student interactions.

Projective identification in action

We noted in our analysis of the data from across the studies that practice educators often appeared mobilized by the student's powerful projections, in a number of ways. First, by experiencing extremes of emotion, including intense anxiety; second, by referring at times to students (and universities) in unprofessional, hostile, and blaming ways; and third, by being unable to think, reflect upon, or contain such feelings or indeed use them to critically consider the student's state of mind and what was being communicated. These projections were so unsettling that sometimes the results were abruptly ended placements, poor assessment reports, or collusion. The latter sometimes took the form of avoiding the task of failing the student—either not addressing concerns quickly enough, making it subsequently difficult to uphold the failed decision because due process had not been followed, or, of more concern, failing to fail the student. We make the case, therefore, that the reluctance or inability to fail a student may well be a form of defensive response to these persecutory projections that induce an anxious state. The narratives of practice educators below illustrate this.

In what we considered to be almost paralysing levels of painful emotion, Lily stated:

> I was incredibly confident with the successful engaged students but with the difficult student my confidence levels went down a lot . . . I was anxious . . . I was worried.

Jennifer recognized she had become part of a dynamic with the student where she "felt like I was working harder than him in his practice placement" yet could not escape from this rescuing dynamic. She stated:

> . . . he [student] took on the role of a child sometimes and puppy dog. I'm the weak one and you're the strong one and it will be in your hands and you're the supervisor . . . [it] carried on, the puppy dog eyes.

This caused Jennifer to experience anger. She stated:

> I got angry with him sometimes. I wasn't angry at him, I was angry at home, I would be smouldering, pissed off . . .

Anger was seen in other narratives, and, in response to the anger felt, practice educators also experienced guilt. Martha reported feeling "terribly guilty", and Daisy stated:

> . . . because at the time I made that decision, the guilt, it was unbearable . . . it was a reality check . . . oh my god, what about her children . . . I felt like I am a rotten shit.

We also noted examples of practice educators' narratives moving away from a professional discourse, which revealed itself in angry and personal comments about the students. For example, Lily described the student as:

> . . . absolutely terrible, she was appalling, she was abysmal and no way should she ever be near clients . . . there were a million difficulties with her . . .

This was seen most starkly in Daisy's narrative, which was shocking, full of profanity, and extreme:

> . . . I just thought . . . I thought, "Fuck you! You are not going to apologize for your fucking behaviour with a period. Every fucking woman in the world gets a period, yes some have difficulties, some get emotional. . . . You've like resorted to like fucking bottom of the barrel . . ."

Daisy makes hurtful and personal comments about the student's body size (the student was significantly overweight) and fantasizes about service users being abusive to the student. She states:

> . . . they'll call you a fat bitch because you are fat . . . it will be their way of releasing, of hurting you.

Some practice educators articulated the persecutory projections in terms of feeling threatened by the students. Mary, for example, stated:

> At the end, when he didn't complete what he was to have completed, I explained, again, that I was going to fail him, and he became sort of aggressive, you know that sort of silent aggression? Intimidation like, you know, what are you doing failing me? It was very unpleasant in his reaction to me.

Carla also expressed fears about what she termed, "the student making damaging claims". She stated:

> It felt like, even my colleague said to me, "She's dangerous, she's going to come in here and wreck somebody's career." Somebody could work their way up for years, and she could come in and say something, and that would be the end of their career. Tons of people just didn't trust her being around.

Lily, a very experienced practice educator of both nursing and social work students, described a student who to "put the fear of God into me" and recognized that the student:

> . . . beat me down really with threats and I allowed myself to be beaten down.

Lily acknowledged that:

> It was the worst career decision I have ever made, and to this day, I
> have a huge regret about it.

This leads to the concern that such projective identificatory processes
thus mobilize practice educators to act out, and a defensive mechanism emerges in turn whereby practice educators cannot fail students.
It appeared to us that to fail the student was akin to acknowledging
practice educators' own failures. Indeed, Terry stated:

> That was the thing I was struggling with through the whole thing.
> How much of her failure was a reflection of my own practice teach-
> ing?

Terry carried on with this theme:

> I would say probably 90% of the time, if the student fails there's
> something wrong with the practice teacher.

We also noted in the retelling of the stories in the research-interview
context the use of present-tense language to explain a past event, so
that it appeared to us that even in the narrating of the story the practice
educators were still mobilized and affected by these projections. It is
important to note, however, that not all practice educators expressed
the same level of emotional distress, and there was evidence of practice
educators managing to fail students in an emotionally contained and
professional manner.

Social work anxieties

Defences against anxiety and pain, although often felt to be an individual concern, are also developed by institutions to protect against
threats. These threats thus arise from a range of possible sources, both
external and internal. Externally these threats may include changes in
governmental policy, legislative change (often in response to moral
panics), and other social change (Halton, 1994). Internally these threats
might concern poor employee relations and, more often, the type of
work the organization is engaged in and who it works with. Defensive
strategies thus emerge in a complex dynamic interplay between individuals and organizations. Given all the continuous reforms within

social work as discussed earlier, it is not surprising that anxiety within social work is high, coupled with the anxieties than emanate from service users and the contested nature of the "primary task"—that is, care and control.

The question then arises as to the nature of the anxieties that affect the social work training system more generally and how these both affect and are symptomatic of the practice educator–student relationship. Perhaps a further pertinent, related question is: Why are they brought to the fore so acutely when issues of failing students emerge? We contend that there are two reasons for this: first, the deeply held unconscious fear of failure, felt by us all; and second, the public perception of social work as a "failing profession"—in short that we cannot get our primary task right, namely to adequately safeguard and protect children from harm. This is made all the more acute and, importantly, public by inspection regimes, audit cultures, performance management, and blaming Public Inquiries and Serious Case Review Reports. Alongside this, social work is imbued with public and political anxiety that emerges so vehemently when a child dies at the hands of her or his parents—namely, because social work has failed to prevent it coming to the public's consciousness (Cooper & Lousada, 2005). The response then is often intense public and political criticism of social work, anxiety-driven policy change, resulting in the construction of further defensive practices and states of mind, which, as so acutely observed in Menzies Lyth's study, may well be obstructing the primary task.

It is not surprising to us, then, that the practice educators most struggling with their task were those in children and family settings. Indeed, the care-versus-control function inherent in social work, which, as Evans and Harris (2004) note, places contradictory demands on social workers, appeared to be played out in practice educator–student relationships via the conflict felt between the nurturer and enabler-of-learning role, versus the assessor role. Lily was able, to some extent, to acknowledge this; she stated:

> . . . there was almost like a maternal feeling about the facilitation of learning but the flipside of that was when I had to become the kind of teller-off or the person who was making judgements . . . I did struggle with that.

This contrasted with an account of a mental health social worker, who, in discussing the practice educator role, stated:

. . . you know it's meant to be a mature student I am dealing with you know, we are entering into this arrangement right, as adults, you know I had my part to play, the student has their part to play . . . I just kind of felt, well, this [failing a student] is going to happen in practice placement . . . this is primarily your responsibility, it's your responsibility at the beginning as well, to think about what you're getting into.

Containment

As Menzies Lyth's work demonstrated so starkly, organizational defences arose in the hospital, which proved unhealthy and psycho-logically damaging, resulting in poor-quality care of patients, poor inter-relations between senior nurses and trainee nurses, and high levels of sickness and attrition rates among nurses. For the practice educators in our studies, they reported that the experience of work-ing with a failing student was stressful, that they felt unsupported by the university and isolated, and that at times they felt threatened by the student. The experience of working with a failing student can all too often leave a lasting legacy on the individual practice educator as well as on the team. Indeed, several practice educators in our studies decided not to take on any further students. The crucial question is, how do practice educators avoid being mobilized by students' projec-tions and, instead, make sense of and reflect upon what is being so forcefully communicated?

It thus seems patent to us from our research into practice learning and subsequent theoretical analysis that containment is key to mini-mizing the negative and damaging impact of projective identification. While social work will always remain an anxiety-infused profession, finding ways to contain these anxieties is crucial. We saw in our studies missed opportunities for practice educators to experience the projec-tions as a form of communication, which could have served to help students make sense of and articulate their own anxieties, psycho-logical processes, and states of mind. The use of Ruch's (2007) work in terms of containment within children and family social work settings, for example, would equally be applicable to practice education. She argues for the need for "safe" spaces that would allow social workers, or in this case practice educators, to explore uncomfortable and difficult emotions to "make sense of the uncertainty and anxiety they encounter on an everyday basis" (p. 662).

As stated earlier, not all practice educators involved in our studies experienced the paralysing levels of emotional pain, although it was still noted as an unpleasant experience. We noted that those practice educators, the majority of whom were, or had been, approved social workers (now called approved mental health practitioners),

1. did not experience any role conflict or strain between the nurturer or enabler of learning and the assessor role of their function;

2   saw failing students as an inevitable part of the job;

3. saw the experience as a learning one;

4. could clearly articulate their responsibilities and boundaries as a gatekeeper to the profession and as a practice educator;

5. saw the student as an adult learner with clear responsibilities;

6. did not internalize the students' failure as their own.

This suggests that the anxieties within social work and practice education can be managed and that projective identificatory mechanisms can be appropriately accommodated, contained, and withstood. This points to a way forward in light of findings, although further research into the psychic strategies employed by such practice educators to withstand the projections of failing students is clearly indicated.

Conclusion

We have argued, therefore, that within social work and social work education there are multiple sources of anxiety and that there is a powerful reinforcing interaction between individuals' everyday, lived experiences of engaging in unconscious defences strategies, as well as organizationally constructed social defences. These interactions operate within a distinct societal, political, and ideological context. Our research to date has thus focused on a particular manifestation of an unconscious defence against anxiety, and we have attempted to use our contemporary research on the issue of assessing failing social work students in practice learning to identify, first, another site where Menzies Lyth's proposition of unconscious defences against anxiety is relevant and, second, how such psychic processes impact on practice educators.

To finish on a reflective note, writing this chapter has been a challenge for us—that is, as social work lecturers who are relatively new to psychoanalytic theory, and are heavily imbued with sociological theories, we were also assailed by fears of "not being good enough". At the same time, we are working in a culture where we are also subject, at times, to the same persecutory and envious projections from students (as well as practice educators) and are sensitive to the same social work anxieties. Such an exploration reminds us starkly of these anxieties. It was interesting to note our own difficulties in thinking when both immersing ourselves in the data and constructing this chapter, as well as our anxious responses.

CHAPTER TWENTY

Unconscious defences against anxiety in a Youth Offending Service

Maxim de Sauma, Sarah Fielding, & Michael Rustin

The idea of unconscious defences against anxiety has undergone a considerable evolution since its original formulations by Elliott Jaques and Isabel Menzies Lyth, as many chapters in this volume make clear. Developments in psychoanalytic theory, as well as the recognition that different occupational and institutional commitments are likely to give rise to different kinds of unconscious anxiety, have both contributed to this. In this chapter, we explore the particular anxieties that we have come to understand through undertaking an experimental kind of therapeutic group work with young offenders. We describe the states of mind of the young people themselves and the impact of these on those who work with them, both as individuals and as organizations. We explore the defences against anxieties which are mobilized in each in the setting of a Youth Offending Service (YOS). We also consider how far the shared understanding of these states of mind can be a positive experience for the young offenders and for those who work with them.

Our psychoanalytically orientated group work intervention was with teenagers aged between 15 and 18 years who had been sentenced to a community order, such as a Youth Rehabilitation Order or an Intensive Supervision and Surveillance Order, within a YOS in a deprived area of London. The group work ran over twelve weekly sessions, arranged with a two-week mid-programme break.[1] The experiences of young people in the group, and those of our own, allowed us to become curious about the institution of the YOS itself, the types of anxieties encountered, and the defences evoked to deal with them.

This work has been undertaken since 2008, and we are currently running our eleventh group programme. This chapter mainly draws on material and experiences from one specific group intervention, which involved five teenagers. The emotional pressures exacted on staff at the YOS (including our group facilitators) and on the dynamics of the team were intense and often replicated the concerns, difficulties, and behaviours of the young people in their care. There was a high turn-over of staff; there was also a consistent group of locum workers, who seemed to manage the work demands by feeling that an escape route was always to hand. The burden of the work at the YOS was so intense that staff described preferring to work 6–9 months of agency work, a time period not dissimilar to the average community sentence for a young person. We have constantly observed the parallels between our clinical group work and the dynamics of the larger institution for which we were providing this particular specialist service.

Before describing the therapeutic work in more detail, we will briefly discuss the context of the YOS.[2] Our project, working in an out-reach capacity with the YOS, began just ten years after the most radical overhaul of the youth justice system in fifty years. The Crime and Dis-order Act (1998) established for the first time a statutory aim of prevent-ing young people offending. Community orders were implemented, trying to prevent offending behaviour without resort to custody. The underlying philosophy of the new service was that young offenders were to be personally responsible for their actions, as were their par-ents; also, under the auspices of the Youth Justice Board, an increasing emphasis was placed on evidence-based practice and outcomes. The other major change was that children were now involved within youth justice from the earlier age of 12 years.

In the current system, young people who are assigned to the YOS are normally between 12 and 18 years of age. They will have been convicted for a variety of offences that could typically include rob-bery, assault, burglary, possession of drugs, threatening or abusive behaviour, or carrying a knife or weapon. Adolescents' delinquency can helpfully be viewed as distinct from adult offending, taking into account their stage of development and the social aspects of ado-lescent delinquency (teenagers tend to commit minor offences with others, and the offence is talked about, witnessed, and shared with peers, whereas adults more often commit crime alone). For the majority of young people, delinquency can be viewed as a developmental crisis or breakdown (Laufer & Laufer, 1984), which requires intervention and support but, hopefully, need not lead on to adult offending behaviour.

These are a vulnerable group of young people, often likely to be Looked After Children or with experiences of loss and family disruption. Although frequently involved in violence towards others, these young people are also likely to have been victims of violence themselves. The mental health needs of young people at the YOS are typically much higher than those of their non-YOS peers, but despite their greater need, they are also less likely to access professional help. The function of the YOS combines notions of punishment and rehabilitation. The requirement of specified hours of attendance at the YOS, and participation in a range of activities there, is intended to fulfil both these aims, with the intention that young people may be able to divert from re-offending and reset their lives towards education, employment, or other developmentally appropriate activities. There are some similarities between the YOS and Adult Probation, where a community order is an alternative to a custodial sentence. Many of the young people refer to their attendance at the YOS as "probation" and "doing time" and are often relieved not to have been "sent down".

The group work programme is designed to be consistent with the aims of the youth justice system, while holding a strong ethos of psychoanalytic applied work within the culture of the Brent Centre for Young People. Other activities available to young people on an order are those concerned with reparation—for example, helping at a local nursing home, making poppies for Remembrance Sunday, or clearing a local graveyard. They also attend appointments with officers who may explore specific issues with them—for example, awareness of knife crime, gang-related topics, problems with home life, setting up meetings with college or apprenticeships, "victim awareness", or substance misuse.

Young people are referred to our group work programme, which is known simply as the "Discussion Group" by their officers. They meet the co-facilitators individually at first, when they are invited to volunteer for the group, but on condition that if they assign themselves to the group, they will remain with it for the full duration and will attend regularly. Their hours attending the group work can be used to count towards the number of hours legally required by the courts to fulfil their orders. Technically, young people can be held to breach—meaning they can be returned to court—if they fail to attend a YOS appointment, but within this group, due to its psychotherapeutic nature and the ethics around mental health interventions, sanctions are not used for young people who miss sessions, although non-attendance is actively explored with them.

The purpose of the Discussion Group

The Brent Centre for Young People is a psychoanalytically orientated service, offering psychotherapeutic help to adolescents. The Centre was founded in 1967 by the psychoanalysts Moses and Egle Laufer, and it has delineated a number of key ideas about adolescent emotional and mental difficulties and breakdown, offering help to young people experiencing a range of difficulties, such as self-harm, suicidality, depression, anxiety, eating problems, sexually risky behaviour, confusions over bodily changes attached to adolescence, school refusal or academic breakdown, difficulties with peers, and delinquency. The Laufers considered delinquency as a manifestation of adolescent breakdown (Laufer, 1995; Laufer & Laufer,1984), and this would also link with Winnicott's (1956) notion of the anti-social tendency, with delinquency being viewed with the cautious optimism that it may have a help-seeking quality, albeit provocatively. We would also understand delinquent behaviour as having a particularly adolescent quality in contrast to adult offending and, of course, as taking place in a social and economic context.

The Centre's outreach project at the YOS offers not only the group work programme, based on its model of psychoanalytic intervention, aimed at intervening at a crucial time for development, but also individual work, where appropriate, and consultation with YOS staff. The Discussion Group was initially a pilot project—we were not sure if it would be an effective way of engaging young people within the YOS, but we had an idea that these young people were more suspicious or hostile towards individual interventions or towards anything seen as "soft" or as a threat to their often necessarily tough exterior. We also knew that most of their offences were likely to have been committed in groups, that there was a strong social aspect to them, and that there might be advantages to young people in working with their peers in a facilitated and containing environment.

This initiative was intended to see if an application of a psychoanalytic approach to young people, seen as a group of six to eight, with two facilitators, could be helpful to them and effective as part of their management within the YOS. The essential starting assumption was that providing some space for reflection for these young people, in which their feelings and anxieties could be put into words, might be helpful to them. We also thought that the experience of being held in mind by two therapists, even over the limited time-span of the group, might be of value to the young people and might also be different from much of their other experience. Both of these initial conjectures and hopes have been fulfilled within the experience of the groups, though not without considerable uncertainties and difficulties. The project has been supported by a research team that has devoted time each week to thinking about the process and outcomes of this work. This provided a supportive thinking space for the group facilitators and maintained a sense of optimism in the face of challenges.

Understanding the work of the YOS

Research on unconscious anxieties in institutions has given attention to the different "primary tasks" that they may have and to the different anxieties that may arise from these. Formally, the primary task of any YOS is defined by the Home Office, where the principal aim of the youth justice system is "to prevent offending by children and young people and requires those involved in the youth justice system to have regard to that aim" (Home Office, 1997). This implies a greater emphasis on rehabilitation than in many other areas of the criminal justice system. Most staff at the YOS have social work or probation backgrounds, with a strong emphasis on welfare in their training, and this seems to give rise to some difficulty and discomfort in combining the aspects of welfare and rehabilitation in this work with the need to also maintain firm boundaries and discipline. External social and political anxieties about the risks of disorder and criminality exert pressure on the service at times. What become obvious, from staff accounts and young people's experiences, in trying to pin down the tasks of the youth offending service are the conflicts and confusion around them. Many officers find the punishment aspect of the task uncomfortable, but there is also some pressure to be seen as "tough" and "not taken for a fool" within the staff team. Above the Central Criminal Court at the Old Bailey in London is an inscription carved into the stone, "Defend the Children of the Poor & Punish the Wrongdoer", which encapsulates the central conflict of the youth justice system—a conflict between law and social welfare, where the young people are both vulnerable and caught doing wrong, both victim and perpetrator. More simply, the staff remark: "Do I have my punishment or welfare hat on?"

It is interesting to note that social and economic factors are generally not considered within any intervention; nevertheless, they impact
significantly on staff and feel a very immediate part of working with
a young person living in a part of London with high levels of poverty
and deprivation. Instead, the YOS offers a range of professional practices that might include reparation, mediation, mentoring, and other
interventions that essentially strive to repair a perceived deficit in the
young person and his family, rather than his environment. (Most of the
young people are male.)

We have particularly noticed staff reports of both guilt (a feeling
connected to taking time off to spend with their own families) and concern around, for example, the Christmas holidays, where the poverty
and social isolation of some young people become especially palpable,
particularly for those young people who are looked after by social
services or in chaotic circumstances. The distress and hopelessness of
staff in recognizing this is painful to bear, and sometimes this becomes
converted into something more manic and excitable—for example, the
idea of having a Christmas party.

A brief note on culture and atmosphere at the YOS

If the reader wants to picture the environment of the YOS, the actual
YOS office is a clean, airy, rather anonymous office space, open-plan,
with lines of computers.[3] Looking exactly like any other office in its
large municipal building, it generates an anxiety of "am I on the right
floor, or in the right place?" The officers "hot-desk"—meaning that
there is little sense of knowing who is in, who sits where. Although the
main aim of the YOS might be thought of in relational terms, of building a relationship with a young person, the office environment conveys
a strong sense of the anti-relational. This relates very much to young
people's experiences of being known, or not known, which we discuss
later in the chapter. Sometimes there is no space. There are more staff
than desks, and staff are encouraged to work away from the building.
Officers are not allowed any personal items on desks, and the office is
paperless: everything is now done on computer screens. There are two
named desks for the duty officers on call, so they can easily be found;
otherwise, all grades of staff, including managers, sit wherever they
can.

Young people are seen away from the office, in a block known as
Customer Services, which has a small series of glass offices in a row,

with a brittle, exposing feel. Privacy is not a key feature, although there are blinds that can be used to increase privacy. The offices are not sound-proofed, and again there are not enough rooms to accommodate the variety of services using them, which unconsciously seems to reflect a strong wish in the institution for an increased reliance on office and "paper work", rather than the more anxiety-provoking contact with troubled young people. Both officers and young people face limitations of resources within the institution, but this is perhaps more intense for the officers, who may feel a responsibility towards the welfare of a young person and may persist in their concern for him, long after he has completed his order.

Having set the scene, we now look more closely at some of the states of mind that young people presented with in group sessions. We have identified four of these states of mind in particular. Within the focus of this book on states of anxiety, we are describing those of young offenders who feel themselves to be lacking recognition, care, and respect, and who are frightened of their capacity to cause damage to themselves and others. Their delinquent status has already been established by the judicial process, which has assigned them to the YOS, which is an additional source of shame. Our argument is that these states of mind were powerfully conveyed in many ways to the group facilitators and to the YOS staff and that understanding them became the central task of this work. We hope to show how these kinds of anxiety and defences against them can be understood and, to a degree, alleviated through a group psychotherapeutic process.

Being known or not known

Young people at the YOS rarely convey a sense of being held in mind. At times, we felt that young people really made sure we were alert to them, noticed them, thought about them—sometimes through provoking us or filling us with despair. At times, a feeling of not being known, not existing, was a state of mind projected into the facilitators, making us feel ignored, disregarded, pushed to the margins of the group, and considered "outside".

Feeling known sometimes appeared in a benign sense, as being contained and held in mind, and sometimes in a more notorious way, being known to the police, for example. The alternative to being known—not to be known at all—was more frightening, and we began to think of the group's primary task as "to get to know each other", as Caroline

Garland (2010) puts it. In our first group session, Kwasi, 16 years old and a Looked After Child, a troubled boy who very much remained in our minds after the group session had finished, told us his state of mind very directly. He talked of the futility of things. He spoke of not caring if he died if he ended up in a fight or something on the street, it wouldn't matter. We took up something of the hopelessness he was feeling, and how difficult it was to protect himself from harm when in that state of mind. He nodded to that and said he didn't mind dying. There was a feeling of quite heavy despair, and yet it was also very articulate, and he seemed hopeful that we could listen. He said several times he didn't mind "speaking his truth here". In Kwasi's case, his need to be known by us, to be understood, feels essential to his very survival. Mason, on the other hand, a hesitant 17-year-old who lives with his mother and disabled sister, has a less benign view of being known, and in the early group sessions he is so fearful of talking that he muffles up his mouth, with his jacket pulled tight around his face, so any communication he makes is mumbled—"he seems to be asking both to be noticed and left alone all at once". He worries about social services involvement and gives the sense of being closed up, suspicious. Mason fears that he will open a Pandora's Box of intervention or intrusion if he opens his mouth, while for Kwasi the risk is of being dropped from another's mind, once he has made contact.

Begir, a 17-year-old refugee who lives with his father, following the death of his mother, arrives to most sessions stoned "and seems to represent something of a mindless state in the group, that some things are too painful to know or think about". Throughout the group sessions, particularly at times when other members have begun to talk more hopefully about the future, or the possibilities of college, Begir breaks into a more frenzied account of stealing mopeds and "burning them up", reminding us that any small sense of development can be quickly burnt up here. Dontrell is a confident, entertaining, and lively 16-year-old who in the early session, alongside a theme of "got to keep your guard up", tells tales of "tags"—the street names of young people they know—a more notorious sense of being known, but also something the group facilitators are shut out from: a state of not knowing. When group members are absent from sessions, as Kian, the youngest in the group at 15 years of age, was for a number of weeks, apparently lost in a daydream kind of time, we realized the importance of not only keeping that missing young person in our minds and helping him back, but also of ensuring that the present group members understood it mattered to us—and them. We learnt one week that Kwasi had walked a number of miles to attend his group session, but on meeting a security officer (not employed by the YOS—our group runs after hours) in reception, he had been turned away, saying he only needed to report in, that there was no group meeting. In fact, we were all waiting for him upstairs. The following week, Kwasi is recognized in reception, early, by our link worker at the YOS, a senior officer, who helps us coordinate the group. He tells us "one of yours is here" and explains that Kwasi's officer had been off sick last week—the week when he couldn't gain entry to the group session either. We thought how dropped from our mind he must have felt last week, and we feel angry that he was sent away. Kwasi's first communication in the group is that he has lost his Oyster card (a travel card in London), "as the wallet isn't strong enough, it keeps falling apart, and if I don't have the wallet it just slides out of my pocket". We had a sense how difficult it was for Kwasi to keep hold of something, how easily things could feel lost. Later in the session, the relief that his name is "registered" and his Oyster card can be restored is palpable.

Kwasi lets us know that when there is a failure in the system of being known, at the moment of not being recognized—of the security officer not knowing the group, of not knowing that his officer is away on sick leave—his sense of development and movement is lost, and literally so in the case of his Oyster card. To not be known here is alienating, frustrating, and impedes growth, but in this large institution it is also a very common experience for staff and young people. It sometimes feels that there just aren't enough resources for people to be known. Relationships are the most important aspect of working with these young people, but they are not central to how the YOS actually sees its work.

We noticed in these early group sessions that for young people to introduce themselves, to volunteer even their name sometimes to their peers, had a dangerous edge to it, as if being known could also pose a threat, particularly in a more paranoid "gang" state of mind. Each member of the group came from a different country, a different cultural background (we work in one of the most diverse boroughs in London), and there was anxiety surrounding what could be known or recognized in each other, when so much felt different or unknown. So, being known came to carry a number of meanings: it could be paranoid, notorious, carry a threat—or be more benign and helpful, although always then with the risk of being dropped. All these aspects of being known are relational, however, and indicate at the very least that one exists.

We were reminded of a previous group, earlier in our experience of working at the YOS, where one 15-year-old boy had been somewhat infamous for committing offences that seemed destined to lead to him being caught—for example, for attempting to steal a mobile phone from a police officer! In the group sessions, this boy would ensure our complete vigilance at all times. Any tiny lapse in our seeming attention to him would give rise to something destructive or explosive—for example, he would run his cigarette lighter across the arm of the chair. After a number of weeks of interpreting this to him, in the sense that we understood his provocative and dangerous actions as ways of ensuring we kept him in mind all the time, he thoughtfully agreed with us—he did need to make sure we hadn't forgotten him. He reminded us that he was one of eight boys in a rather chaotic household. We knew his mother was very depressed, his father in prison. Kwasi similarly, with his despairing talk of violence towards himself in the first session, ensures he has a firm place in our minds.

Interestingly, as Kwasi increasingly felt present in our minds (he never failed to be amazed that we remembered things he had talked about in the previous session), he began to talk with more hopefulness—sitting a literacy exam that went OK, thinking about college for the year ahead. This was a more general shift in the group for everyone, as they begin to feel a little more known—Kian tells us of being a year ahead in science, doing well at school, despite causing trouble; Dontrell, too, talks about his wish to vote to change things and whether he might study media at college.

The problems of time

Linked to this theme of fragile self is a feeling that the reality of time can be hard to grasp at the YOS. Young people's relationships to past and future can feel unthinkable. Although the YOS and the frame of the group has the capacity to represent reality and limits, with appointment times and measured time periods, even staff at the YOS struggle with time, rarely knowing, for example, when an order ends. We see Kian "disappear" from the group for four weeks; when he returns, he is shocked to learn he has missed so many sessions—he can't believe it. He wonders later if time could be mixed up, when he wants it, what about a group on Sundays? Weekends are boring. Any missing time, any break, is painful. His genuine confusion leads the group to talk about daydream time, reality, the difficulty of living beyond a present moment. Some of this feels tangibly adolescent. However, this fluidity and confusion around time takes on particular meanings within the YOS, where many young people sullenly describe "doing time"—having been ordered by the court to complete a community sentence of a fixed time. Regardless of the depth of resentment or shame, "doing time" doesn't seem to involve counting the days, however. Endings typically come as a surprise to all parties, denying the importance of a worked-through ending for both young person and officer. In this way, time can operate as a defence against being known.

Individual appointments with officers at the YOS are rarely attended on time, and this is tolerated by a duty-officer system, which will see young people "reporting in" at any time of their appointed day, benignly stretching the requirement to return young people to court, but also reducing contact between a young person and his allocated officer, with whom he may have and need a relationship. We have noticed in our own experience of conducting staff meetings that YOS staff also use time in this way—drifting in and out, making a "touch-and-go" contact with us, but always ready to be called out.

Within the group, a limit of twelve weeks is made clear from the start. The boys complain initially that the group is too long. From the mid-point of the group, there is more urgency—time is running out. Anxieties around the two-week break, and the eventual ending, are to be talked over, again and again. Time is important for adolescents, something needing to be worked with. At the YOS, the danger is of ignoring time. Development can be experienced as a threat, something forceful, inevitable—not an uncommon reaction to puberty. Young people often hit crisis points with exams or other rituals that symbolize a move towards adulthood. Begir represents the dangers of skirting around developmental tasks, lost and stoned on the margins, with no school or work place. Sometimes there is a sense of a traumatic relationship to time, like when Kian announces to us in his confusion, "The present is the time I know." It can feel as if the past bursts into interactions and actions, but it rarely emerges as a narrative. Officers mostly know little about a young person's past; there is a sense of curiosity being dangerous—these young people present with deprived and hard-to-hear histories.

Time at the YOS is very different from our psychoanalytic sense of time, where time is measured, noticed, early or late, used or wasted; perhaps most importantly, time is contact with another person, someone who knows something of you.

Latent depression and despair

One of the most pervasive feelings encountered at the YOS is that of despair and hopelessness, often linked to the complex circumstances and histories young people present with and to the difficulties of trying to work towards a change. The despair can feel so deadening that we sometimes felt relief at encountering more aggressive or hostile feelings, or manic activity within the group, which at least superficially felt more lively.

In Session 11, the group have just returned from a week's break in the programme, and the end of the group is very present in the material. Following a discussion of Mason "coming off tag",[4] the conversation turns to the summer again—the long break, school holidays, the group finishing, and the break we have just had. Kian is particularly talkative and seems afraid of what might happen over the summer, particularly with the Olympics. There is a feeling that the police will not cope (and that presumably we cannot cope with their more explosive or despairing feelings). It might be like the recent riots again. The conversation becomes more frantic, with missiles, airplanes being shot down, curfews for terrorists. We talked about the summer really not feeling safe. This is briefly acknowledged by a worried-looking Kian, before the group shifts to a more excitable feeling of the "biggest-ever McDonalds" near the Olympic Park—would it be serving the biggest-ever burger? Mason is the only one in the group unmoved by this more manic excitement, commenting, "still the same shit food". Here, we see something of the difficulties of facing painful realities. Mason's feeling of "shit food" seems doubly despairing, with no hope that the group might provide something more thoughtful or nourishing.

In the final session, our sense of hopelessness—for not being able to provide enough (certainly not the biggest-ever burger)—also comes up, alongside the boys' feelings of concern about the future. The boys have planned a special final meeting, asking us for pizzas to mark the ending. They are pleased that we remember the pizzas for the final session, although as they arrive for the session they are convinced we will have forgotten. We talk to them about the mixed feelings of endings, of feeling let down, and the importance of talking about that together today. Begir arrives late; he looks tired, grey around the edges, a reminder that the group hasn't been enough, that these boys remain worrying and vulnerable. He acknowledges our concern that we didn't see him last week, "just slept last week" he says in a defeated, worn-out way.

The session becomes distracted at this point, with excitable banter about something from school between Dontrell and Kian, while Kwasi and Mason look on quietly. We say how difficult it seems to stay with something serious today, and we take up the worry everyone shared about Begir last week and the concerns this week about our last session. Begir drops his headphones and begins to engage. He seems reassured that we are making quite an effort to think with him. He openly tells the group how he feels, getting into more trouble than he was before the group started, or sleeping all the time. There is a hint of excitement about the trouble, but it has a weary quality, as if his manic defence is no longer working. We say something about the trouble—the excitement feels like a temporary relief, but the feelings underneath stay the same? Begir, surprisingly, agrees with this. He talks about his feeling of hopelessness—if he's not in trouble, what does he do? He speaks with longing about returning to his home country.

The yearning for his home country, which he left as a refugee, was profound here, alongside a feeling of not being able to get on track developmentally—trouble is all he knows. At times in the group, it felt as if thinking was something that was intrinsically connected to depressive pain and this painful sense of hopelessness, and it therefore needing to be avoided. We feel this acutely in the countertransference.

Humiliation and fears of being exposed

A significant proportion of the young people in our group have had relatively difficult or traumatized earlier experiences—for example, coming to the UK as a refugee or an economic migrant, loss of a parent through death or separation, loss of a family through being placed in institutional care, loss of school place/exclusion, parents' mental health difficulties, domestic violence at home—and it may be that these were predisposing causes for later developmental difficulties. Within this context, we came to think about how a state of humiliation and fears of being exposed recurred throughout the group in different ways, and how this might link to the vulnerable histories with which young people presented.

One particularly prominent example of the themes of shame and exposure involved a shocked discussion of someone Dontrell knew who had been "filmed on the toilet". This video had been circulating at school. The story was that a friend had slept over at a friend's house and had then taken this film surreptitiously. They laugh raucously as they share this story, but there is an underlying horror and a very exposed persecutory feeling. Our feeling in the transference was around the risks of feeling exposed in the group, a real feeling of being "caught with your pants down", in a very shameful way. When we addressed the sense of humiliation underneath the more jokey atmosphere, Dontrell says something about the disrespect of having a friend over to your house, your Mum cooks them dinner, they have the benefit of the gas and electricity that your family has paid for—and then you take a picture of your friend "taking a shit". That is disrespectful, says Dontrell, with some authority, to the rest of the group, who nod in agreement. We think here about the importance of a firm boundary that can allow the group to feel safe. Later in the group, they talk similarly about a drunk man who has lost control of himself, wet himself. All the shame and humiliation is projected outside the group, but it feels clear to us that the group feels a risky business here: there's a real worry about what is inside them and what can be shown safely. We were aware at times that we were hesitant in taking up the negative transference, or addressing this more directly, as there was a feeling of something brittle and fragile in the group and that we needed to tread softly.

The fear of exposure is replicated in the YOS staff team, albeit with a different quality. One of our tasks is to offer a regular space for discussing cases—the young people with whom officers are working—in a team meeting. The anxiety in attending this is palpable, with staff concerned about "exposing" their practice, a constant feeling that they might be pulled up for something they have done wrong. There is little sense that it could be a more benign and helpful meeting, although this changes gradually, as the reality of attending this meeting is not the same as the imagined fear. It struck us, however, how dangerous it could feel for both young people and staff to "lose face".

At times any sense of humiliation within the group could feel explosive, carrying a risk of violence. Thinking about the young people's histories, we understood that earlier exposure to violence and abuse would also have involved recurring humiliations and a sense of cumulative trauma, where a slight can become a massive insult. Dontrell arrived to one session fuelled with adrenalin, his face frozen in a furious grimace. His hoody was up, pulled around his face as if to shield him, and he looks tight, ready to fight like a boxer. He is too tense to sit down. We wonder what happened, and we learn, through a torrent of swear words that have an evacuative quality, that he has just met someone downstairs who spat on him once. He is disgusted and describes wanting to fight this other boy, in graphic, horrible terms, suggestive of bodily violation—"shank him up so bad". The rest of the group becomes excited, full of bravado, in response to this. It feels very precarious to talk to them about violence as a defence against the humiliation—although slowly we do talk, and Dontrell manages to sit down and talk about the incident. It turned out that it was over a year ago that the boy had spat on him, but something of this "disrespect" had been held onto and quickly reactivated.

The importance of being known, of existing in another's mind—a crucial aspect of our work at the YOS—can easily be disrupted by this feeling of shame. As Erikson (1950/1977) comments: "he who is ashamed would like to force the world not to look at him, not to notice his exposure. He would like to destroy the eyes of the world. Instead he must wish for his own invisibility" (p. 227). Behind the humiliation is a fear of contempt (or what the young people call "disrespect"), which is also a fear of emotional abandonment. We found Bion's ideas about thinking and containment particularly relevant in working with this group and, in terms of shame, were reminded of Bion's understanding of a failure in containment, where a child felt he was dying and no one noticed (Bion, 1970, cited in Morgan-Jones 2010, p. 183). This can be played out in a rather concrete way at the YOS, where young people on the fringes of gang activity, for example, may place themselves in repeating situations of risk of harm—which is dealt with both by manic denial and by provocation of concern.

The question of defences

We have so far described different states of mind—for example, of being known, of despair, of humiliation, and of fear of exposure—which were pervasive in our group work, but these also occur within the YOS institution itself in differing ways. We were left with feelings of being provoked, excluded, confused, struggling to think, frightened, caught up with something more manic, or left with a bleak hopelessness. These were feelings that had real intensity and could be difficult to bear even with support, supervision, and the ongoing interest and curiosity of the research team. Isabel Menzies Lyth (1960) highlighted in her observations of nursing practice that the task of understanding an institution involves bringing workers into direct emotional contact with difficult tasks and supporting them to deploy their capacities fully.

What defences are mobilized against these unbearable feelings, and where are they located? Among the young people themselves, it seems that the main defence is to try *not* to know, to simply blot out discomfort and anxiety through existing in a kind of limbo; it also involves project-ing feelings of confusion, hopelessness, and anger into others, includ-ing the YOS officers and ourselves. Their defensive structures, like their attachment to the group, have a volatile, ephemeral quality. We felt that one of our tasks was to contain rapidly changing states of mind long enough for them to be recognized and named.

We as conductors of these groups sought to stay in touch with the states of feeling mobilized within the group, while being aware of how difficult this could be. We were able to share experiences with each other and take part in a supervision group to help us process these feelings. We also had the resources of training and a tradition of theory and practice to keep us "on task". Perhaps the most significant defence we found ourselves falling into was to become too passive, to be so anx-ious about a potentially negative reaction from the young people that it came to seem an achievement for us and the group just to survive. But looking back, it seems clear to us now that we did more than this, and that some development did take place.

Within the YOS itself, we were constantly reminded of what a dif-ficult job its officers had, being on the receiving end of challenging and provocative projections and, possibly most difficult to bear, the sense of despair. Perhaps the predominant defence of the YOS as an institution was to avoid the relational aspect of its task, to lose sight of the idea that a central task should be building a relationship with the young people, whatever else also has to be done. The impersonal office environment we described seems to be symptomatic of this denial. It has been put to us that the apparent confusion of the YOS about its purposes, and its difficulties in organizing itself to keep these in mind, was a symp-tom of a deeper problem—that is, the ambivalence of the wider society towards young people who, in different ways, appear to "fail" and who then enact their despair and resentment in antisocial acts, of which they themselves are often also victims. While society seems to have designed, in the YOS, an enlightened approach to young offenders, there may be larger systemic reasons, connected with an environment of poverty and inequality and a pervasive desire to blame, that make it difficult for it to fulfil its mission.

Learning and development in the wider context of the YOS

However, for all these defensive responses, we also encountered unex-pected hope for the adolescents placed in the group. Kwasi walking for a number of miles to attend a session was one moving example of commitment and meaning. Despite the difficulties we describe, the fact is that the young people mostly did establish and maintain a relationship with the group, and with us. They were curious about us—where did we live, what music did we like, could we imagine what their lives were like? We heard, too, how important their relationship to the officers was, even if they could be superficially dismissive or contemptuous of them. The two-week break we instituted proved to be a valuable preparation for the ending of the group; also, after the group had ended, following up the young people individually signified our continuing interest in them, sometimes beyond the end of their order (a time when most young offenders re-offend). From our follow-up meetings, we had some evidence that young people were engaging with college or school, had reduced or stopped offending, and were somehow "getting over" the setback of their original community order and conviction. The idea that they could access a part of themselves that was not humiliated or afraid, which did feel recognized and remembered, seemed to allow some hope. Begir—who had presented himself as hopelessly beyond help or intervention during the group, smoking cannabis and sleeping during the day, "burning up mopeds", and no plans for the future—perhaps surprised us the most at follow-up. He spoke of visiting grandparents in his home country and seemed to have recovered a sense of a good object, someone who cared. He began to think about how to stop being in trouble and about what to do with his life. He was even open to the suggestion of "talking to someone" at the Brent Centre if he felt he needed to in the future—he was openly grateful for the experience of the group. We felt that something of the group had been established in his mind and had helped him to feel contained enough that he might now mobilize a more hopeful part of himself.

Our findings may have relevance to the larger systems responsible for working with young offenders, such as the YOS. We believe there is an organizational design that would enable this service to keep in mind the importance of holding these young people in mind, while at the same time recognizing that its two necessary functions of setting firm boundaries for the young people and developing a relationship with them are not in contradiction and need not be confused with each other. So far as the YOS is concerned, the immediate question is who holds the officers emotionally in mind to carry out their tasks. The defences against something more relational at the YOS may appear, at first glance, safer or easier to maintain, but the task of preventing reoffending demands a different approach. Staff need the right support and understanding to work with the extreme anxieties and provocation they inevitably encounter. There is a wider question too, since defences against the anxieties of knowing and of relationships are widespread in many fields of work beyond youth offending, and these raise larger issues about our contemporary social system.

Acknowledgements

Grateful thanks to Danny Goldberger, child and adolescent psychotherapist, who was the co-facilitator of this group, with Sarah Fielding. We also gratefully acknowledge the contributions to this research project from Anna Honeysett, Adam Kay, Mariachiara Zappa, Maria Papadima, Korina Soldatic, and Aylish O'Driscoll. And, of course, thanks to all the staff at the Brent Centre for Young People.

Notes

1. We are grateful to Margaret Rustin for suggesting the two-week break, as a helpful way of thinking about separation and absence before the actual ending of the group.

2. Young people's material, including names and personal details, have been changed to ensure confidentiality. All young people gave consent within our research project for their material to be shared for publication in this way.

3. We should make clear that this is a different environment from that of the Brent Centre, which occupies a large house converted for its psychotherapeutic work and is where the group facilitators have their "secure base".

4. Some young people are put on electronic curfew for part of their community order, meaning they have to be back at home at certain times, recorded electronically by a "tag" attached to their ankle.

REFERENCES

Alford, C. F. (1997). *What Evil Means to Us*. Ithaca, NY: Cornell University Press.

Allen, G. (2011). *Early Intervention: The Next Steps—An Independent Report to Her Majesty's Government*. London: HMSO.

Alvarez, A. (1992). *Live Company: Psychoanalytic Psychotherapy with Autistic, Borderline, Deprived and Abused Children*. London: Routledge.

Amado, G. (1995). Why psychoanalytical knowledge helps us understand organizations: A discussion with Elliott Jaques. *Human Relations, 48* (4): 351–357.

Anderson, D. (2007). Reading water: Risk, intuition, and insight. In: M. J. McNamee (Ed.), *Philosophy of Risk and Adventure Sports* (pp. 71–79). London: Routledge.

Apter, M. J. (1992). *The Dangerous Edge: The Psychology of Excitement*. New York: Free Press.

Armstrong, D. (2004). Emotions in organizations: Disturbance or intelligence. In: C. Huffington, W. Halton, D. Armstrong, & J. Pooley (Eds.), *Working Below the Surface: The Emotional Life of Contemporary Organizations*. London: Karnac.

Armstrong, D. (2005a). *Organization in the Mind: Psychoanalysis, Group Relations and Organizational Consultancy*. London: Karnac.

Armstrong, D. (2005b). Psychic retreats. In: *Organization in the Mind: Psychoanalysis, Group Relations and Organizational Consultancy* (pp. 69–89). London: Karnac.

Armstrong, D. (2007). The dynamics of lateral relations in changing organizations worlds. *Organisational and Social Dynamics, 7* (2): 193–210.

Armstrong, D. (2012a). *The "Tavistock Group" within War Psychiatry in Britain.* Paper presented at Conference on Psychoanalysis in the Age of Totalitarianism, London (September 21–22).

Armstrong, D. (2012b). Terms of engagement: Looking backwards and forwards at the Tavistock enterprise. *Organisational and Social Dynamics, 12* (1): 106–121.

Arnaud, G. (2012). The contribution of psychoanalysis to organization studies and management: An overview. *Organization Studies, 33* (9): 1121–1135.

Autor, D. H., & Dorn, D. (2013). How technology wrecks the middle class. *The New York Times,* 24 August.

Bain, A. (1998). Social defences against organisational learning. *Human Relations, 51* (3): 413–429.

Bain, A., & Barnett, L. (1986). *The Design of a Day Care system in a Nursery Setting for Children Under Five: An Abridged Version of a Report of an Action Research Project.* Document No. 2T347. London: Tavistock Institute of Human Relations.

Balint, M. (1959). *Thrills and Regressions,* London: Hogarth Press.

Ballatt, J., & Campling, P. (2011). *Intelligent Kindness.* London: Royal College of Psychiatrists.

Barnes, E. (1963). Changing hospital attitudes. *International Journal of Nursing Studies, 1*: 11–16.

Barts Health NHS Trust (2013). *Independent Investigation into the Services Provided at The Haven, Whitechapel.* Available at: www.thebureauinvestigates. com/2013/12/27/get-the-report-investigation-into-whitechapel-sexual-assault-referral-centre

Beck, U. (1992). *Risk Society: Towards a New Modernity.* London: Sage, 1998.

Bell, D. (1996). Primitive mind of state. *Psychoanalytic Psychotherapy, 10* (1): 45–47.

Benjamin, J. (1988). *The Bonds of Love: Psychoanalysis, Feminism, and the Problem of Domination.* New York: Random House.

Benjamin, J. (2009). A relational psychoanalysis perspective on the necessity of acknowledging failure in order to restore the facilitating and containing features of the intersubjective relationship (the shared third). *International Journal of Psychoanalysis, 90*: 441–450.

Beveridge, W. (1942). *Social Insurance and Allied Services. Report by Sir William Beveridge.* London: HMSO.

Bick, E. (1968). The experience of the skin in early object relations. *International Journal of Psychoanalysis, 49*: 484–486. Reprinted in: A. Briggs, *Surviving Space: Papers on Infant Observation.* London: Karnac, 2002.

Binnie, A., & Titchen, B. (1999). *Freedom to Practise: The Development of Patient-Centred Nursing.* Oxford: Butterworth Heinemann.

Bion, W. R. (1948). Psychiatry at a time of crisis. *British Journal of Medical Psychology, 21* (2): 81–89. Reprinted in: *Cogitations*. London: Karnac, 1994.

Bion, W. R. (1961). *Experiences in Groups and Other Papers*. London: Tavistock Publications.

Bion, W. R. (1962a). *Learning from Experience*. New York: Basic Books; reprinted London: Karnac, 1984.

Bion, W. R. (1962b). A theory of thinking. In: *Second Thoughts* (pp. 110–119). London: Heinemann, 1967; reprinted London: Karnac, 1984.

Bion, W. R. (1963). *Elements of Psychoanalysis*. London: Heinemann; reprinted London: Karnac, 1984.

Bion, W. R. (1965). *Transformations: Change from Learning to Growth*. London: Heinemann; reprinted London: Karnac, 1984.

Bion, W. R. (1967). *Second Thoughts*. London: Heinemann; reprinted London: Karnac, 1984.

Bion, W. R. (1970a). *Attention and Interpretation: A Scientific Approach to Insight in Psycho-Analysis and Groups*. London: Tavistock Publications; reprinted London: Karnac, 1984.

Bion, W. R. (1970b). Container and contained. In: *Attention and Interpretation: A Scientific Approach to Insight in Psycho-Analysis and Groups* (pp. 72–82). London: Tavistock Publications; reprinted London: Karnac, 1984.

Bion, W. R. (1991). *A Memoir of the Future*. London: Karnac.

Bion, W. R. (1997). *War Memoirs 1917–1919*. London: Karnac.

Black, D. (2004). Sympathy reconfigured. *International Journal of Psychoanalysis, 85*: 579–596.

Black, M. (1993). *The Growth of Tameside Nursing Development Unit*. London: The King's Fund.

Bloom, P. (2013). Cutting off the king's head!: Traversing the fantasy of sovereignty toward a discipline beyond control. In: G. Arnaud & B. Vidaillet (Eds.), *Re-Working Lacan at Work*. Paris: ESCP Europe.

Boccara, B. (2013). Socioanalytic dialogue. In: S. Long (Ed.), *Socioanalytic Methods*. London: Karnac.

Boehm, C. (1999). *Hierarchy in the Forest: The Evolution of Egalitarian Behavior*. Cambridge, MA: Harvard University Press.

Boehm, C. (2000). Conflict and the evolution of social control. *Journal of Consciousness Studies, 7* (1–2): 79–101.

Boehm, C. (2012). *Moral Origins*. New York: Basic Books.

Bollas, C. (1987). *The Shadow of the Object: Psychoanalysis of the Unthought Known*. New York: Columbia University Press.

Boltanski, L., & Chiapello, E. (2005). *The New Spirit of Capitalism*. London: Verso.

Bolton, W., & Roberts, V. (1994). Asking for help: Staff support and sensitivity groups re-visited. In: A. Obholzer & V. Z. Roberts (Eds.), *The Unconscious at Work: Individual and Organizational Stress in the Human Services*. London: Routledge.

Bott, E. (1955). Conjugal roles and social networks. *Human Relations, 8*: 345–384.

Bowlby, J. (1977). The making and breaking of affectional bonds: Aetiology and psychopathology in the light of attachment theory. *British Journal of Psychiatry, 130*: 201–210.

Boxer, P. J. (2012). *The Architecture of Agility: Modeling the Relation to Indirect Value within Ecosystems*. Saarbrücken: Lambert Academic.

Boxer, P. J. (2013). Managing the risks of social disruption; What can we learn from the impact of social networking software? *Socioanalysis, 15*: 32–44.

Boxer, P. J. (2014). Leading organisations without boundaries: "Quantum" organisation and the work of making meaning. *Organisational and Social Dynamics, 14* (1): 130–153.

Boyle, R. P., & Coughlin, G. (1994). Conceptualising and operationalising cultural theory. In: D. J. Coyle & R. J. Ellis (Eds.), *Politics, Policy and Culture*. Boulder, CO: Westview Press.

Brehony, K. J., & Nawrotzki, K. D. (2010). From weak social democracy to hybridized neo-liberalism: Early childhood education in Britain since 1945. In: K. Hagemann, K. H. Jarausch, & C. Allemann-Ghionda (Eds.), *Children, Families and States: Time Policies of Childcare, Preschool, and Primary Education in Europe*. New York: Berghahn Books.

Breivik, G. (2007a). The quest for excitement and the safe society. In: M. J. McNamee (Ed.), *Philosophy of Risk and Adventure Sports* (pp. 10–24). London: Routledge.

Breivik, G. (2007b). Can BASEjumping be morally defended. In: M. J. McNamee (Ed.), *Philosophy of Risk and Adventure Sports* (pp. 168–184). London: Routledge.

Bridger, H. (1990). The discovery of the therapeutic community. In: E. Trist & H. Murray (Eds.), *The Social Engagement of Social Science, A Tavistock Anthology, Vol. I: The Socio-Psychological Perspective* (pp. 68–87). London: Free Association Books.

Briggs, A. (1972). *The Report of the Committee on Nursing*. Cmnd 5115. London: HMSO.

Briggs, J. (1970). *Never in Anger: Portrait of an Eskimo Family*. Cambridge, MA: Harvard University Press.

Britton, R. (1989). The missing link: Parental sexuality in the Oedipus complex. In: *The Oedipus Complex Today: Clinical Implications* (pp. 83–101). London: Karnac.

Britton, R. (1992). Keeping things in mind. In: R. Anderson (Ed.), *Clinical Lectures on Klein and Bion* (pp. 102–113). London: Routledge.

Britton, R. (1998a). Before and after the depressive position: Ps(n)→ D(n)→ Ps(n+1). In: *Belief and Imagination* (pp. 69–81). London. Routledge.

Britton, R. (1998b). *Belief and Imagination*. London: Routledge.

Broadhurst, K., Wastell, D., White, S., Hall, C., Peckover, S., Thompson, K., et al. (2010). Performing "Initial Assessment": Identifying the latent conditions for error at the front-door of local authority children's services. *British Journal of Social Work, 40* (2): 352–370.

Brooker, L. (2010). Constructing the triangle of care: Power and professionalism in practitioner/parent relationships. *British Journal of Educational Studies, 58* (3): 181–196.

Brymer, E. (2010). Risk taking in extreme sports: A phenomenological perspective. *Annals of Leisure Research, 13* (1/2): 218–239.

Brymer, E., & Gray, T. (2009). Dancing with nature: Rhythm and harmony in extreme sports participation. *Journal of Adventure Education & Outdoor Learning, 9* (2): 135–149.

Burchell, G., Gordon, C., & Miller, P. (Eds.) (1991). *The Foucault Effect: Studies in Governmentality* (pp. 1–48). Chicago, IL: University of Chicago Press.

Burke, W. W. (2011). *Organization Change: Theory and Practice* (3rd edition). Thousand Oaks, CA: Sage.

Burke, W. W., & Litwin, G. H. (1992). A causal model of organizational performance and change. *Journal of Management, 18* (3): 532–545.

Butler Report (1975). *Regional Secure Units*. London: HMSO.

Castells, M. (2012). *Networks of Outrage and Hope: Social Movements in the Internet Age*. Cambridge: Polity Press.

Chamberlain, L. (2001). *The Secret Artist: A Close Reading of Sigmund Freud*. New York: Seven Stories.

Clarke, J., Gewirtz, S., & McLaughlin, E. (Eds.) (2000). *New Managerialism, New Welfare?* London: Sage.

Cole, A. (2013). Care workers cast off bureaucracy. *Guardian*, 17 October. Available at: www.theguardian.com/social-care-network/2013/oct/16/care-workers-cast-off-bureaucracy

Cooper, A. (1996). Psychoanalysis and the politics of organizational theory. *Journal of Social Work Practice, 10* (2): 137–145.

Cooper, A. (2005). Surface and depth in the Victoria Climbié Inquiry Report. *Child and Family Social Work, 10*: 1–9.

Cooper, A. (2009a). Be quiet and listen: Emotion, public policy and social totality. In: S. Day-Sclater, D. Jones, & H. Price (Eds.), *Emotion: New Psychosocial* Perspectives (pp. 169–182). London: Routledge.

Cooper, A. (2009b). Hearing the grass grow: Emotional and epistemological challenges of practice-near research. *Journal of Social Work Practice, 23* (4): 429–442.

Cooper, A. (2010). Legend, myth and idea: On the fate of a great paper. *British*

Journal of Psychotherapy, 26 (2): 219–227. [Special Issue—Isabel Menzies Lyth: A Symposium in Honour of Her Life and Work]

Cooper, A. (2011). How to (almost) murder a profession: The unsolved mystery of British social work. In: J. Adlam, A. Aiyegbusi, P. Kleinot, A. Motz, & C. Scanlon (Eds.), *The Therapeutic Milieu under Fire*. London: Jessica Kingsley.

Cooper A. (2014). A short psychosocial history of British child abuse and protection: Case studies in problems of mourning in the public sphere. *Journal of Social Work Practice, 28* (3): 271–285. [Special Issue: Child Protection after Munro: Reflections Three Years On]

Cooper, A., & Dartington, T. (2004). The vanishing organization: Organizational containment in a networked world. In: C. Huffington, W. Halton, D. Armstrong, & J. Pooley (Eds.), *Working Below the Surface: The Emotional Life of Contemporary Organizations*. London: Karnac.

Cooper, A., & Lousada, J. (2005). *Borderline Welfare: Feeling and Fear of Feeling in Modern Welfare*. London: Karnac.

Coyle, D. J. (1994). The theory that would be King. In: D. J. Coyle & R. J. Ellis, *Politics, Policy and Culture*. Boulder, CO: Westview Press.

Craib, I. (1994). *The Importance of Disappointment*. London: Routledge.

Crociani-Windland, L., & Hoggett, P. (2012). Politics and affect. *Subjectivity, 5*: 161–175.

Croisdale-Appleby, D. (2014). *Re-Visioning Social Work Education: An Independent Review*. London: Department of Health. Available at: www.gov.uk/government/uploads/system/uploads/attachment_data/file/285788/DCA_Accessible.pdf

Cummins, A. (2002). The road to hell is paved with good intentions: Quality assurance as a defence against anxiety. *Organisational and Social Dynamics, 2* (1): 99–119.

Cunnane, D., & Warwick, R. (2013). Francis Report: What went wrong with NHS Leadership? *Guardian Professional*, 14 February.

Dalio, R. (2011). *Principles*. Available at: www.bwater.com/Uploads/FileManager/Principles/Bridgewater-Associates-Ray-Dalio-Principles.pdf

Dartington, T. (2010). *Managing Vulnerability*. London: Karnac.

Darzi, A. (2008). *High Quality Care for All: NHS Next Stage Review Final Report*. CM 7432. Richmond: Office of Public Sector Information.

De Bianchedi, E. T., Scalozub De Boschan, L., De Cortiñas, L. P., & De Piccolo, E. G. (1988). Theories on anxiety in Freud and Melanie Klein: Their metapsychological status. *International Journal of Psychoanalysis, 69*: 359–368.

Derivatives Strategy (2000). *The World According to Ray Dalio*. Available at: www.derivativesstrategy.com/magazine/archive/2000/1000qa.asp

Dewar, B., & Nolan, M. (2013). Caring about caring: Developing a model to implement compassionate relationship centred care in an older people care setting. *International Journal of Nursing Studies, 50:* 1247–1258.

DfE (2012). *The Revised Early Years Foundation Stage.* London: Department for Education.

DfE (2013). *More Great Childcare: Raising Quality and Giving Parents More Choice.* London: Department for Education.

Dicks, H. V. (1970). *50 Years of the Tavistock Clinic.* London: Routledge & Kegan Paul.

DiMaggio, P. J. (1988). Interest and agency in institutional theory. In: L. G. Zucker (Ed.), *Institutional Patterns and Organisations: Culture and Environment.* Cambridge, MA: Ballinger.

DoH (1991). *The Children Act 1989 Guidance and Regulations, Volume 2: Family Support, Day Care and Educational Provision for Young Children.* Department of Health. London: HMSO.

DoH (1999). *Making a Difference: Strengthening the Nursing, Midwifery and Health Visiting Contribution to Health and Healthcare.* London: Department of Health.

DoH (2002). *Requirements for Social Work Training.* London: Department of Health.

DoH (2006). *From Values to Action: The Chief Nursing Officer's Review of Mental Health Nursing.* London: Department of Health.

Douglas, M. (1970). *Natural Symbols: Explorations in Cosmology.* London: Routledge, 2003).

Douglas, M. (1982). Cultural bias. In: *In the Active Voice.* London: Routledge & Kegan Paul.

Douglas, M. (1986). *How Institutions Think.* New York: Syracuse University Press.

Du Gay, P. (Ed.) (2005). *The Values of Bureaucracy.* Oxford: Oxford University Press.

Ebert, P., & Robertson, S. (2007). Adventure, climbing excellence and the practice of "bolting". In: M. J. McNamee, *Philosophy of Risk and Adventure Sports.* London: Routledge.

Edelman, M. (1964). *The Symbolic Uses of Politics.* Chicago, IL: University of Illinois Press.

Elfer, P. (2006). Exploring children's expressions of attachment in nursery. *European Early Childhood Education Research Journal, 14* (2): 81–95.

Elfer, P. (2009). *5000 Hours: Facilitating Intimacy in the Care of Children under Three Attending Full Time Nursery.* Unpublished doctoral dissertation, University of East London, London.

Elfer, P. (2012). Emotion in nursery work: Work discussion as a model of critical professional reflection. *Early Years: An International Journal of Research and Development, 32* (2): 129–141.

Elfer, P. (2013). Emotional aspects of nursery policy and practice—progress and prospect. *European Early Childhood Education Research Journal*. Available online at: www.tandfonline.com/doi/full/10.1080/1350293X.2013.798464

Elfer, P., & Beasley, G. (1991). *Registration of Childminding and Day Care: Using the Law to Raise Standards*. London: HMSO.

Elfer, P., & Dearnley, D. (2007). Nurseries and emotional well being: Evaluating an emotionally containing model of professional development. *Early Years: An International Journal of Research and Development, 27* (3): 267–279.

Elfer, P., & Page, J. (2014). *Babies in Nursery: Needs and Numbers. Interviews with Nursery Managers Regarding Their Views on Working with Babies in Nursery*. Manuscript in preparation.

Emery, F. E. (1997). Introduction. In: E. Trist, F. Emery, & H. Murray (Eds.), *The Social Engagement of Social Science, Vol. 3: The Socio-Ecological Perspective*. Philadelphia, PA: University of Pennsylvania Press. Available at: www.moderntimesworkplace.com/archives/ericsess/sessvol3/sessvol3.html

Emery, F. E., & Trist, E. L. (1965). The causal texture of organizational environments. *Human Relations, 18* (1): 21–32.

Emirbayer, M., & Mische, A. (1998). What is agency? *American Journal of Sociology, 103* (4): 962–1023.

Epstein, S., & Fenz, W. D. (1965). Steepness of approach and avoidance gradient in humans as a function of experience: Theory and experiment. *Journal of Experimental Psychology* (July): 1–12.

Erikson, E. H. (1950). *Childhood and Society*. London: Triad/Paladin Books, 1977; New York: W. W. Norton, 1993.

Ersser, S. (1997). *Nursing as a Therapeutic Activity: An Ethnography*. Aldershot: Avebury.

Ersser, S., & Tutton, E. (1991). *Primary Nursing in Perspective*. London: Scutari.

Evans, A., Traynor, M., & Glass, N. (2013). An exploration of jealousy in nursing: A Kleinian analysis. *Nursing Inquiry, 24* (2): 171–178.

Evans, M. (2007). Being driven mad: Towards understanding borderline and other disturbed states of mind through the use of the counter transference, *Psychoanalytic Psychotherapy, 21* (3): 216–232.

Evans, M. (2008). Tuning into the psychotic wavelength: Psychoanalytic supervision for mental health professionals. *Psychoanalytic Psychotherapy, 22* (4): 248–261.

Evans, M. (2009). Tackling the theory–practice gap in mental health nurse training. *Mental Health Practice, 13* (2): 21–24.

Evans, M. (2011). Pinned against the ropes; Understanding anti-social personality disordered patients through use of the counter-transference. *Psychoanalytic Psychotherapy, 25* (2): 143–156.

Evans, T., & Harris, J. (2004). Street-level bureaucracy, social work and the (exaggerated) death of discretion. *British Journal of Social Work, 34* (6): 871–895.

Fabricius, J. (1991). Running on the spot, or can nursing really change? *Psychoanalytic Psychotherapy, 5* (2): 97–108.

Fabricius, J. (1995). Psychoanalytic understanding and nursing: A supervisory workshop with nurse tutors, *Psychoanalytic Psychotherapy, 9* (1): 17–29.

Fabricius, J. (1999). Reflections on the crisis in nursing. *Psychoanalytic Psychotherapy, 13* (3): 203–206.

Fay, E. (2008). Derision and management. *Organization, 15*: 831.

Fenichel, O. (1946). *The Psychoanalytic Theory of Neurosis*. London: Routledge & Kegan Paul; New York: W. W. Norton, 1974.

Ferguson, H. (2005). Working with violence, the emotions and the psychosocial dynamics of child protection: Reflections on the Victoria Climbié case. *Social Work Education, 24* (7): 781–795.

Field, F. (2010). *The Foundation Years: Preventing Poor Children Becoming Poor Adults. Report of the Independent Review on Poverty and Life Chances*. London: HMSO.

Finch, J. (2010). *Can't Fail, Won't Fail—Why Practice Assessors Find it Difficult to Fail Social Work Students: A Qualitative Study of Practice Assessors' Experience of Assessing Marginal or Failing Social Work Students*. DSW thesis, University of Sussex, Falmer. Available at:. http://sro.sussex.ac.uk /2370

Finch, J. (2013). *A Critical Exploration of Practice Assessment Panels: Participation, Power, Emotion and Decision Making in Relation to Failing Social Work Students*. York: Higher Education Academy. Available at: www.heacademy .ac.uk/resources/detail/resources/detail/disciplines/hsc/Social-Work-and-Social-Policy/A_critical

Finch, J. (2014). "Running with the fox and hunting with the hounds": Social work tutors' experiences of managing students failing in practice learning settings. *British Journal of Social Work*. Epub ahead of publication.

Finch, J., & Poletti, A. (2013). "It's been hell": Italian and British practice educators' narratives of working with struggling or failing social work students in practice learning settings. *European Journal of Social Work, 17* (1): 135–150.

Finch, J., Schaub, J., & Dalrymple, R. (2014). Projective identification and the fear of failing: Making sense of practice educators' experiences of failing social work students in practice learning settings. *Journal of Social Work Practice: Psychotherapeutic Approaches in Health, Welfare and the Community, 28* (2): 139–145.

Finch, J., & Taylor, I. (2013). "Failing to fail?" Practice educators' emotional experiences of assessing failing social work students. *Social Work Education, 32* (2): 244–258. [Special Edition: Field Education in Social Work]

Flynn, R. (2001). Impediments to organisational effectiveness: Social defences and shame in the workplace. *Socio-Analysis 3* (2): 109–122.

Foss, N. J., & Klein, P. G. (2012). *Organizing Entrepreneurial Judgement: A New Approach to the Firm.* Cambridge: Cambridge University Press.

Foucault, M. (1975). *Surveiller et punir. Naissance de la prison.* Paris: Editions Gallimard. [*Discipline and Punish: The Birth of the Prison.* London: Allen Lane, 1977.]

Francis, R. (2013). *The Report of the Mid Staffordshire NHS Trust Public Inquiry.* Public Inquiry Chaired by Robert Francis QC. London: HMSO.

Freud, S. (1911b). Formulations on the two principles of mental functioning. *Standard Edition, 12.*

Freud, S. (1914g). Remembering, repeating and working through. *Standard Edition, 12.*

Freud, S. (1920g). *Beyond the Pleasure Principle, Standard Edition, 18*: 3–64.

Freud, S. (1921c). *Group Psychology and the Analysis of the Ego. Standard Edition, 18*: 67–143.

Freud, S. (1925h). Negation. *Standard Edition, 19.*

Freud, S. (1926d [1925]). *Inhibitions, Symptoms and Anxiety. Standard Edition, 20.*

Freud, S. (1927c). *The Future of an Illusion. Standard Edition, 21.*

Freud, S. (1933a). *New Introductory Lectures on Psycho-Analysis. Standard Edition, 22.*

Frosh, S. (2012). *A Brief Introduction to Psychoanalytic Theory.* Basingstoke: Palgrave.

Gabriel, Y. (2012). Organizations in a state of darkness: Towards a theory of organizational miasma. *Organization Studies, 33* (9): 1137–1152.

Garelick, A. (2012). Doctors' health: Stigma and the professional discomfort in seeking help. *The Psychiatrist, 36*: 81–84.

Garland, C. (2010). *The Groups Book. Psychoanalytic Group Therapy: Principles and Practice.* London: Karnac.

Geertz, C. (1983). From the native's point of view: On the nature of anthropological understanding. In: *Local Knowledge* (pp. 55–72). New York: Basic Books.

Giddens, A. (1990). *The Consequences of Modernity.* Cambridge: Polity Press.

Giddens, A. (1991). *Modernity and Self-Identity.* Cambridge: Polity Press.

Giddens, A. (1992). *The Transformation of Intimacy.* Cambridge: Polity Press.

Giddens, A. (1994). *Beyond Left and Right.* Cambridge: Polity Press.

Giddens, A. (1998). *The Third Way.* Cambridge: Polity Press.

Gidman, J. (2001). The role of the tutor: A literature review. *Nurse Education Today, 21*: 359–365.

Gilbert, T. (2005). Trust and managerialism: Exploring discourses of care. *Journal of Advanced Nursing, 52* (4): 454–463.

Girard, R. (1972). *Violence and the Sacred.* Baltimore, MD: Johns Hopkins University Press, 1979.

Glossop, C. (2002). Student nurse attrition: Use of an exit-interview procedure to determine students' leaving reasons. *Nurse Education Today, 22* (5): 375–386.

Glyn, A. (2006). *Capitalism Unleashed.* Oxford: Oxford University Press.

Goddard Report (1953). *The Work of Nurses in Hospital Wards (Nuffield).* London: Nuffield Provincial Hospitals Trust.

Goffman, E. R. (1961). *Asylums.* New York: Doubleday Anchor.

Goodrich, J., & Cornwell, J. (2012). *The Contribution of Schwartz Center Rounds® to Hospital Culture.* Available at: www.kingsfund.org.uk/sites/files/kf/field/field_publication_file/contribution-schwartz-center-rounds-goodrich-cornwell-may12.pdf

Grandin, T., & Johnson, C. (2009). *Making Animals Happy: How to Create the Best Life for Pets and Other Animals.* London: Bloomsbury.

Greenfield, S. (2012). Nursery home visits: Rhetoric and reality. *Journal of Early Childhood Research. 10* (1): 100–112.

Grosz, S. (2014). *The Examined Life: How We Lose and Find Ourselves.* London: Vintage.

Guignard, F. (2014). Psychic development in a virtual world. In: A. Lemma & L. Caparrotta (Eds.), *Psychoanalysis in the Technoculture Era.* New York: Routledge.

Hall, C., Parton, N., Peckover, S., & White, S. (2010). Child-centric information and communication technology (ICT) and the fragmentation of child welfare practice in the UK. *Journal of Social Policy, 39* (3): 393–413.

Halton, W. (1994). Unconscious aspects of organizational life. In: A. Obholzer & V. Z. Roberts (Eds.), *The Unconscious at Work: Individual and Organizational Stress in the Human Services* (pp. 11–18). London: Routledge.

Harrison, T. (2000). *Bion, Rickman, Foulkes and the Northfield Experiments.* London: Jessica Kingsley.

Hartley, P., & Kennard, D. (2009). *Staff Support Groups in the Helping Professions.* London: Routledge.

Harvey, D. (1991). *The Condition of Post-Modernity.* Oxford: Blackwell.

Harvey, D. (2005). *A Brief History of Neoliberalism.* Oxford: Oxford University Press.

Hatcher, B. G. (1997). Coral reef ecosystems: How much greater is the whole than the sum of the parts? *Coral Reefs, 16* (Suppl.): 77–91.

Hegel, G. (1806). *The Phenomenology of Spirit,* trans. A. V. Miller. Oxford: Oxford University Press, 1979.

Hewison, A., & Wildman, S. (1996). The theory–practice gap in nursing: A new dimension. *Journal of Advanced Nursing, 244*: 754–761.

Heymans, A., Kennedy, R., & Tischler, L. (Eds.) (1986). *The Family as Inpatient.* London: Free Association Books.

Hinshelwood, R. D., & Skogstad, W. (2000). *Observing Organisations: Anxiety, Defence and Culture in Health Care.* London: Routledge.

Hirschhorn, L. (1988). *The Workplace Within: Psychodynamics of Organizational Life.* Cambridge, MA: MIT Press, 1990.

Hirschhorn, L., & Horowitz, S. (2013). *Extreme Work Environments: Beyond Anxiety and Social Defense.* Paper presented at the ISPSO 2013 Annual Meeting, Oxford.

Hochschild, A. (1983). *The Managed Heart: Commercialization of Human Feeling.* Berkeley, CA: University of California Press.

Hoggett, P. (1992). *Partisans in an Uncertain World: The Psychoanalysis of Engagement.* London: Free Association Books.

Hoggett, P. (1998). The internal establishment. In: P. Bion Talamo, F. Borgogno, & S. Merciai (Eds.), *Bion's Legacy to Groups.* London: Karnac.

Hoggett, P. (2005). Conflict, ambivalence and the contested purpose of public organizations. *Human Relations, 59* (2): 175–194.

Hoggett, P. (2008). What's in a hyphen? Reconstructing psychosocial studies. *Psychoanalysis, Culture and Society, 13*: 379–384.

Hoggett, P. (2010). Government and the perverse social defence. *British Journal of Psychotherapy, 26* (2): 202–213. [Special Issue—Isabel Menzies Lyth: A Symposium in Honour of Her Life and Work]

Hoggett, P. (2013). Governance and social anxieties. *Organisational and Social Dynamics, 13* (1): 69–78.

Hollway, W., & Jefferson, T. (2013). *Doing Qualitative Research Differently: A Psychosocial Approach.* London: Sage.

Home Office (1997). *New National and Local Focus on Youth Crime.* London.

Hopkins, J. (1988). Facilitating the development of intimacy between nurses and infants in day nurseries. *Early Child Development and Care, 33*: 99–111.

Hopper, E. (2002). *The Social Unconscious.* London: Jessica Kingsley.

House of Commons Education Committee (2013). *Foundation Years: Sure Start Children's Centres. Fifth Report of Session 2013–14. Volume 1.* HC 364–1. London: HMSO.

Hoyle, L. (2004). From sycophant to saboteur: Responses to organizational change: In C. Huffington, D. Armstrong, W. Halton, L. Hoyle, & J. Pooley (Eds.), *Working Below the Surface: The Emotional Life of Contemporary Organizations* (pp. 87–106). London: Karnac.

HSE (2000). *The Scale of Occupational Stress: The Bristol Stress and Health at Work Study.* London: Health & Safety Executive.

Huffington, C. (2008). The system in the room: The extent to which coaching can change the organization. In: D. Campbell & C. Huffington (Eds.), *Organizations Connected: A Handbook of Systemic Consultation.* London: Karnac.

Hussein, S., Moriarty, J., Manthorpe, J., & Huxley, P. (2008). Diversity and progression among students starting social work qualifying programmes in England between 1995 and 1998: A quantitative study. *British Journal of Social Work, 38* (8): 1588–1609.

Hutchings, M., Ward, P., & Bloodworth, K. (2013). "Caring around the clock": A new approach to intentional rounding. *Nursing Management, 20* (5): 24–30.

Ilundain-Agurruza, J. (2007). Kant goes skydiving: Understanding the extreme by way of the sublime. In: M. J. McNamee (Ed.), *Philosophy of Risk and Adventure Sports.* London: Routledge.

Jackson, D., Firtko, A., & Edenborough, M. (2007). Personal resilience as a strategy for surviving and thriving in the face of workplace adversity: A literature review. *Journal of Advanced Nursing, 60* (1): 1–9.

Jackson, E. (2002). Mental health in schools: What about the staff? Thinking about the impact of work discussion groups in school settings. *Journal of Child Psychotherapy, 28* (2): 129–146.

Jackson, E. (2008). The development of work discussion groups in educational settings. *Journal of Child Psychotherapy, 34* (1): 62–82.

James, N. (1992). Care = organisation + physical labour + emotional labour. *Sociology of Health and Illness, 14* (4): 489–509.

Jaques, E. (1951). *The Changing Culture of a Factory: A Study of Authority and Participation in an Industrial Setting.* London: Tavistock Publications; reprinted London: Routledge, 2001. Also in: E. Trist & H. Murray (Eds.), *The Social Engagement of Social Science, Vol. 1: The Socio-Psychological Perspective.* London: Free Association Books, 1990.

Jaques, E. (1953). On the dynamics of social structure: A contribution to the psychoanalytical study of social phenomena deriving from the views of Melanie Klein. *Human Relations, 6* (1): 3–24.

Jaques, E. (1955). Social systems as a defence against persecutory and depressive anxiety. In: M. Klein, P. Hermann, & R. E. Money-Kyrle (Eds.), *New Directions in Psychoanalysis* (pp. 478–498). London: Tavistock Publications; reprinted London: Karnac, 1985.

Jaques, E. (1956). *Measurement of Responsibility: A Study of Work, Payment and Individual Capacity.* London: Tavistock Publications.

Jaques, E. (1989). *Requisite Organisation: The CEO's Guide to Creative Structure and Leadership.* Aldershot: Gower.

Jaques, E. (1995). Why the psychoanalytical approach to understanding organizations is dysfunctional. *Human Relations, 48* (4): 343–349.

Jaques, E. (1998). *Requisite Organization.* Arlington, VA: Cason Hall.

Judt, T. (2010). *Ill Fares the Land*. London: Penguin.

Kahn, W. (1992). To be fully there: Psychological presence at work. *Human Relations, 43* (4): 321–347.

Kahneman, D. (2013). *Thinking, Fast and Slow*. New York: Farrar, Straus & Giroux.

Keat, R., & Urry, J. (1975). *Social Theory as Science*. London: Routledge.

Kernberg, O. F. (1973). Psychoanalytic object-relations theory, group processes, and administration. *Annual of Psychoanalysis, 1*: 363–386.

Kerr, J. H., & Mackenzie, S. H. (2012). Multiple motives for participating in adventures ports. *Psychology of Sport and Exercise, 13* (5): 649–657.

Khaleelee, O. (2010). From autonomy to dependency? *British Journal of Psychotherapy, 26* (2): 213–218. [Special Issue—Isabel Menzies Lyth: A Symposium in Honour of Her Life and Work]

Kierkegaard, S. (1980). *The Concept of Anxiety*. Princeton, NJ: Princeton University Press.

Kirsner, D. (2004). The intellectual odyssey of Elliott Jaques: From alchemy to science. *Free Associations, 11* (55): 179–204.

Klein, M. (1930). The importance of symbol formation in the development of the ego. In: *Writings, Vol. 1: Love, Guilt and Reparation and Other Works* (pp. 219–232). London: Hogarth Press, 1975; reprinted London: Karnac, 1992.

Klein, M. (1935). A contribution to the psychogenesis of manic-depressive states. In: *Writings, Vol. 1: Love, Guilt and Reparation and Other Works* (pp. 262–289). London: Hogarth Press, 1975; reprinted London: Karnac, 1992.

Klein, M. (1940). Mourning and its relation to manic-depressive states. In: *Writings, Vol. 1: Love, Guilt and Reparation and Other Works* (pp. 344–369). London: Hogarth Press, 1975; reprinted London: Karnac, 1992.

Klein, M. (1946). Notes on some schizoid mechanisms. In: *Writings, Vol. 3: Envy and Gratitude and Other Works* (pp. 1–24). London: Hogarth Press, 1975; reprinted London: Karnac, 1993.

Klein, M. (1952). Some theoretical conclusions regarding the emotional life of the infant. In: *Writings, Vol. 3: Envy and Gratitude and Other Works* (pp. 61–93). London: Hogarth Press, 1975; reprinted London: Karnac, 1993.

Klein, M. (1957). Envy and gratitude. In *Writings, Vol. 3: Envy and Gratitude and Other Works* (pp. 176–235). London: Hogarth Press, 1975; reprinted London: Karnac, 1993.

Kraemer, S. (2011). The dangers of this atmosphere: A Quaker connection in the Tavistock Clinic's development. *History of the Human Sciences, 24*: 82–102.

Krantz, J. (2010). Social defences and twenty-first century organisations. *British Journal of Psychotherapy, 26* (2): 192–201. [Special Issue—Isabel Menzies Lyth: A Symposium in Honour of Her Life and Work]

Krantz, J. (2011). Reflective citizenship: An organizational perspective. In: L. Gould, A. Lucey, & L. Stapley (Eds.), *The Reflective Citizen: Organizational and Social Dynamics* (pp. 149–162). London: Karnac.

Krantz, J. (2013). Work culture analysis and reflective space. In S. Long (Ed.), *Socioanalytic Methods: Discovering the Hidden in Organisations and Social Systems* (pp. 23–44). London: Karnac.

Krantz, J., & Gilmore, T. (1990). The splitting of leadership and management as a social defense. *Human Relations, 43* (2): 183–284. Reprinted in: B. Sievers (Ed.), *Psychoanalytic Studies of Organizations: Contributions from the International Society for the Psychoanalytic Study of Organizations (ISPSO).* London: Karnac, 2009.

Krantz, J., & Gould, L. (2005). *Bricks Without Mortar: The Decline of Sentience in Global Organizations.* Paper presented at the OPUS Conference.

Kratz, C. (1979). *The Nursing Process.* London: Balliere Tindall.

Kurtz, C. F., & Snowden, D. J. (2003). The new dynamics of strategy: Sense-making in a complex and complicated world. *IBM Systems Journal, 42* (3). Available at: http://ieeexplore.ieee.org/search/searchresult.jsp?newsea rch=true&queryText=The+new+dynamics+of+strategy&x=40&y=16

Lacan, J. (1959–1960). *The Seminar of Jacques Lacan, Book VII: The Ethics of Psychoanalysis.* London: Routledge, 1992.

Lacan, J. (1966a). The subversion of the subject and the dialectic of desire in the Freudian unconscious. In: *Écrits: The First Complete Edition in English* (pp. 671–702). New York: W. W. Norton, 2006.

Lacan, J. (1966b). The instance of the letter in the unconscious or reason since Freud. In: *Écrits: The First Complete Edition in English* (pp. 412–444). New York: W. W. Norton, 2006.

Lacan, J. (1975). The nucleus of repression. In: J.-A. Miller (Ed.), *The Seminar of Jacques Lacan, Vol. 1 (1953–1954)* (pp. 187–199). Cambridge: Cambridge University Press, 1988.

Lakatos, I. (1970). Falsification and the methodology of scientific research programmes. In: I. Lakatos & A. Musgrave, *Criticism and the Growth of Knowledge* (pp. 91–196). Cambridge: Cambridge University Press.

Laming, L. (2009). *The Protection of Children in England: A Progress Report.* London: HMSO.

Lancet (2013). The NHS: Free and caring or a market commodity [Editorial]. *Lancet, 382*: 571.

Lane, D. A., & Maxfield, R. R. (2005). Ontological uncertainty and innovation. *Journal of Evolutionary Economics, 15* (1): 3–50.

Laufer, M. (1995). *The Suicidal Adolescent.* London: Karnac.

Laufer, M., & Laufer, E. (1984). *Adolescence and Developmental Breakdown: A Psychoanalytic View.* New Haven, CT: Yale University Press; reprinted London: Karnac, 1995.

Lawlor, D. (2009). A case study in the functioning of social systems as a defence against anxiety: Rereading 50 years on. *Clinical Child Psychology and Psychiatry, 14* (4): 523–530.

Lawrence, W. G. (1985). Management development . . . some ideals, images and realities. In: A. D. Colman & M. H. Geller (Eds.), *Group Relations Reader, Vol. 2.* Jupiter, FL: A. K. Rice Institute.

Lawrence, W. G. (2005). *Introduction to Social Dreaming.* London: Karnac.

Layton, L. (2008). Editor's introduction. *Psychoanalysis, Culture and Society, 13*: 339–340. [Special Issue: British Psychosocial Studies]

Leach, P., Barnes, J., Nichols, M., Goldin, J., Stein, A., Sylva, K., Malmberg, L. E., & the FCCC team (2006). Child care before 6 months of age: A qualitative study of mothers' decisions and feelings about employment and non-maternal care. *Infant and Child Development: An International Journal of Research, 15* (5): 471–502.

Lees, A. (2014). *Spotlights and Shadows: A Social Work Perspective on Information Sharing to Safeguard Children.* Doctoral thesis, University of Southampton, Southampton.

Lees, A., Meyer, E., & Rafferty, J. (2013). From Menzies Lyth to Munro: The problem of managerialism. *British Journal of Social Work, 43* (3): 542–558.

Lewin, K. (1997). *Resolving Social Conflicts and Field Theory in Social Science.* Washington, DC: American Psychological Society.

Long, S. (2006). Organizational defenses against anxiety: What has happened since the 1955 Jaques paper? *International Journal of Applied Psychoanalytic Studies, 3* (4): 279–295.

Long, S. (2008). *The Perverse Organisation and Its Deadly Sins.* London: Karnac.

Long, S. (Ed.) (2013). *Socioanalytic Methods.* London: Karnac.

Long, S., & Harney, M. (2013). The associative unconscious. In: S. Long (Ed.), *Socioanalytic Methods: Discovering the Hidden in Organisations and Social Systems* (pp. 3–22). London: Karnac.

Lousada, J., & Cooper, A. (2005). *Borderline Welfare: Feeling and Fear of Feeling in Modern Welfare.* London: Karnac.

Lucey, A. (2013). *Containment in Contemporary Organizations.* Paper presented at ISPSO Annual Meeting, Oxford.

Maben, J., Latter, S., & Macleod Clark, J. (2007). The sustainability of ideals, values and the nursing mandate: Evidence from a longitudinal qualitative study. *Nursing Inquiry, 14* (2): 99–113.

Macaulay, C., & Hirons, P. (Eds.) (in press). *Patient Journeys.* London: Radcliffe.

Maccoby, M. (2000). Narcissistic leaders: The incredible pro's and the inevitable cons. *Harvard Business Review* (January–February): 69–77.

Mackintosh, C. (2000). Is there a place for "care" within nursing? *International Journal of Nursing Studies, 37*: 321–327.

Mahoney, J., & Thelen, K. (2010). *Explaining Institutional Change: Ambiguity, Agency and Power*. New York: Cambridge University Press.

Main, T. F. (1957). The ailment. *The British Journal of Medical Psychology, 30*: 129–145.

Maratos, A., Birdsall, N., Benson, L., Tanner, C., Scott-Stewart, M., Bogal, S., et al. (2014). *Sharing, Openness and Supervision: The Use of Cognitive Analytic Therapy in Reflective Practice: A Randomised Trial of Reflective Practice on Six Inpatient Wards*. Manuscript in preparation.

Mars, G. (2008). Corporate cultures and the use of space: An approach from cultural theory. In: *Innovation: European Journal of Social Science Research, 21* (3): 181–204.

Mason, P. (2013). *Why It's Still Kicking off Everywhere: The New Global Revolutions* (2nd edition). London: Verso.

Mathers, S., Eisenstadt, N., Sylva, K., Soukakou, E., & Erkey-Stevens, K. (2014). *Sound Foundations: A Review of the Research Evidence on Quality of Early Childhood Education and Care for Children under Three*. London: The Sutton Trust.

Mathers, S., Sylva, K., & Joshi, H. (2007). *Quality of Childcare Settings in the Millennium Cohort Study*. Department of Educational Studies, University of Oxford and Institute of Education, University of London. London: HMSO.

McAfee, A. (2012). *The Great Decoupling of the US Economy* [Blog]. Available at: http://andrewmcafee.org/2012/12/the-great-decoupling-of-the-us-economy

McDowall Clark, R., & Baylis, S. (2012). "Wasted down there": Policy and practice with the under-threes. *Early Years: An International Journal of Research and Development, 32* (2): 229–242.

McGuire, J., & Richman, N. (1986). The prevalence of behavioural problems in three types of preschool group. *Journal of Child Psychology and Psychiatry, 27*: 455–472.

McLuhan, M. (1964). *Understanding Media: The Extensions of Man* New York: McGraw-Hill.

Melamed, L. (1996). *Escape to the Futures*. New York: Wiley.

Melanie Klein Trust (2014). *Unconscious Phantasy*. Available at: www.melanie-klein-trust.org.uk/unconscious-phantasy

Meltzer, D. (1968). Terror, persecution and dread: A dissection of paranoid anxieties. *International Journal of Psychoanalysis, 49*: 396–401.

Meltzer, D. (1973). Terror, persecution and dread. In: *Sexual States of Mind* (pp. 99–106). Strath Tay: Clunie Press.

Meltzer, D. (1975). *Explorations in Autism*. Strath Tay: Clunie Press.

Menzies, I. (1960). A case study in the functioning of social systems as a defence against anxiety: A report on a study of the nursing service of a general hospital. *Human Relations, 13* (2): 95–121. Reprinted in: I. Menzies

Lyth, *Containing Anxiety in Institutions: Selected Essays* (pp. 43–85). London: Free Association Books, 1988.

Menzies Lyth, I. (1976). *The Psychological Welfare of Young Children Making Long Stays in Hospital*. Unpublished paper, Tavistock Institute of Human Relations, London.

Menzies Lyth, I. (1988). *Containing Anxiety in Institutions: Selected Essays*. London: Free Association Books.

Menzies Lyth, I. (1989). Day care of children under five: An action research study. In: *The Dynamics of the Social: Selected Essays, Vol. 2*. London: Free Association Books.

Menzies Lyth, I. (1990). A psychoanalytical perspective on social institutions. In: E. L. Trist & H. Murray (Eds.), *The Social Engagement of Social Science: The Socio-Psychological Perspective* (pp. 463–475). London: Free Association Press.

Menzies Lyth, I. (1999). Facing the crisis. *Psychoanalytic Psychotherapy, 13* (3): 233–231.

Menzies Lyth, I., Robertson, J., Scott, S. M., & Gwynne, G. (1971). *An Action Research Study of the Day Care of Children under Five*. Report to the Department of Health and Social Security. London: Tavistock Institute of Human Relations.

Miller, E. J. (1959). Technology, territory and time: The internal differentiation of complex production systems. *Human Relations, 12*: 243–272.

Miller, E. J. (1976). *Task and Organisation*. London: Free Association Books.

Miller, E. J. (1993). *From Dependency to Autonomy: Studies in Organisation and Change*. London: Free Association Books.

Miller, E. J. (1998). A note on the protomental system and groupishness: Bion's basic assumptions revisited. *Human Relations, 51* (12): 1495–1508. Reprinted in: P. Bion Talamo, F. Borgogno, & S. Merciai (Eds.), *Bion's Legacy to Groups*. London: Karnac, 1998.

Miller, E. J., & Gwynne, G. V. (1972). *A Life Apart: A Pilot Study of Residential Institutions for the Physically Handicapped and the Young Chronic Sick*. London: Tavistock Publications.

Miller, E. J., & Rice, A. K. (1967). *Systems of Organization: Task and Sentient Systems and Their Boundary Control*. London: Tavistock Publications.

Miller, J.-A. (1968). Action of the structure. *The Symptom, 10* (2009, Spring). Available at: www.lacan.com/thesymptom/?p=423

Milton, J., & Davison, S. (1997). Observations of staff-support groups with time-limited external facilitation in a psychiatric institution. *Psychoanalytic Psychotherapy, 11* (2): 135–145.

Mintzberg, H. (1983). *Structure in Fives: Designing Effective Organizations*. London: Prentice-Hall International.

MoH (1965). *Day Care of Children*. Ministry of Health, Circular 5/65, 10 April. London: HMSO.

MoH & MoE (1945). *Nursery Provision for Children under Five*. Ministry of Health & Ministry of Education, Circular 221/45, 14 December. London: HMSO.

Morgan, G. (1986). *Images of Organization*. London: Sage.

Morgan-Jones, R. (2010). *The Body of the Organisation and Its Health*. London: Karnac.

Mouzelis, N. (1995). *Sociological Theory: What Went Wrong?* Oxford: Routledge.

Mouzelis, N. P. (2008). *Modern and Postmodern Social Theorizing*. New York: Cambridge University Press.

Munro, E. (2010). *The Munro Review of Child Protection: Part One—A Systems Analysis*. London: Department for Education. Available at: www.gov.uk/government/publications/munro-review-of-child-protection-part-1-a-systems-analysis

Munro, E. (2011a). *The Munro Review of Child Protection: Interim Report—The Child's Journey*. London: Department for Education. Available at: www.gov.uk/government/publications/munro-review-of-child-protection-interim-report-the-childs-journey

Munro, E. (2011b). *The Munro Review of Child Protection: Final Report—A Child-Centred System*. CM 8062. London: Department for Education. Available at: www.gov.uk/government/publications/munro-review-of-child-protection-final-report-a-child-centred-system

Murphey, M. G. (1993). *The Development of Peirce's Philosophy*. Cambridge, MA: iHackett Publishing.

Murray, H. (1990). The transformation of selection procedures: The War Office Selection Boards. In: E. L. Trist & H. Murray (Eds.), *The Social Engagement of Social Science: A Tavistock Anthology. Vol. 1: The Socio-Psychological Perspective* (pp. 45–67). London: Free Association Books.

Narey, M. (2014). *Making the Education of Social Work Consistently Effective*. London: Department for Education. Available at: www.gov.uk/government/uploads/system/uploads/attachment_data/file/287756/Making_the_education_of_social_workers_consistently_effective.pdf

Nutbrown, C. (2012). *Foundations for Quality: The Independent Review of Early Education and Childcare Qualifications*. The Nutbrown Review. London: Department for Education.

Obholzer, A. (1989). Psychoanalysis and the political process. *Psychoanalytic Psychotherapy, 4* (1): 55–66.

Obholzer, A. (1994a). Authority, power and leadership: Contributions from group relations training. In: A. Obholzer & V. Roberts (Eds.), *The Unconscious at Work: Individual and Organizational Stress in the Human Services* (pp. 39–47). London: Routledge.

Obholzer, A. (1994b). Managing social anxieties in public sector organisations. In: A. Obholzer & V. Z. Roberts (Eds.), *The Unconscious at Work:*

Individual and Organizational Stress in the Human Services (pp. 169–178). London: Routledge.

Ochs, P. (1998). *Peirce: Pragmatism and the Logic of Scripture*. Cambridge: Cambridge University Press.

Ofsted (2013). *Evaluation Schedule for Inspections of Registered Early Years Provision. Guidance and Grade Descriptors for Inspecting Registered Early Years Provision from 4 November 2013*. London: HMSO.

Ofsted (2014). *The Report of Her Majesty's Chief Inspector of Education, Children's Services and Skills—Early Years (2012/2013)*. London: HMSO.

Ogden, T. (1989). On the concept of a contiguous-autistic position. *International Journal of Psychoanalysis, 70*: 127–141.

O'Hagan, A. (2012). Our paedophile culture. *London Review of Books, 34* (No. 5–8, 8 November).

Orme, J., MacIntyre, G., Green Lister, P., Cavanagh, K., Crisp, B., Hussein, S., et al. (2009). What (a) difference a degree makes: The evaluation of the new social work degree in England. *British Journal of Social Work, 39*: 161–178.

Osgood, J. (2004). Time to get down to business? The response of early years practitioners to entrepreneurial approaches to professionalism. *Journal of Early Childhood Research, 2* (1): 5–24.

O'Shaughnessy, E. (1981). A clinical study of a defensive organization. *International Journal of Psychoanalysis, 62*: 359–370.

O'Shaughnessy, E. (1992). Enclaves and excursions. *International Journal of Psychoanalysis, 73*: 603–611.

Page, J., & Elfer, P. (2013). The emotional complexity of attachment interactions in nursery. *European Early Childhood Education Research Journal, 24* (1). Available at: www.tandfonline.com/doi/abs/10.1080/1350293X .2013.766032#.VCHHARZlxTE

Palfrey, J., & Gasser, U. (2008). *Born Digital: Understanding the First Generation of Digital Natives*. New York: Basic Books.

Palmer, B. (2002). The Tavistock Paradigm: Inside, outside and beyond. In: R. D. Hinshelwood & M. Chiesa (Eds.), *Organisations, Anxiety and Defences: Towards a Psychoanalytic Social Psychology* (pp. 158–182). London: Whurr.

Papadopoulos, N. (2010). *The Psychoanalytic Underpinnings of the Later Work of Elliott Jaques and Its Normative Reception*. Paper presented at the ISPSO Annual Meeting, Elsinore, Denmark.

Parton, N. (2008). Changes in the form of knowledge in social work: From the "Social" to the "Informational"? *British Journal of Social Work, 38* (2): 253–269.

Patman, D. (2013). Socioanalysis and the electronic matrix. *Socioanalysis, 15*: 17-31.

Patterson, M., Nolan, M., Rick, J., Brown, J., & Adams, R. (2011). *From Met-*

rics to Meaning: Culture Change and Quality of Acute Hospital Care for Older people. Available at: www.nets.nihr.ac.uk/__data/assets/pdf_file/0003/64497/FR-08-1501-93.pdf

Pearson, A. (1985). *The Effects of Introducing New Norms in a Nursing Unit and an Analysis of the Process of Change.* Doctoral thesis, Department of Social Science and Administration, Goldmith's College, University of London.

Pearson, A. (Ed.) (1988). *Primary Nursing: Nursing in the Burford and Oxford Nursing Development Units.* London: Croom Helm.

Pearson, A., Punton, S., & Durant, I. (1992). *Nursing Beds: An Evaluation of the Effects of Therapeutic Nursing.* Harrow: Scutari Press.

Pearson, A., Vaughan, B., & Fitzgerald, M. (1996). *Nursing Models for Practice.* Oxford: Butterworth Heinemann.

Pecotic, B. (2002). The life of Isabel Menzies Lyth. *Organisational and Social Dynamics, 2* (1): 2–44.

Peirce, C. S. (1905). Issues of pragmaticism. *The Monist, 15* (4): 481–499.

Peirce, C. S. (1908). A neglected argument for the reality of God. *The Hibbert Journal, 7* (October): 90–112.

Penn, H. (2007). Childcare market management: How the United Kingdom Government has reshaped its role in developing early childhood education and care. *Contemporary Issues in Early Childhood, 8* (3): 192–207.

Petriglieri, G., & Petriglieri, J. L. (2010). Identity workspaces: The case of business schools. *Academy of Management Learning & Education, 9* (1): 44–60.

Pickersgill, T. (2001). The European Working Time Directive for doctors in training. *British Medical Journal, 323*: 1266.

Piper, H., & Smith, H. (2003). "Touch" in educational and child care settings: Dilemmas and responses. *British Educational Research Journal, 29* (6): 879–894.

Plunkett, J., & Pessoa, J. P. (2013). *A Polarising Crisis? The Changing Shape of UK and US Labour Markets for 2008 to 2012.* London: Resolution Foundation.

Porter, M. E., & Kramer, M. R. (2011). Creating shared value: How to reinvent capitalism—and unleash a wave of innovation and growth. *Harvard Business Review* (January–February): 2–17.

Prensky, M. (2011). *From Digital Natives to Digital Wisdom: Hopeful Essays for 21st Century Learning.* New York: Corwin.

Procter, S., Wallbank, S., & Dhaliwall, J. (2013). What compassionate care means. *Health Service Journal,* 28 February. Available at: www.hsj.co.uk/comment/what-compassionate-care-means/5055438.article

Pruitt, L. P., & Barber, M. (2004). Savage inequalities indeed: Inequalities and urban school reform. In: S. Cyntrybaum & D. A Noumair (Eds.), *Group Dynamics, Organizational Irrationality and Social Complexity: Group Relations Reader 3* (pp. 303–320). Jupiter, FL: A. K. Rice Institute.

RCN (2013). *RCN Employment Survey.* London: Royal College of Nursing.

Available at: www.rcn.org.uk/__data/assets/pdf_file/0005/541292/ Employment_Survey_2013_004_503_FINAL_100214.pdf

RCN (2014). *Frontline First: More Than Just a Number—March 2014 Special Report*. London: Royal College of Nursing. Available at: www.rcn.org .uk/__data/assets/pdf_file/0007/564739/004598.pdf

Reder, P., & Duncan, S. (2004). From Colwell to Climbié: Inquiring into fatal child abuse. In: N. Stanley & J. Manthorpe (Eds.), *The Age of the Inquiry* (pp. 92–115). London: Routledge.

Redfern, S. (1996). Individualised patient care: Its meaning and practice in a general setting. *NT Research, 1* (1): 22–33.

Registered Mental Nurse (1960). Defence mechanisms in nursing: A review by a Registered Mental Nurse. In: I. Menzies Lyth: *Containing Anxiety in Institutions: Selected Essays* (pp. 89–94). London: Free Association Books, 1988.

Revans, R. (1959). *The Hospital as an Organism: A Study in Communication and Morale*. Paper presented at the Sixth International Meeting of the Institute of Management Science, Paris, September. Preprint No. 7. London: Pergamon.

Rey, H. (1994). *Universals of Psychoanalysis in the Treatment of Psychotic and Borderline States*. London: Free Associations Books.

Rice, A. K. (1958). *Productivity and Social Organization: The Ahmedabad Experiment*. London: Tavistock Publications.

Rice, A. K. (1963). *The Enterprise and Its Environment*. London: Tavistock.

Rice, A. K. (1965). *Learning for Leadership: Interpersonal and Intergroup Learning*. London: Karnac, 1999.

Rickman, J. (1938). Does it take all kinds to make a world? Uniformity and diversity in communities. In: P. King (Ed.), *No Ordinary Psychoanalyst: The Exceptional Contributions of John Rickman* (pp. 159–183). London: Karnac, 2003.

Rizq, R. (2012). The perversion of care: Psychological therapies in a time of IAPT. *Psychodynamic Practice, 18:* 7–25.

Roberts, J. (2011). Trust and early years childcare: Parents' relationships with private, state and third sector providers in England. *Journal of Social Policy, 40* (4): 695–715.

Roberts, V. Z. (1994). The self-assigned impossible task. In: A. Obholzer & V. Z. Roberts (Eds.), *The Unconscious at Work: Individual and Organizational Stress in the Human Services*. London: Routledge.

Robertson, J., & Robertson, J. (1953). *A Two-Year-Old Goes to Hospital* [Film]. Ipswich: Concord Video & Film Council.

Robertson, J., & Robertson, J. (1958). *Going to Hospital with Mother* [Film]. Ipswich: Concord Video & Film Council.

Robertson, J., & Robertson, J. (1989). *Separation and the Very Young*. London: Free Association Books.

Rosenfeld, H. (1971). A clinical approach to the psychoanalytic theory of the life and death instincts: An investigation into the aggressive aspects of narcissism. *International Journal of Psychoanalysis, 52*: 169–178.

Rozenholtz, S. J. (1989). Workplace conditions that affect teacher quality and commitment: Implications for teacher induction. *The Elementary School Journal, 4*: 421–438.

Ruch, G. (2007). Reflective practice in child care social work: The role of containment. *British Journal of Social Work, 37* (4): 659–680.

Rustin, M. E. (2005). Conceptual analysis of critical moments in Victoria Climbié's life. *Child and Family Social Work, 10*: 11–19.

Rustin, M. E., & Bradley, J. (2008). *Work Discussion: Learning from Reflective Practice in Work with Children and Families.* London: Karnac.

Rustin, M. J. (2004). Learning from the Victoria Climbié Inquiry. *Journal of Social Work Practice, 18* (1): 9–18.

Rustin, M. J. (2011). *The Psychology of Neo-Liberalism.* Paper presented at OPUS Conference, London (November).

Rustin, M. J. (2013). A relational society. *Soundings, 54*: 23–36.

Rutter, M. (1979). *Fifteen Thousand Hours: Secondary Schools and Their Effect on Children.* Cambridge, MA: Harvard University Press.

Rycroft-Malone, J., Seers, K., Titchen, A., Harvey, G., Kitson, A., & McCormack, B. (2004). What counts as evidence in evidence-based practice. *Journal of Advanced Nursing, 47* (1): 81–90.

Salvage, J., & Wright, S. (Eds.) (1995). *Nursing Development Units: A Force for Change.* Harrow: Scutari Press.

Sandel, M. (2013). This much I know. *The Observer,* 27 April.

Sapolsky, R. (2000). Stress hormones: Good and bad. The effects of stress and stress hormones on human cognition: Implications for the field of brain and cognition. *Neurobiology of Disease, 7* (5): 540–542.

Savage, J. (1995). *Nursing Intimacy: An Ethnographic Approach to Nurse-Patient Interaction.* London: Scutari Press.

Schaub, J., & Dalrymple, R. (2011). *"She Didn't Seem Like a Social Worker": Practice Educators Experiences and Perceptions of Assessing Failing Social Work Students on Placement.* Available at: www.swapbox.ac.uk/1151

Schaub, J., & Dalrymple, R. (2013). Surveillance and silence: New considerations in assessing difficult social work placements. *Journal of Practice Teaching and Learning, 11* (3): 79–97. [Special Edition: Failing Students]

Schoeck, H. (1966). *Envy: A Theory of Social Behaviour.* New York: Harcourt Brace & World.

Schwartz, H. S. (1992). *Narcissistic Process and Corporate Decay: The Theory of the Organization Ideal.* New York: New York University Press.

Scott, W. R. (2008). *Institutions and Organizations* (3rd edition). Thousand Oaks, CA: Sage.

Segal, H. (1957). Notes on symbol formation, *International Journal of Psychoanalysis, 38*: 391–397. Reprinted in: *The Work of Hanna Segal: A Kleinian Approach to Clinical Practice*. London: Free Association Books, 1986.

Segal, H. (1991). *Dream, Phantasy and Art*. London: Routledge.

Service, E. (1975). *Origin of the State and Civilization: The Process of Cultural Evolution*. New York: W. W. Norton.

Shapiro, E., & Carr, A. W. (1991). *Lost in Familiar Places*. New Haven, CT: Yale University Press.

Simon, J. (2002). Taking risks: Extreme sports and the embrace of risk in advanced liberal societies. In: T. Baker & J. Simon (Eds.), *Embracing Risk: The Changing Culture of Insurance and Responsibility*. Chicago, IL: University of Chicago Press.

6, P. (2011). *Explaining Political Judgement*. New York: Cambridge University Press.

6, P. (2014). *Elementary Forms of Social Organisation: Developing the Neo-Durkheimian Institutional Approach*. Manuscript in preparation.

6, P., & Mars, G. (2008). *The Institutional Dynamics of Culture, Vol. 1*. Farnham: Ashgate.

Sjoholm, C. (2013). *The Time of the Phallus? Object and Desire in the 21st Century*. Paper presented at the Love and Politics Workshop at the Netherlands Institute of Cultural Analysis, Holland.

Smith, G. (1986). Resistance to change in geriatric care. *International Journal of Nursing Studies, 23* (1): 61–70.

Smith, P. (1992). *The Emotional Labour of Nursing: How Nurses Care*. London: Macmillan.

Smith, P. (2012). *The Emotional Labour of Nursing Revisited: Can Nursing Still Care?* London: Palgrave Macmillan.

Spillius, E. B. (1990). Review of *Containing Anxiety in Institutions* and *The Dynamics of the Social: Selected Essays* by Isabel Menzies Lyth. *International Journal of Psychoanalysis, 71*: 366–368.

Spillius, E. B., Milton, J., Garvey, P., & Couve, C. (2011). *The New Dictionary of Kleinian Thought*. London: Routledge.

Stanley, K., Cooke, G., & Bellamy, K. (2006). *Equal Access? Appropriate and Affordable Childcare for Every Child*. London: Institute for Public Policy Research.

Stavrakakis, Y. (2007). *The Lacanian Left: Psychoanalysis, Theory, Politics*. New York: SUNY Press.

Stein, M. (2000). After Eden: Envy and the defences against anxiety paradigm. *Human Relations, 53* (2): 193–211.

Stein, M. (2011). A culture of mania: A psychoanalytic view of the incubation of the 2008 credit crisis. *Organization 18* (2): 173–186.

Steiner, J. (1985). Turning a blind eye: The cover up for Oedipus. *International Review of Psychoanalysis, 12*: 161.

Steiner, J. (1993). *Psychic Retreats: Pathological Organizations in Psychotic, Neurotic and Borderline Patients*. London: Routledge.

Stokes, J. (1994). The unconscious at work: Teams, groups and organization. In: A. Obholzer & V. Z. Roberts (Eds.), *The Unconscious at Work: Individual and Organizational Stress in the Human Services*. London: Routledge.

Stokes, J. (1999). Why do we work? In: D. Taylor (Ed.), *Hearts and Minds*. London: Duckworth.

Suedfeld, P. (2001). Applying positive psychology in the study of extreme environments. *Journal of Performance in Extreme Environments, 6* (1). Available at: http://docs.lib.purdue.edu/cgi/viewcontent.cgi?article=1020&context=jhpee

SWTF (2009). *Facing up to the Task—The Interim Report of the Social Work Taskforce*. London: Department of Health & Department for Children, Schools and Families.

Taylor, F. (1911). *The Principles of Scientific Management*. New York: Harper & Row.

Taylor, H., Beckett, C., & McKeigue, B. (2008). Judgements of Solomon: Anxieties and defences of social workers involved in care proceedings. *Child and Family Social Work, 13*: 23–31.

Thalassis, N. (2007). Soldiers in psychiatric therapy: The case of Northfield Military Hospital 1942–1946. *Social History of Medicine, 20*: 351–368.

Thaler, R. T., & Sunstein, C. R. (2008). *Nudge: Improving Decisions about Health, Wealth and Happiness*. New Haven, CT: Yale University Press.

Theodosius, C. (2008). *Emotional Labour in Health Care: The Unmanaged Heart of Nursing*. Abingdon: Routledge.

Thompson, M. (2008). *Organising and Disorganising*. Axminster: Triarchy Press.

Thompson, M., Ellis, R., & Wildavsky, A. (1990). *Cultural Theory*. Boulder, CO: Westview Press.

Tickell, C. (2011). *The Early Years: Foundations for Life, Health and Learning. An Independent Report on the Early Years Foundation Stage to Her Majesty's Government*. London: HMSO.

Tischler, L., & Heymans, A. (1986). Nurse–therapist supervision. In: A. Heymans, R. Kennedy, & L. Tischler (Eds.), *The Family as Inpatient*. London: Free Association Books.

Titchen, A. (2000). *Professional Craft Knowledge in Patient-Centred Nursing and the Facilitation of Its Development*. Oxford: Ashdale Press.

Torres, N. (2013). Gregariousness and the mind: Bion and Trotter, an update. In: N. Torres & R. D. Hinshelwood (Eds.), *Bion's Sources*. London: Routledge.

Traynor, M., Stone, K., Cook, H., Gould, D., & Maben, J. (2014). Disciplinary processes and the management of poor performance among UK nurse: Bad apple or systemic failure? A scoping study. *Nursing Inquiry, 21* (1): 51–58.

Trevithick, P. (2011). Understanding defences and defensiveness in social work. *Journal of Social Work Practice, 25* (4): 389–412.

Trist, E. (1950). Culture as a psycho-social process. In: E. L. Trist & H. Murray (Eds.), *The Social Engagement of Social Science, Vol. 1: The Socio-Psychological Perspective.* London: Free Association Books, 1990.

Trist, E. (1977). A concept of organizational ecology. *Australian Journal of Management, 2* (2): 161–175.

Trist, E. (1985). Working with Bion in the 1940s: The group decade. In: M. Pines (Ed.), *Bion and Group Psychotherapy.* London: Routledge & Kegan Paul.

Trist, E. (1989). The assumptions of ordinariness as a denial mechanism: Innovation and conflict in a coal mine. *Human Resource Management, 28* (2): 253–264.

Trist, E., Higgins, G. W., Murray, H., & Pollock, A. (1990). The assumption of ordinariness as a denial mechanism: Innovation and conflict in a coal mine. In: E. Trist & H. Murray (Eds.), *The Social Engagement of Social Science, Vol. 1: The Socio-Psychological Perspective* (pp 476–493). London: Free Association Books.

Trist, E., & Murray, H. (1990a). Historical overview. In: E. Trist & H. Murray (Eds.), *The Social Engagement of Social Science, Vol. 1: The Socio-Psychological Perspective* (pp. 1–34). London: Free Association Books.

Trist, E., & Murray, H. (1990b). Introduction. In: E. Trist & H. Murray (Eds.), *The Social Engagement of Social Science, Vol. 1: The Socio-Psychological Perspective* (pp. 37–38). London: Free Association Books.

Tucker, S. (2010). An investigation of the stresses, pressures and challenges faced by primary school head teachers in a context of organizational change in schools. *Journal of Social Work Practice, 24* (1): 63–74.

Tuckett, D. (2012). *Minding the Markets: An Emotional Finance View of Financial Instability.* Basingstoke: Palgrave Macmillan.

Turkle, S. (2011). *Alone Together: Why We Expect More from Technology and Less from Each Other.* New York: Basic Books.

Tustin, F. (1981). *Autistic States in Children.* London: Routledge & Kegan Paul.

Tutton, E., Seers, K., & Langstaff, D. (2008). Professional nursing culture on a trauma unit: Experiences of patients and staff. *Journal of Advanced Nursing, 61* (2): 145–153.

Tutton, E., Seers, K., & Langstaff, D. (2012). Hope in orthopaedic trauma: A qualitative study. *International Journal of Nursing Studies, 49* (7): 872–879.

Tutton, E., Seers, K., Langstaff, D., & Westwood, M. (2011). Staff and patient views of the concept of hope on a stroke unit: A qualitative study. *Journal of Advanced Nursing, 68* (9): 2061–2069.

Twight, M. F., & Martin, J. (1999). *Extreme Alpinism: Climbing Light, Fast and High.* Seattle, WA: The Mountaineers.

UKCC (1986). *Project 2000: A New Preparation for Practice.* London: United Kingdom Central Council. Available at: www.nmc-uk.org/Documents /Archived%20Publications/UKCC%20Archived%20Publications/ Project%202000%20A%20New%20Preparation%20for%20Practice%20 May%201986.pdf

Vygotsky, L. S. (1978). *Mind in Society: The Development of Higher Psychological Processes.* Cambridge, MA: Harvard University Press.

Waddell, M., & Williams, G. (1991). Reflections on perverse states of mind. *Free Associations, 22*: 203–213.

Wallbank, S. (2013). Maintaining professional resilience through group restorative supervision. *Community Practitioner, 86* (8): 26–28.

Warman, A., & Jackson, E. (2007). Recruiting and retaining children & families' social workers: The potential of work discussion groups. *Journal of Social Work Practice, 21* (1): 35–48.

Wastell, D., White, S., Broadhurst, K., Peckover, S., & Pitthouse, A. (2010). Children's services in the iron cage of performance management: Street-level bureaucracy and the spectre of Svejkism. *International Journal of Social Welfare, 19*: 310–320.

Waterhouse, L., & McGhee, J. (2009). Anxiety and child protection: Implications for practitioner–parent relations. *Child and Family Social Work, 14* (4): 481–490.

Weber, M. (1948). Bureaucracy. In: *From Max Weber: Essays in Sociology* (pp. 196–244), ed. H. H. Gerth & C. W. Mills. Oxford: Routledge, 2009.

Weick, K. E. (1996). Drop your tools: An allegory for organizational studies. *Administrative Science Quarterly* (June): 301–313.

Wells, L. (1995). Group as a whole: A systemic socioanalytic perspective on interpersonal and group relations. In: J. Gillette, & M. McCollom (Eds.), *Groups in Context: A New Perspective on Group Dynamics.* Lanham, MD: University Press of America.

White, S., Hall, C., & Peckover, S. (2009). The descriptive tyranny of the Common Assessment Form: Technologies of categorization and professional practice in child welfare. *British Journal of Social Work, 39*: 1197–1217.

Wilkinson, R., & Pickett, K. (2009). *The Spirit Level: Why Equality Is Better for Everyone.* London: Penguin.

Williams, R. (1977). *Marxism and Literature.* Oxford: Oxford University Press.

Williams, R. (1993). *Drama from Ibsen to Brecht.* London: Hogarth Press.

Wilsford, D. (2010). The logic of policy change: Structure and agency in political life. *Journal of Health Politics, Politics and Law, 35* (4): 663–680.

Winnicott, D. W. (1947). Hate in the countertransference. In: *Through Pae-diatrics to Psychoanalysis* (pp. 194–203). London: Hogarth Press, 1975; reprinted London: Karnac, 1984.

Winnicott, D. W. (1956). The anti-social tendency. In: *Through Paediatrics to Psychoanalysis* (pp. 306–315). London: Hogarth Press, 1975; reprinted London: Karnac, 1984 .

Wood, J. (1987). *A Theory of Small Group Structure*. Doctoral thesis, Yale University, New Haven, CT, & University of Michigan, Ann Arbor, MI.

Woodburn, J. (1982). Egalitarian societies. *Man, New Series, 17* (3): 431–451.

Woodhouse, D., & Pengelly, P. (1991). *Anxiety and the Dynamics of Collaboration*. Aberdeen: Aberdeen University Press.

Wood Report (1947). *Working Party on the Recruitment and Training of Nurses (Majority Report)*. London: HMSO.

Wulf, J. (2012). *The Flattened Firm—Not as Advertised*. Working paper. Boston, MA: Harvard Business School.

Yakeley, J., Schoenberg, P., Morris, R., Sturgeon, D., & Majid, S. (2011). Psychodynamic approaches to teaching medical students about the doctor–patient relationship: Randomised controlled trial. *The Psychiatrist, 135*: 308–313.

INDEX

Innutiaq, 153
in-service training [INSET], 271
INSET: *see* in-service training
instant lateral communication, 17
"instinctive groupishness", 156
Institute of Psychoanalysis, 52, 178
institution(s):
    authoritarian: *see* authoritarian
        institutions
    formal and informal, and cultural
        theory, 94–96
    total: *see* total institutions
    unconscious anxieties for, origins and
        consequences of, 6
    varieties of, 12–15
institutional anxiety(ies), 137
    containment of, 312–313
institutional defence(s), 4, 145, 257
    in hospital and prison, 176–186
    obsessional, 130
    obsessive, 140
institutional processes, 4, 231
    as principal sources or generators of
        anxiety and defence, 6
    psychoanalytic thinking as valuable
        resource for study of, 12
institutional splitting, 259
institutional support, and leadership, 129
institutional thought-styles, 95, 96
instrumentality, of late capitalism, 216
instrumental vs. substantive ways of
    functioning, 215–216
instrumental thinking, 215
Intensive Supervision and Surveillance
    Order, 315
intentional rounding, 120
inter-agency information-sharing and
    collaboration, 251
internal establishment, 6, 53
internal gang, 10
internal market, 137
    and effect of survival anxiety on
        healthcare system, 132–133
internet, 67, 204, 220
interpersonal anxiety(ies), 78
interpersonal dynamics, 18
interpersonal psychoanalysis, 44
interpersonal repressive techniques, 31
introjected identification, 234
introjection and projection, cycle of, 60,
    63, 217
introjective identification, processes of,
    12
Inuit Eskimos, Utku, 153
irrational states of mind, 6
isolating, disconnection of all emotion
    from ideas and actions as, 29

Jackson, D., 121
Jackson, E., xvi, 6, 19, 269–283, 297
James, N., 116
Jaques, E., 265
    on anxiety in institutional settings, 6
    on bad impulses projected into groups
        as defence against paranoid
        anxiety, 265
    contributions of, 93–94
    first to use phrase "social defences
        against anxiety", 148, 177
    ground-breaking work in 1950s, x
    and Menzies Lyth, respective views on
        organizational dynamics, 1, 5, 18,
        19, 28, 34, 39, 56, 76, 90–91, 160,
        177, 223–224, 234, 315
    organization as container for anxieties
        of members, 51
    on paranoid-schizoid and depressive
        anxiety in conflict between
        managers and trade union
        leaders, 22
    "phantasy form" of organization, 35
    on psychoanalysis as dysfunctional in
        organizations, 107
    roles occupying different levels in
        hierarchy corresponding to
        different timespans of discretion,
        77
    theoretical ambivalence of, 241
    on unconscious defences against
        anxiety, 1
        grounded in Klein's work on
        paranoid-schizoid and depressive
        anxiety, 4–6
    work-related anxieties, 163
Jefferson, T., 50
job interviews, 40
Jobs, S., 203
Johns, J., 185
Johnson, A., 212
Johnson, C., 42, 46
Jolly, R., 224
Joshi, H., 295
jouissance, 195
Judt, T., 220

Kahn, W., 31, 35
Kahneman, D., 199
Kant, I., 195
Karnac, H., 179
Kay, A., 332
Keat, R., 107
"keep death at bay" service, 55
Kennard, D., 151, 157
Kennedy, R., 178, 185
Kernberg, O. F., 161